I0753210

HISTORIC PHOTOS OF
TALLAHASSEE

TEXT AND CAPTIONS BY ANDREW N. EDEL

TURNER
PUBLISHING COMPANY

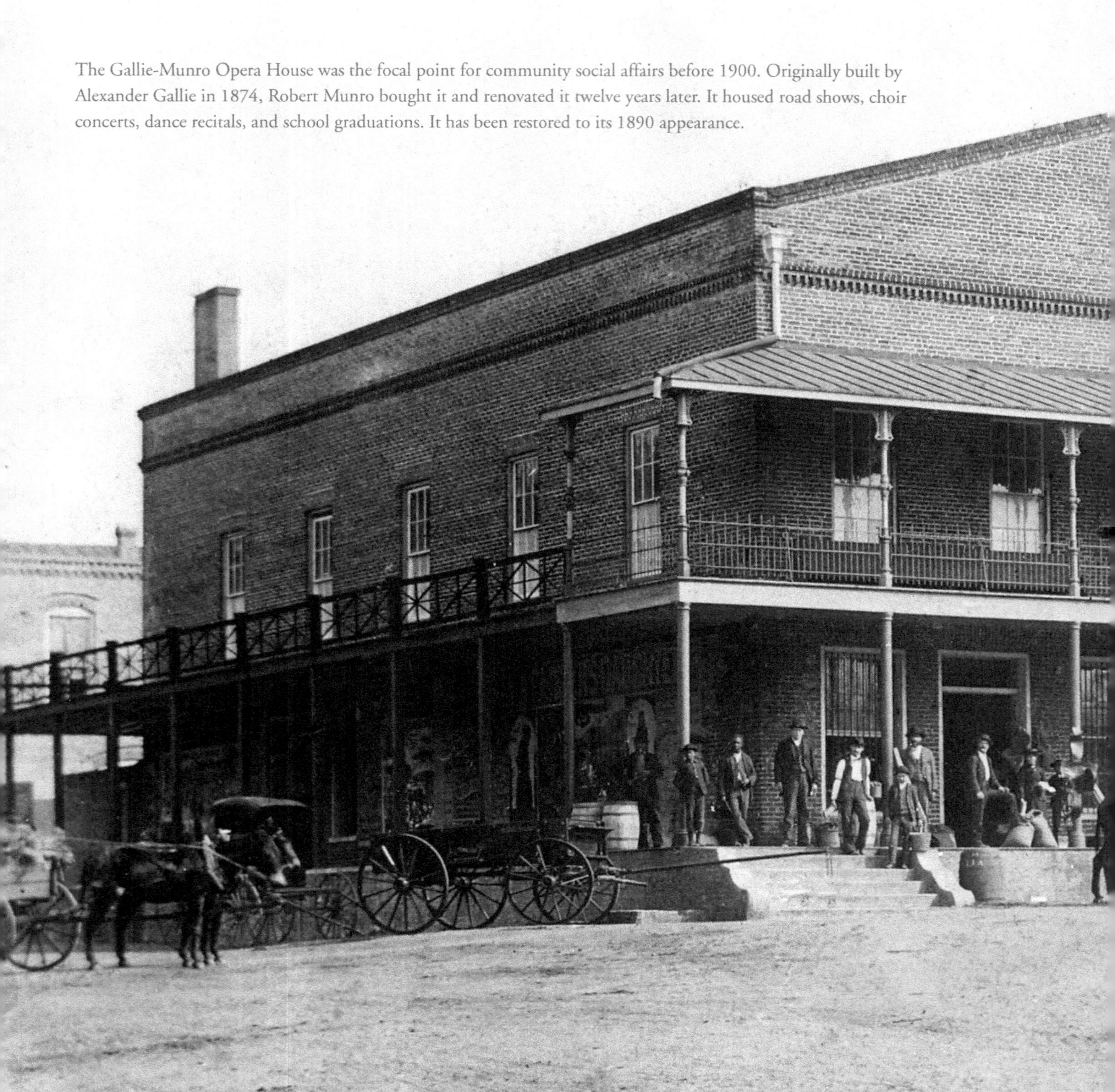

The Gallie-Munro Opera House was the focal point for community social affairs before 1900. Originally built by Alexander Gallie in 1874, Robert Munro bought it and renovated it twelve years later. It housed road shows, choir concerts, dance recitals, and school graduations. It has been restored to its 1890 appearance.

HISTORIC PHOTOS OF
TALLAHASSEE

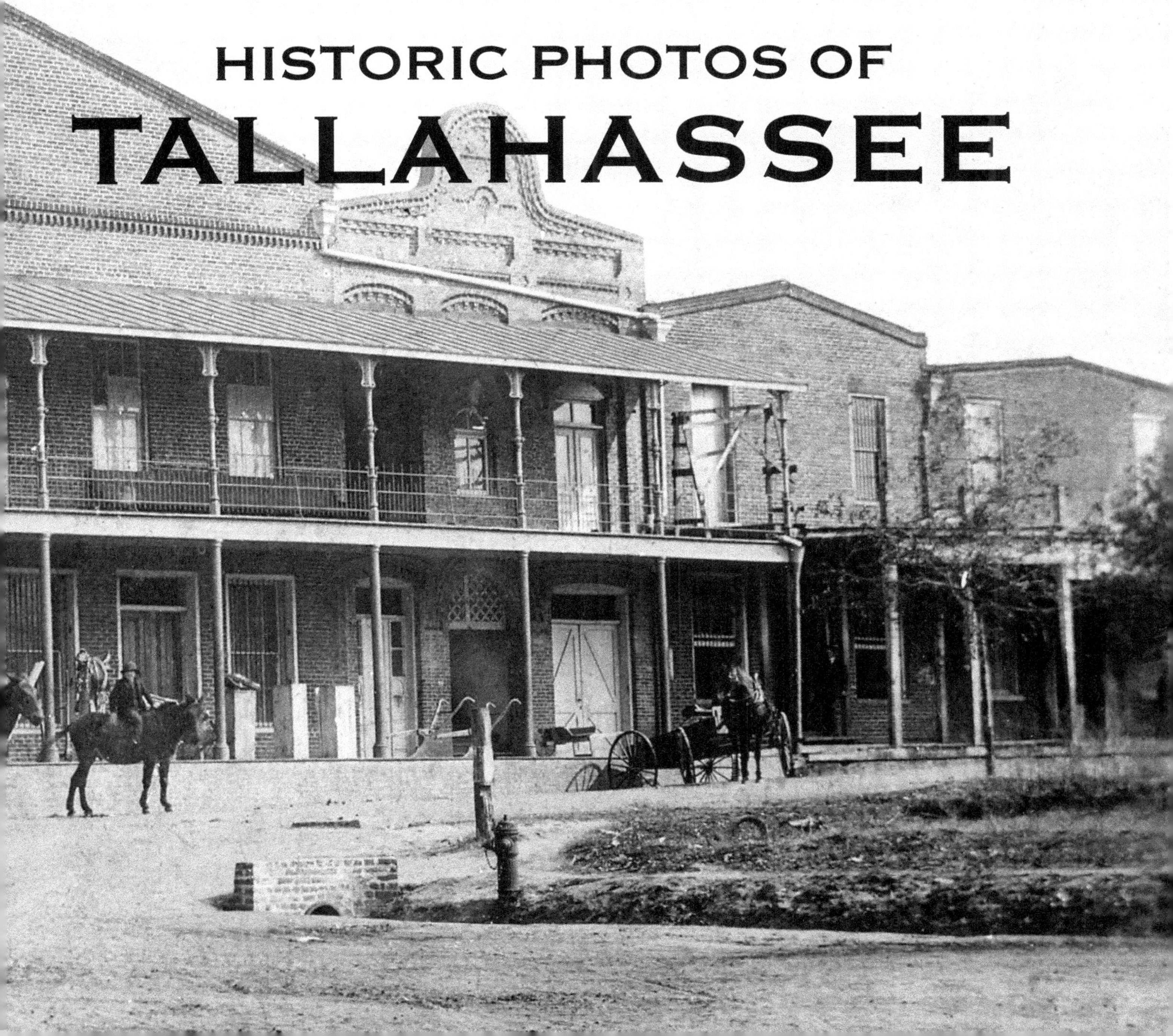

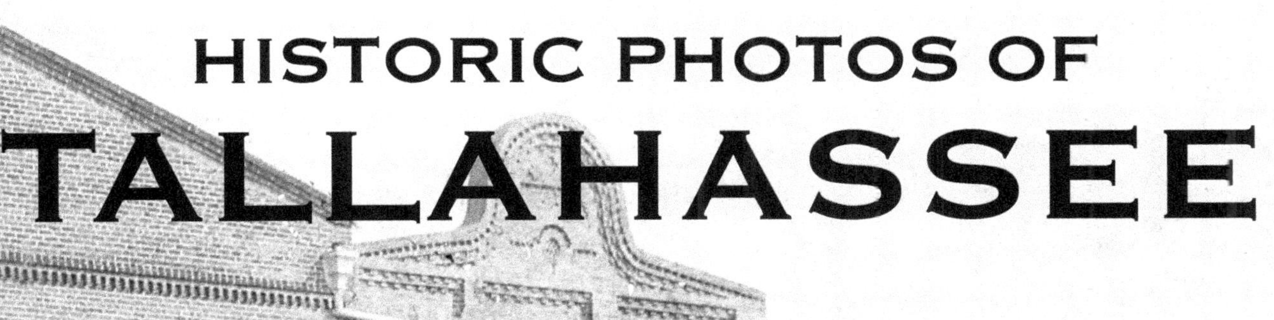

Turner Publishing Company
www.turnerpublishing.com

Historic Photos of Tallahassee

Library of Congress Control Number: 2006937076

ISBN-10: 1-59652-324-7
ISBN-13: 978-1-59652-324-1

Printed in the United States of America

ISBN 978-1-68336-939-4 (hc)

Contents

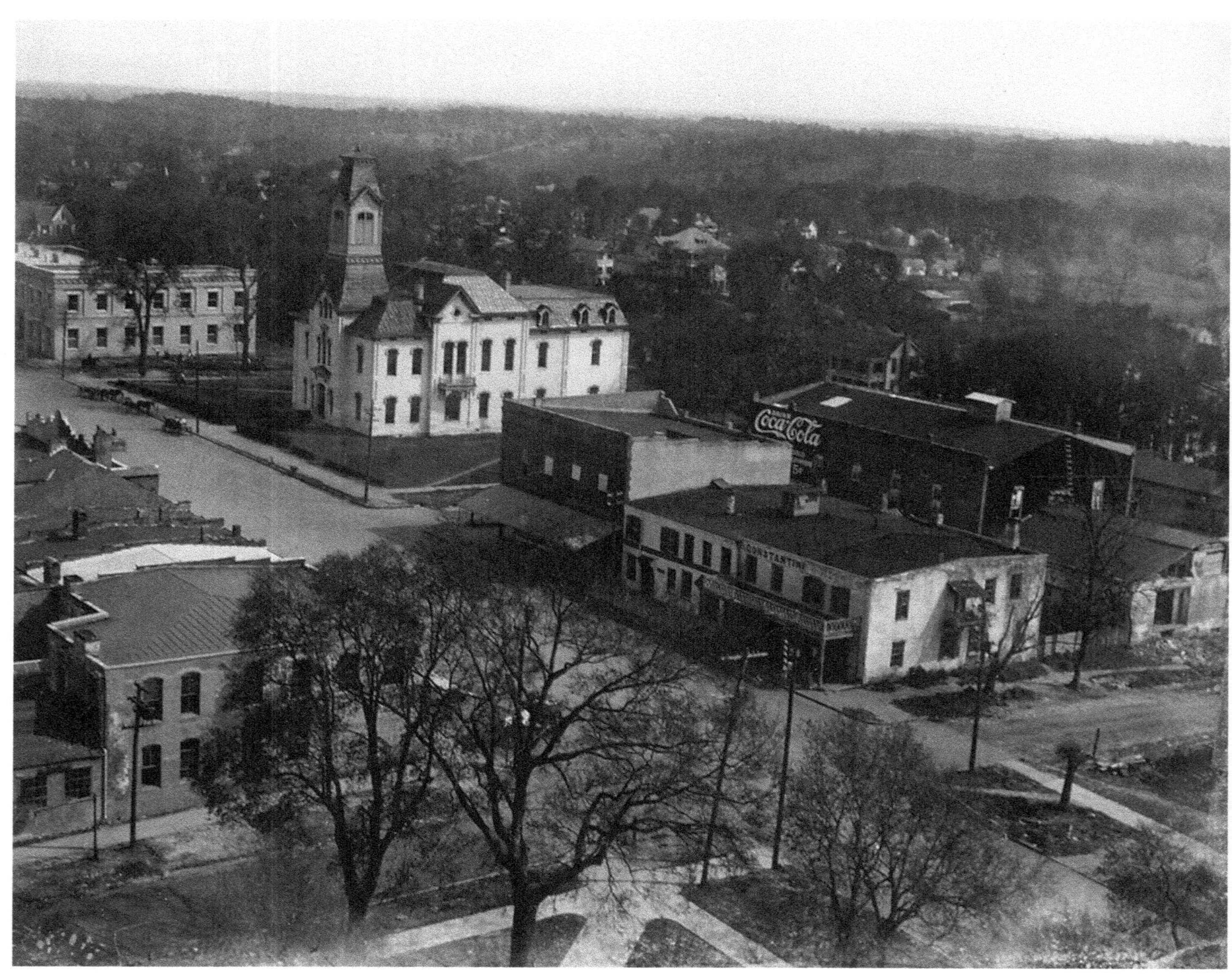

Added in 1902, the cupola on the new capitol dome was the highest spot in Tallahassee and afforded great views of the area. This view, taken around 1914, shows the east side of Monroe Street and the Leon County Courthouse, with its tower.

Acknowledgments

This volume, *Historic Photos of Tallahassee,* is the result of the cooperation and efforts of many individuals and organizations. It is with great thanks that we acknowledge in particular the valuable contribution of the State Archives of Florida, Erik Robinson, and N. Adam Watson, Photographic Archivist at the archives.

This project represents countless hours of review and research. The researchers and writer have reviewed thousands of photographs. We greatly appreciate the generous assistance of the archives listed here, without whom this project could not have been completed.

The goal in publishing this work is to provide broader access to a set of extraordinary photographs. The aim is to inspire, provide perspective, and evoke insight that might assist officials and citizens, who together are responsible for determining Tallahassee's future. In addition, the book seeks to preserve the past with respect and reverence.

With the exception of touching up imperfections caused by the vicissitudes of time and cropping where necessary, no other changes have been made. The focus and clarity of many images is limited to the technology of the day and the skill of the photographer who captured them.

We encourage readers to reflect as they explore Tallahassee, stroll along its streets, or wander its neighborhoods. It is the publisher's hope that in making use of this work, longtime residents will learn something new and that new residents will gain a perspective on where Tallahassee has been, so that each can contribute to its future.

—Todd Bottorff, Publisher

Preface

The photographic history of Tallahassee is well documented. At least four books of historic photographs have been published, thousands of images are available online at the State Archives, and many more have been included in other websites, articles, and videos. There are, however, compelling reasons for another book of historic photographs of Tallahassee. First, owing to the sheer number of extant photographs, even those familiar with the city's history will likely discover new images. Those unfamiliar with the city's past will reap a fresh glimpse into the rich photographic history of this community. Second, in addition to photographs, every book or portfolio offers its own commentary and perspective on the past. The focus of this volume is on Tallahassee's rich cultural heritage amid its lovely natural setting.

Individually, photographs offer an unspoiled glimpse of another place and time. Aided with informative text about specific elements, the viewer can draw his own insights and interpretation. As a collection, photographs constitute a history of a community's challenges, growth, and change. To help the viewer visually experience the historical continuity of Tallahassee, the images are arranged chronologically.

The materials used in developing the captions and overall perspective of the book are the product of many hours of research at the Florida State Library and Archives, Florida State University library, Supreme Court library, and Old Capitol collections.

Many in the general public have gained a cursory knowledge of Tallahassee in recent years. As the state capital of Florida, it is the setting for national news stories about the entire state. Every year thousands of people come to Tallahassee, some to attend the universities, others to work for the state government, and many as tourists to visit the state capital. For all those wishing to discover more about Tallahassee the goal of this work is to provide some insight and perspective about its traditions, history, people, and culture.

Summaries of each of the four eras provide historical background for the photographs. Section 1, A Capital Beginning, briefly describes the founding of the city, and spans the Civil War to the turn of the century. Section 2, A Capital Idea, covers the impact of education and government in the first two decades of the twentieth century. Section 3, A Capital City, traces the city's growth from a small rural town. Section 4, A Capital Complex, covers capital expansion from the beginning of World War II to the 1970s.

In each era the selection of photographs together with the captions and introduction provides a broad perspective on the development of Tallahassee. Various aspects are traced from period to period—the economy, civic improvements, education, state government, and social trends.

Tallahassee is situated in a garden spot of green hills, year-round flowers, and majestic oaks draped with Spanish moss. Walking around Tallahassee, one covers the same ground traversed by Apalachee Indians and Spanish conquistadors. Desoto, Osceola, Andrew Jackson, governors, presidents, slaves, and adventurers all walked the land. The origin of the Native American word *tallahassee* is generally translated "old fields" or "abandoned villages." Perhaps "ghost town" is a more apt translation, for it evokes the romanticism of Tallahassee—a city with a strong sense of its past in a timeless natural setting.

It is hoped that this work will add to the understanding of the unique cultural heritage of Tallahassee.

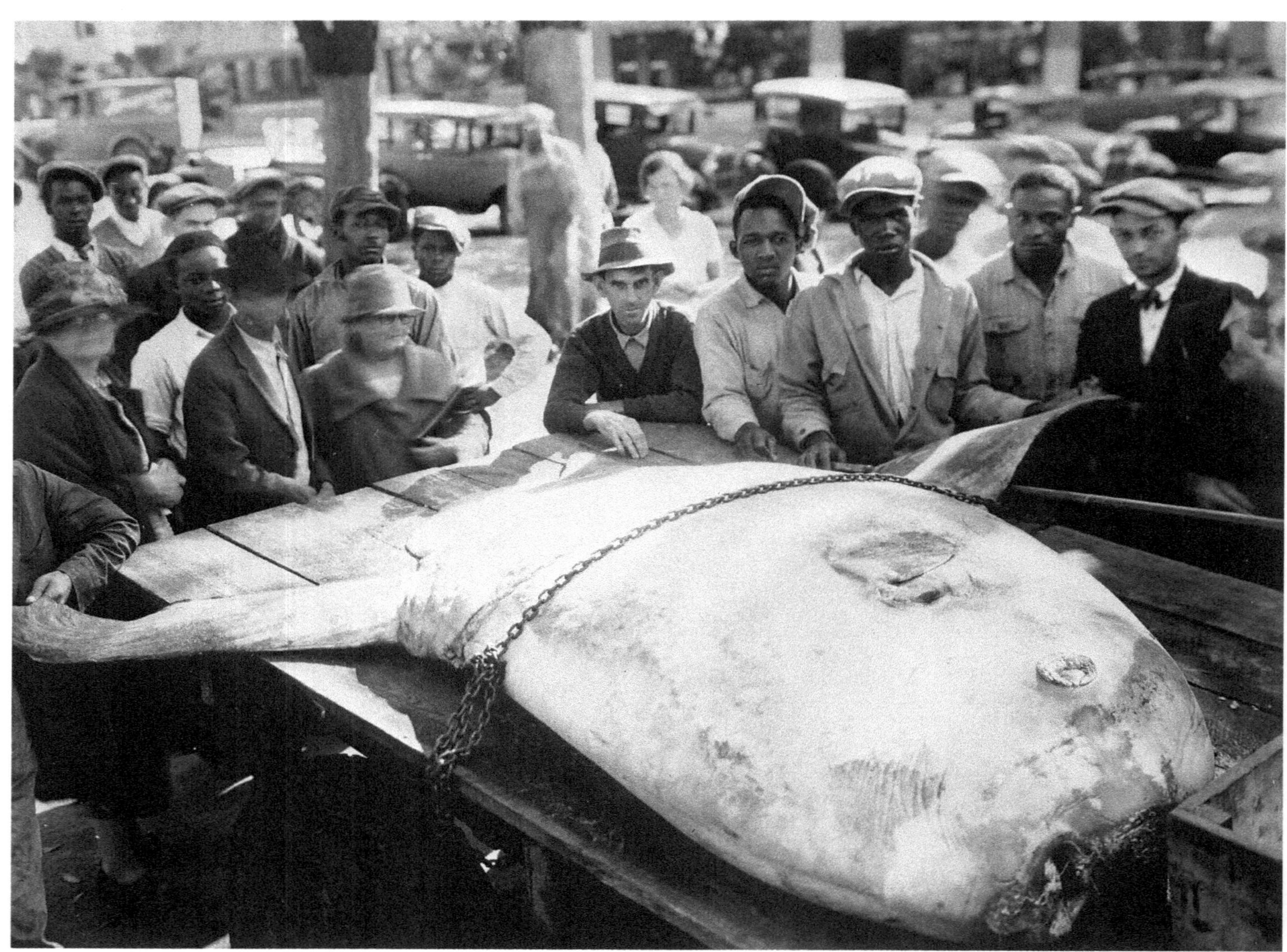

This rare mola was caught off St. Marks, Florida, and brought to Tallahassee on the back of a truck. Only 20 miles from the little fishing village of St. Marks, Tallahassee is close to the Gulf of Mexico. Fishing and water sports have long been a favorite pastime.

A Capital Beginning

(1824–1900)

The Adams-Onis treaty, ratified in 1821, transferred East and West Florida from Spain to the United States. The territory of Florida was formed the next year retaining the two former capitals of St. Augustine and Pensacola. The Territorial Council selected the little Indian village of Tallahassee as the site for a new capitol in 1823. A lawless place, gunfights and duels were common in the new town; Ralph Waldo Emerson called it "a grotesque place of land speculators and desperados." The year 1841 proved particularly disastrous with a yellow fever epidemic, major bank failure, and a terrible fire. Despite these setbacks, a state constitution was adopted and in 1845 Tallahassee became the capital of the 27th state of the Union. As the cotton economy continued to prosper, Tallahassee grew as the social and economic hub of the nearby slave-worked cotton plantations.

In 1861 Florida joined the Confederacy, proclaiming the Ordinance of Secession on the capitol steps. Four years later, the city declared that "Tallahassee was the only Confederate capital east of the Mississippi River not captured during the Civil War." After the war, reconstruction brought economic and social challenges to Tallahassee as newly freed slaves or freemen required jobs, education, and basic subsistence. During this period attempts to return to the pre-war cotton economy failed owing to disease, a declining market, and lack of financing. Without an agricultural base, there was virtually no growth from 1865 to 1876. At the capitol, state politics went through a stormy period of appointed governors, carpetbaggers, and a newly empowered faction of freed slaves.

After the 1876 election, Democrats and old Southern political factions gradually gained control of state government, focusing on stimulating business and a return to pre-war social stability. As the economy grew, the former slave community, politically and socially, was suppressed.

Tallahassee's economy is still dependent on agriculture, but Leon County farmers diversified into other products including tobacco, nuts, pears, grapes, and sugar cane. The 1880s brought an economic recovery and up to the turn of the century the population grew at a rate of 20 percent. During that time, Tallahasseans struggled to become more "metropolitan," adding many civic improvements—animal control laws, street-lamps, free mail delivery, sidewalks, an opera house, a luxurious residential district, a grand hotel, and even a streetcar line.

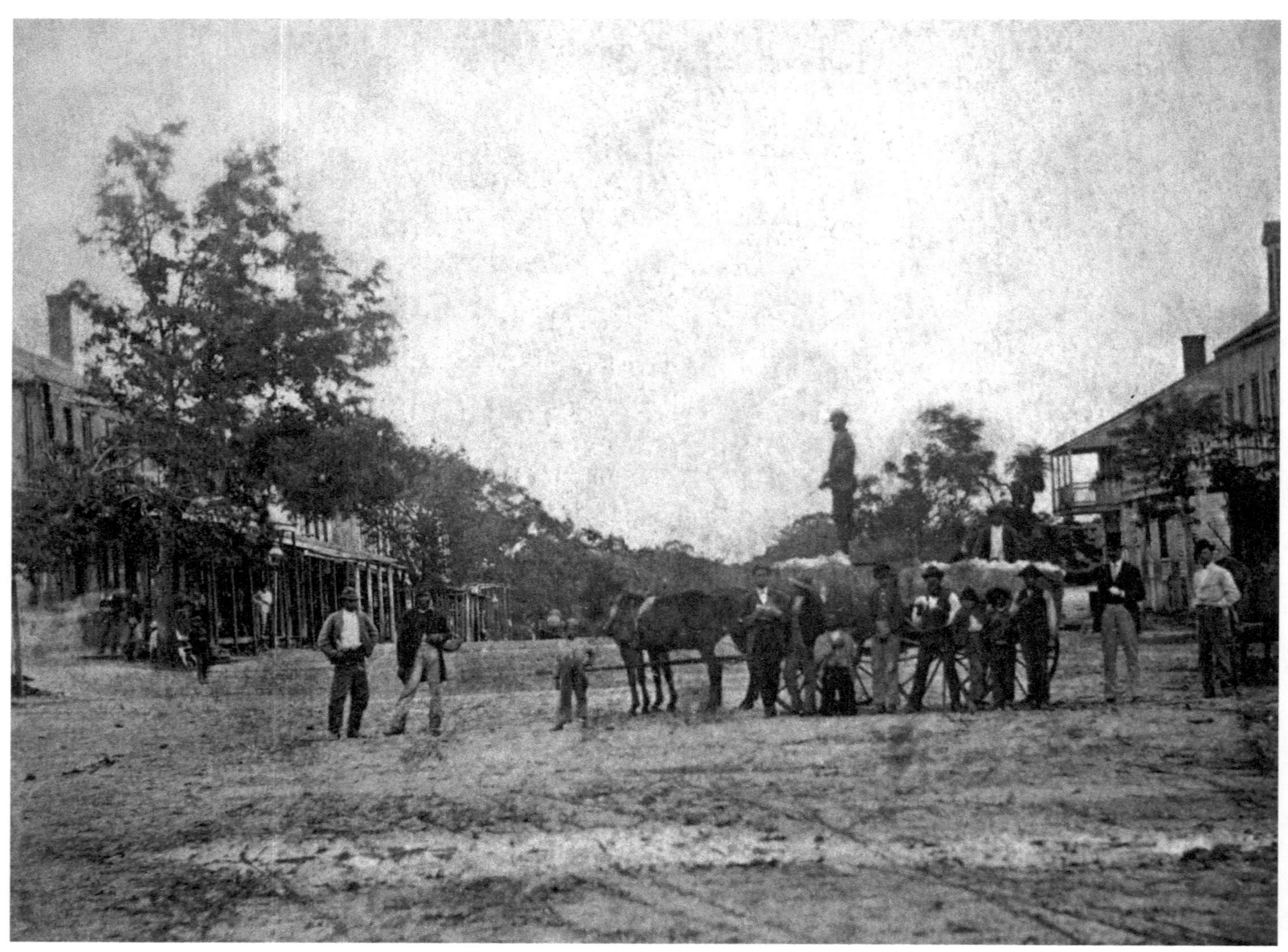

Although founded as the capital city of Florida, over a decade after the Civil War Tallahassee still looked like a frontier town, with few buildings and wide, rough dirt streets. Residents pose with a horse-drawn wagon in the middle of town on Monroe Street. The Phoenix building at right burned in 1877.

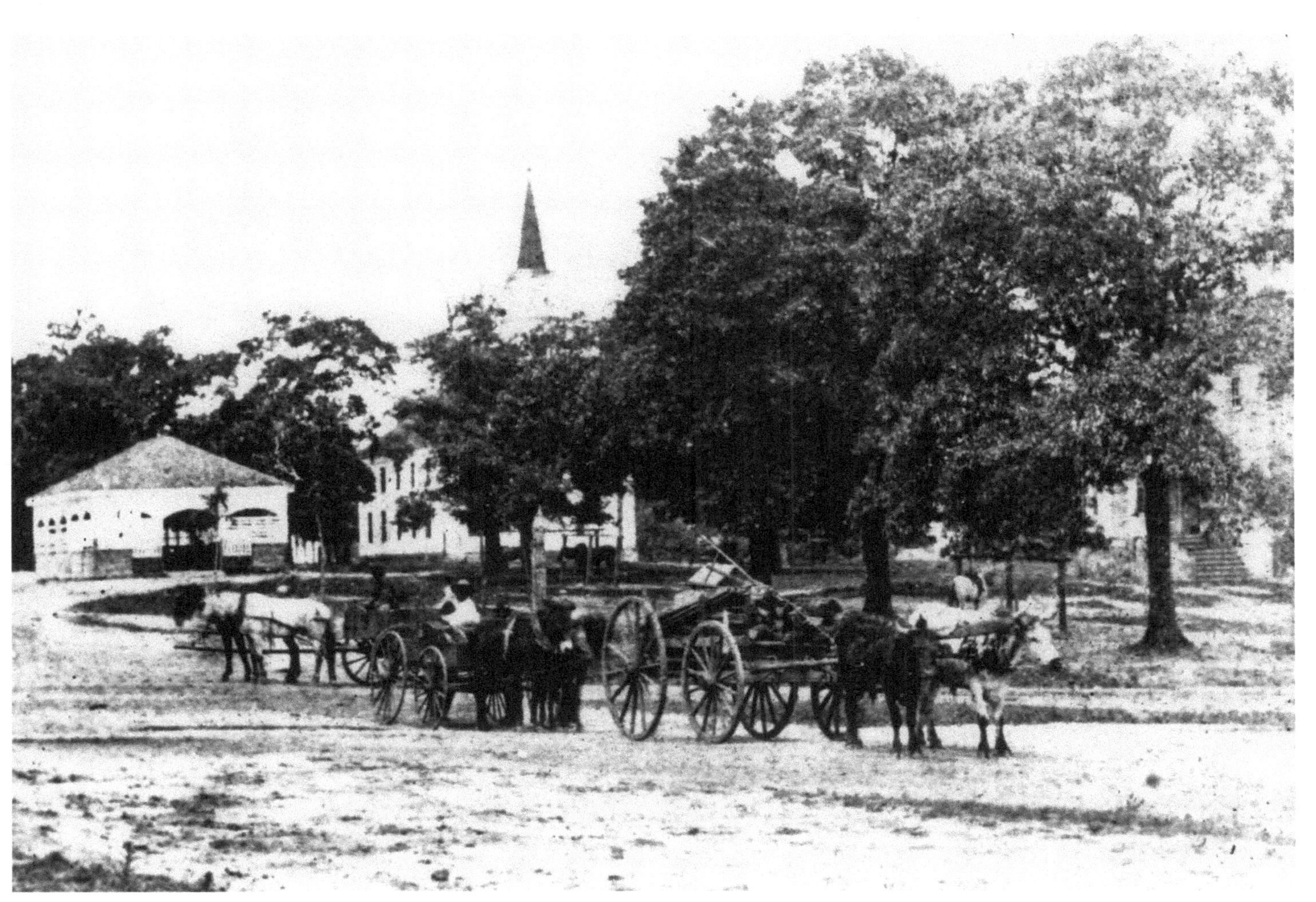

Ox carts pause on Park Avenue, prominent center of early Tallahassee. On the far left, the market place operated daily and was regulated by the city. The First Presbyterian Church, at center, was often used as a city hall for political speeches. The courthouse, partly obscured by trees, burned in 1879.

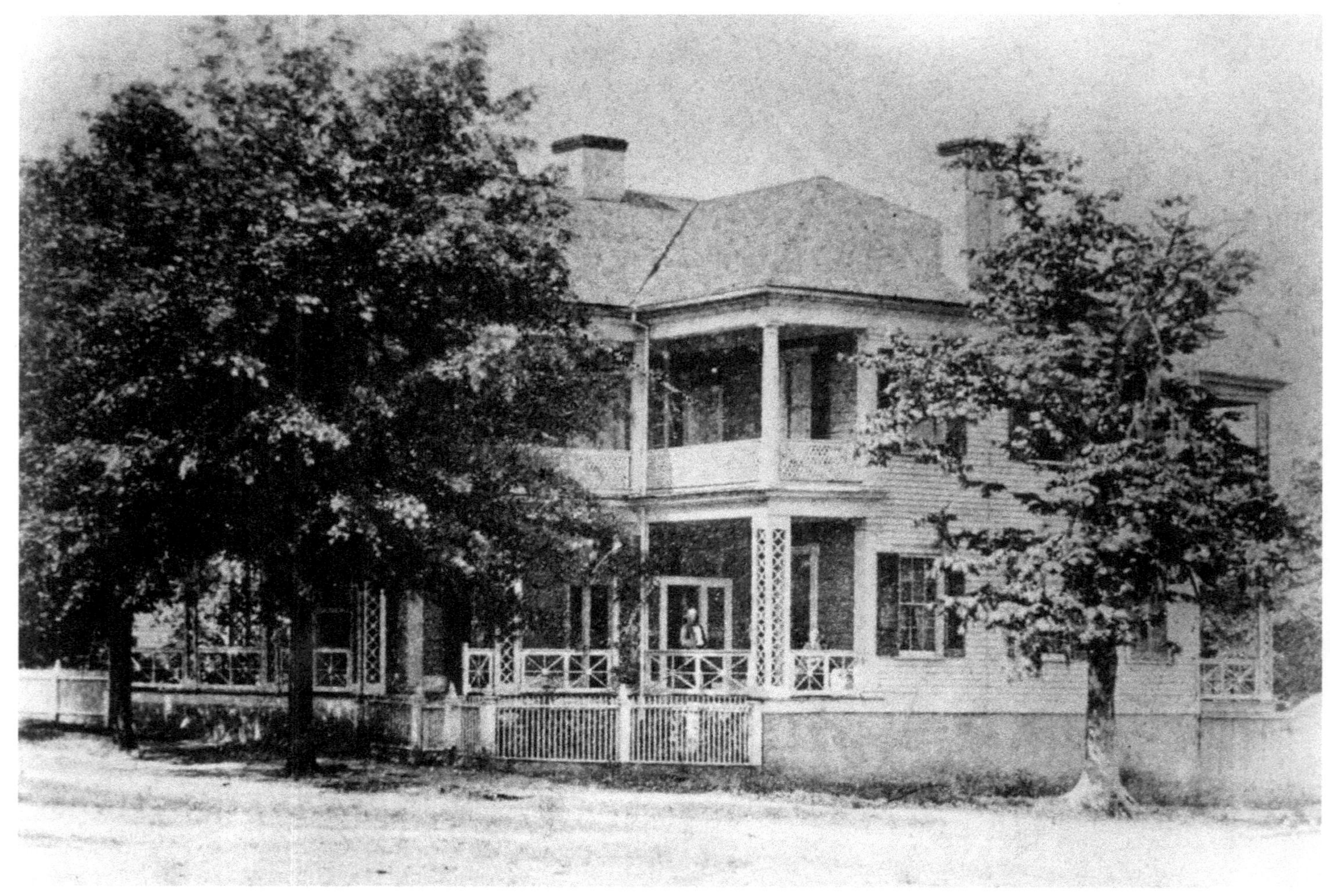

Governor Harrison Reed lived in this home while serving as governor from 1868 to 1872. Until 1905 Florida's governors had to obtain their own lodging. Reed, the first elected governor after the Civil War, served during the turbulent Reconstruction period. His own party tried to impeach him four times.

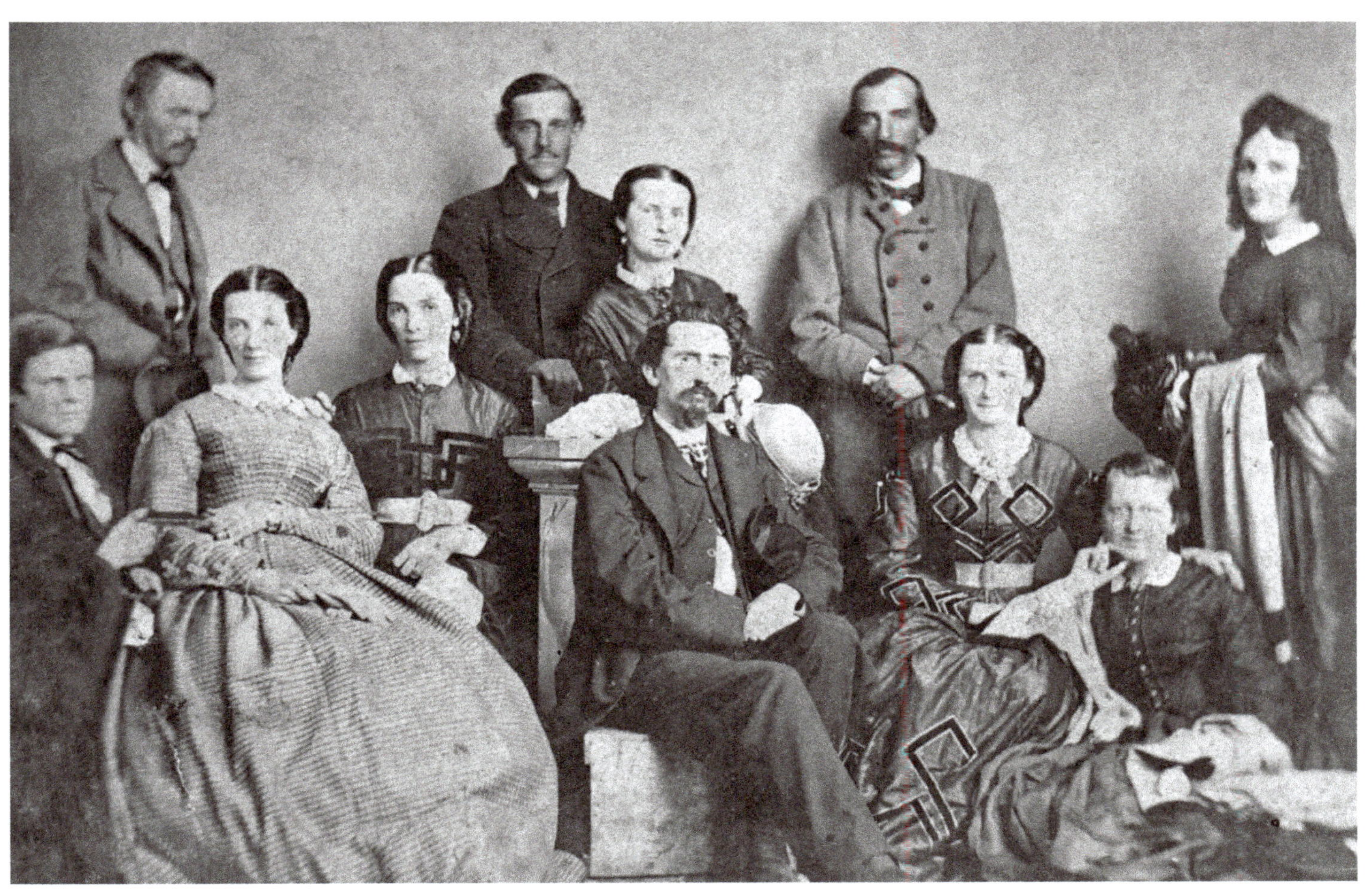

The wedding of Florence Holland and William Bull took place at Greenwood Plantation after the end of the Civil War in 1865. The bridegroom had just been mustered out of the Confederate army after being imprisoned for two years at Johnson's Island in Lake Erie. Bull sits at center with his bride on his right (the third person from left).

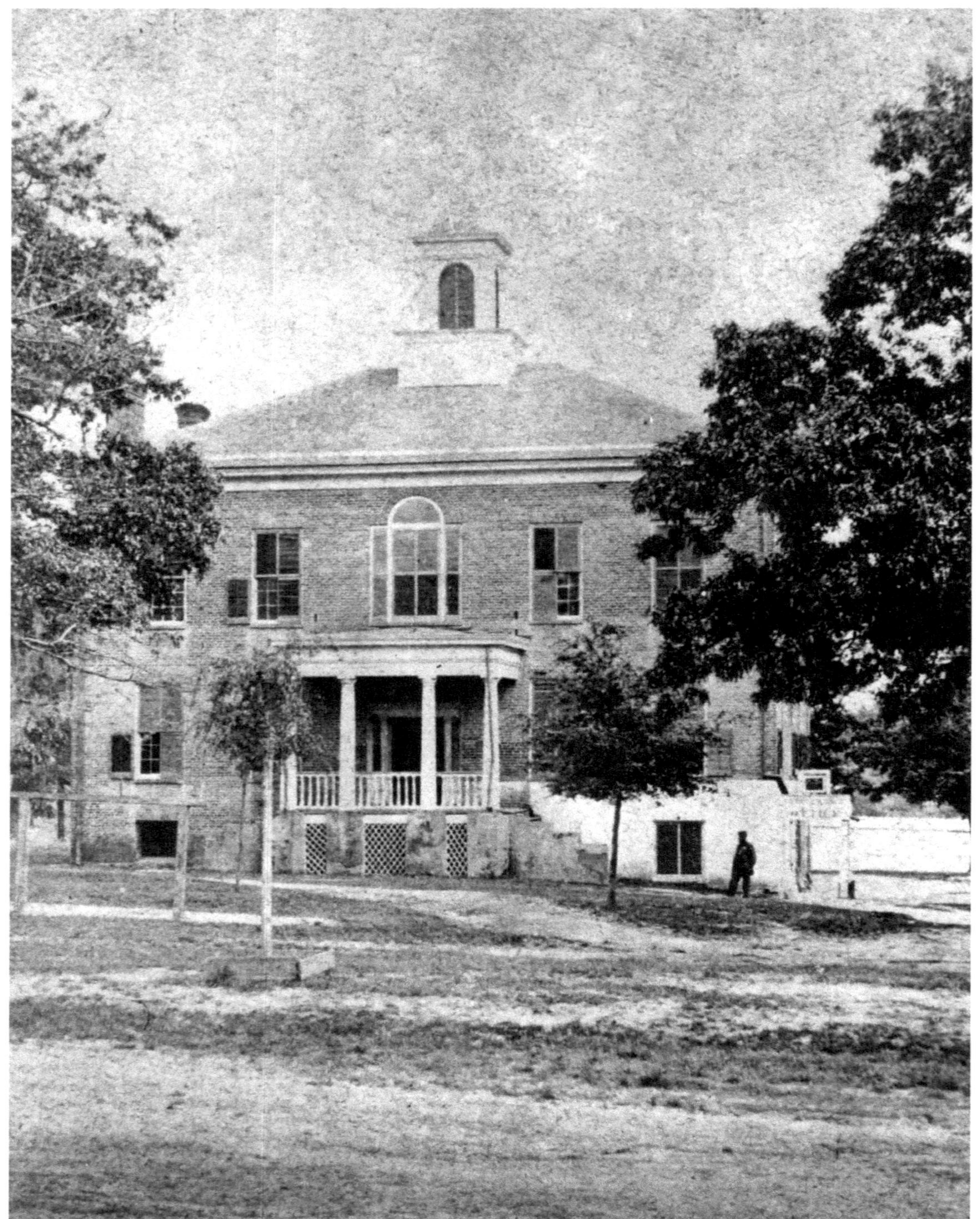

Completed in April 1833, the first Leon County courthouse was located on Park Avenue in the heart of Tallahassee. It burned in 1879. Created in 1824, Leon County was the seventh county in Florida. Its fertile soil and central location made it the most affluent and populated county in antebellum Florida.

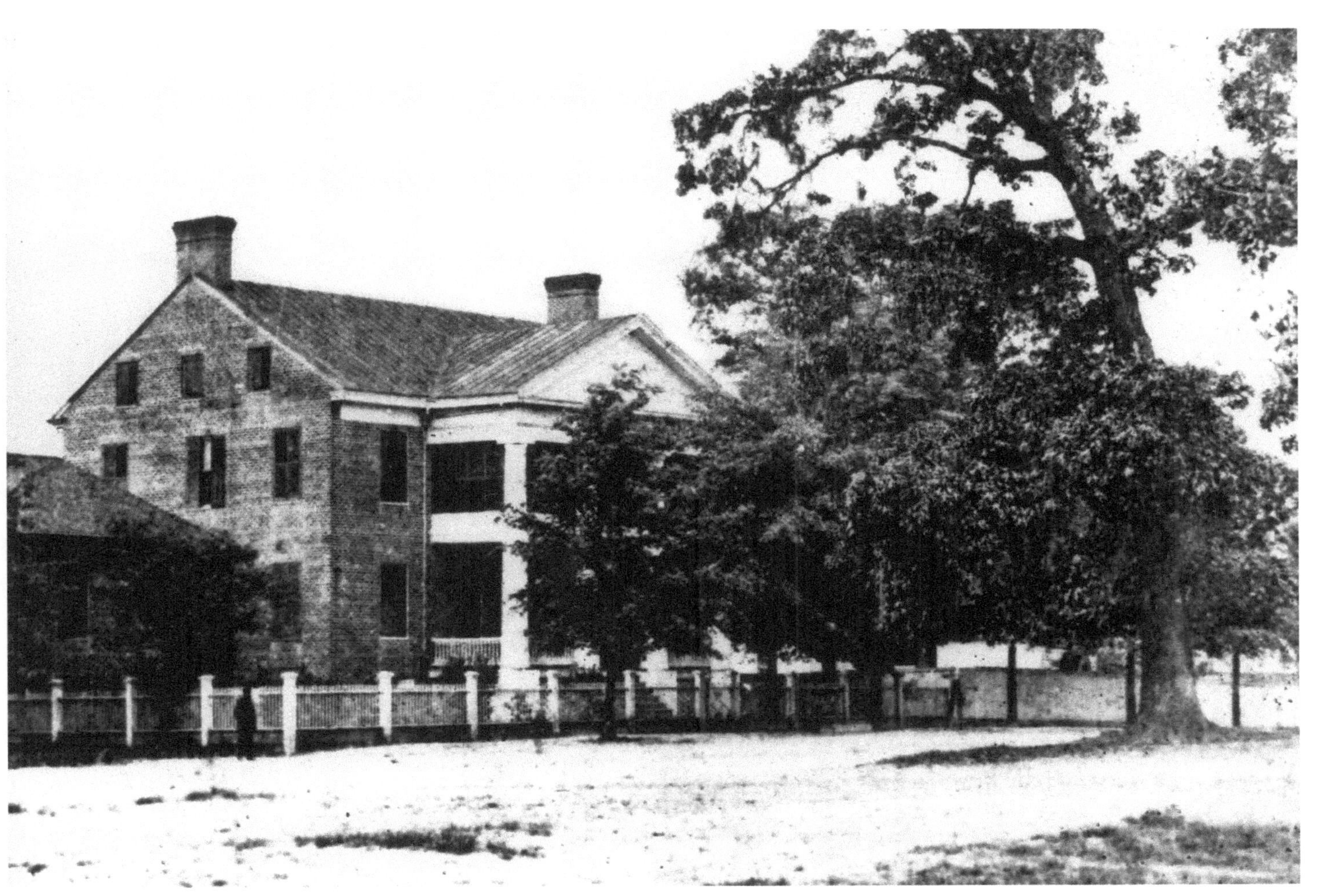

One of Tallahassee's oldest residences, the Columns was located on the southwest corner of Adams Street and Park Avenue. Built ca. 1830 and moved in 1971 to the northwest corner of Park Ave. and Duval St., it has served as private home, bank, boardinghouse, restaurant, library, and home of the chamber of commerce.

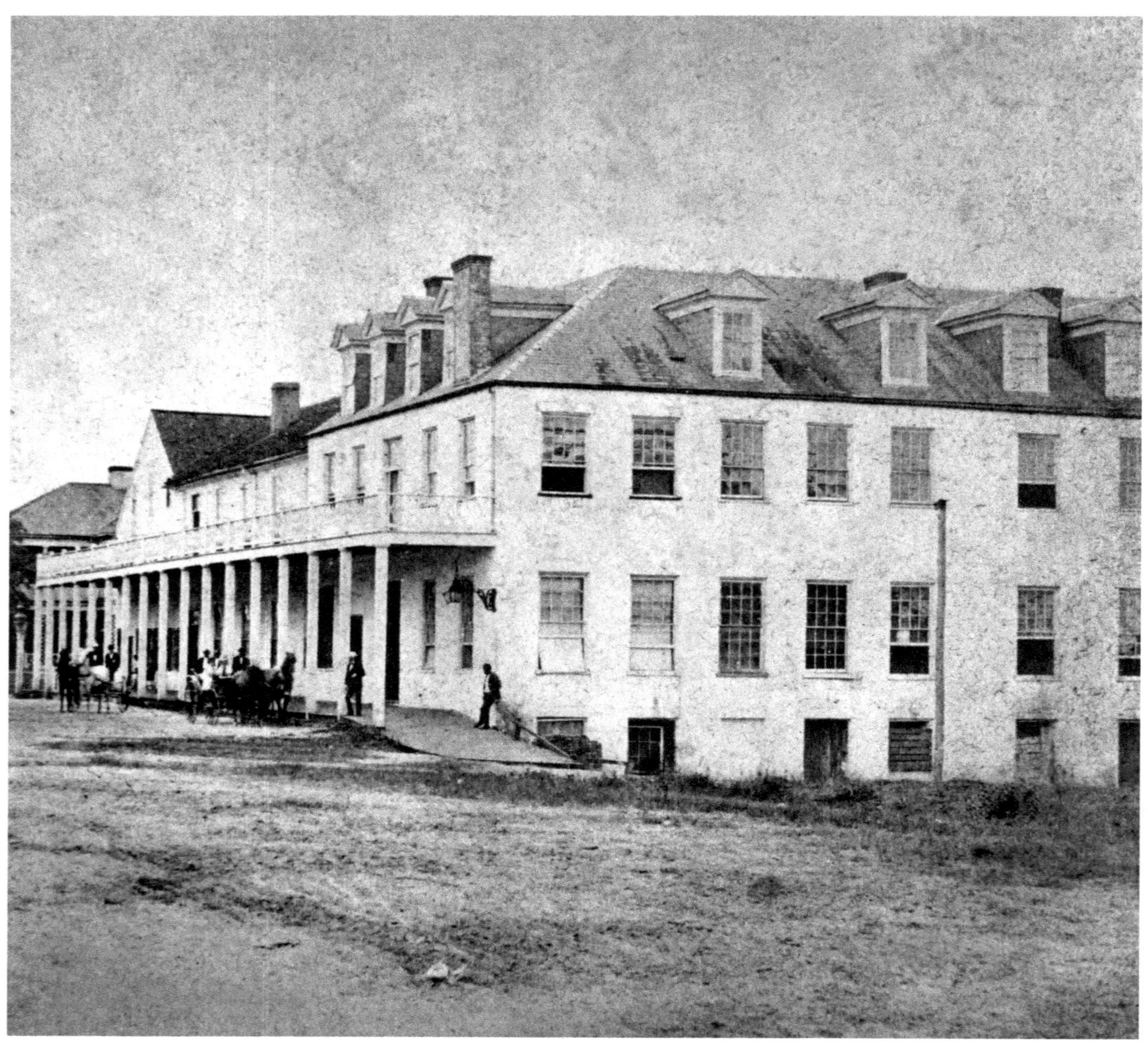

The Morgan Hotel on Adams Street across from the Capitol had many names and owners. Originally built in 1834 by Thomas Brown, who later became governor, it was first known as Brown's Inn. It was called the City Hotel in 1839, the Adelphi in 1840, and finally the Morgan Hotel. It was destroyed by fire in 1886.

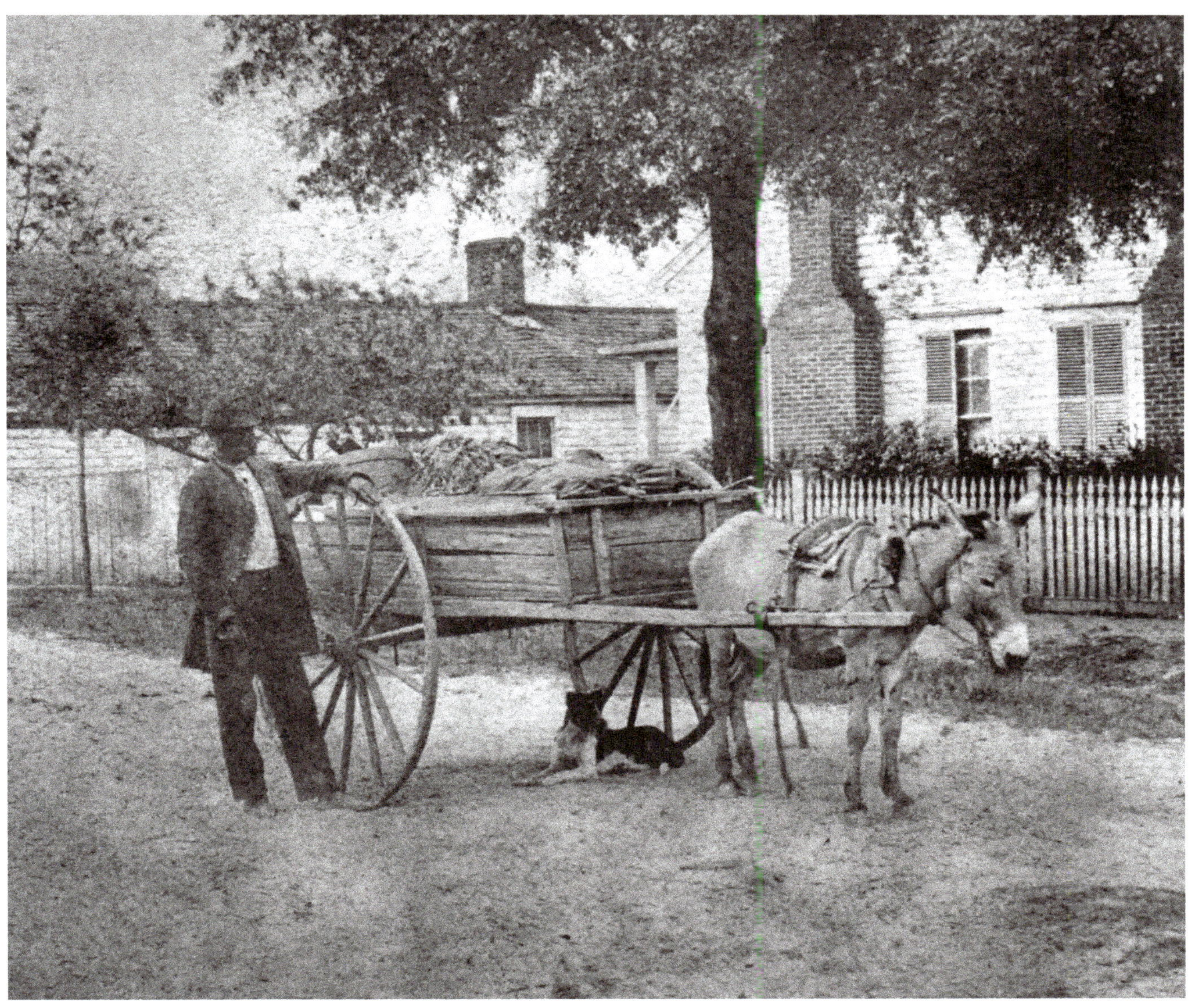

In 1874, a man with his mule cart pauses near the Davis home at the southwest corner of Park Avenue and Duval Street. Converted from a two-story log house for the Tatum family, it had also served as a Masonic lodge and schoolhouse. Born in the house, Jennie Tatum later lived there with her husband, Mayor Fcster Gilmore.

This is the oldest known photograph of Florida's Old Capitol, probably the west side, between 1845 and 1870. The Greek Revival structure was designed by architect Cary W. Butt of Mobile, Alabama. Construction began in 1839, but funds ran out and it was not completed until 1845, when Florida became a state. The total cost was $55,000.

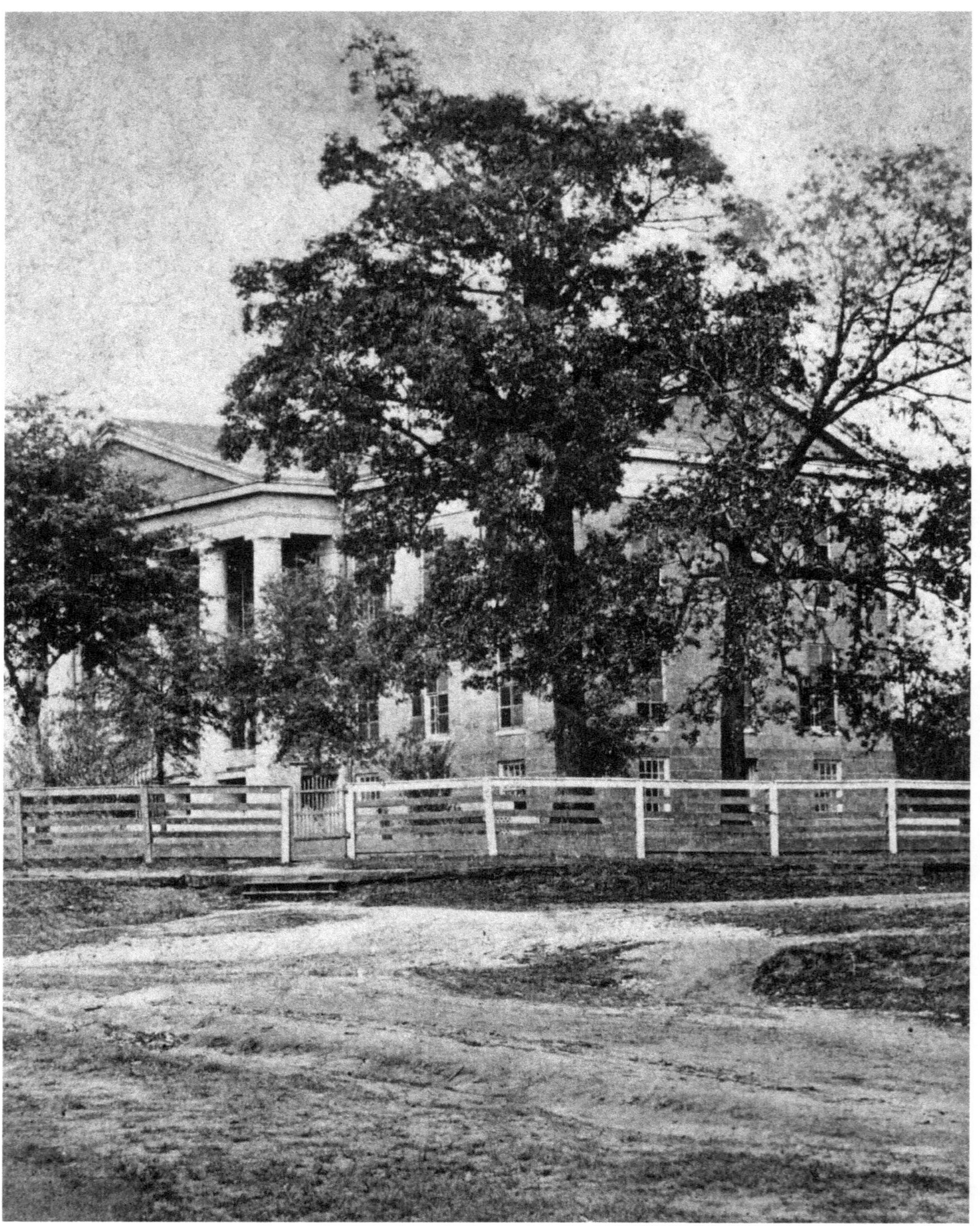

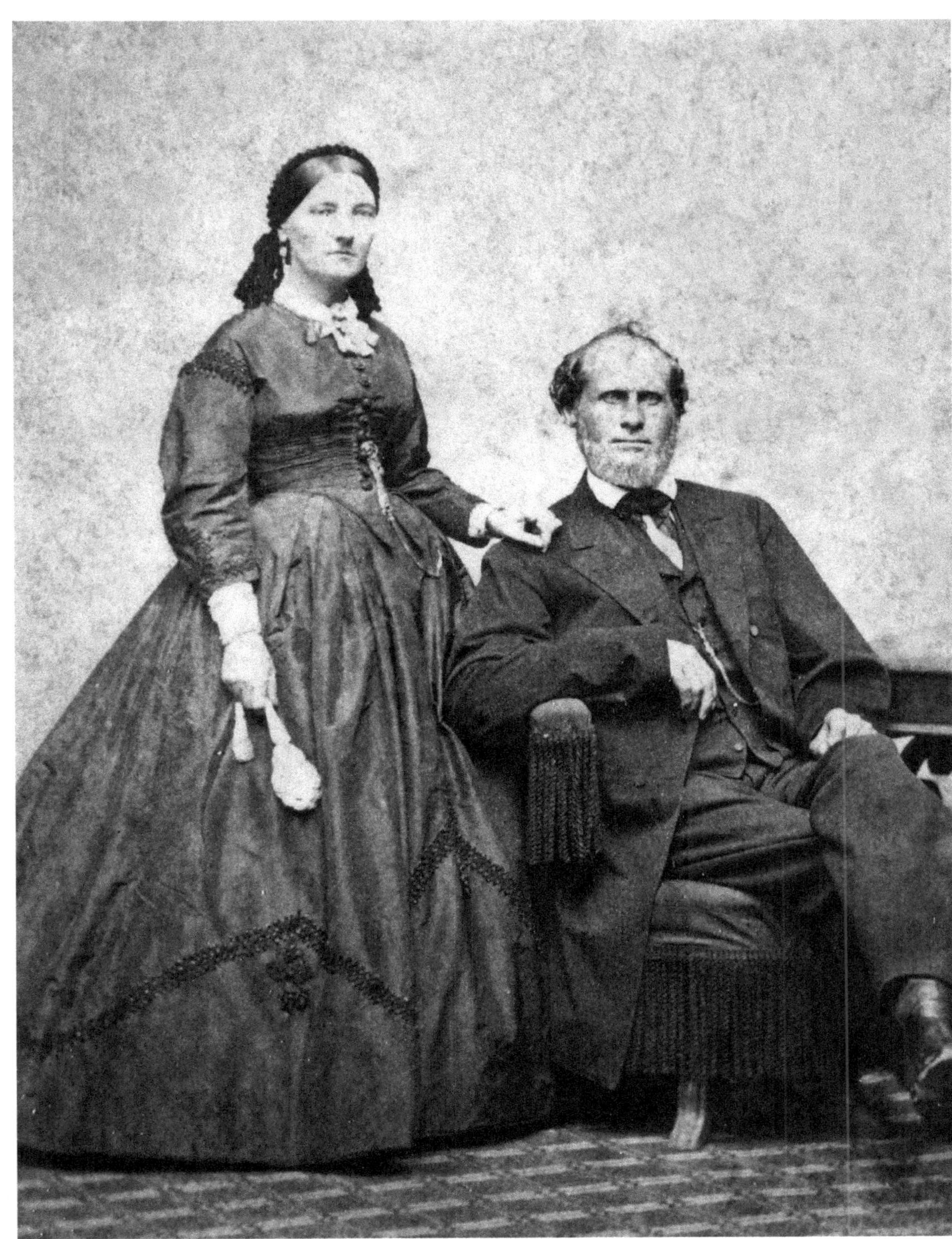

Arriving in 1840 at the age of twenty-six, Perez Bonney Brokaw established a profitable livery stable business in Tallahassee. By 1850 he was able to acquire a sizable property and that same year married Cornelia Tatum. After Cornelia's death, Perez married her sister Elizabeth, shown with him here in 1875.

Erected in 1840, this was the first of three Trinity Methodist churches to stand at the northeast corner of Park and Duval. It was leveled in 1892 to make way for the second church, constructed the next year. The second church was demolished in August 1962 to make way for the third structure.

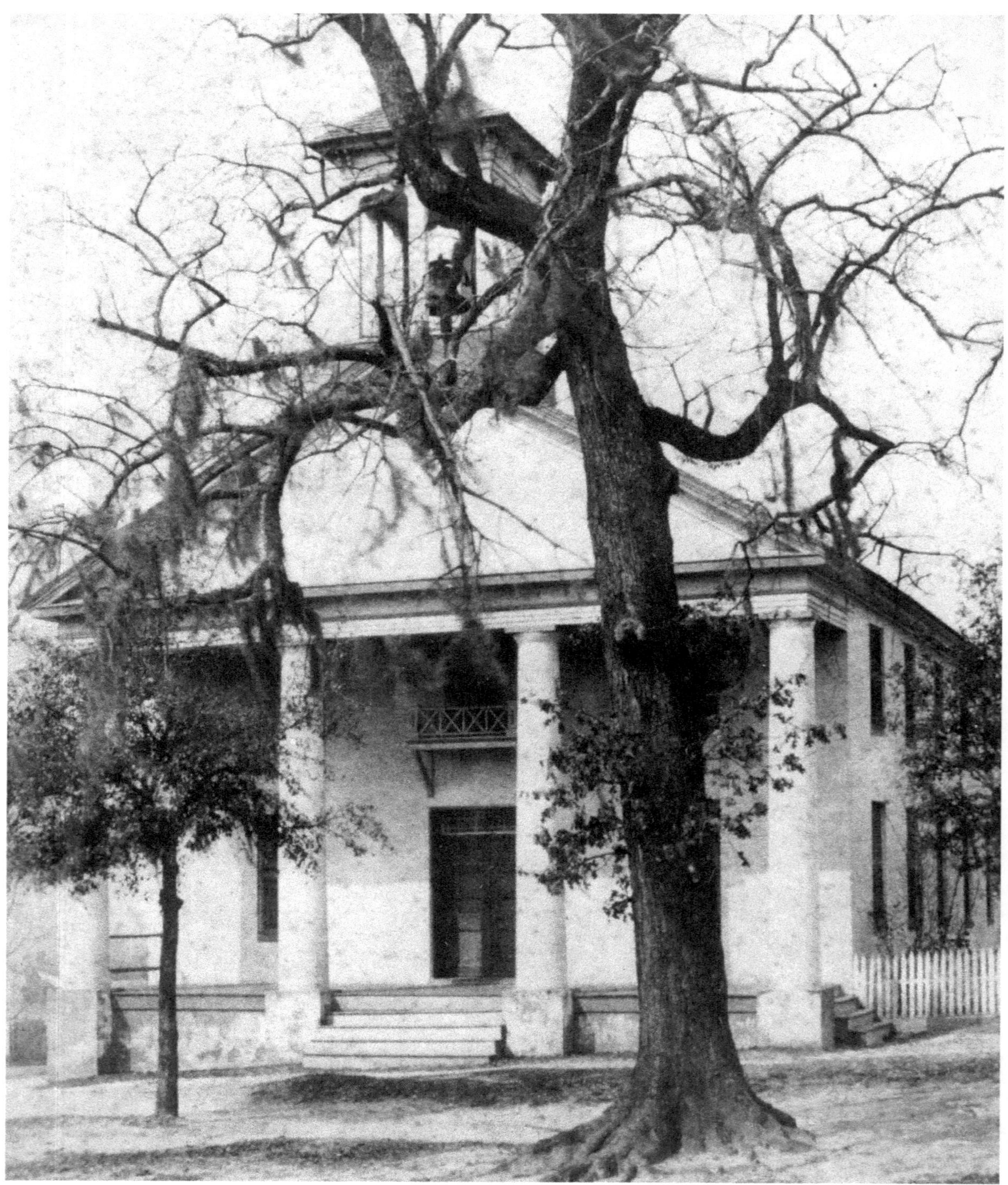

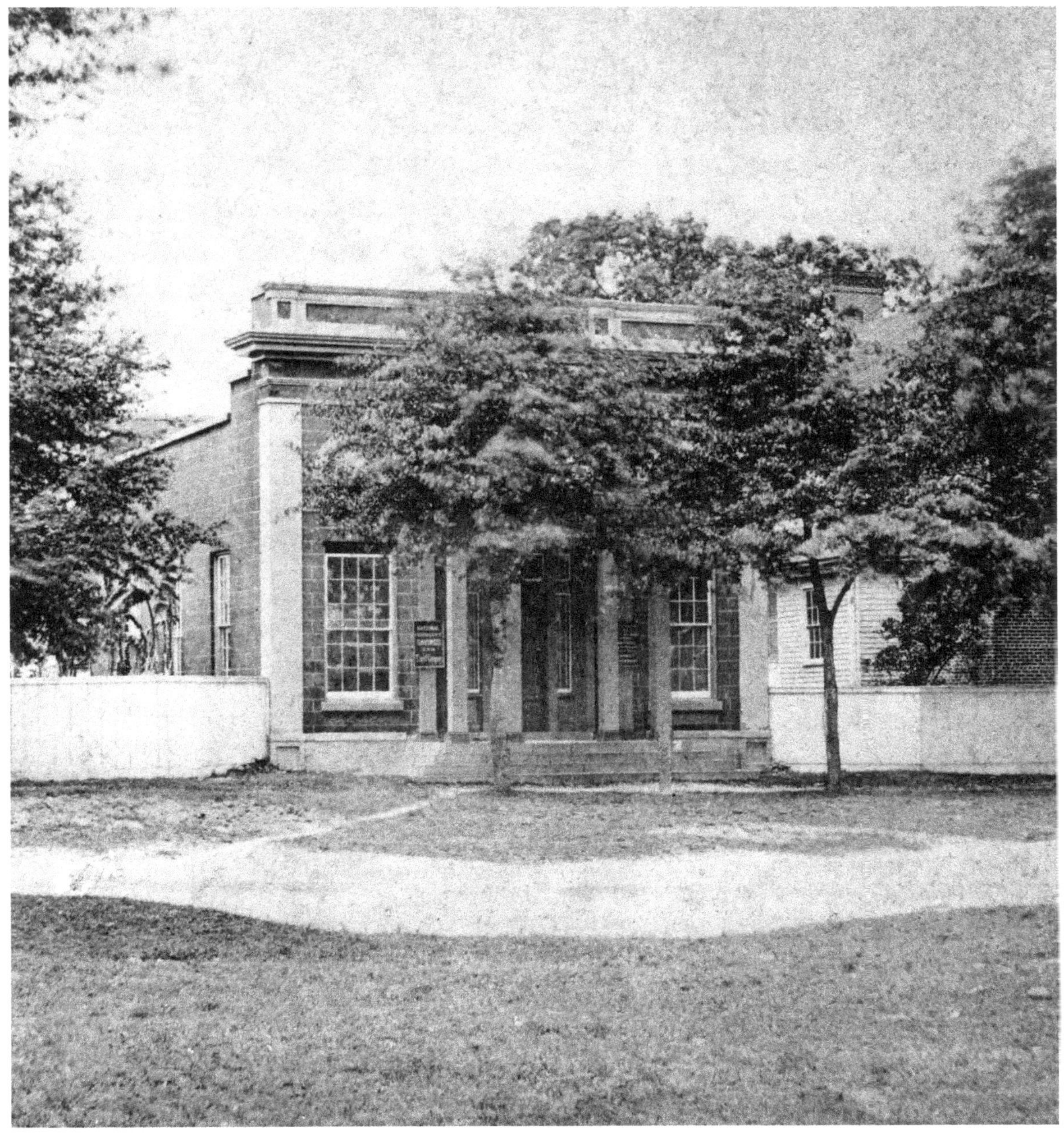

Chartered by the Florida Territorial Legislative Council as a planter's bank in 1833, this building opened in 1841 as the Union Bank. The bank failed by 1843 owing to crop failures, the Second Seminole War, and mismanagement. After the Civil War it reopened as the Freedman's Savings and Trust Bank for former slaves.

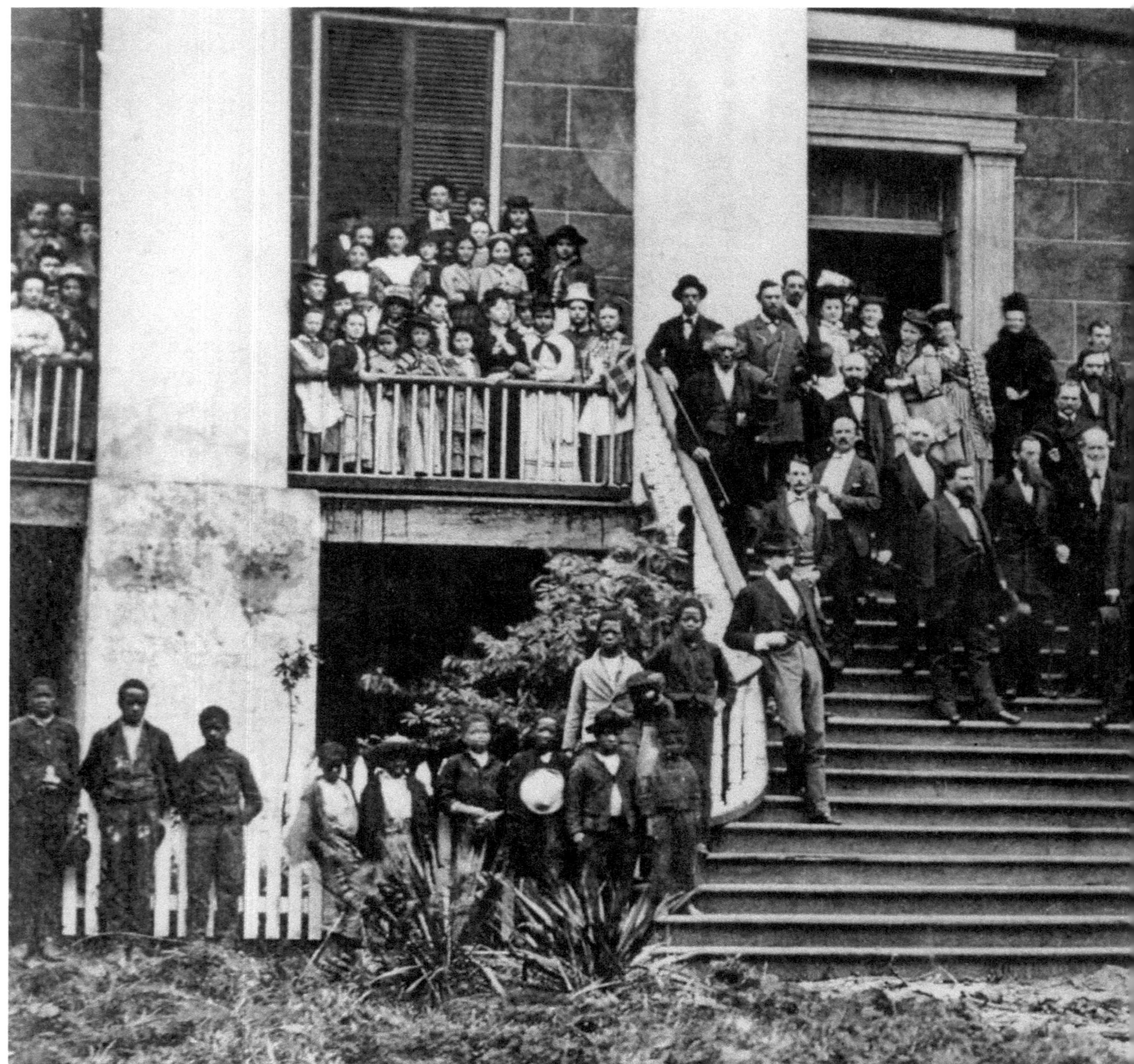

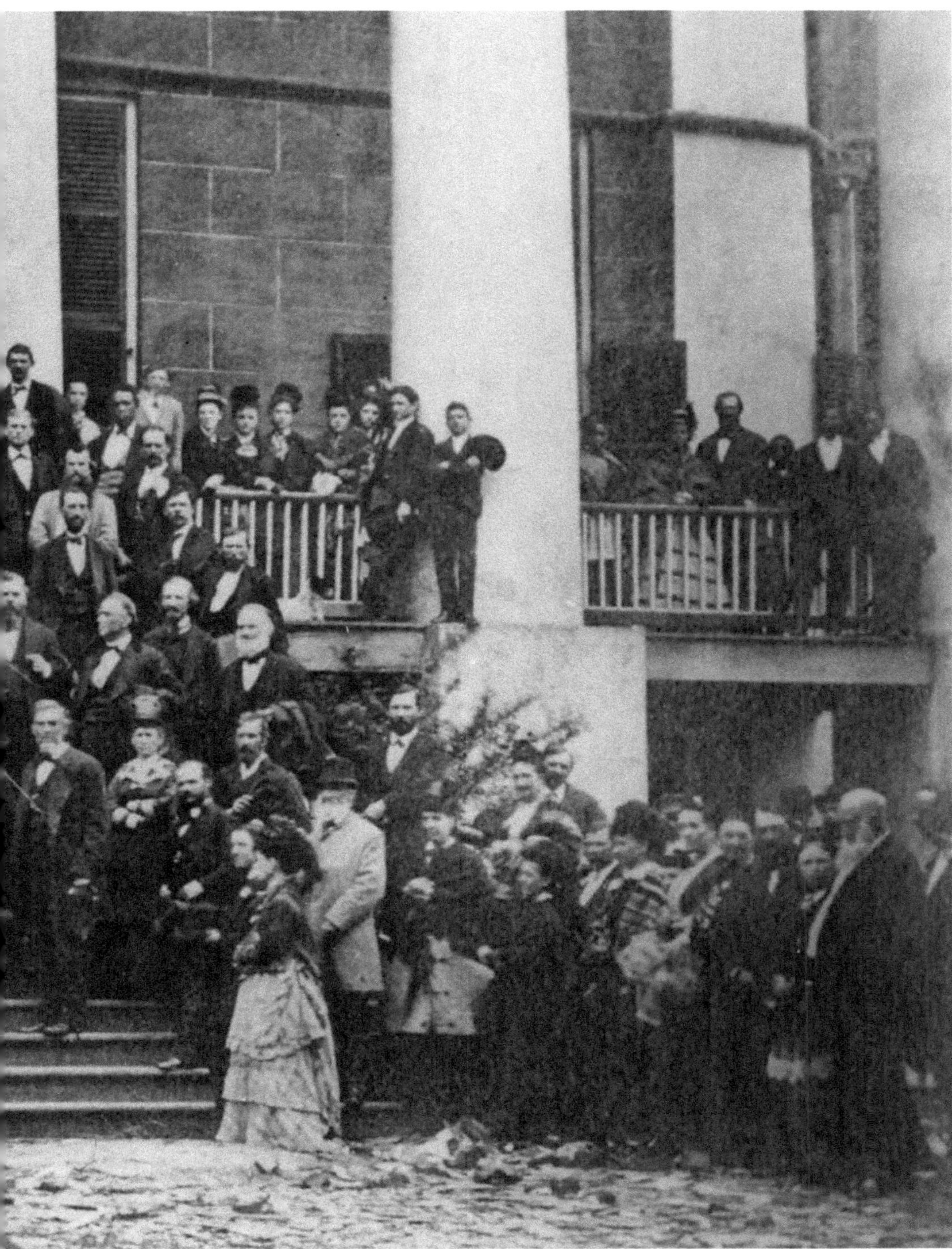

Outside an unkempt capitol in 1875, Governor Marcellus Stearns, center front, greets Harriet Beecher Stowe, the lady in black on the 6th step. Mrs. Stowe, famous abolitionist author of *Uncle Tom's Cabin,* settled in Florida after the Civil War, where she helped establish schools for the children of former slaves.

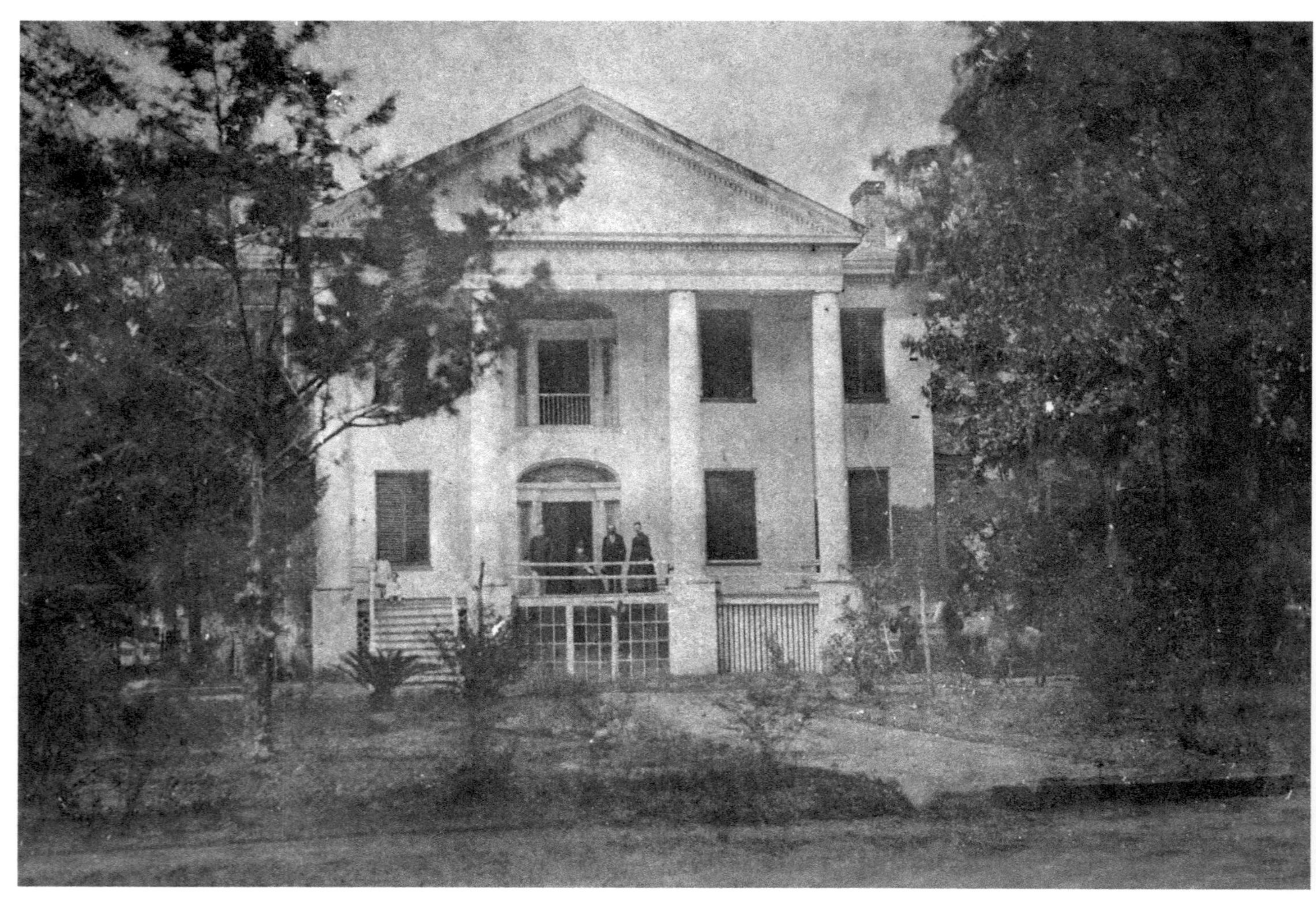

The Grove was Tallahassee's most famous antebellum house. It was the residence of territorial governor Richard Keith Call from 1836 to 1839 and 1841 to 1844, and the thirty-third governor Leroy Collins from 1955 to 1961. Ellen Call Long, seated in the center, was the daughter of Governor Call. The house has remained in the Call family since the 1830s.

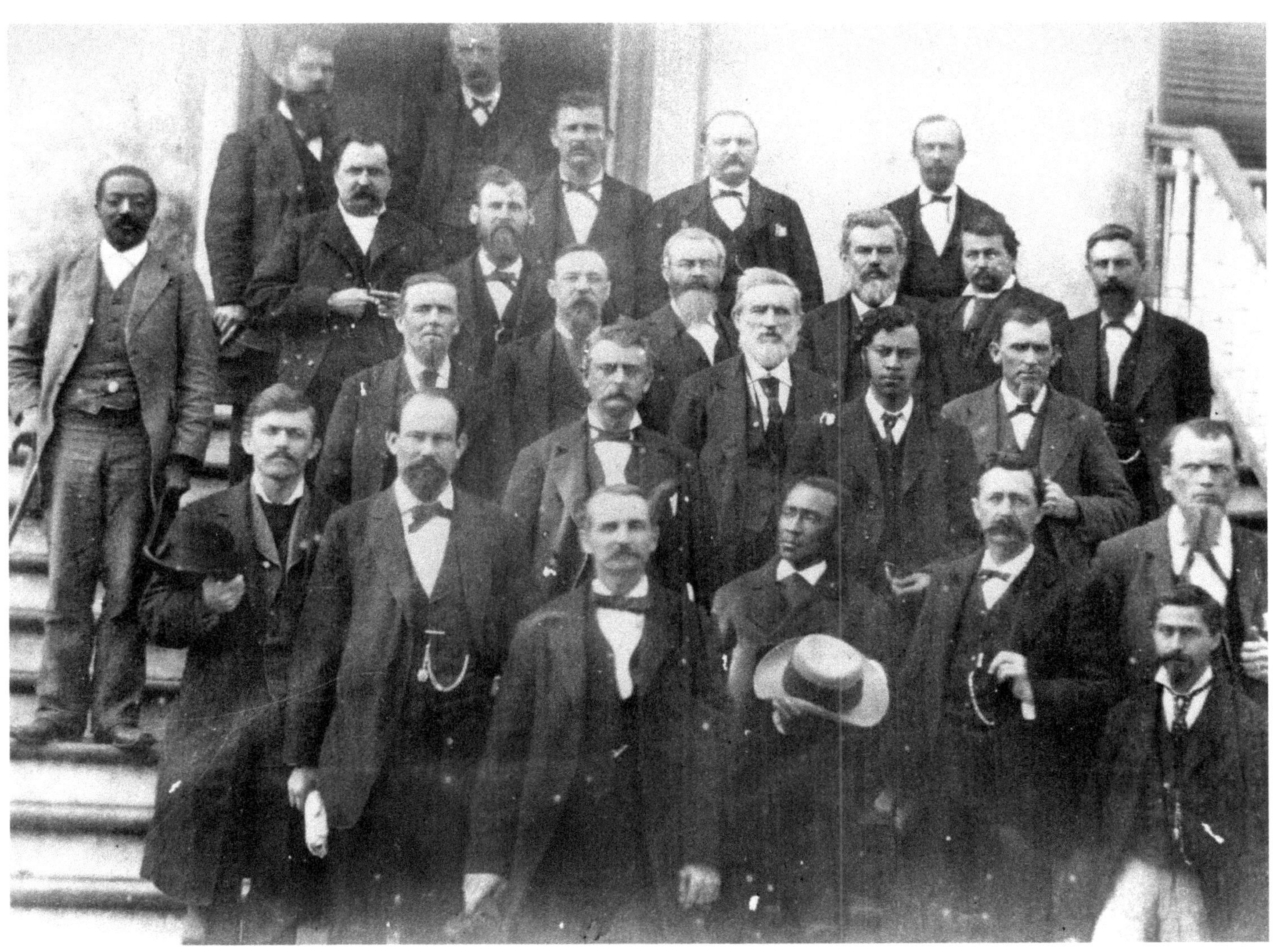

Legislators pose for a group portrait at the capitol. Reconstruction brought a new political make-up to Florida. Democrat senator John Wallace, visible at left with cane, wrote *Carpet Bag Rule in Florida,* while Robert Meacham, third row from back and third from right, with beard, was a minister and a Republican senator.

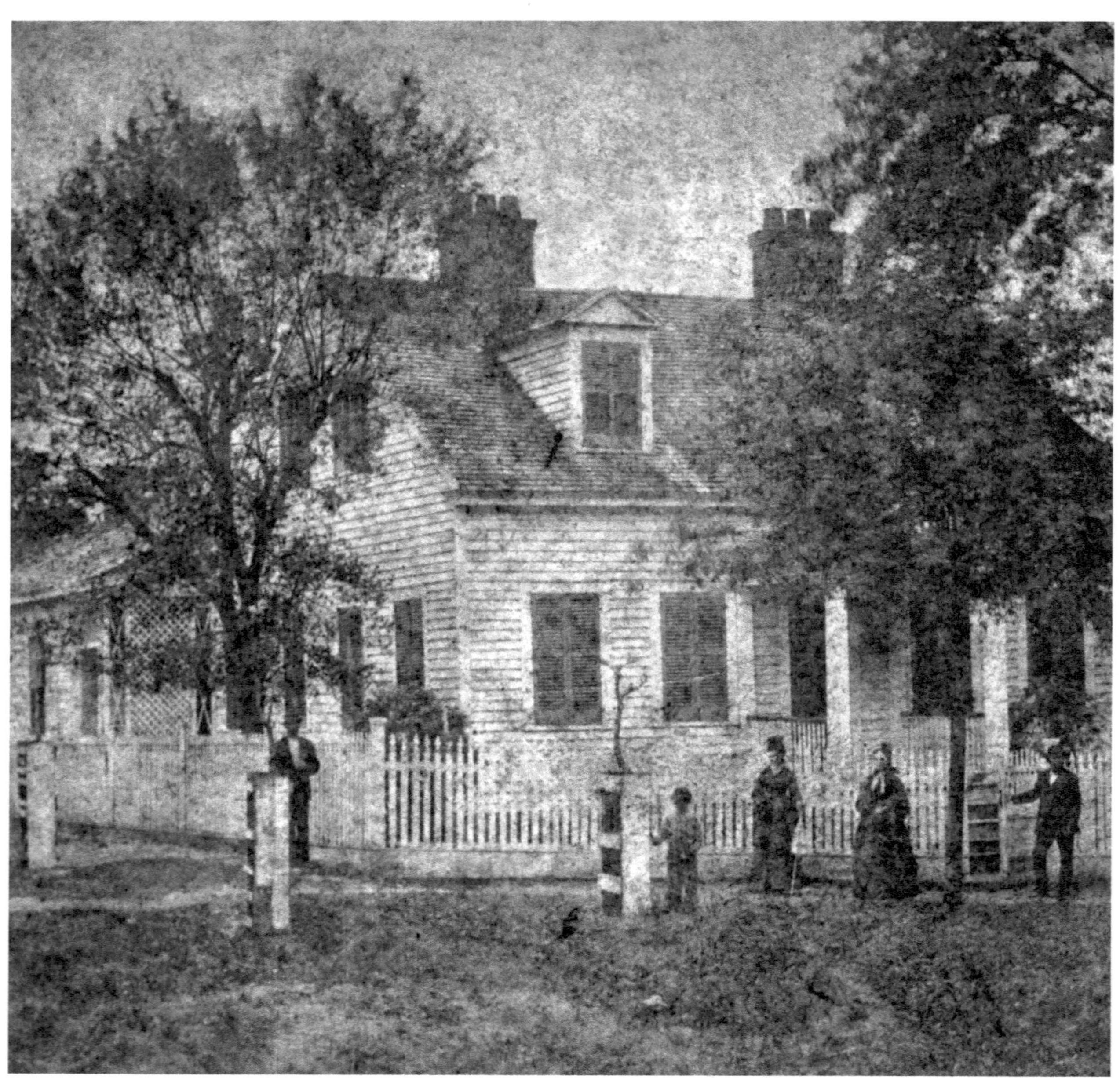

Mr. and Mrs. Selim W. Myers, a Tallahassee Jewish family, stand in front of their home at 701 South Adams Street in 1874. Originally built for his parents sometime before 1845, the house was inherited by Selim, a watchmaker. Myers Park is named in honor of Selim's son, Frederick Towle Myers, president of the 1897 Florida Senate.

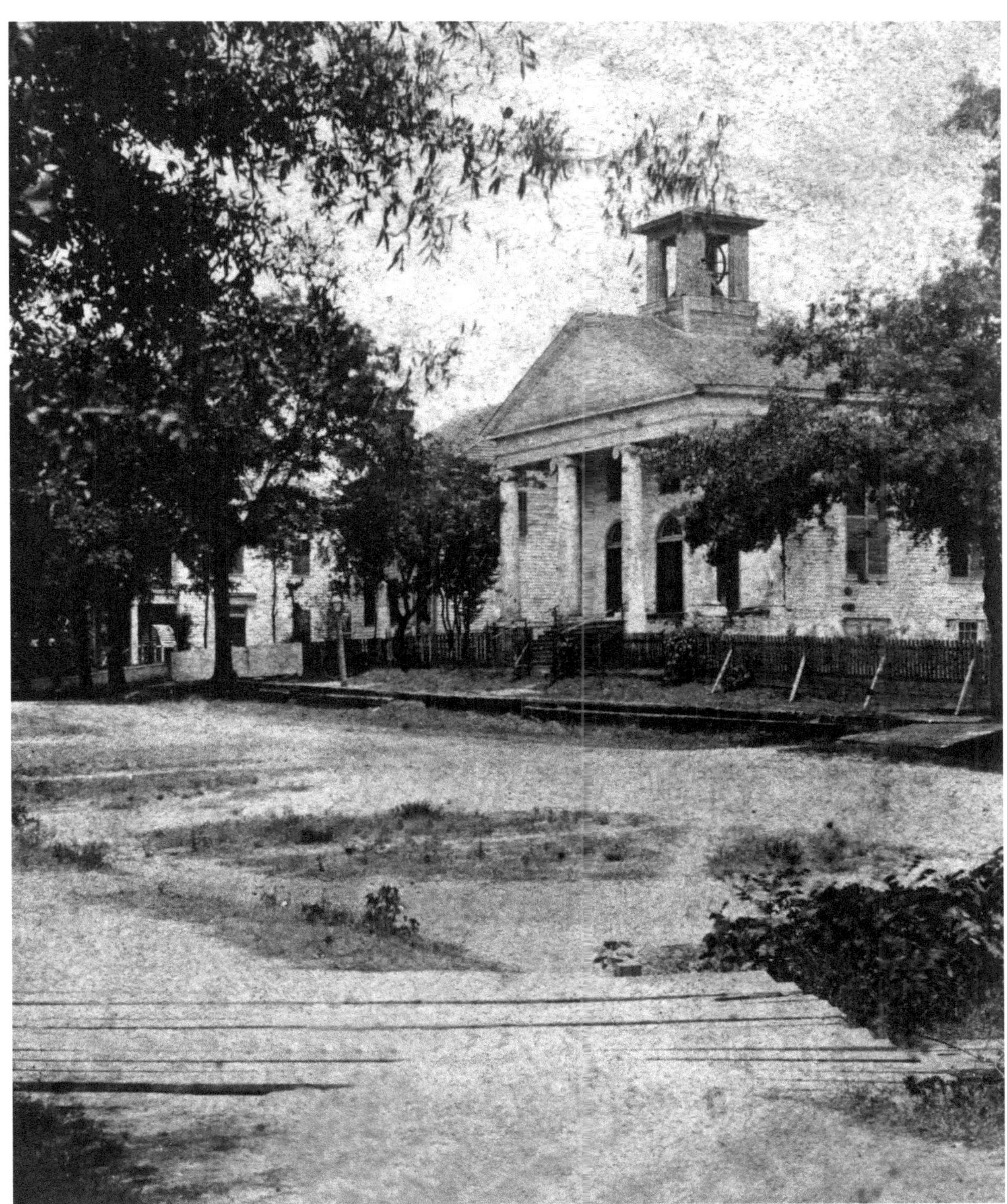

Organized in 1829 as the third Episcopal congregation in Florida, St. Johns Episcopal church has ministered to many generations of Tallahasseans. Built by John Lavinus around 1837 for $10,000, this wooden building was destroyed by fire on January 19, 1879. The second church building, built of brick, became a Tallahassee landmark.

Produce and goods, many from the outlying farms and plantations, were sold fresh daily at this marketplace on Park Avenue, shown sometime in the 1870s. After emancipation, many former slaves in the area found themselves back working on the plantations, only now with contracts approved by the Freedman's Bureau.

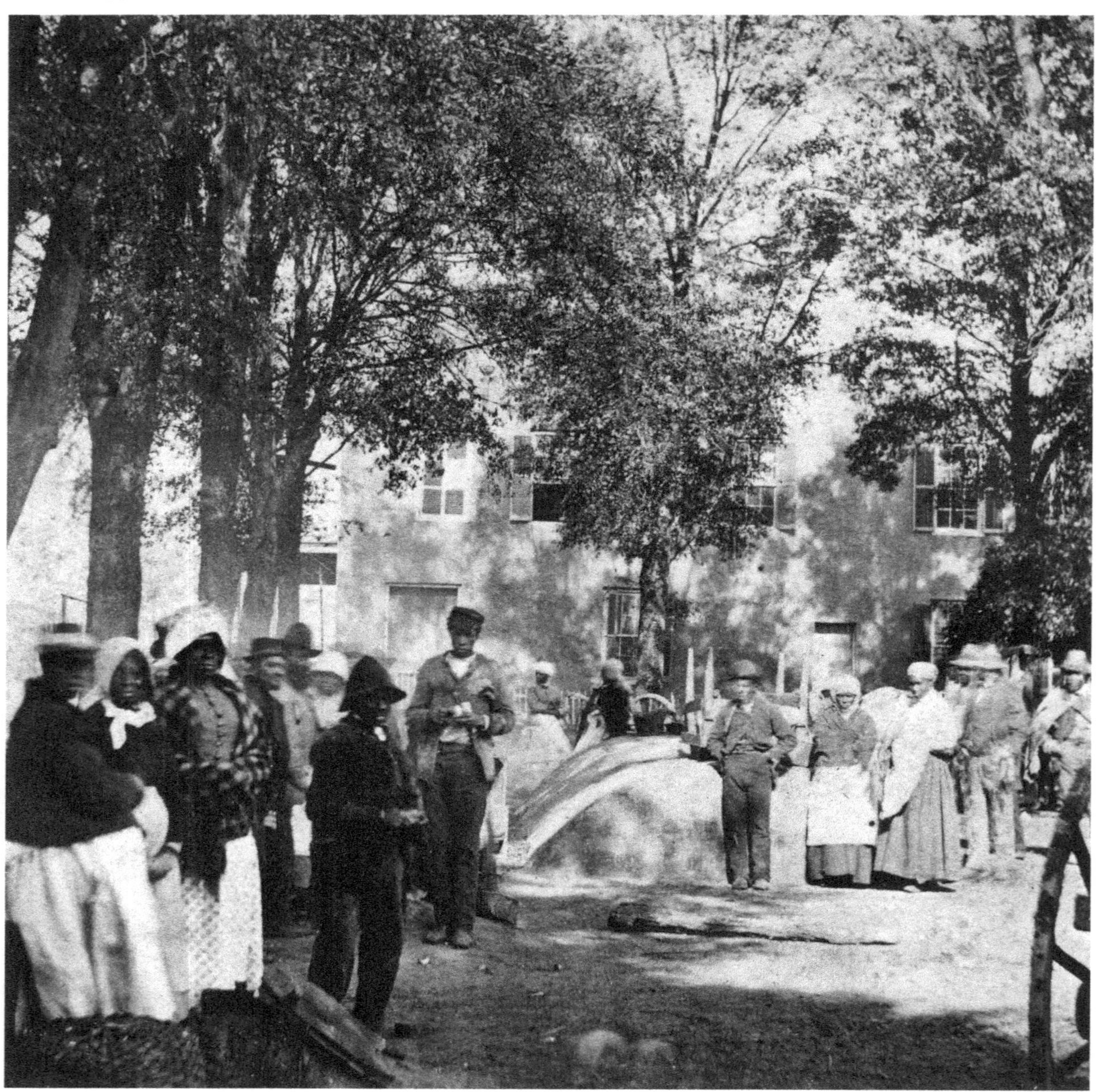

The first Catholic church in Tallahassee was built on the northeast corner of Park and Gadsden in 1845 but burned in 1847. Shown here is the second building, the Church of St. Mary, which cost about $2,500 in 1853. The Catholic Church has a long heritage in the area, dating to the Christmas mass celebrated by Spanish explorer Hernando DeSoto's expedition in 1539.

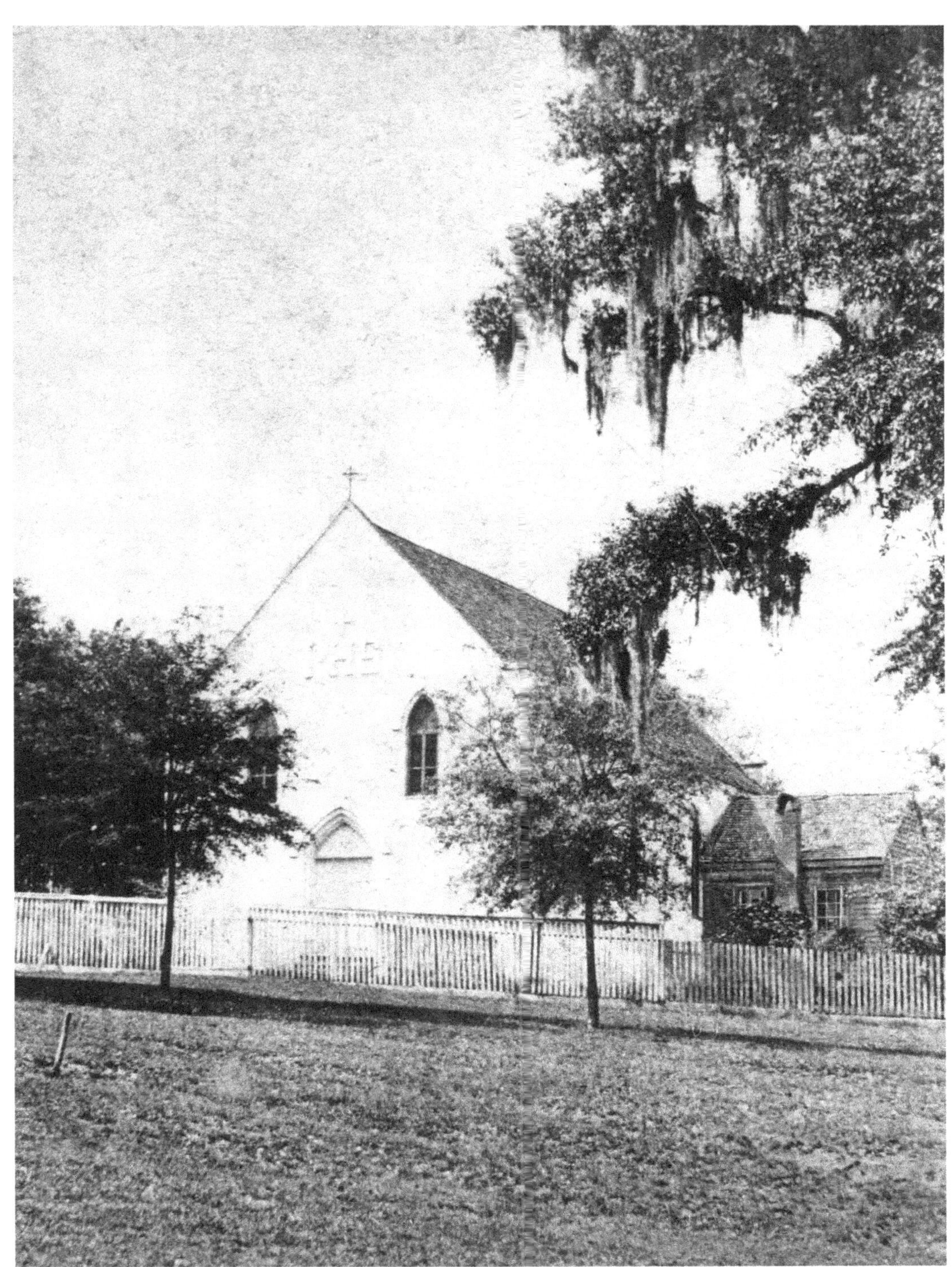

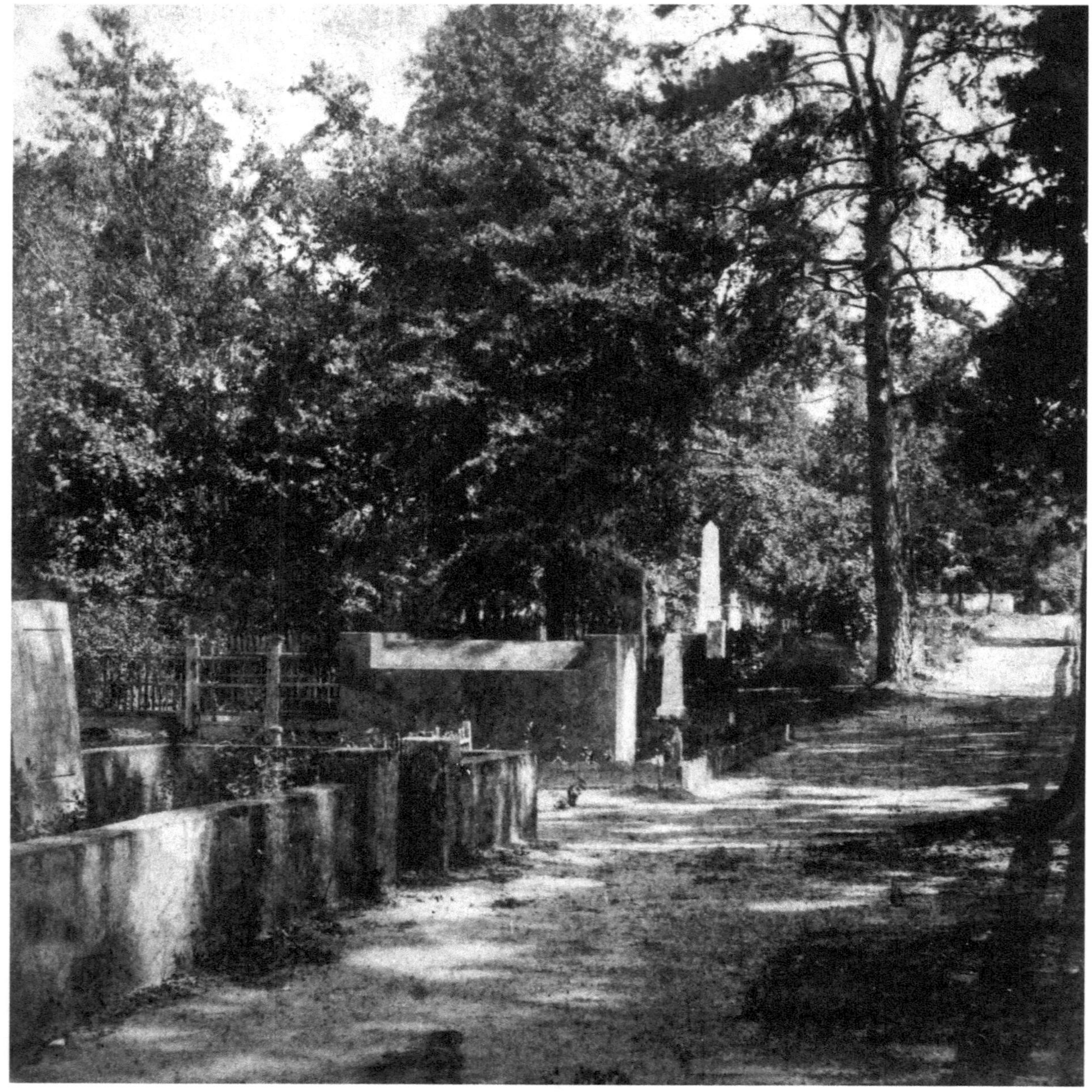

The Old City Cemetery was laid out by the Territorial Legislature in 1829 as the "Public Burying Ground," the city's first public cemetery. Interred here are a Florida governor, Confederate and Union Civil War casualties, African American leaders, legislators, and victims of the 1841 yellow fever epidemic.

In 1885, the Florida Railway and Navigation Company was consolidated from many north Florida railroad lines, some dating back to the old Tallahassee Railroad Company, chartered in 1835. This inspection team poses in front of an engine, originally of the Indiana, Peru and Chicago line, named the *C. B. Robinson.*

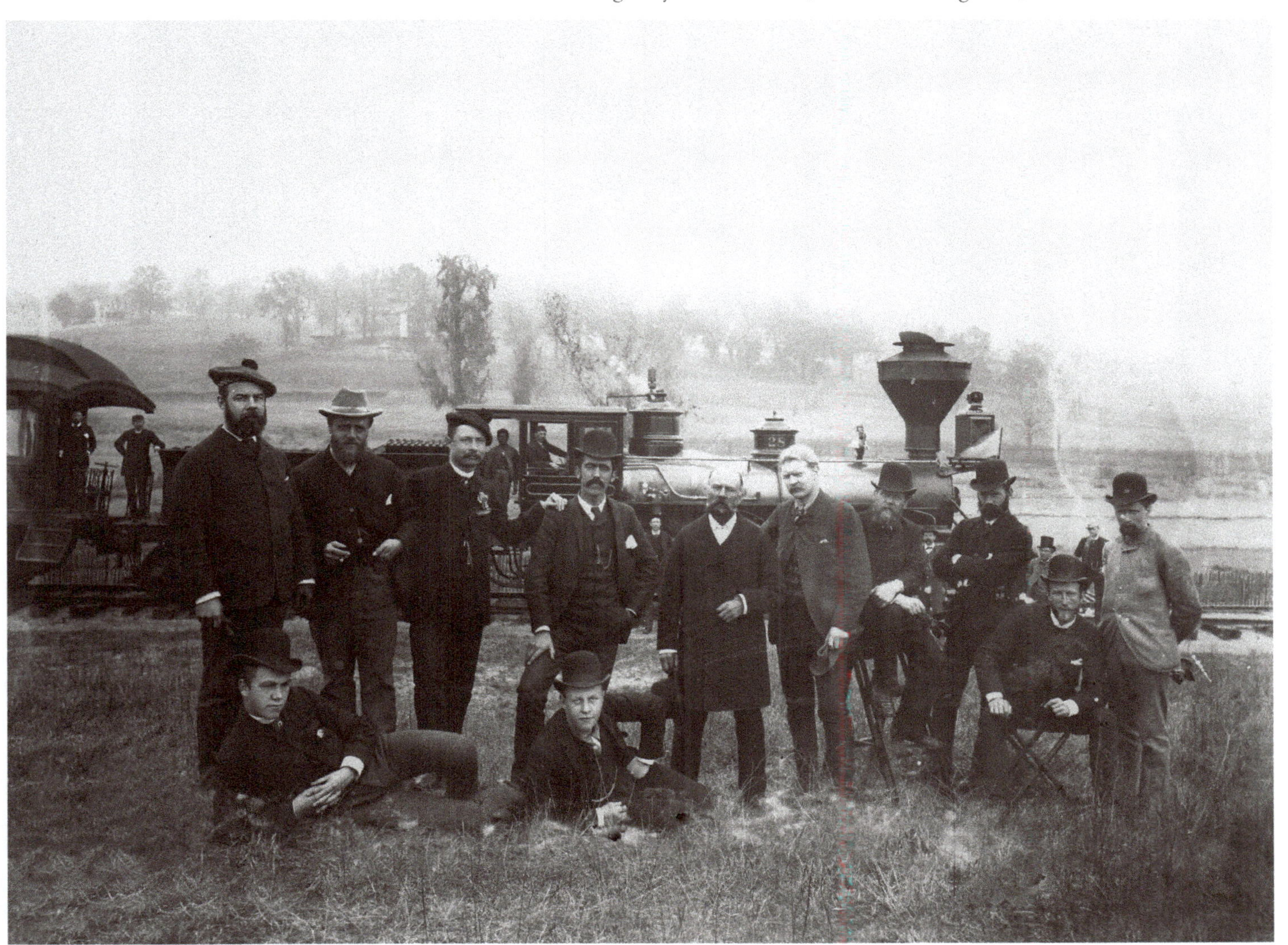

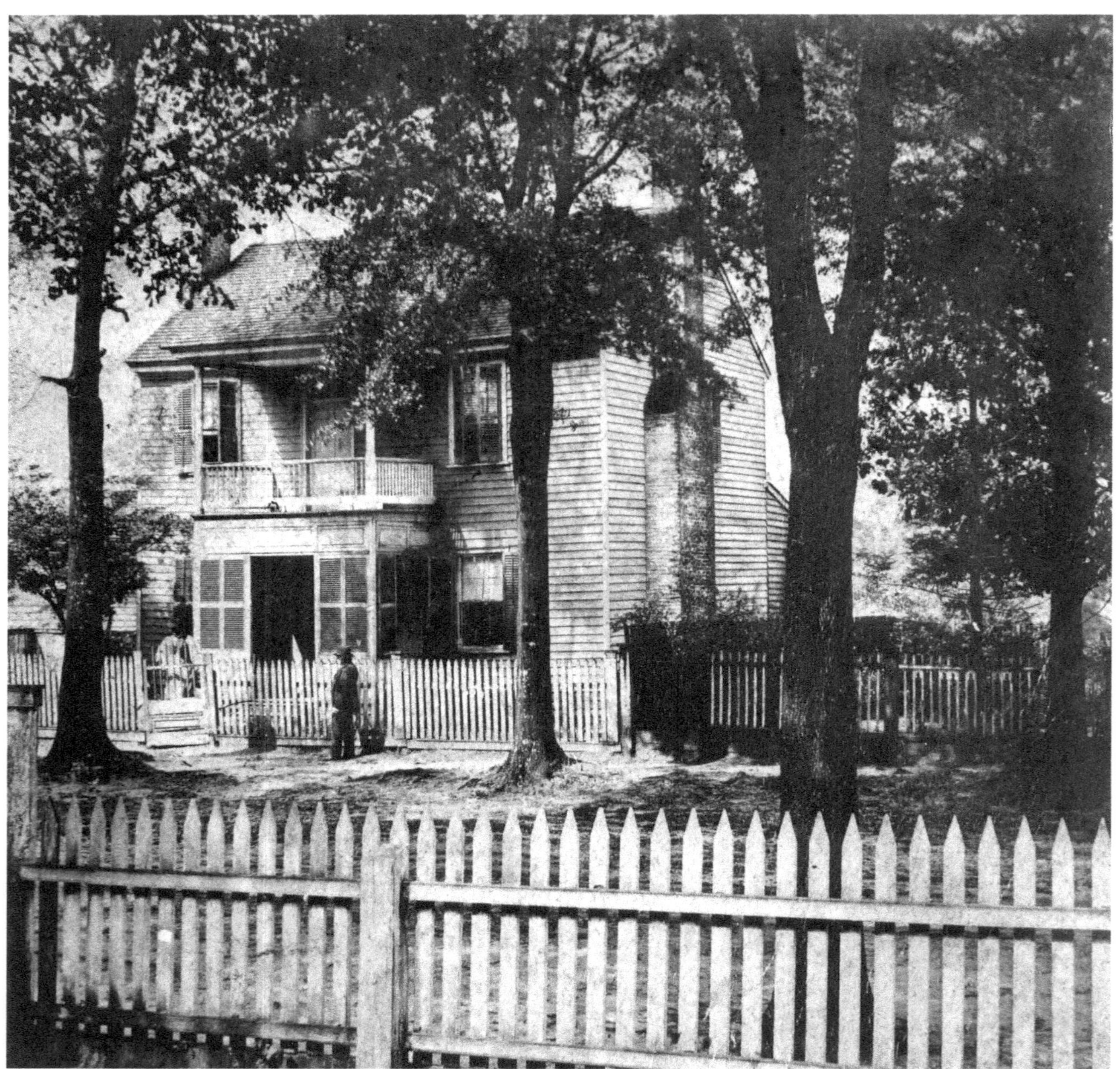

This home of Thomas Blake Byrd at 635 Calhoun Street was built for Matthew Lively, a druggist, in 1865 and sold to Willie P. Byrd in 1882. A few years later Willie's brother, Thomas, moved his family into the house from the nearby town of Miccosukee. The family owned and operated T. B. Byrd and Son Grocery Store until the 1960s.

Governor William D. Bloxham entertains guests at his city residence. Elected in 1880, Bloxham, a Leon County resident, moved from his plantation southeast of Tallahassee to this house on Calhoun Street. With him are (left to right) George Lewis, Willie Bloxham, Mrs. Bloxham, Governor Bloxham, Mrs. George Lewis.

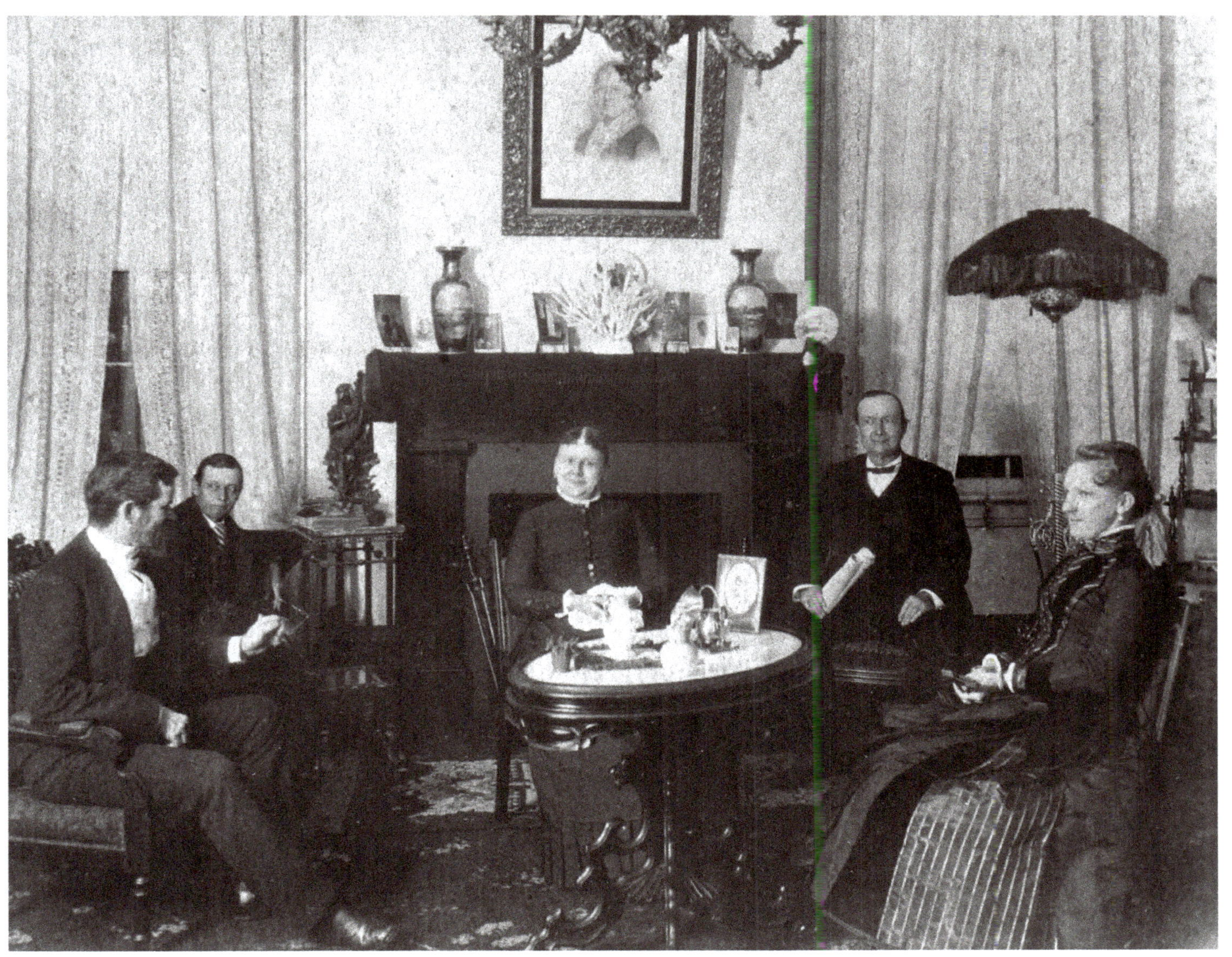

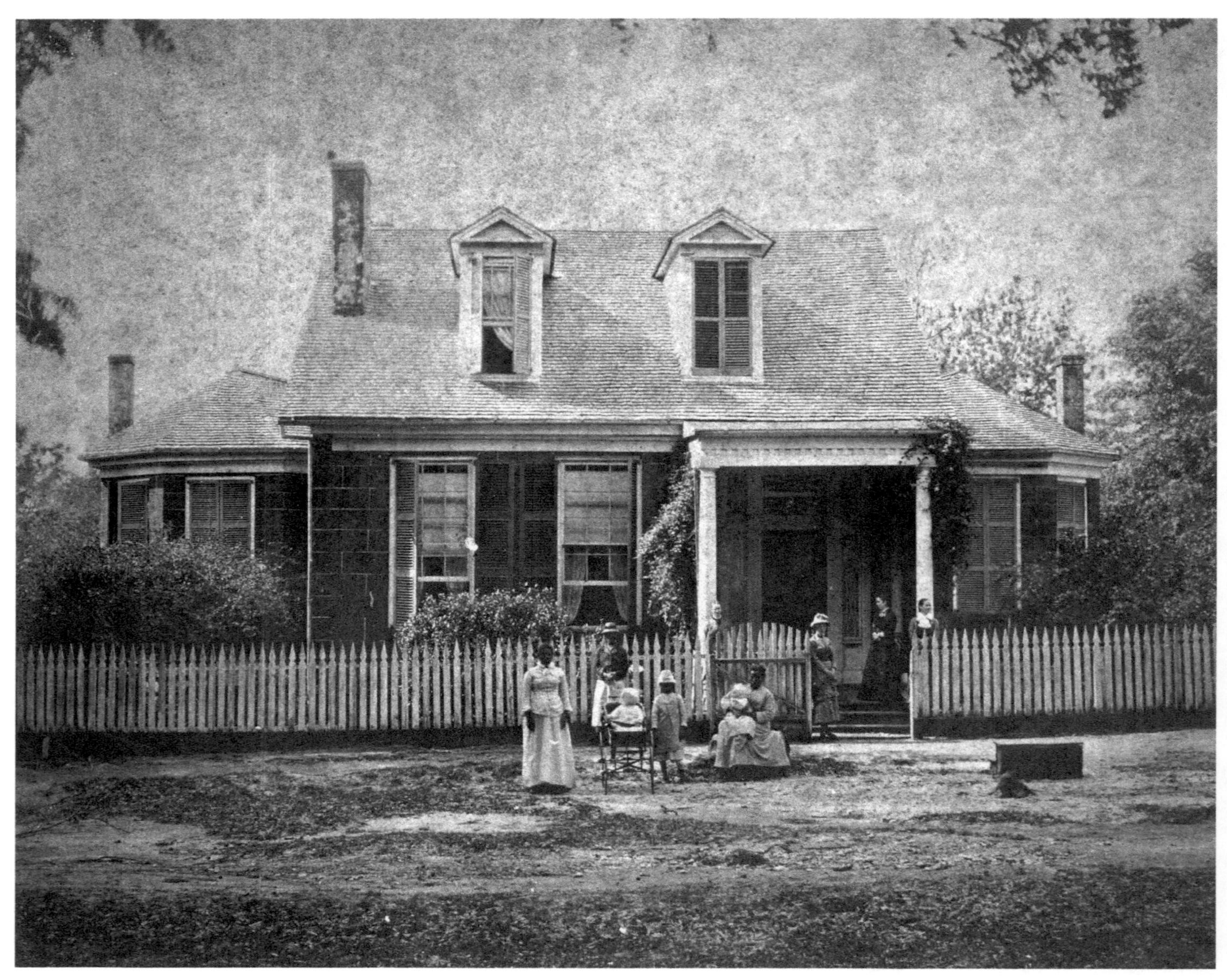

In 1888, the Flagg family and servants pose in front of their home on McCarty Street, later renamed Park Avenue. Originally built in 1840 by Captain Richard Shine purportedly with materials from the earlier territorial capitol, it was remodeled in 1894 by the Chittenden family. The house has served as hospital, boardinghouse, and dining spot.

The steamboat *Walkatomica* met train travelers from the Tallahassee and St. Marks terminal, providing leisurely excursions to Newport, Carrabelle, and St. Teresa, all popular recreation spots. A round-trip ticket for train and steamer was $2.25. Launched in June 1885, the *Walkatomica* burned in October 1898.

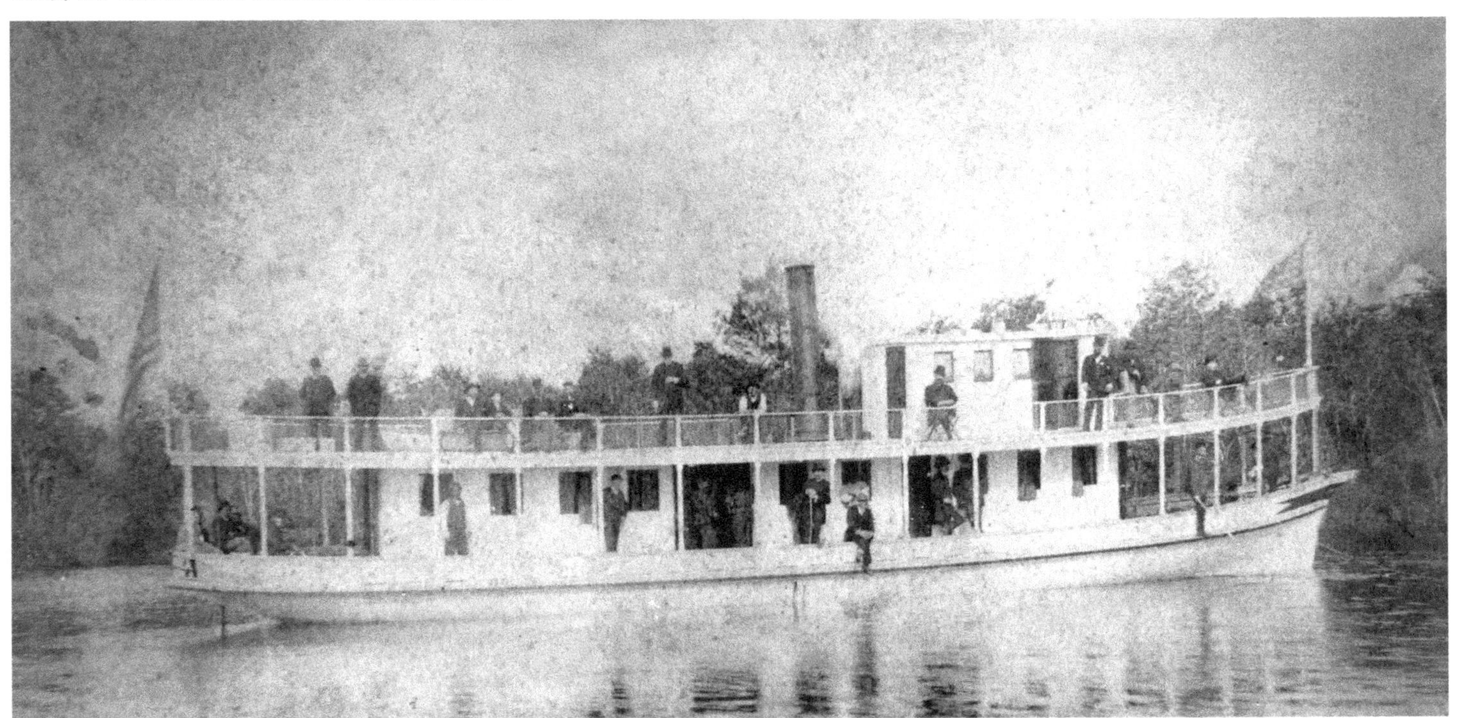

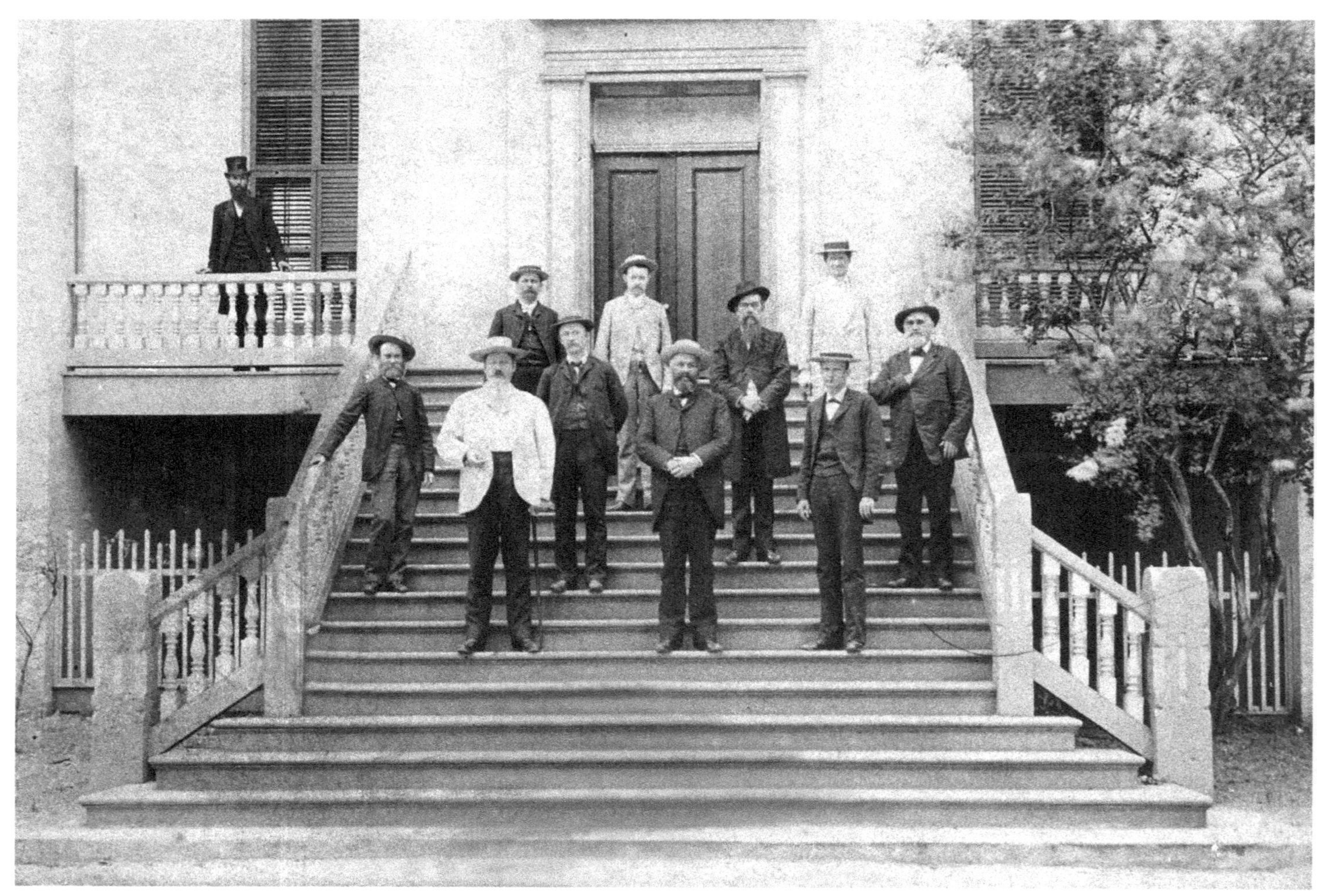

Florida's 14th governor Edward Aylsworth Perry (front center, hands clasped) and cabinet pause for a photograph on the Capitol steps in 1885. During his administration, Florida adopted a new constitution and established a state board of education. In October 1885, surprised capitol visitors were greeted by an ostrich roaming the fenced grounds, a present to the governor.

Florida State University traces its beginnings to 1851 when the state legislature established the West Florida Seminary. The seminary officially opened in 1857 in this building, constructed by the city three years earlier on a site formerly known as Gallows Hill. The building was leveled in 1891 for the new College Hall.

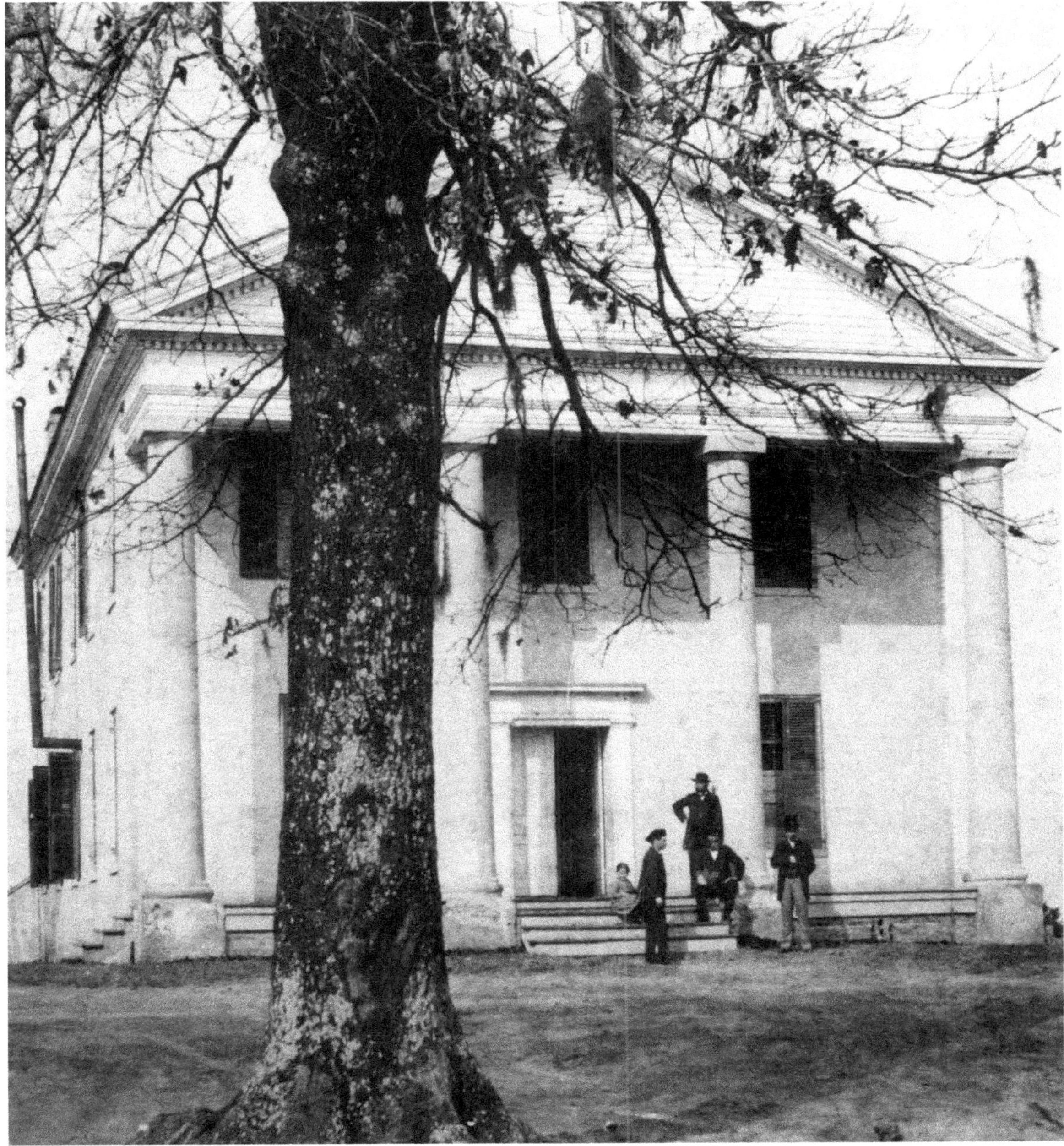

Owned by Emile Dubois, this vineyard operated from 1884 to 1904. Located at the site of the seventeenth-century Spanish mission San Luis de Apalachee, it has yielded archaeological evidence of a Spanish fort, church, and residences, as well as an Apalachee council house and Indian village. The site is now an interpretive park.

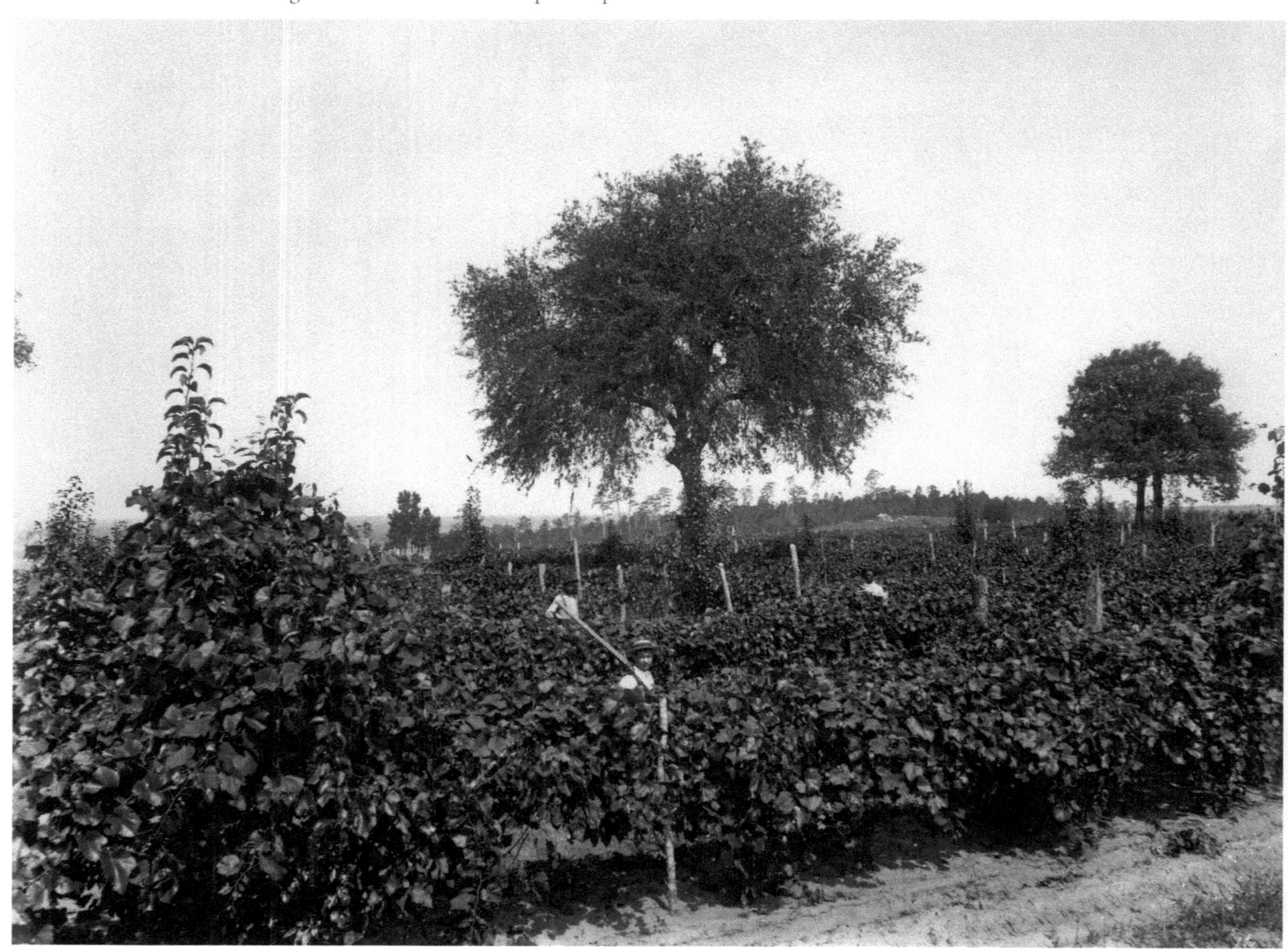

Members of the 1885 Florida Senate gather on the Capitol steps for a group portrait. At right holding a coat is Secretary of the Senate William MacWilliams, and next to him, the lieutenant governor and president of the Senate Milton H. Mabry, later a Florida Supreme Court justice.

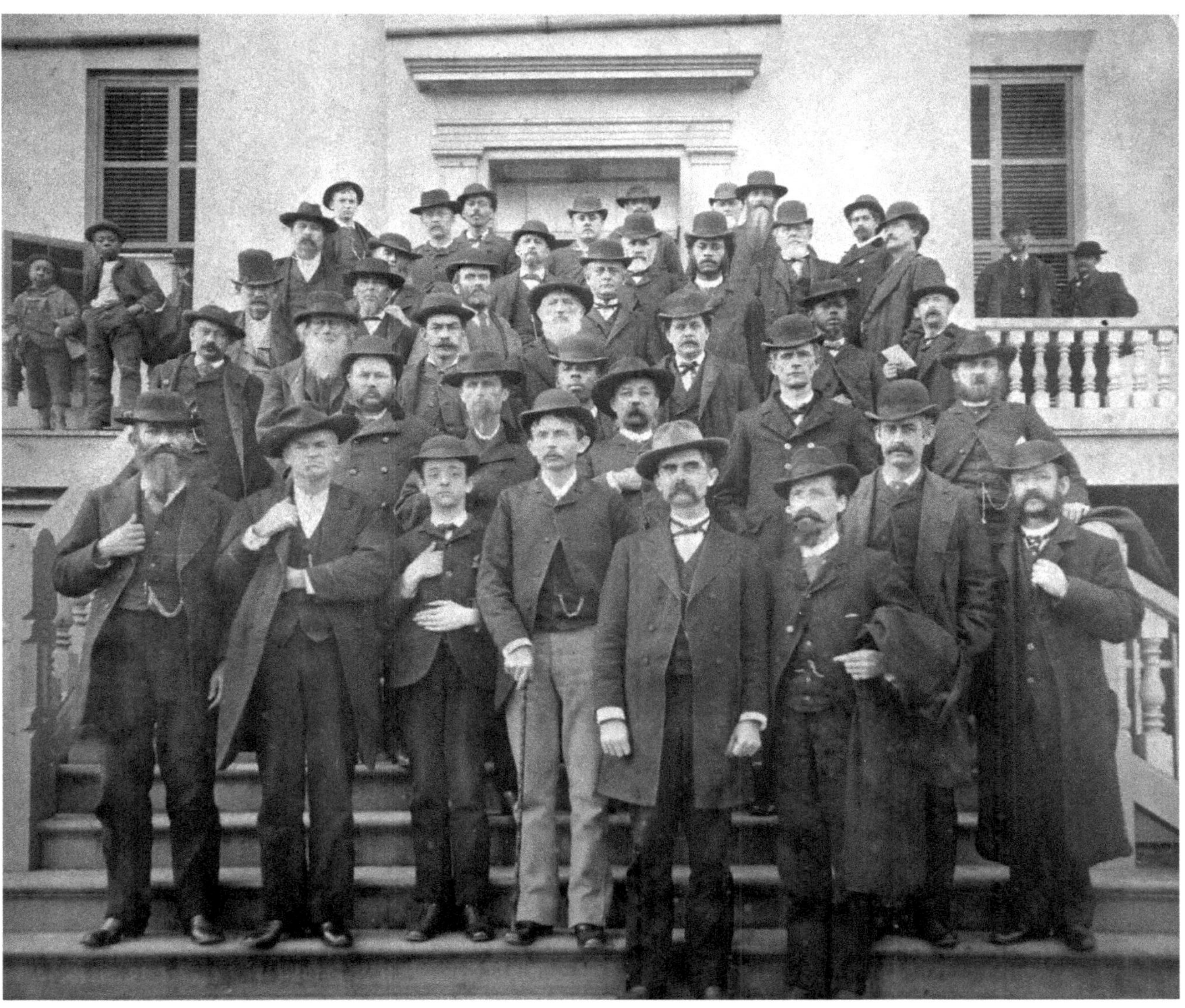

Following Spread: Tallahassee photographer Alvan Harper captured this image of two boys and crew of the Florida Railway and Navigation Company engine number 16. Harper's photograph reflects local pride felt toward the railroads—some of it owing to the presence of a railroad shop facility, the only industrial plant located in Tallahassee in the 1880s.

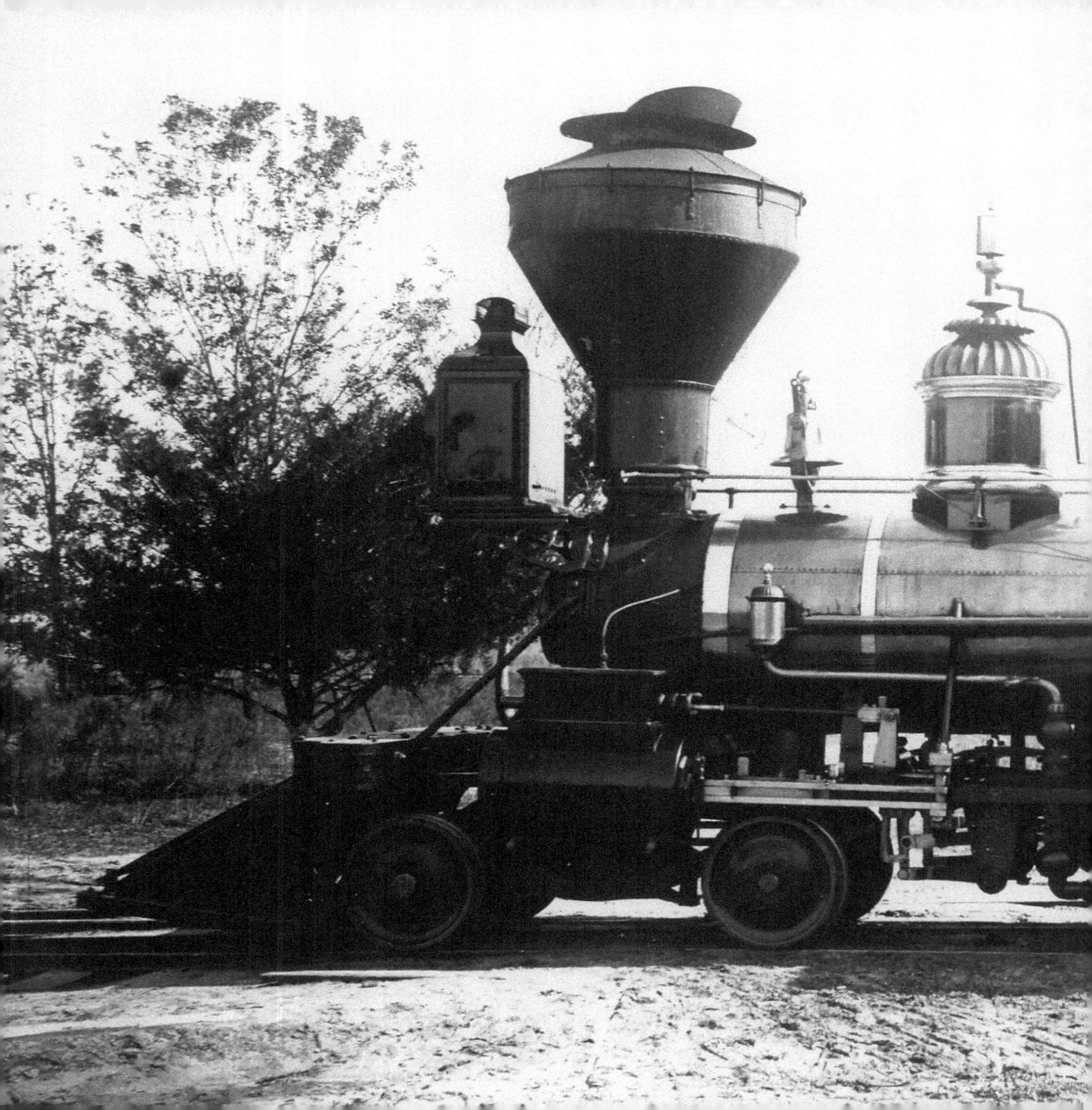

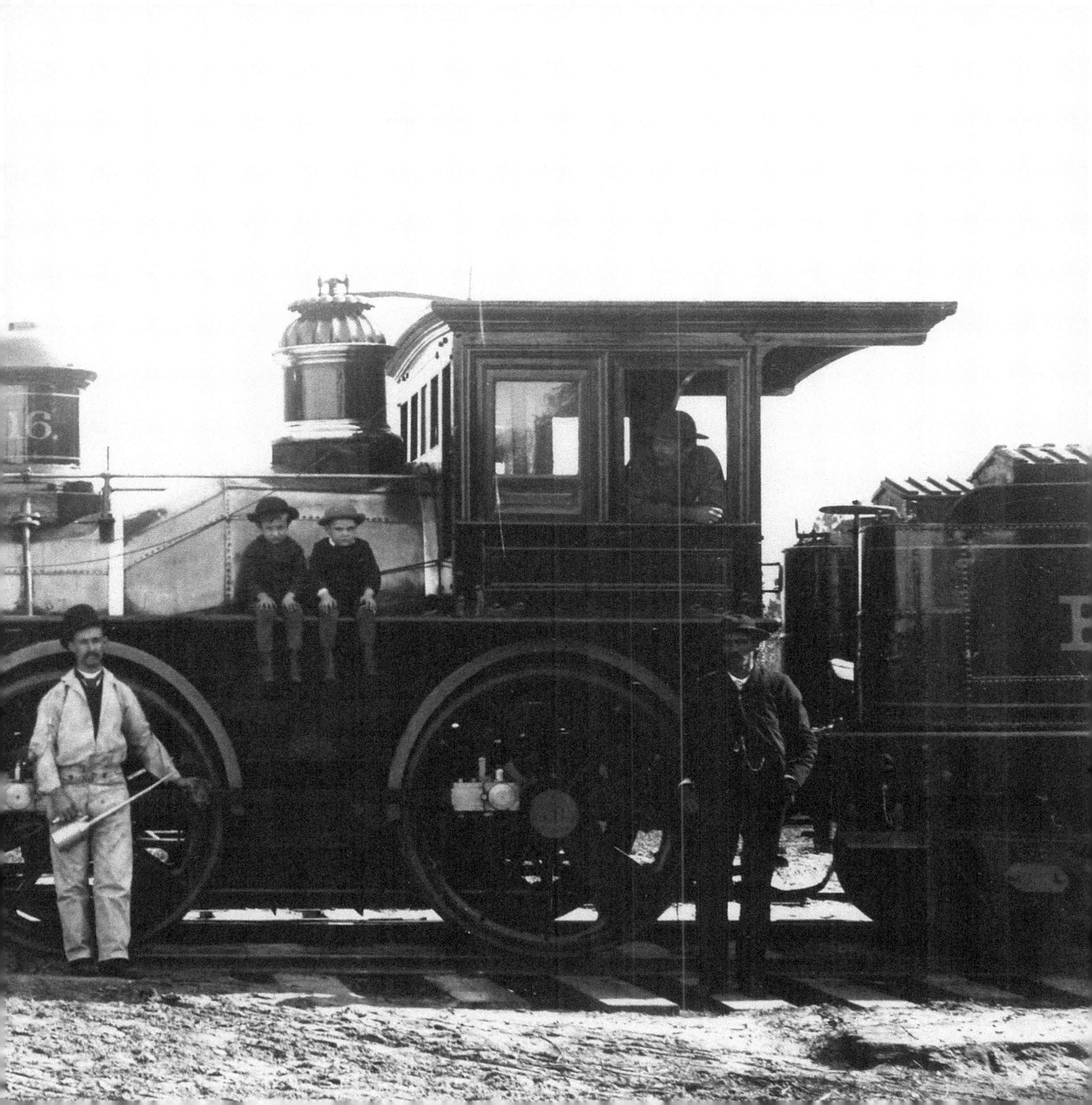
16.

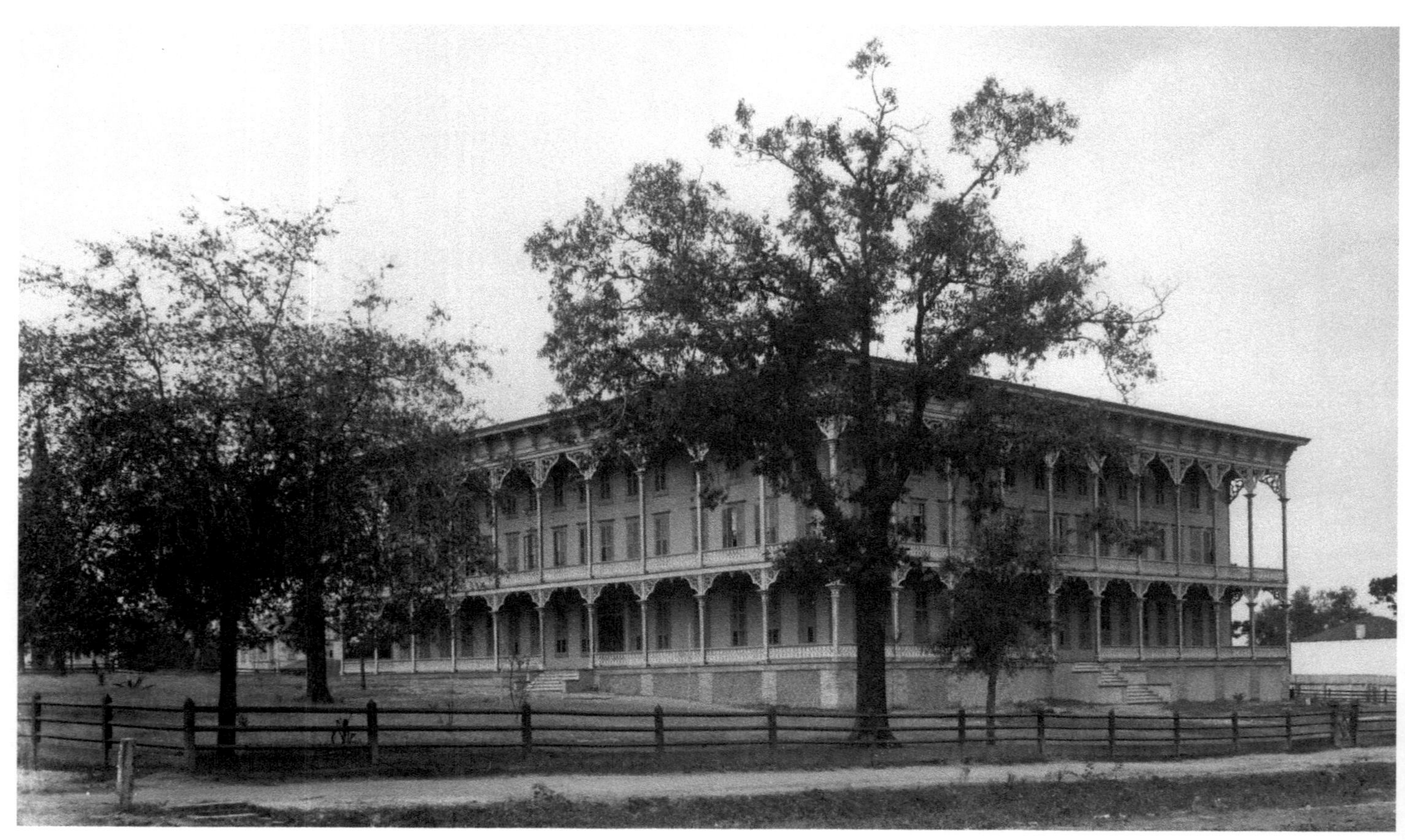

Landscaped with roses, hyacinths, and tulips, the Leon Hotel was a first-class hotel for a capital city. Also located at this prime site on Park Avenue was the first courthouse, which burned in 1879; the first Leon Hotel, burned in 1885; the second Leon Hotel, burned in 1925; and the post office, built in 1935.

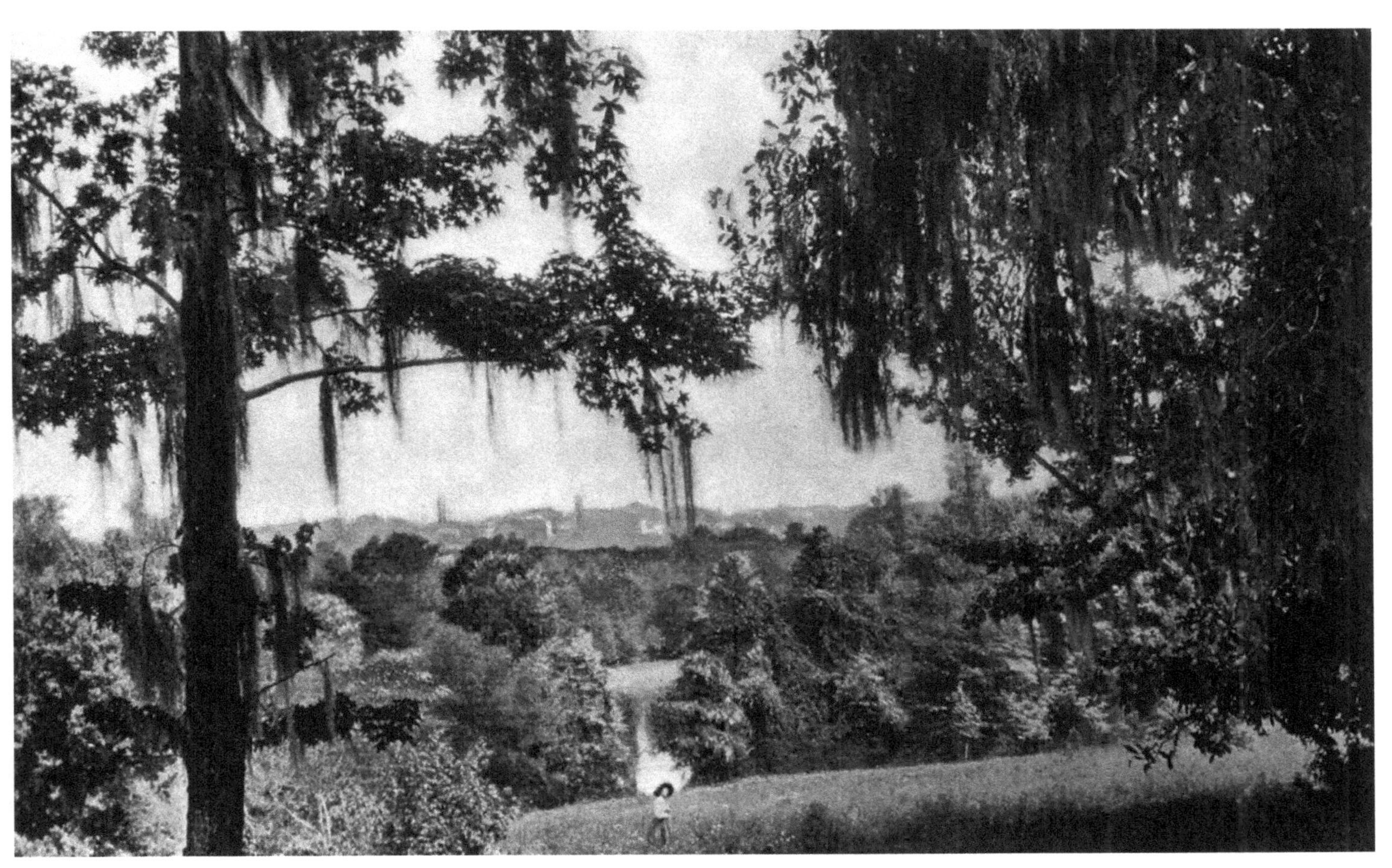

A scenic view of the hill country with Mrs. Alvan Harper at "Lake and Plantation," about one mile east of the Capitol. In 1824, John Lee Williams, one of two commissioners looking for a new capitol site, noted that "a more beautiful country can scarcely be imagined, it is high, rolling, and well watered."

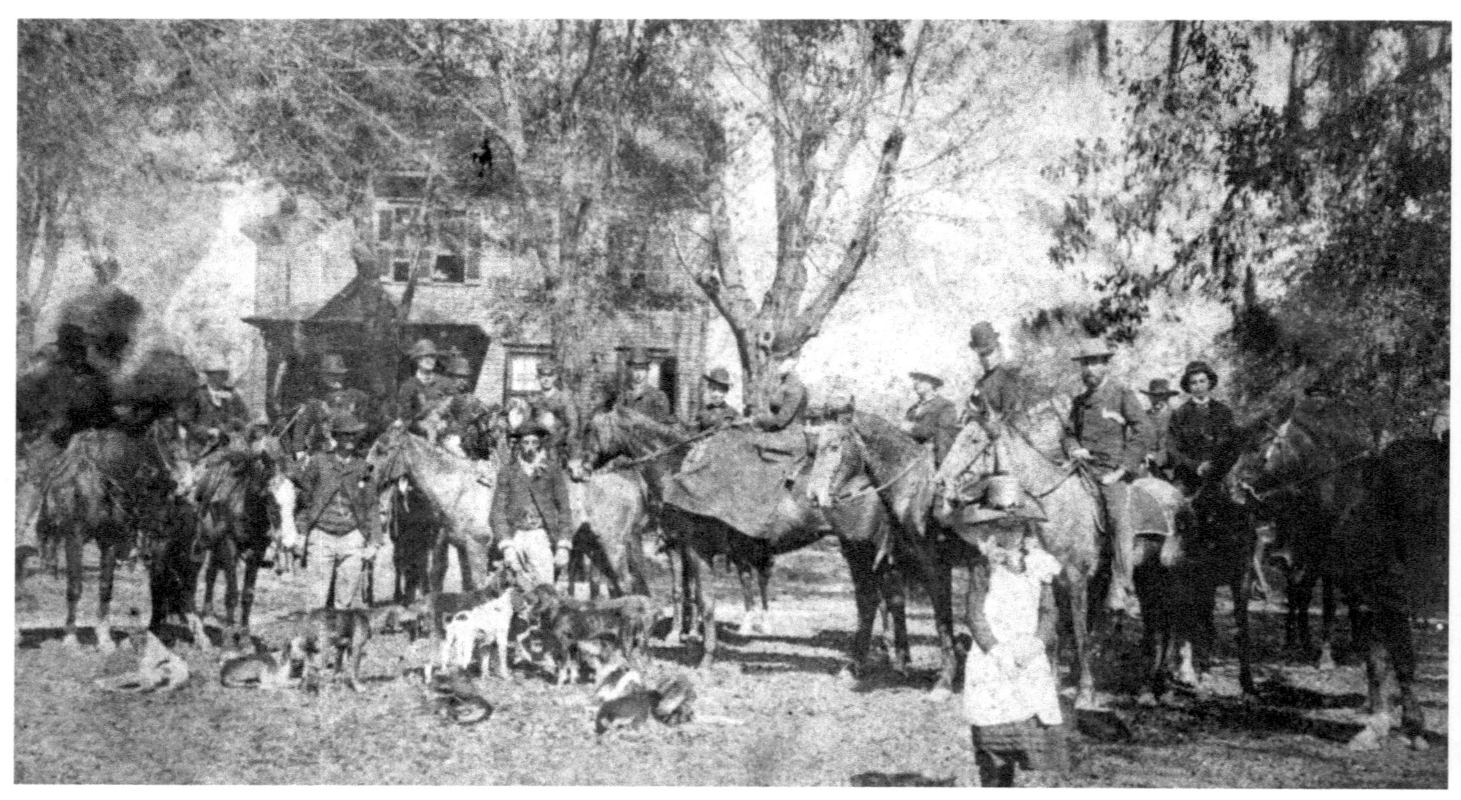

The well-to-do of 1894 Tallahassee enjoyed many interesting diversions. Gathering for a fox hunt are members of three prominent estates and the local sheriff. Quail hunting became a profitable local business. The area is still considered a prime territory for quail hunting.

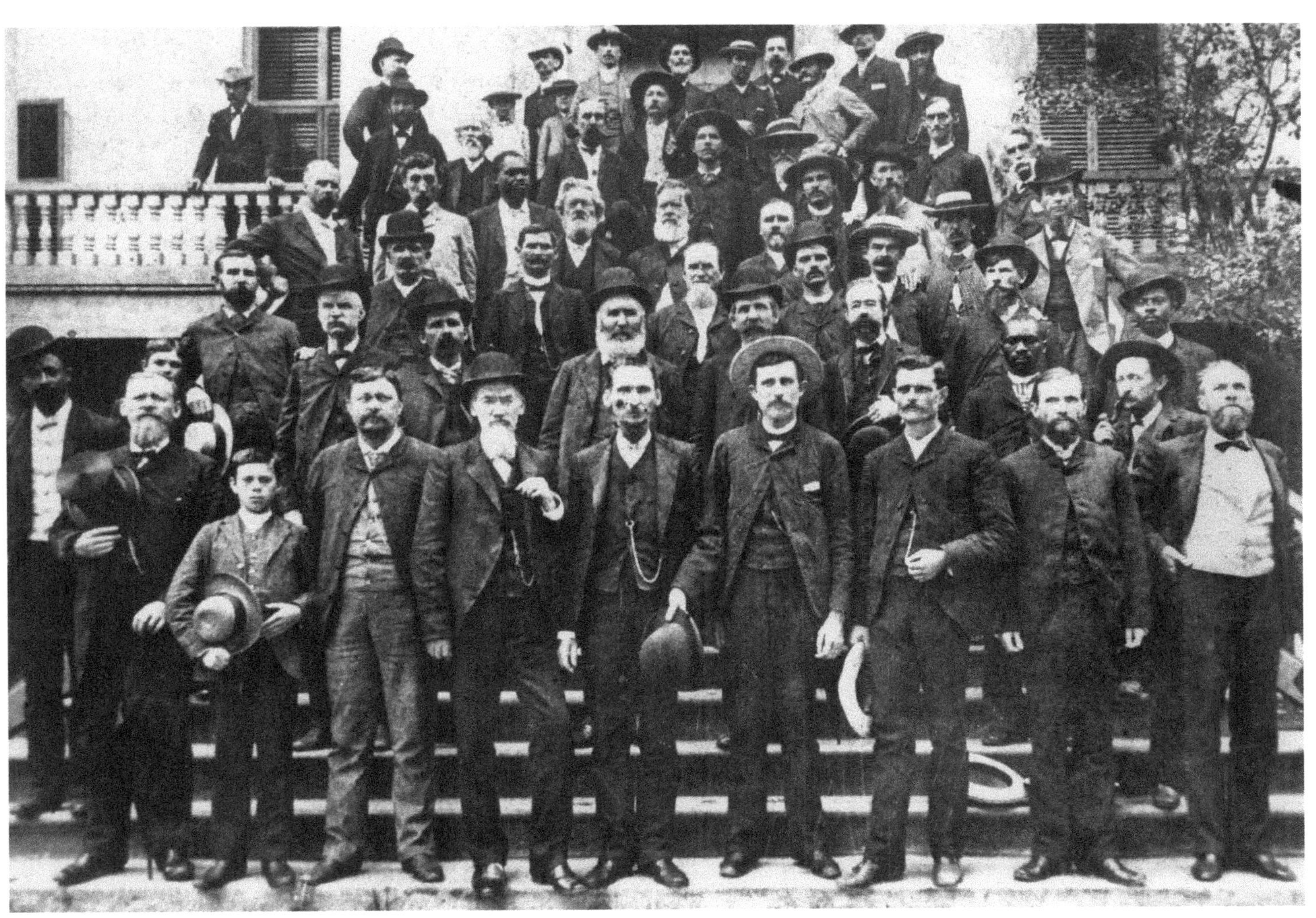

Members of the 1887 Florida legislature gather on the Capitol steps for a group portrait, dressed in three-piece suits, adorned with pocket watches, and wearing derby, bowler, and straw hats. A page boy stands in the front row.

Tallahassee produced its share of "town characters," people with colorful names and habits that added spice to the community. "Uncle" Liberty sits on the steps with George Gwynn, Jr., son of a local doctor.

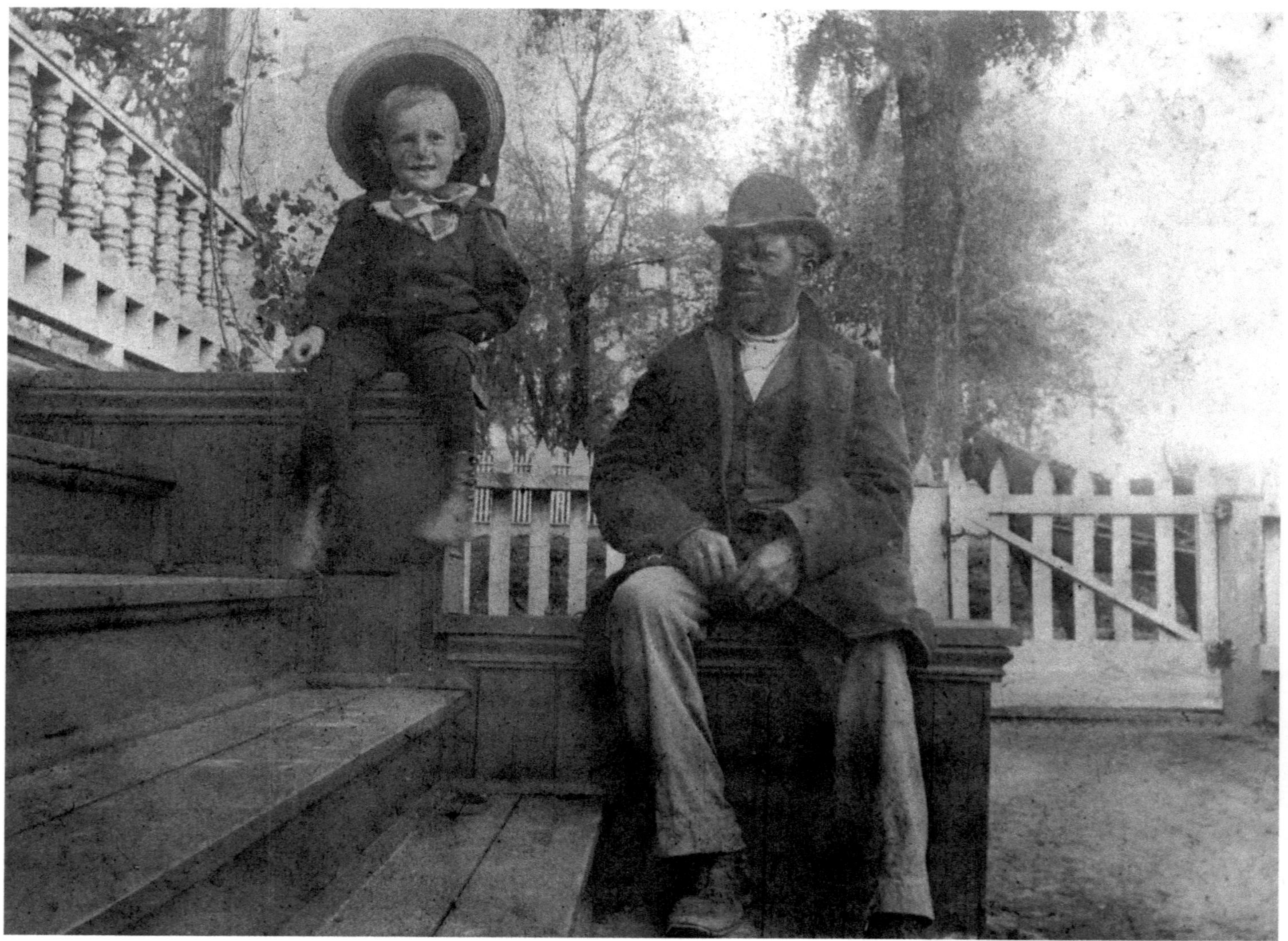

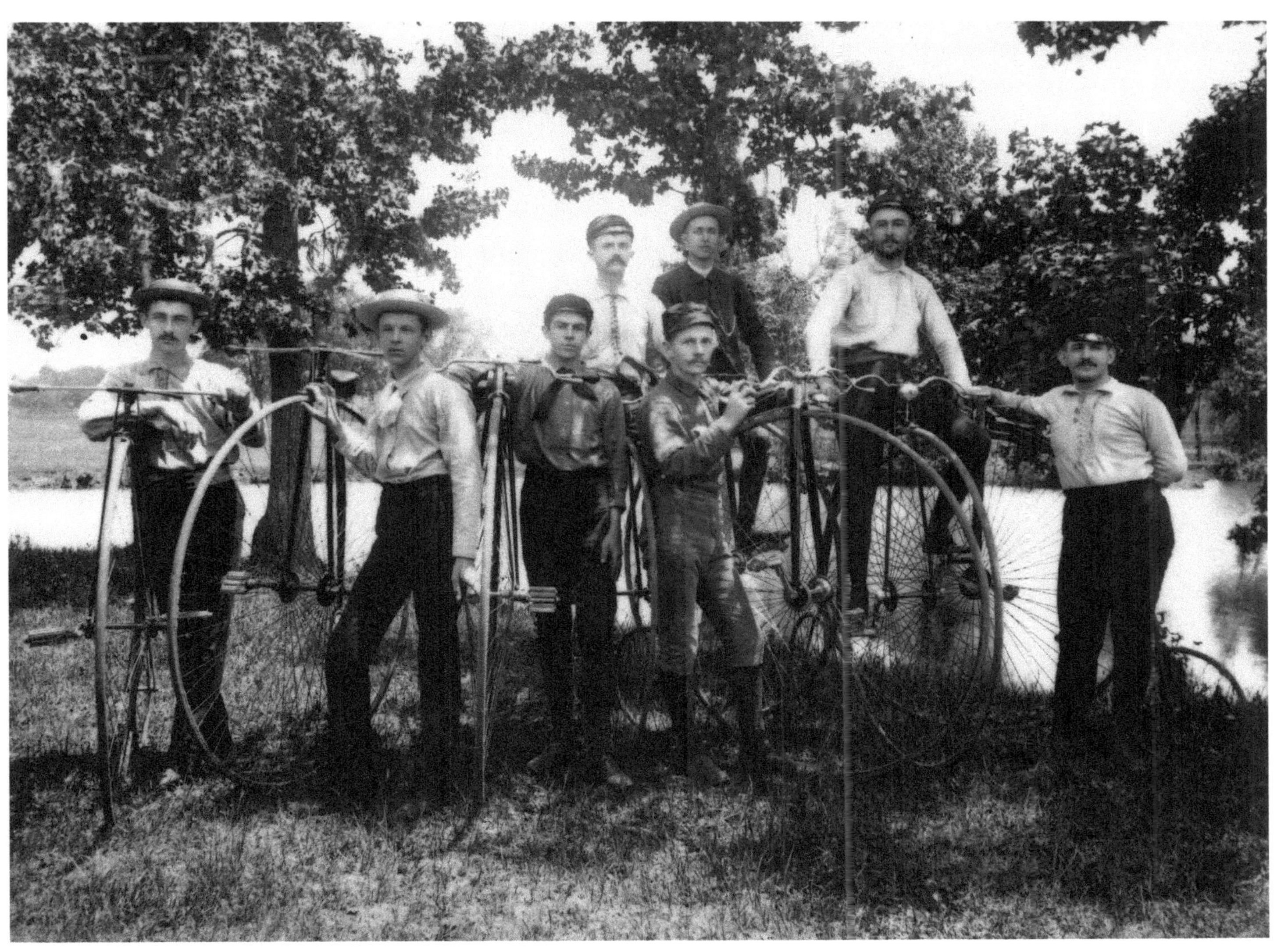

Eight men of the Florida Cycling Club proudly show their penny-farthing bicycles. Tallahassee's well-to-do young men enjoyed this popular activity. In the back row are Captain Louis H. Strumm, at left, and Laurie A. Perkins, at right, who turn up in other photographs by Alvan Harper.

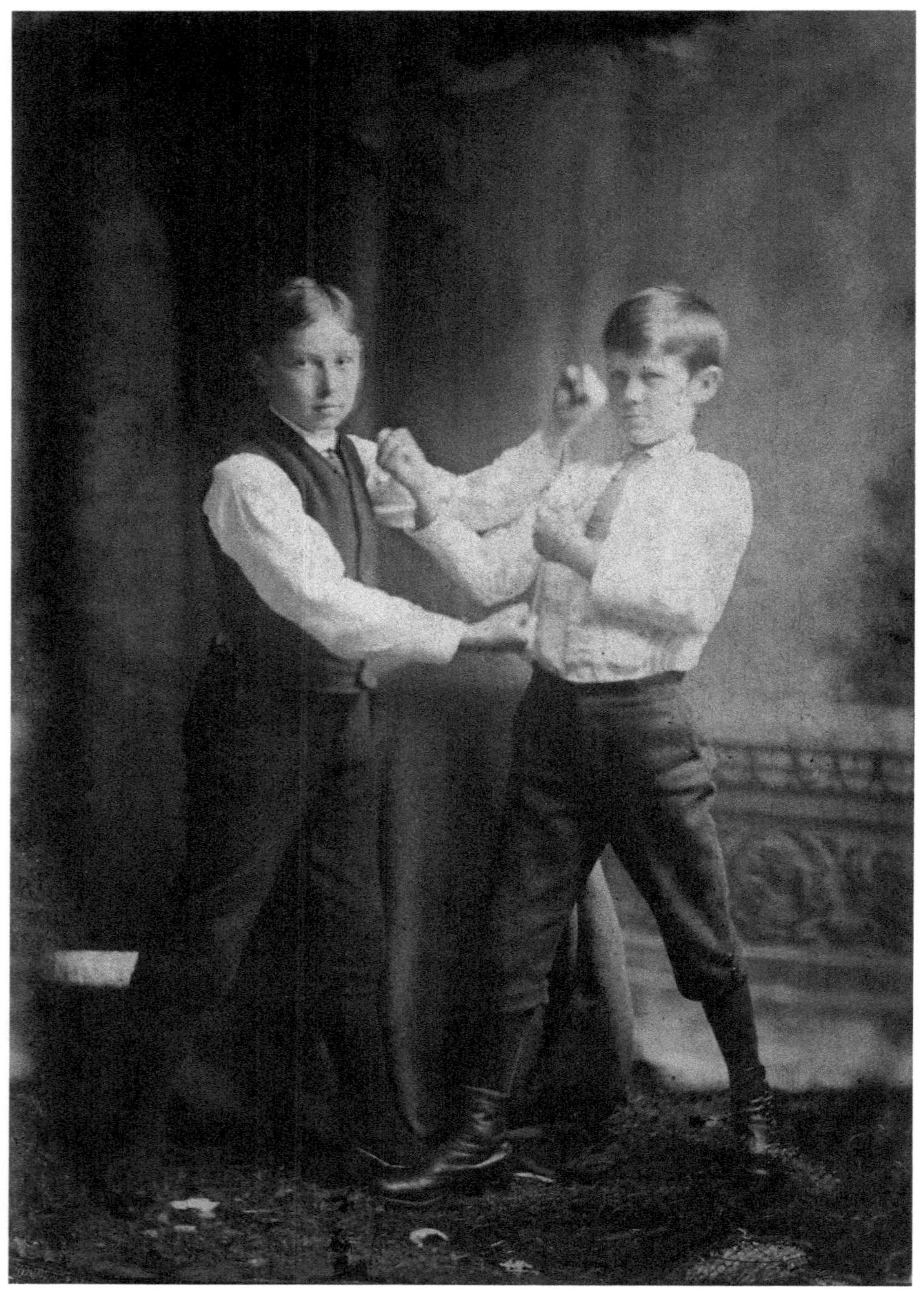

John Henderson and John Morgan (of the Morgan Hotel) pose for a "fight." Well-to-do children were often photographed engaged in sporting activities. Tallahassee social groups were nicknamed "golddusters" (the upper and middle class); "hominy huskers" (the agricultural poor); and "depot greasers" (those who lived or worked near railroads).

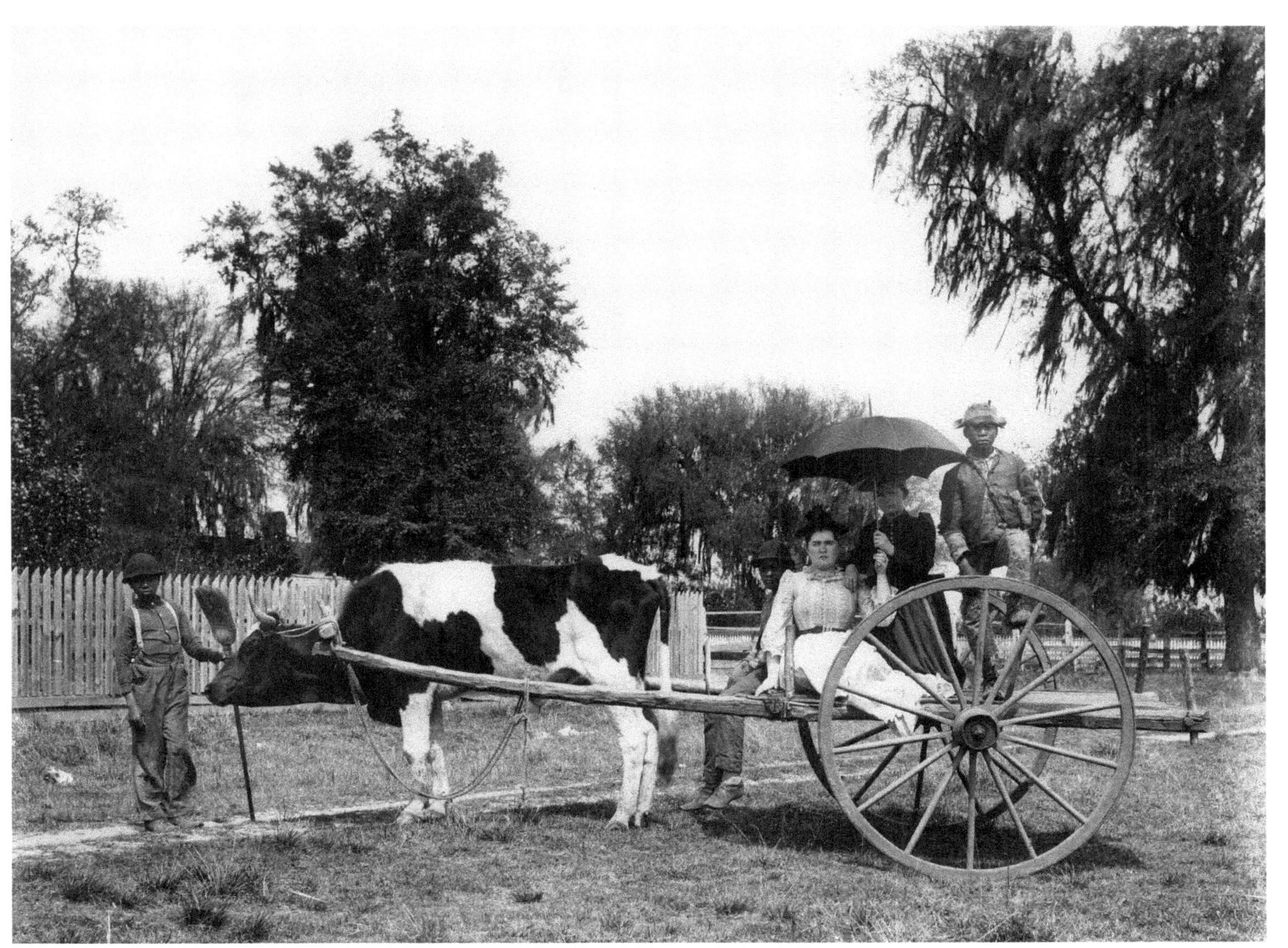

Another Alvan Harper photograph of four children and an adult on an ox cart, taken between 1885 and 1910. Harper's photographs show people at work and leisure, often outdoors at their home.

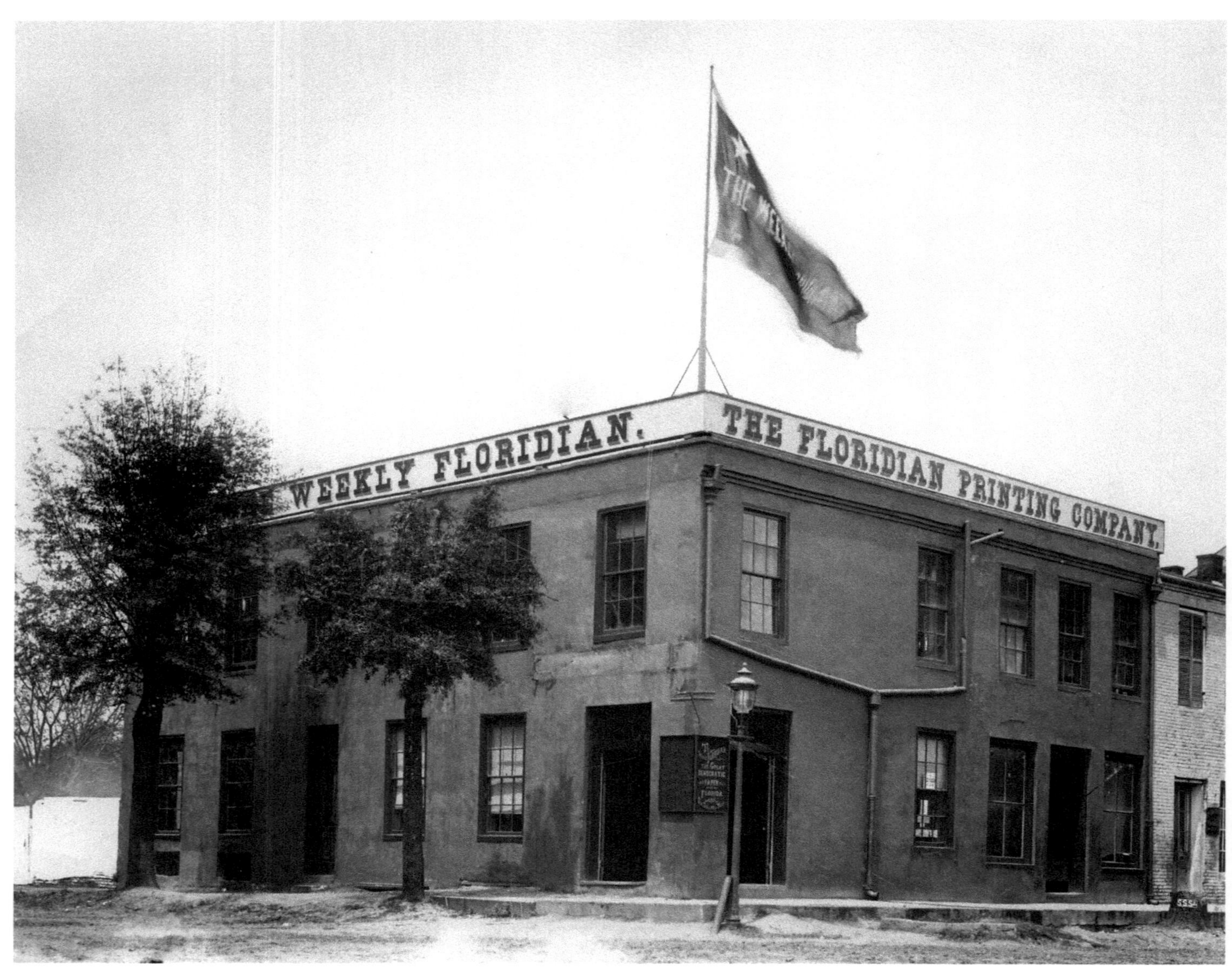

The sign behind the street-lamp reads "The Weekly Floridian—The Great Democratic Paper of Florida—One Dollar a Year." Established in 1829, it was one of the earliest newspapers in Florida. Through the *Floridian,* its editor and longtime owner, Charles E. Dyke, exerted a strong influence on public opinion and state legislation.

Alvan S. Harper lived in Tallahassee from 1884 until his death in 1911 and owned a photographic studio for most of that period. In 1946 some 2,000 glass negatives were discovered in the attic of Harper's former home. Now in the State Archives of Florida, the Harper Collection is a valuable resource on Tallahassee.

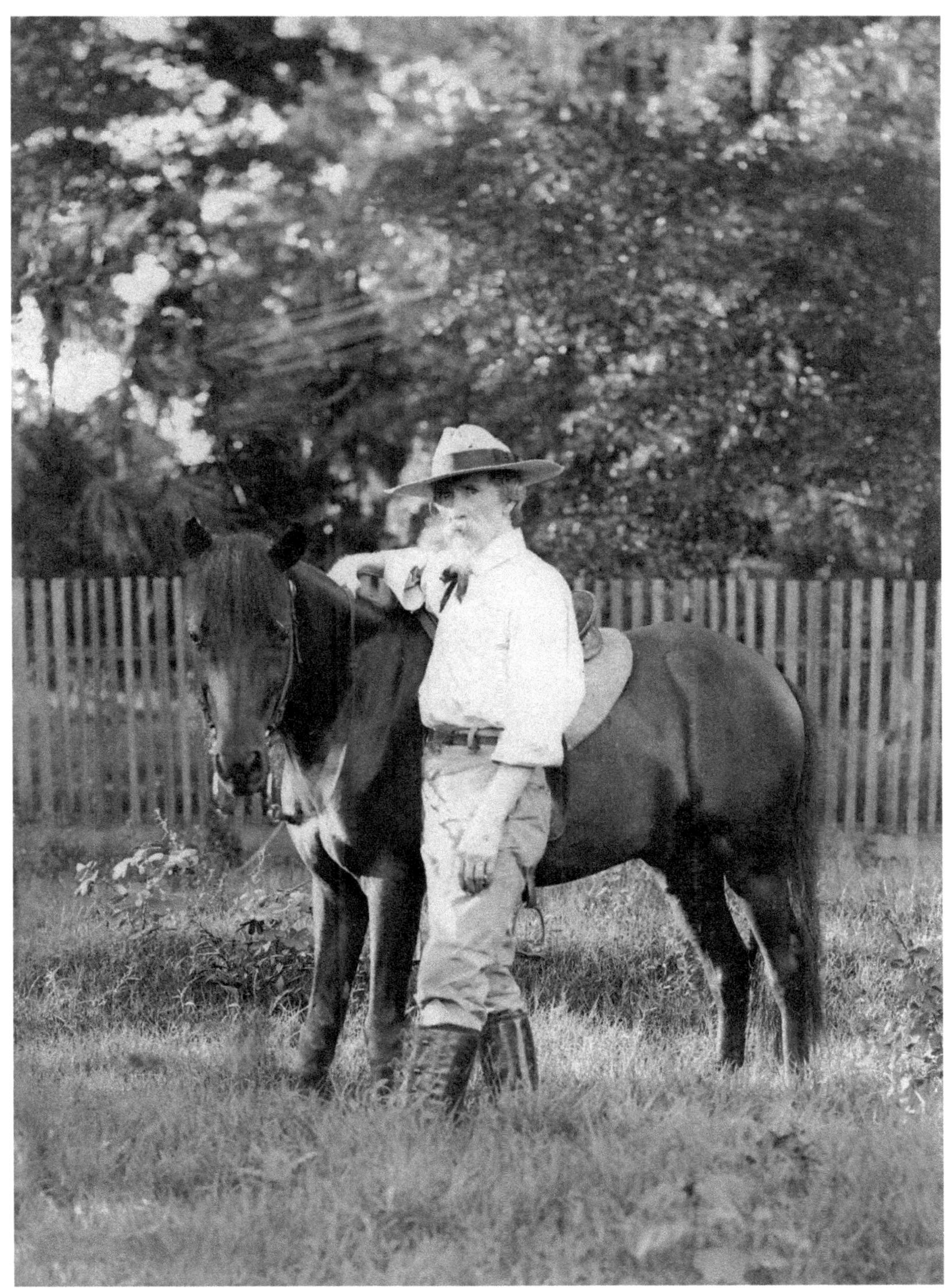

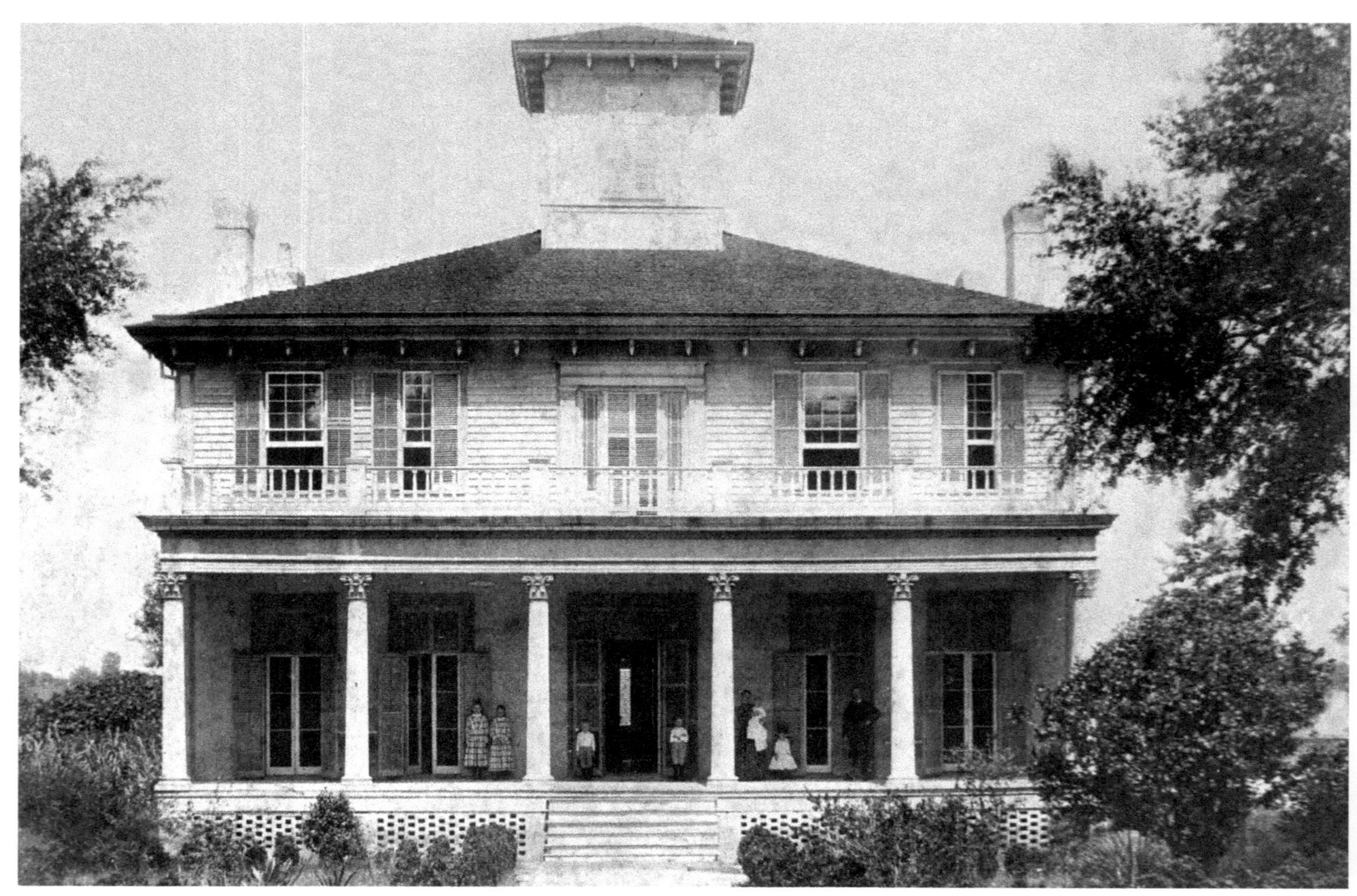

The Brokaw-McDougall House on North Meridian Street was built in the early 1850s for Perez Brokaw. His daughter Phebe married a Scottish immigrant, Alexander McDougall. After Phebe's death in 1883, Alexander married her sister Eliza. On the porch is Alexander McDougall with his children and wife Eliza, who holds an infant.

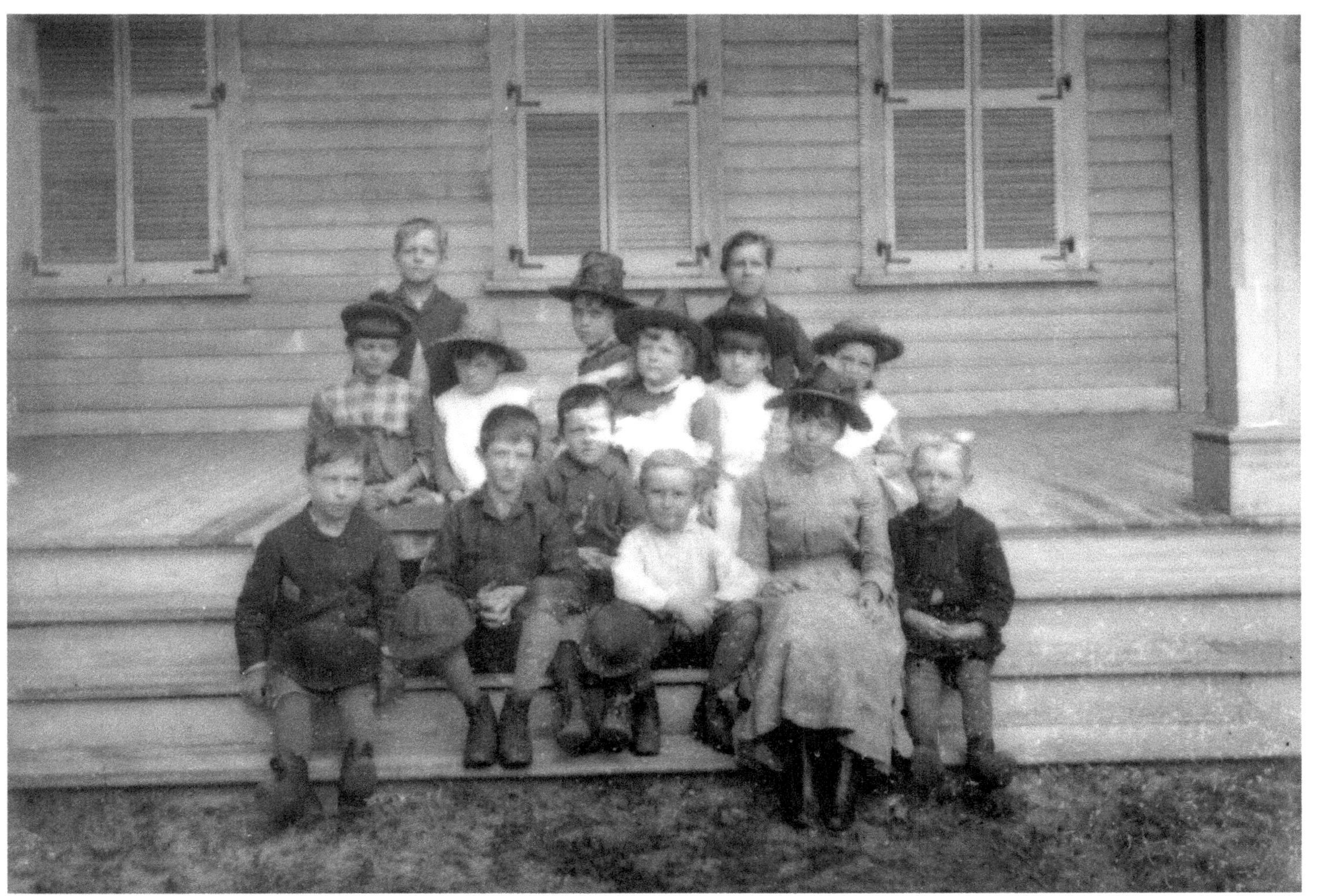

This Tallahassee teacher and her students are sitting for their class photograph ca. 1900. According to custom, the girls are wearing hats while the boys hold theirs. African American students went to separate schools. During this time the State of Florida increased funding to schools and started providing textbooks.

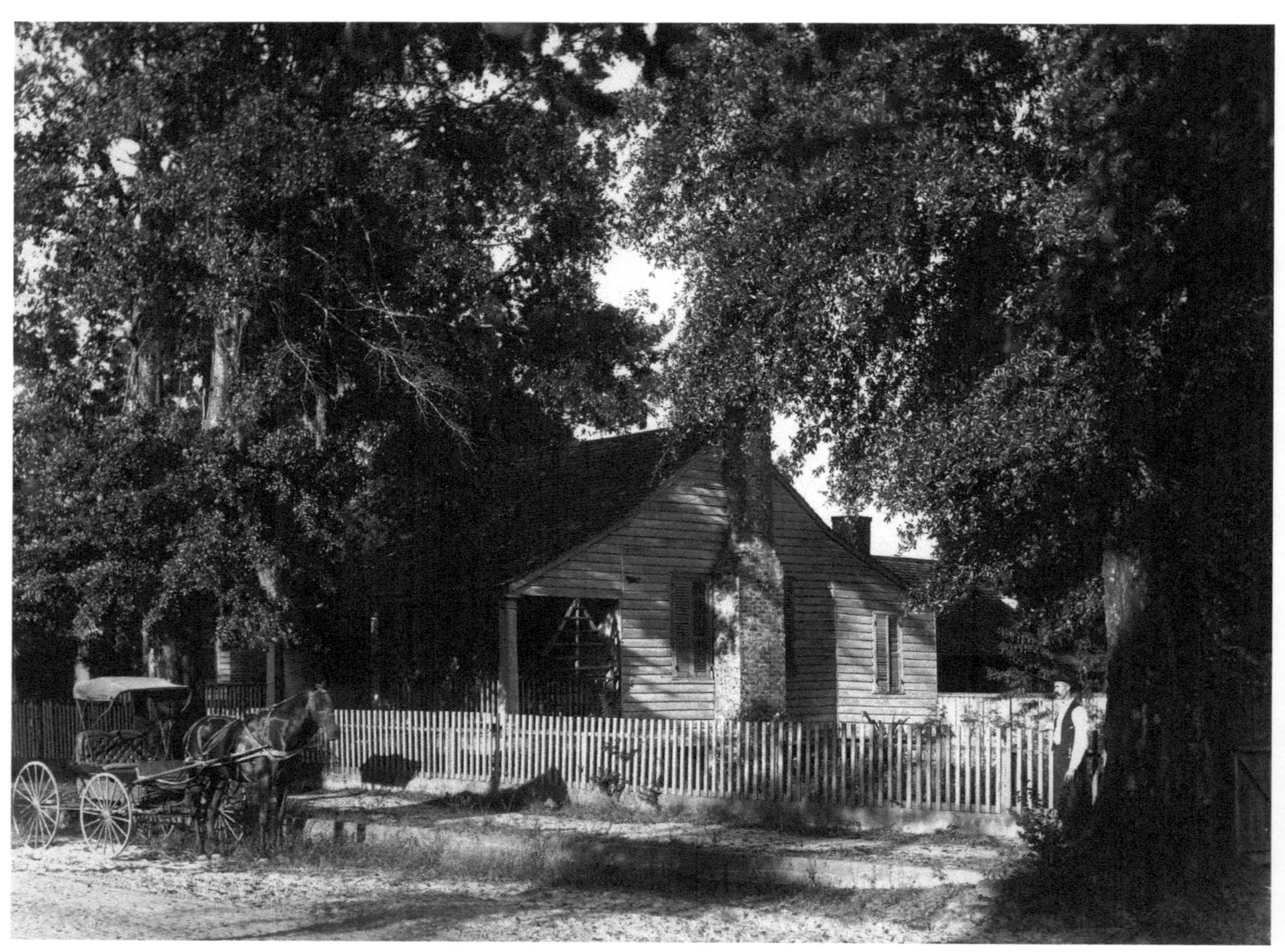

A typical Tallahassee neighborhood ca. 1900. At left a horse and buggy waits parked, at left a man, perhaps the owner, stands beside a tree. Noteworthy are the dirt road, large oak trees, open porch, picket fence, and window shutters, closed to keep out the sun. Street signs and house numbers were not seen in Tallahassee until 1902.

These laborers are boiling cane syrup. After the Civil War, the cotton economy never regained its prewar prosperity. Leon County farmers tried many alternative agricultural crops, including tobacco, nuts, pears, grapes, and sugar cane. The cane was cut and its juice squeezed out; the raw juice was then boiled into syrup in the large brick fireplace.

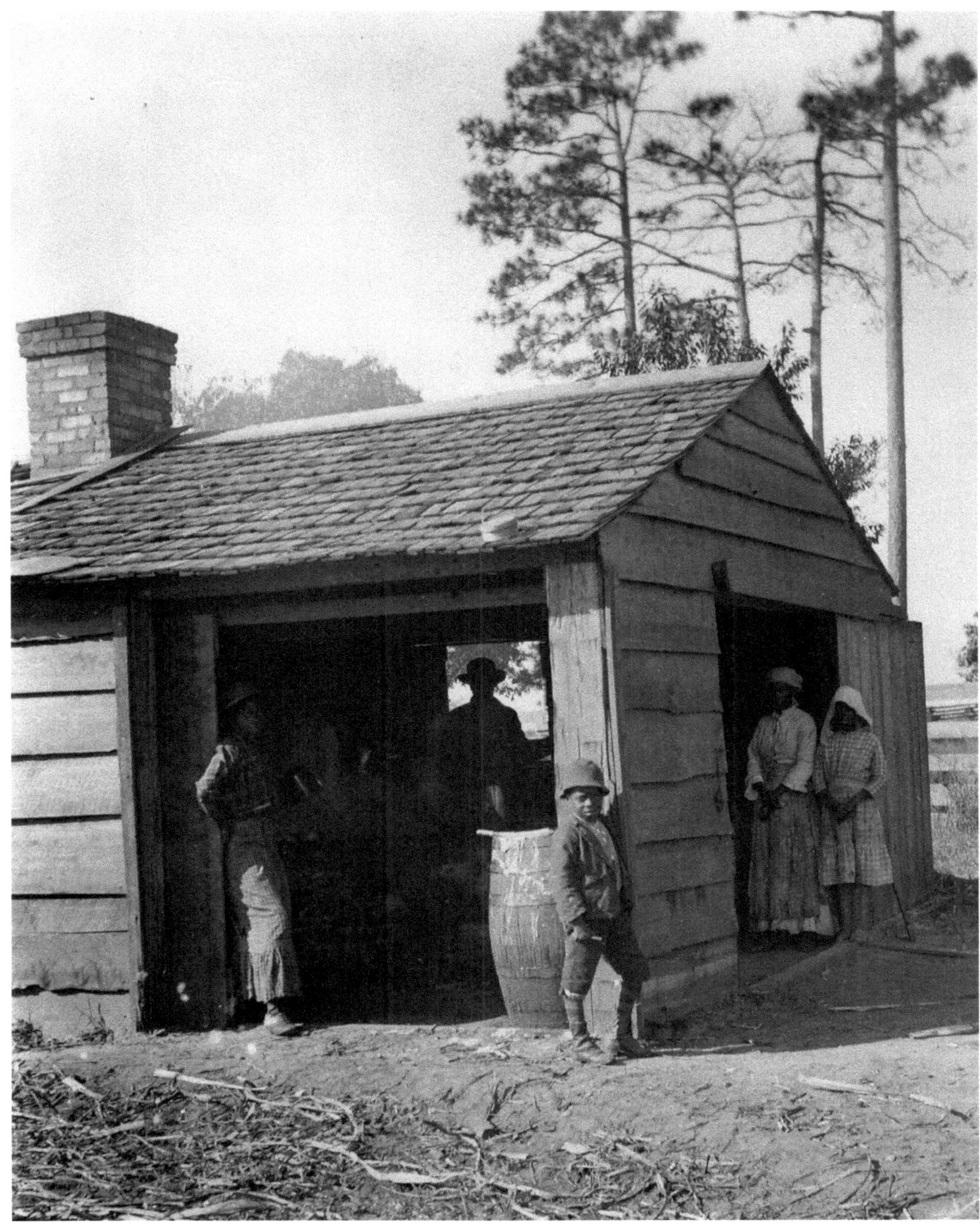

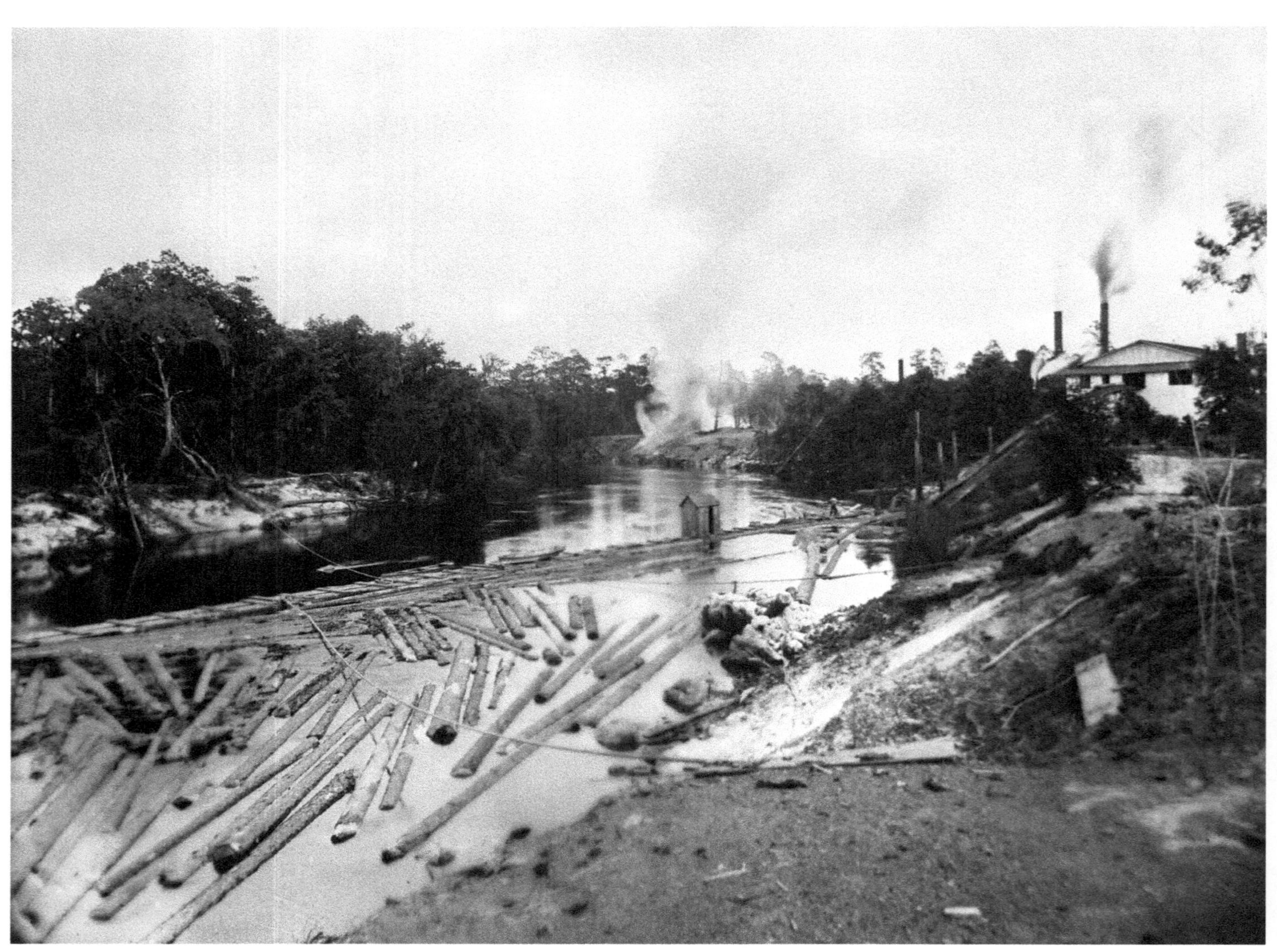

This sawmill is believed to have been on the Ochlocknee River, near Tallahassee. As mill fires increased, mills posted "No Smoking" signs, but most were ignored. One lumber mill superintendent noted in his diary, "Posted a sign in the mill according to instructions, 'No Smoking,' I had a lighted cigar in my mouth at the time."

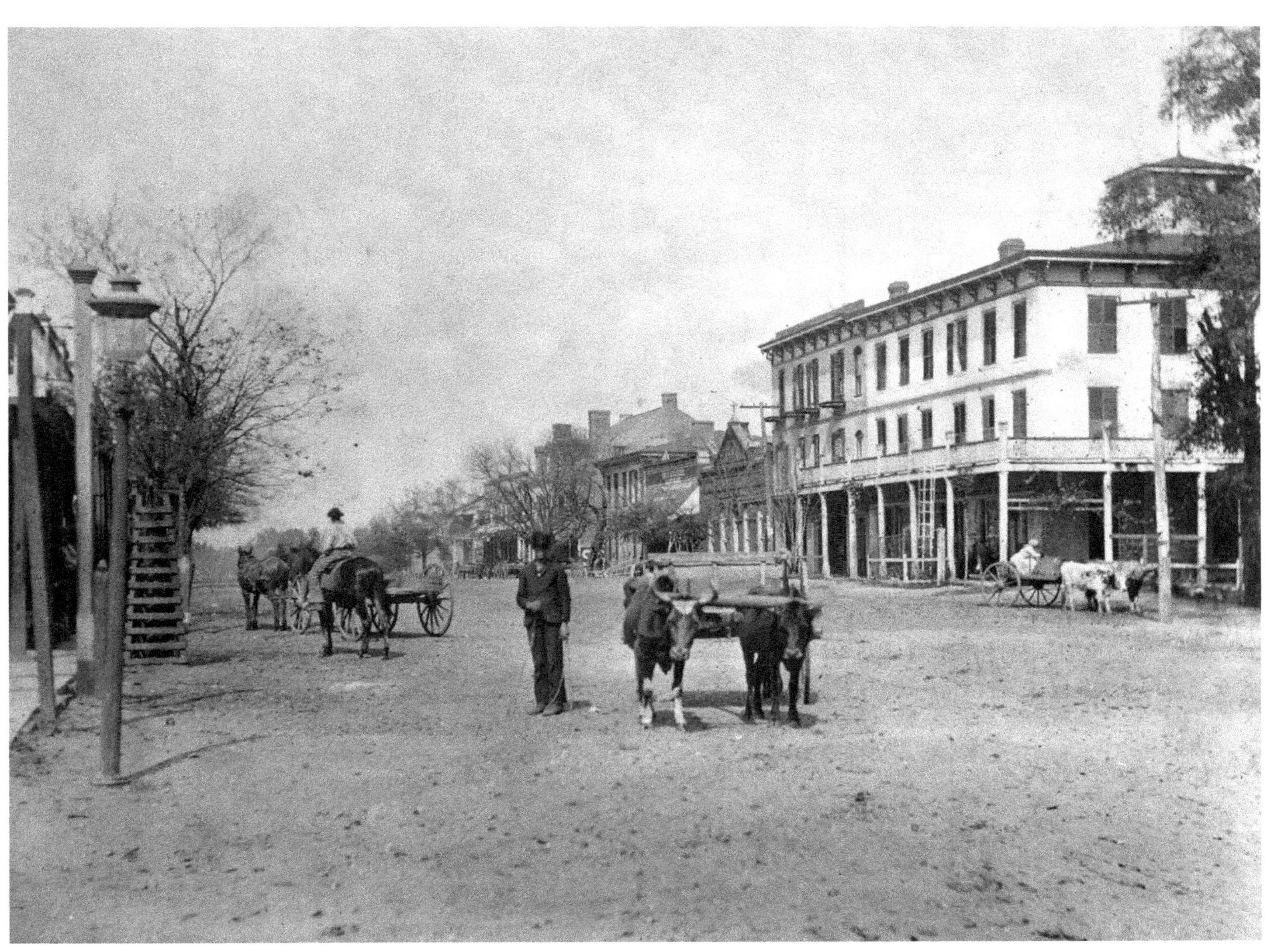

Ox carts trudge down a wide Monroe Street. Economic prosperity motivated civic improvements during the 1880s and 1890s, including animal control and gas lamps (one is visible at left). A gas factory was built, pipes laid, and iron posts installed for the street-lamps. The gas lamps were turned on a few days before Christmas, 1888.

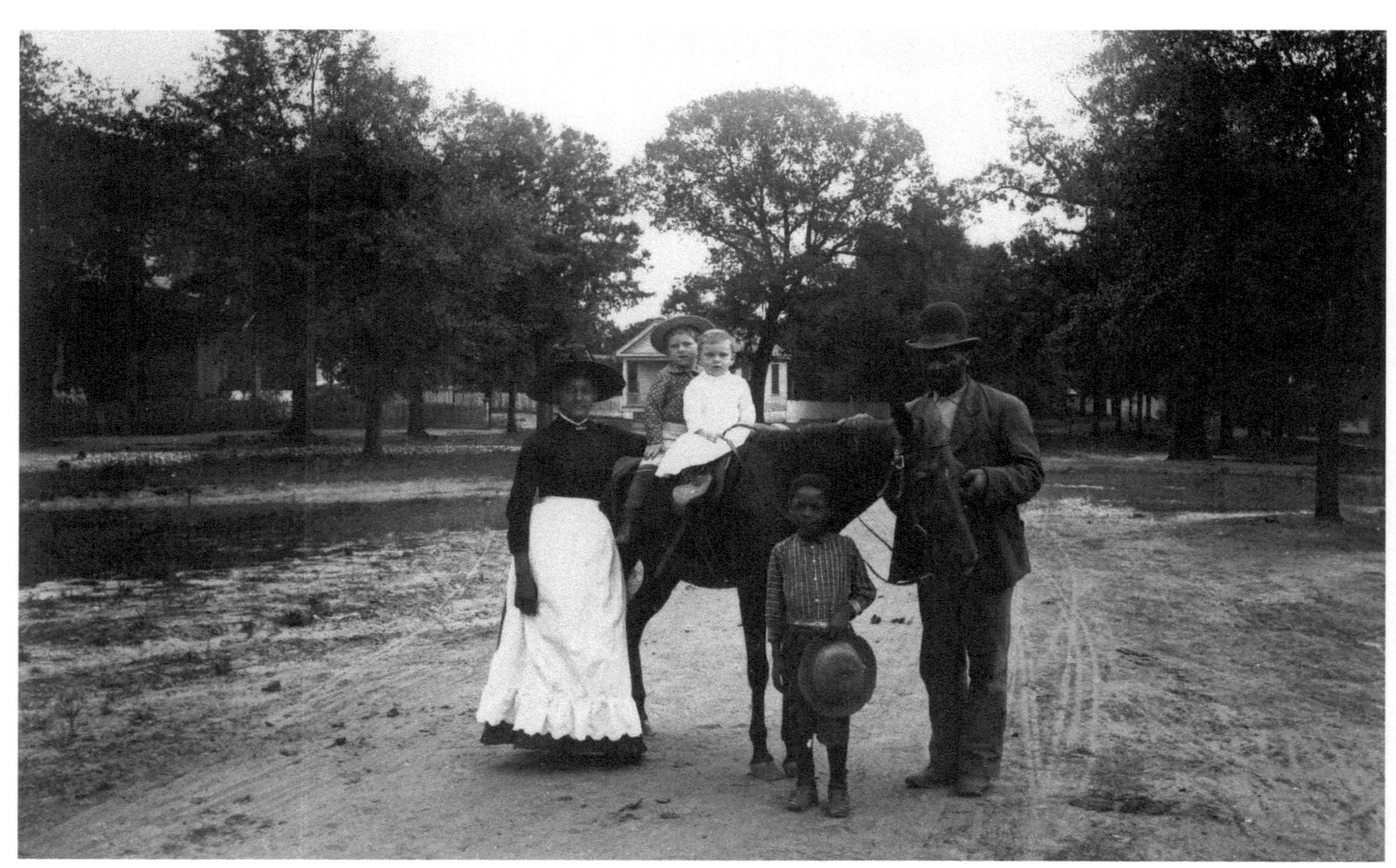

Members of the Winthrop and Merritt families ca. 1890. Mary the nurse, Matthew the coachman, and their son Eddie pose with Francis and Guy Winthrop (on horseback), descendants of a wealthy Massachusetts family. During Reconstruction, many blacks in Tallahassee found employment as servants to wealthy whites.

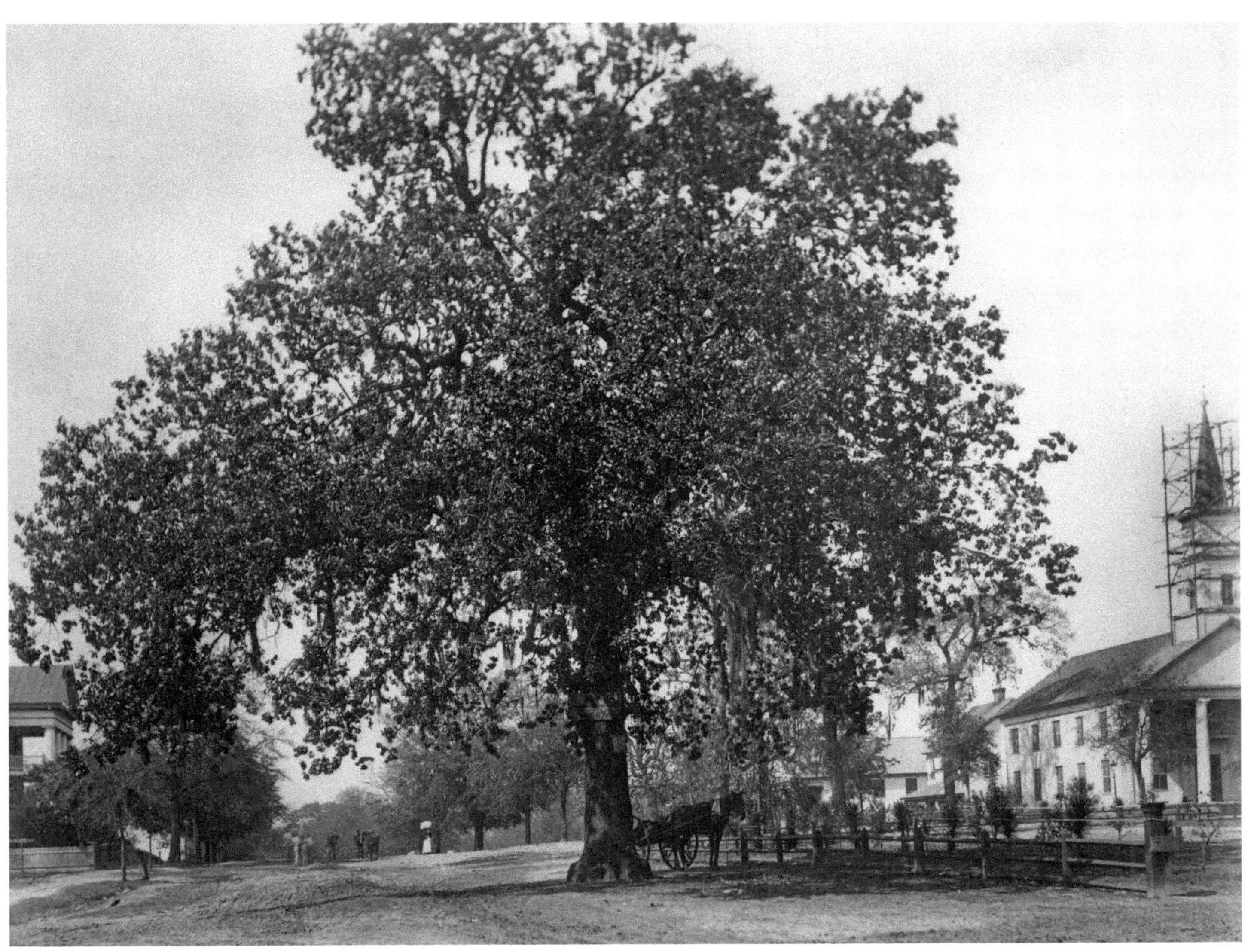

On Park Avenue ca. 1890, the Columns building is visible on the far left and the First Presbyterian Church, with scaffolding around the steeple, on the right. Around this time the ladies of the Tallahassee Improvement Association started a project to save "grand old shade trees, the noble oaks of Tallahassee."

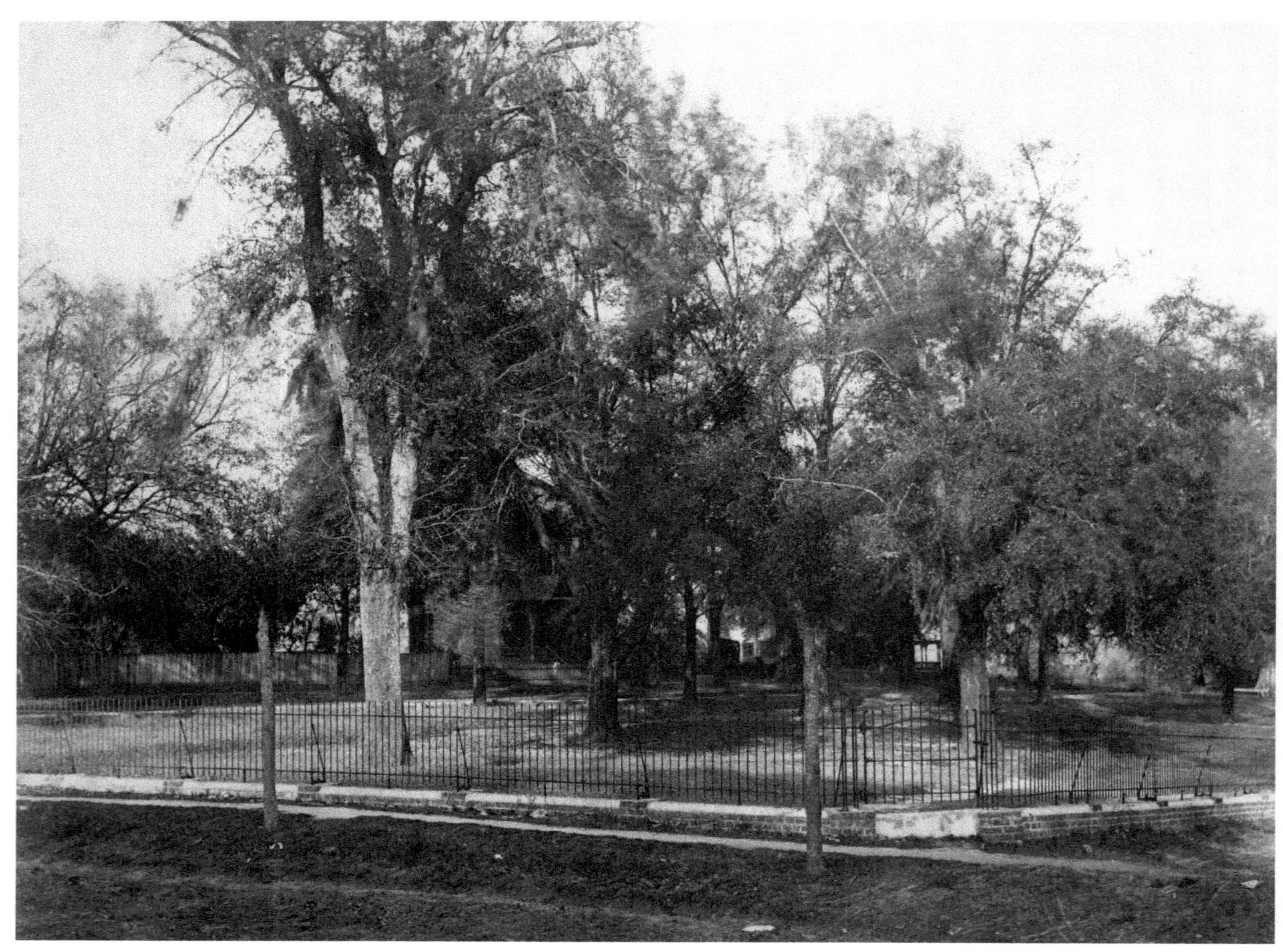

Lewis Park is one of a chain of five parks on Park Avenue. Originally a 200-foot stretch of open ground, this area was designed as a field for firing armaments, in case of Indian attack. Built by Captain William C. Lewis in 1885, Lewis Park became one of the main social gathering spots of the city, hosting parades, parties, picnics, and fairs.

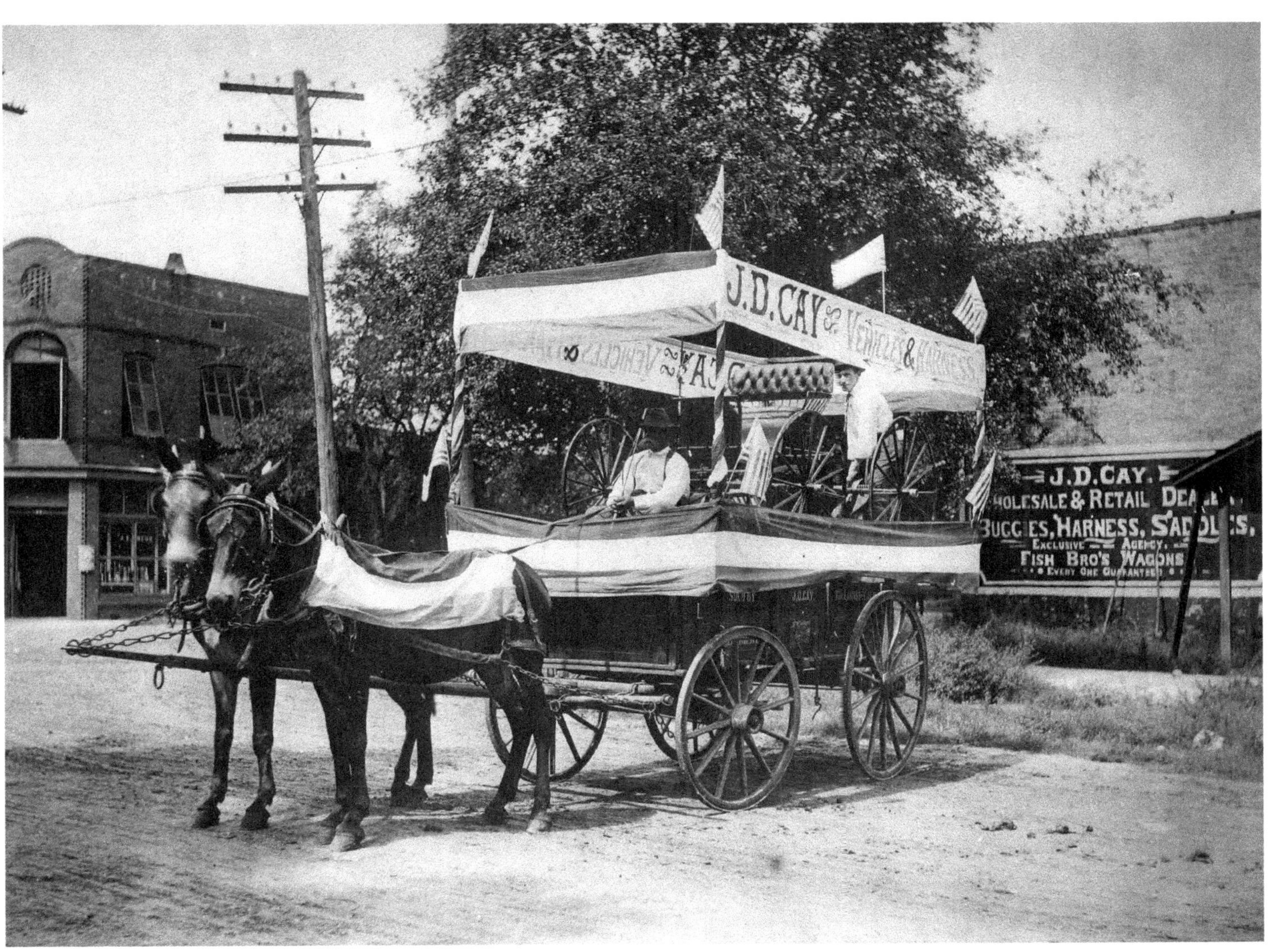

John David Cay came to Tallahassee in the late 1800s with his wife, Georgia Winn, and family. He entered the turpentine and naval stores business, and later owned a livery stable. Advertising his livery stable is a parade entry, shown here, which consisted of a light carriage atop a heavy-duty wagon.

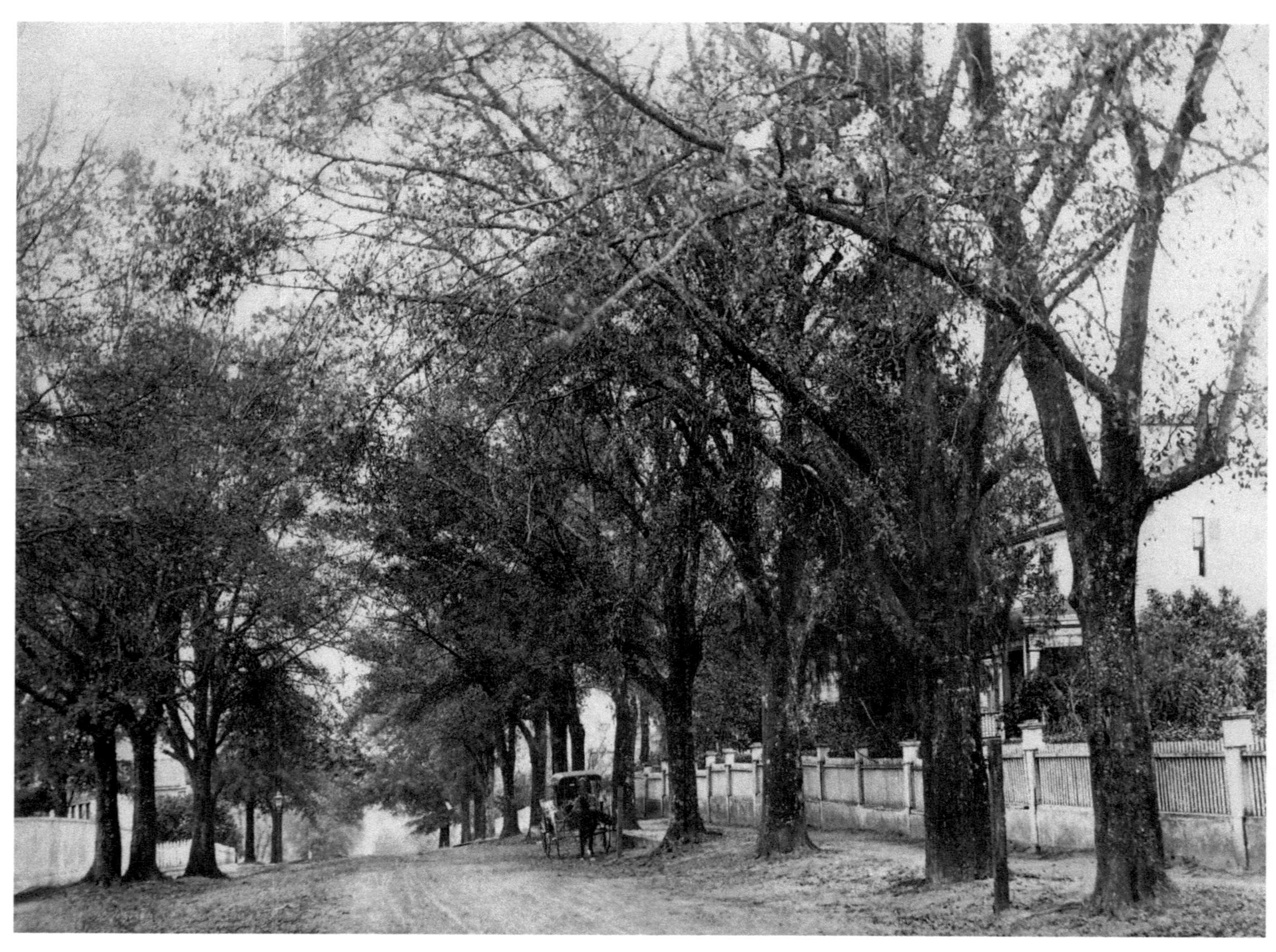

Tallahassee's old oaks, draped with Spanish moss, gracefully span the area's roads. These canopy roads, some following old Native American or Spanish trails, radiate from Tallahassee like spokes on a wheel. Once the source of goods and supplies coming from the plantations to Tallahassee, they are now designated scenic drives.

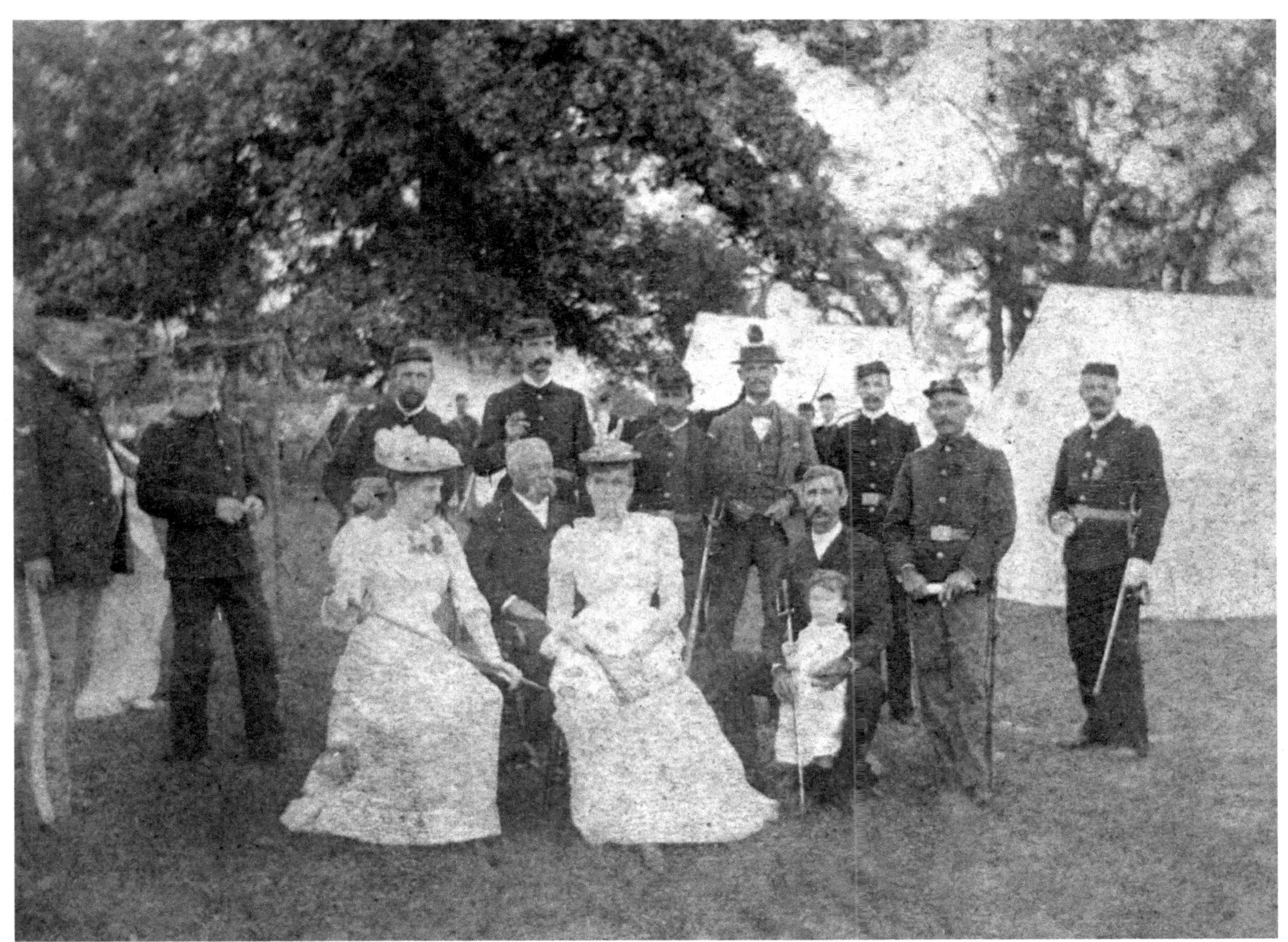

Governor Francis P. Fleming (1889–1893), fourth man from the left, visits the Florida State Troops. Established in 1887, the State Troops became the National Guard in 1909. During his administration, Fleming called for a special session of the legislature to establish a state board of health in order to deal with a yellow fever epidemic.

Erected for John G. Anderson in 1850, this house boasted Italian marble and French crystal chandeliers, and two double parlors. Napoleon Bonaparte Broward used it as the governor's mansion when he took office in 1905, until 1907. Bought by Allie Yawn Brown in the 1920s, it came to be known as the Brown House. Its leveling gave rise to the local preservation movement.

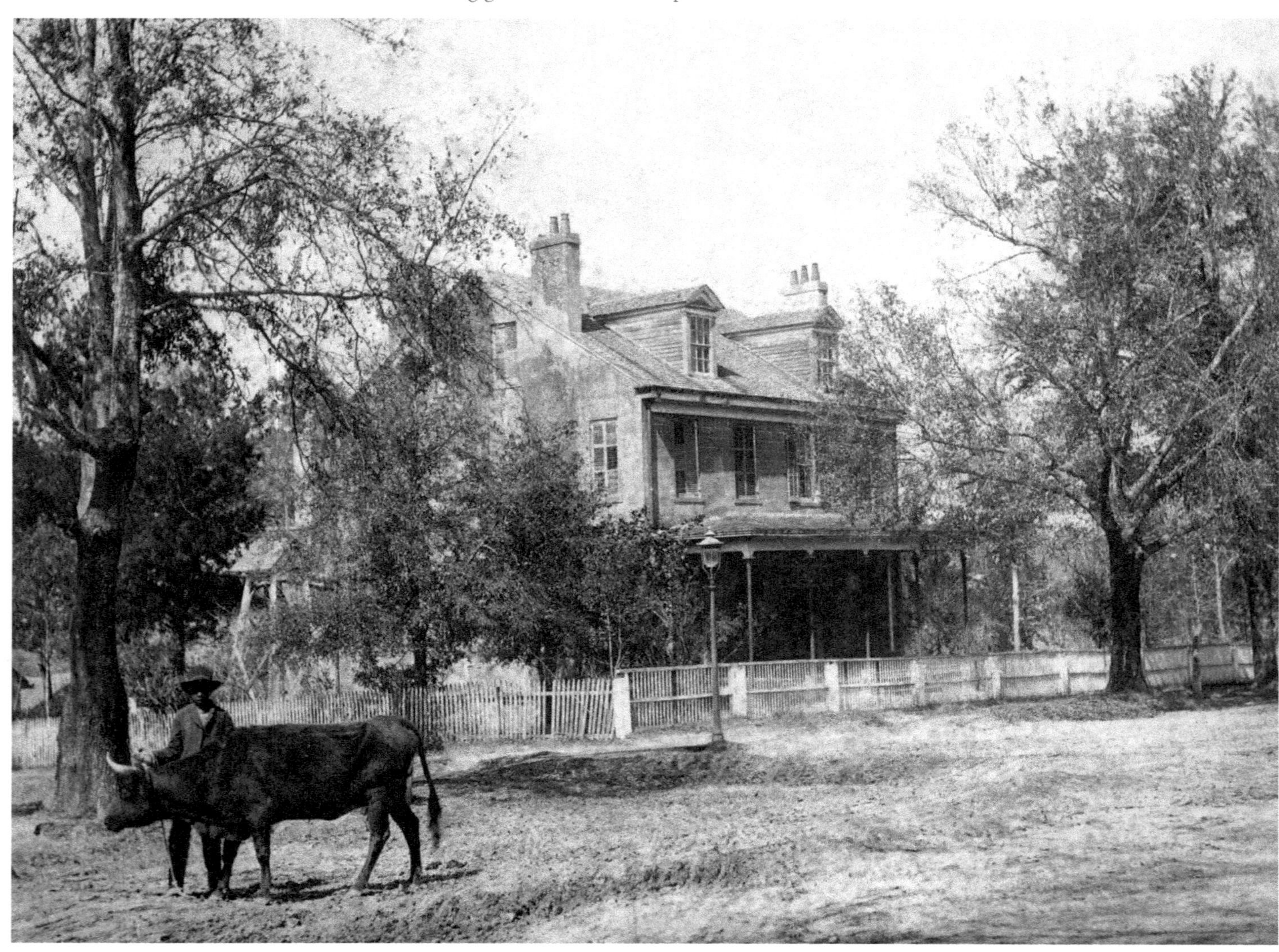

Built around 1858, this freight depot served many railroad lines, including the Florida Central, Seaboard Coastline, and Amtrak as a renovated passenger station. The town's first railroad was the Tallahassee–St. Marks line with mule-drawn cars. Completed in 1837, it provided transport to the gulf port of St. Marks.

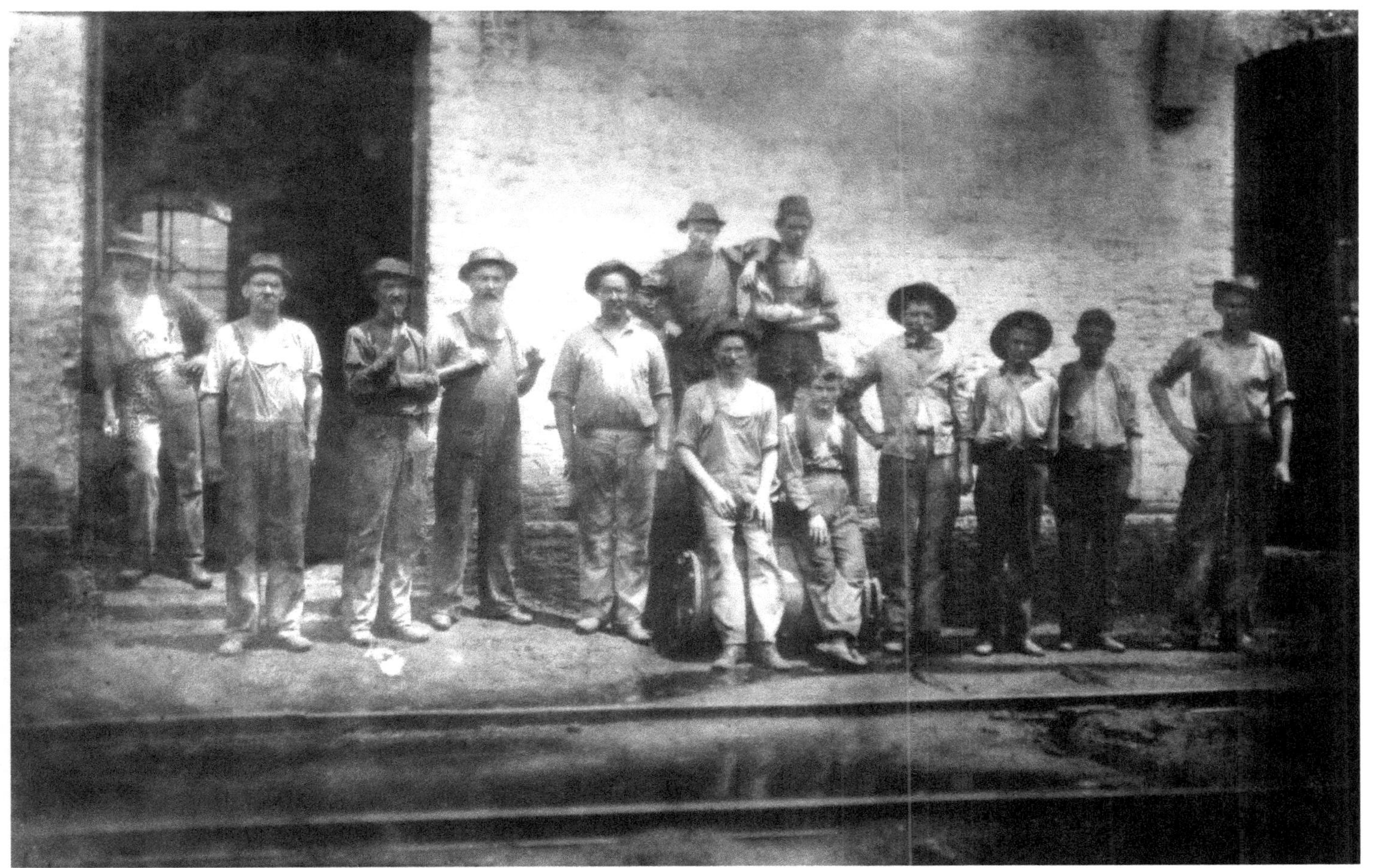

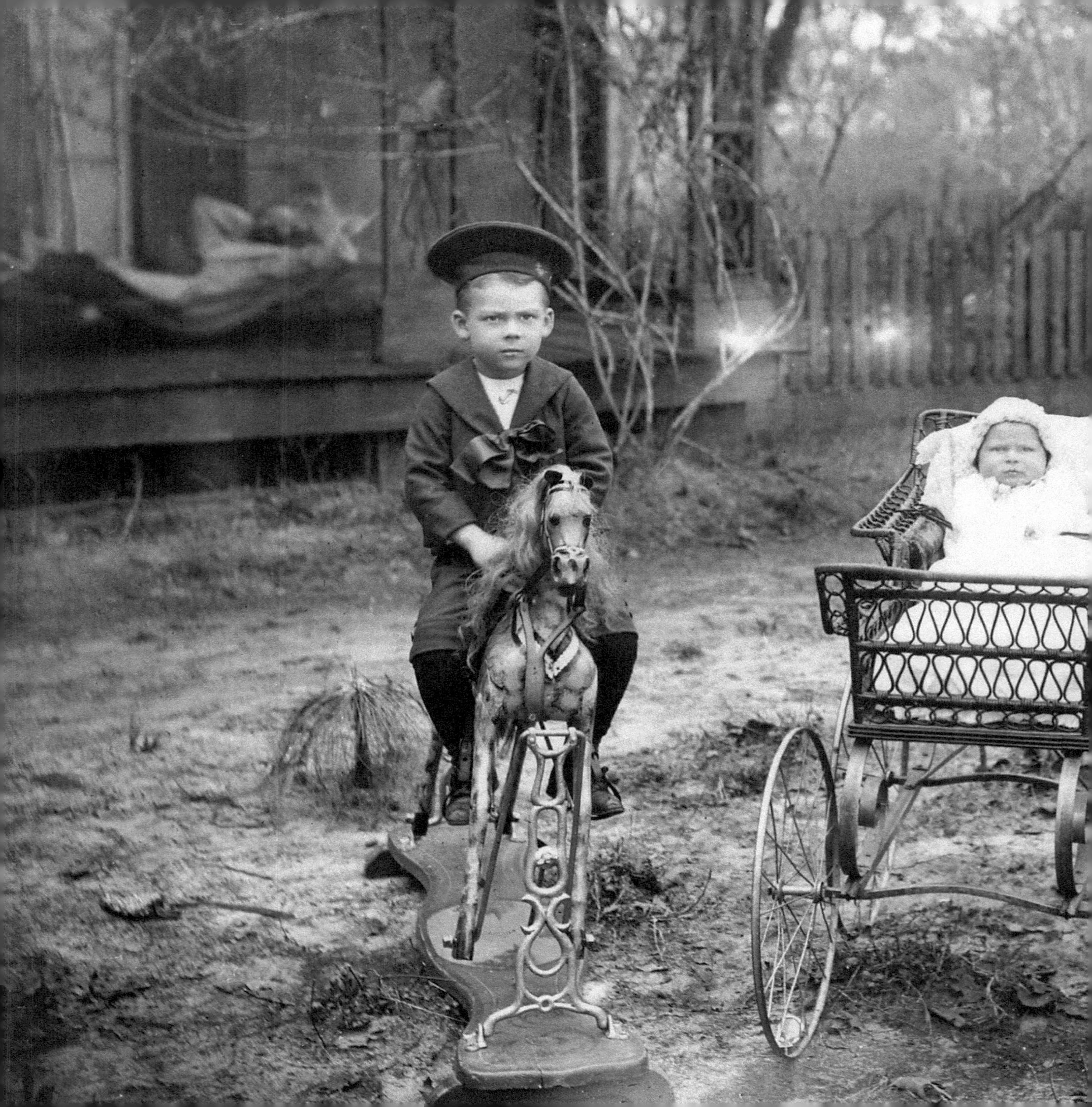

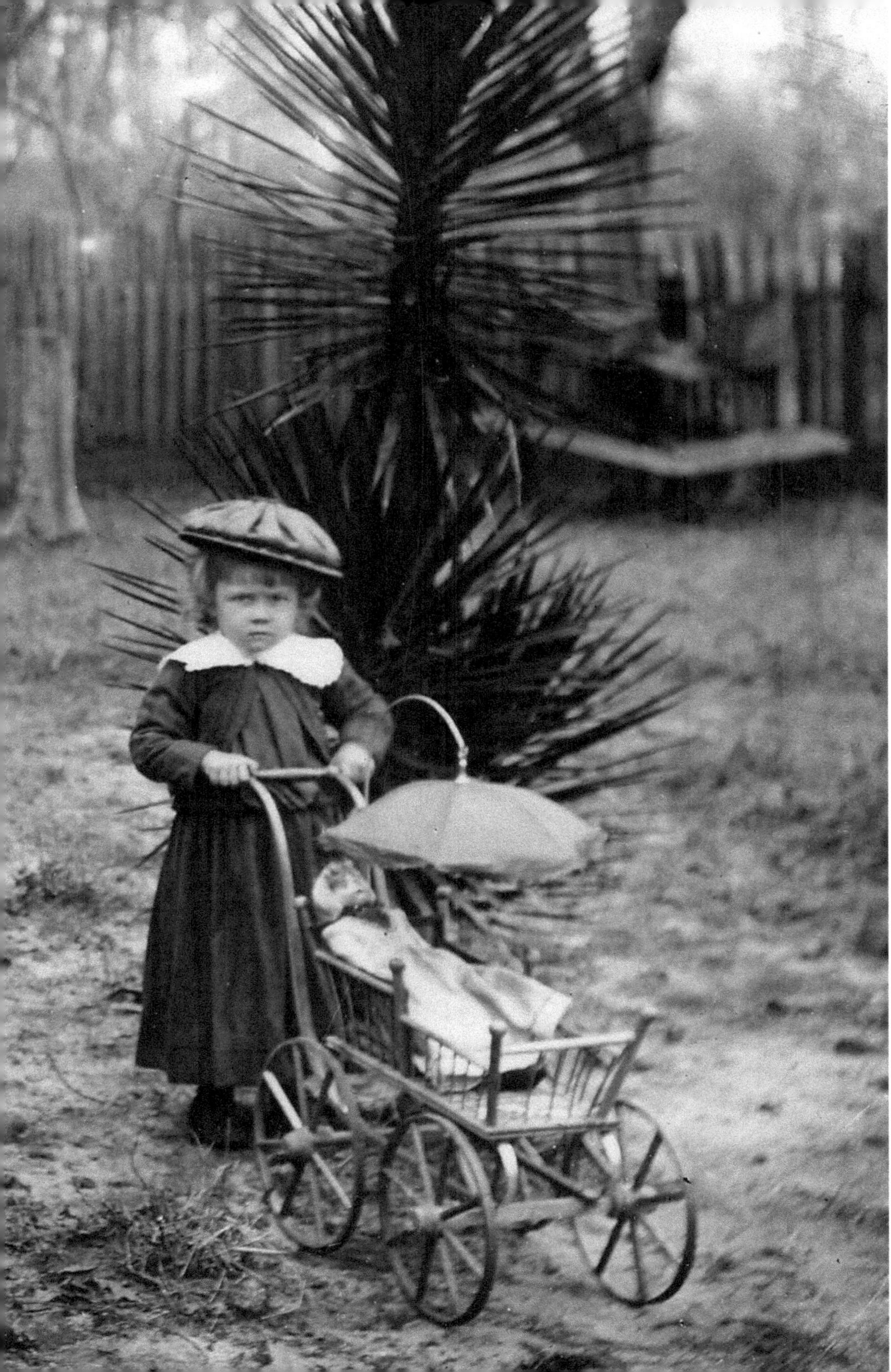

Three children with their toys pose in the yard for a portrait sometime in the late nineteenth century. Tallahassee children learned very early in life to avoid the spikes of the Spanish bayonet plant—behind the little girl at right. An interested onlooker reclines in a hammock on the porch at left.

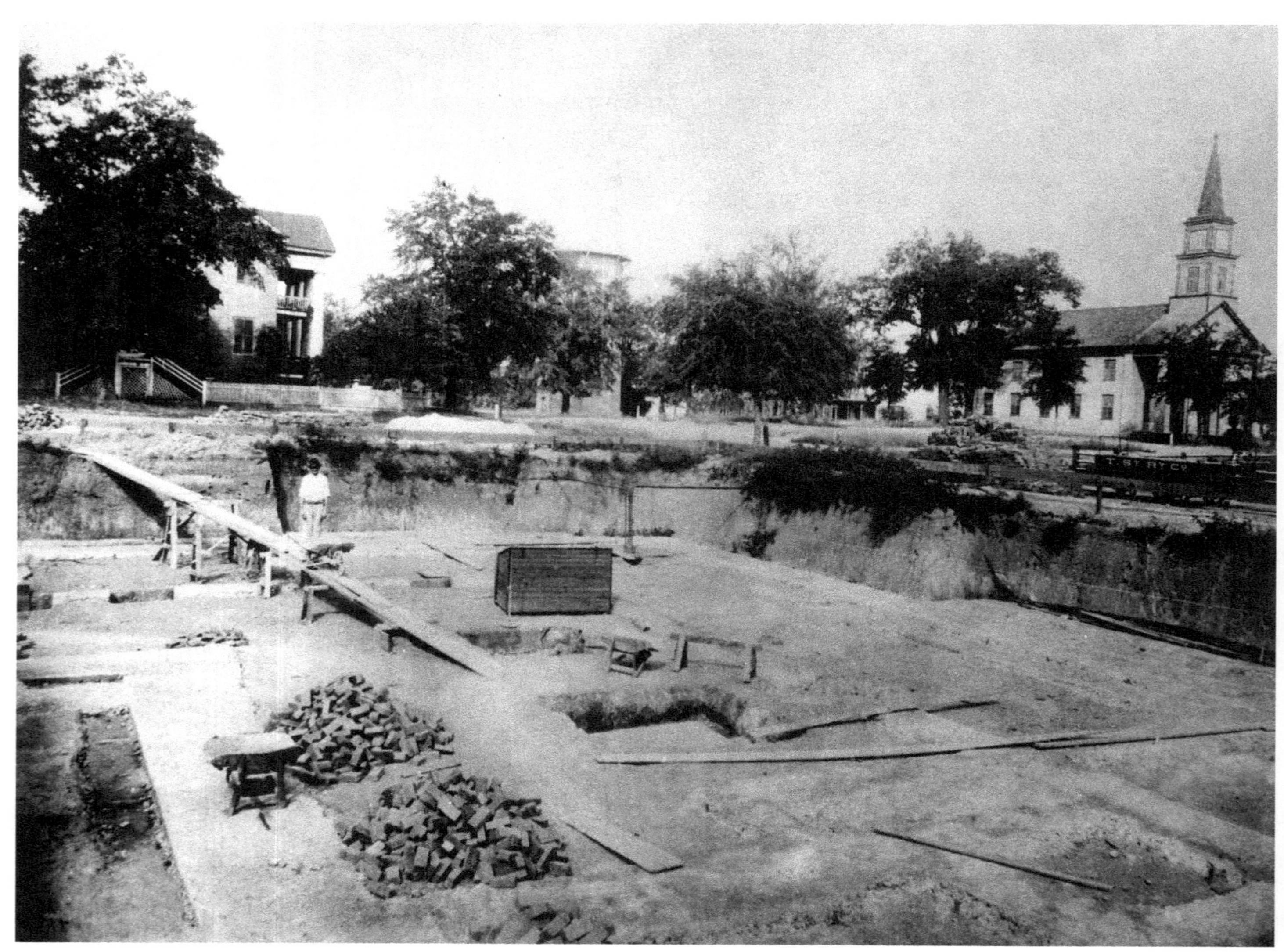

A view of construction on the Tallahassee post office about 1892. Located on the southeast corner of Adams and Park, it became city hall in 1936 and was leveled in 1964. In 1972 the Tallahassee Hilton Hotel was built on the site.

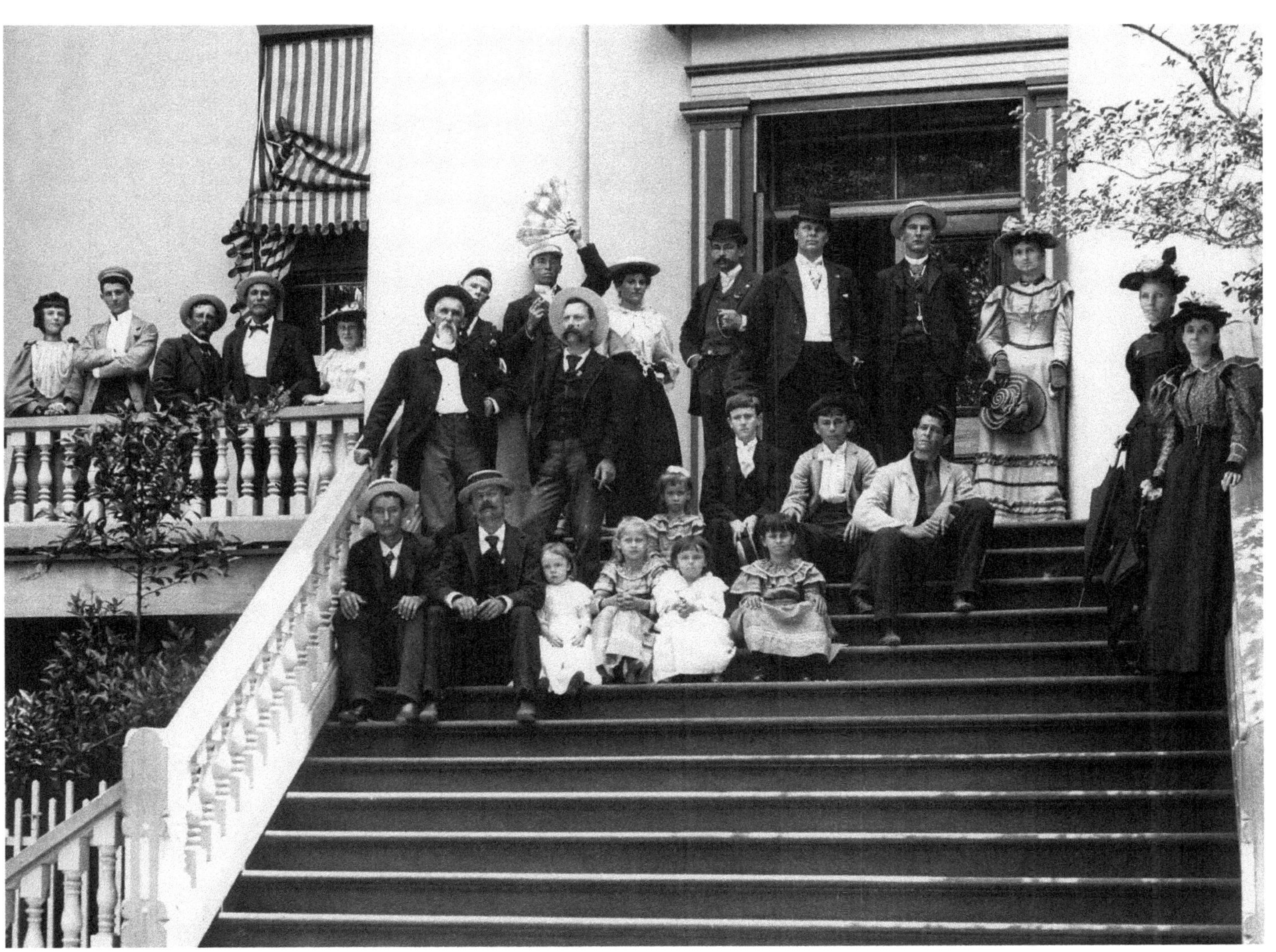

John Fowler's family and company pause for a group portrait on the steps of the capitol in 1893. Improvements following Harriet Beecher Stowe's visit almost twenty years earlier are noticeable. Renovations to the building, in 1891, included a new roof with added cupola, water closets, fountains, and fresh whitewash.

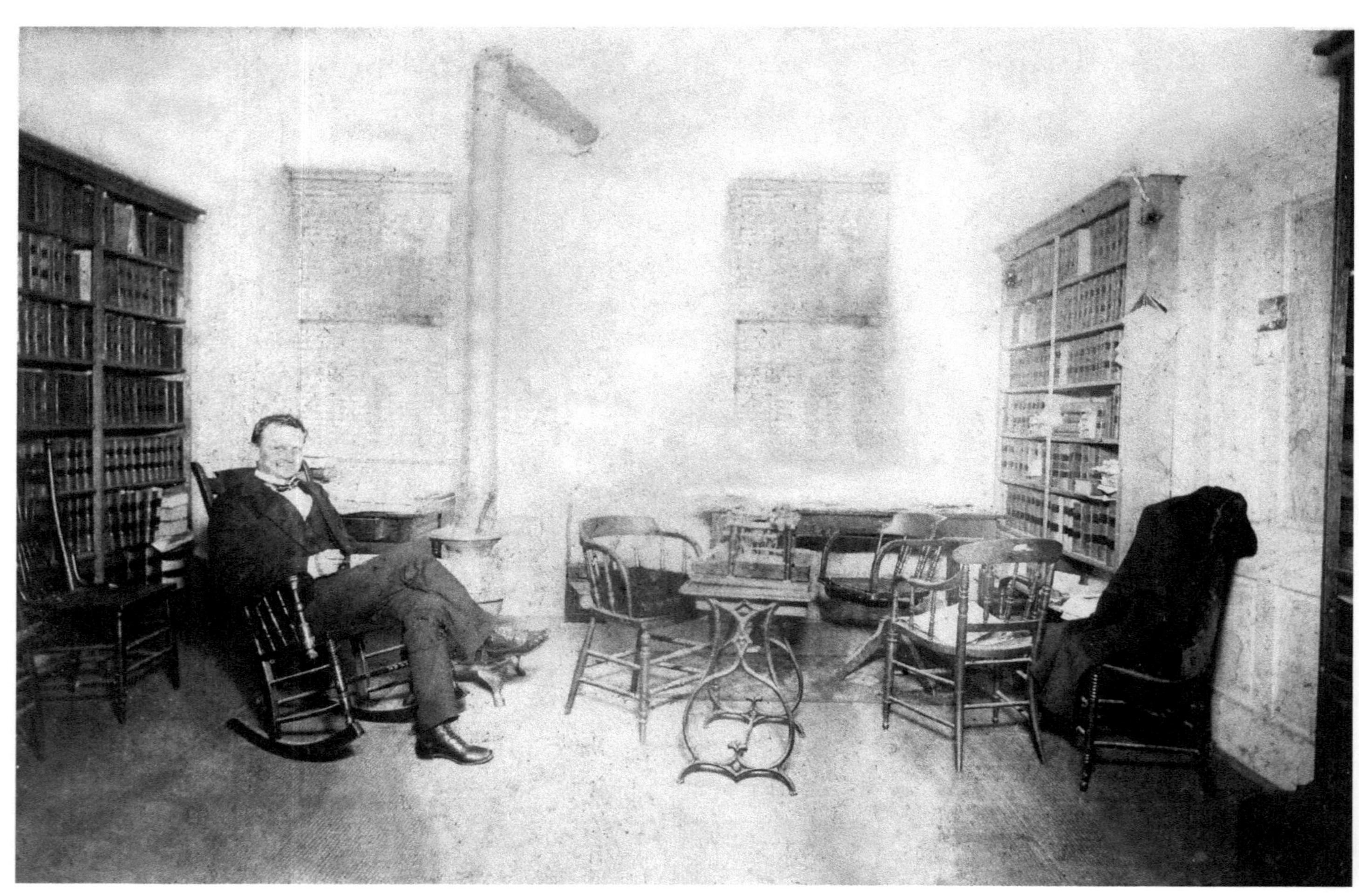

Supreme Court justice George P. Raney sits in his office during his 1885–1894 term. He was also a state representative, senator, and attorney general. Raney noted that this image was "taken by a tramp artist at his own request; but of course I had to subscribe after the work was exhibited. Do not be beguiled if you do not want to pay." Posterity applauds the artist for recording Raney's countenance, and thanks Raney for paying up.

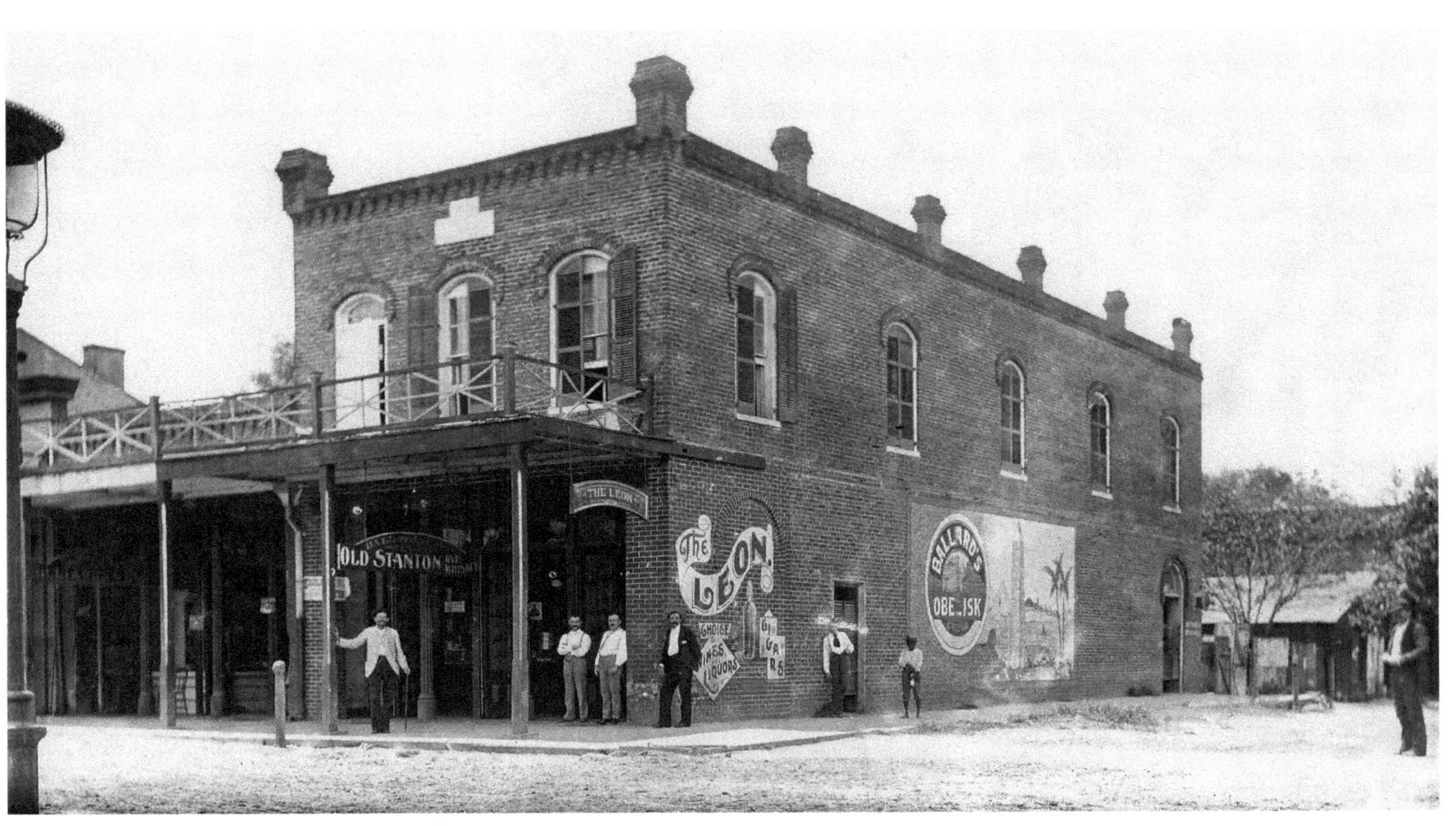

Lively's corner, at the southwest corner of Monroe and College, was originally built in 1875 as Lively's drugstore. In 1892 the popular Leon Bar operated as liquor store, bar, and pool room, and was a target of temperance advocates. It closed when the town went dry in 1904, and was later opened as another drugstore and as an office building.

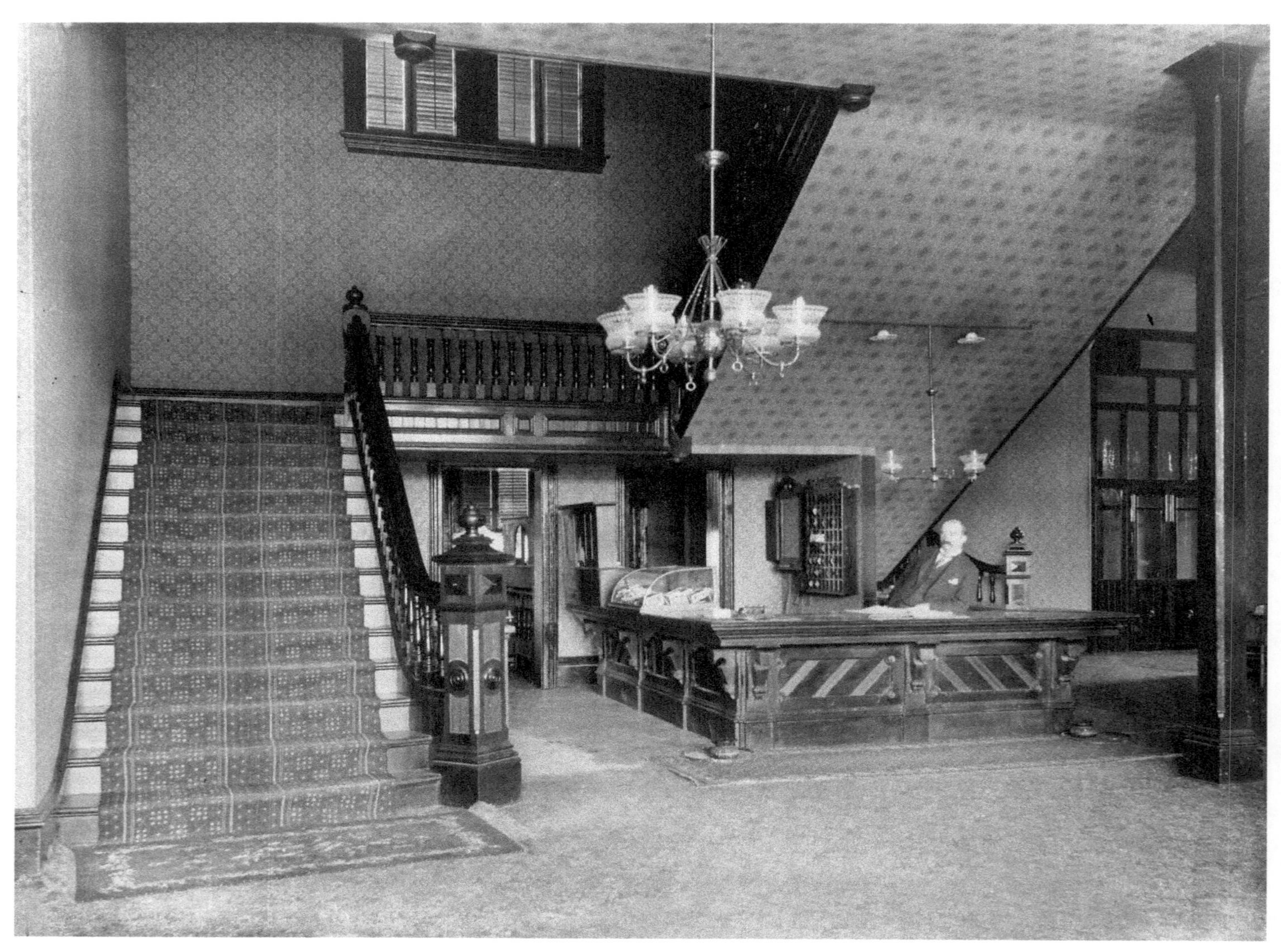

Manager Oglesby leans on the lobby desk of the luxurious Leon Hotel. It featured gas lighting, running water, a dining room, telegraph office, and a barbershop. Governor William Sherman Jennings and family lived at the Leon Hotel for a few years. His son recalled "sliding down the highly polished railings of the Leon Hotel."

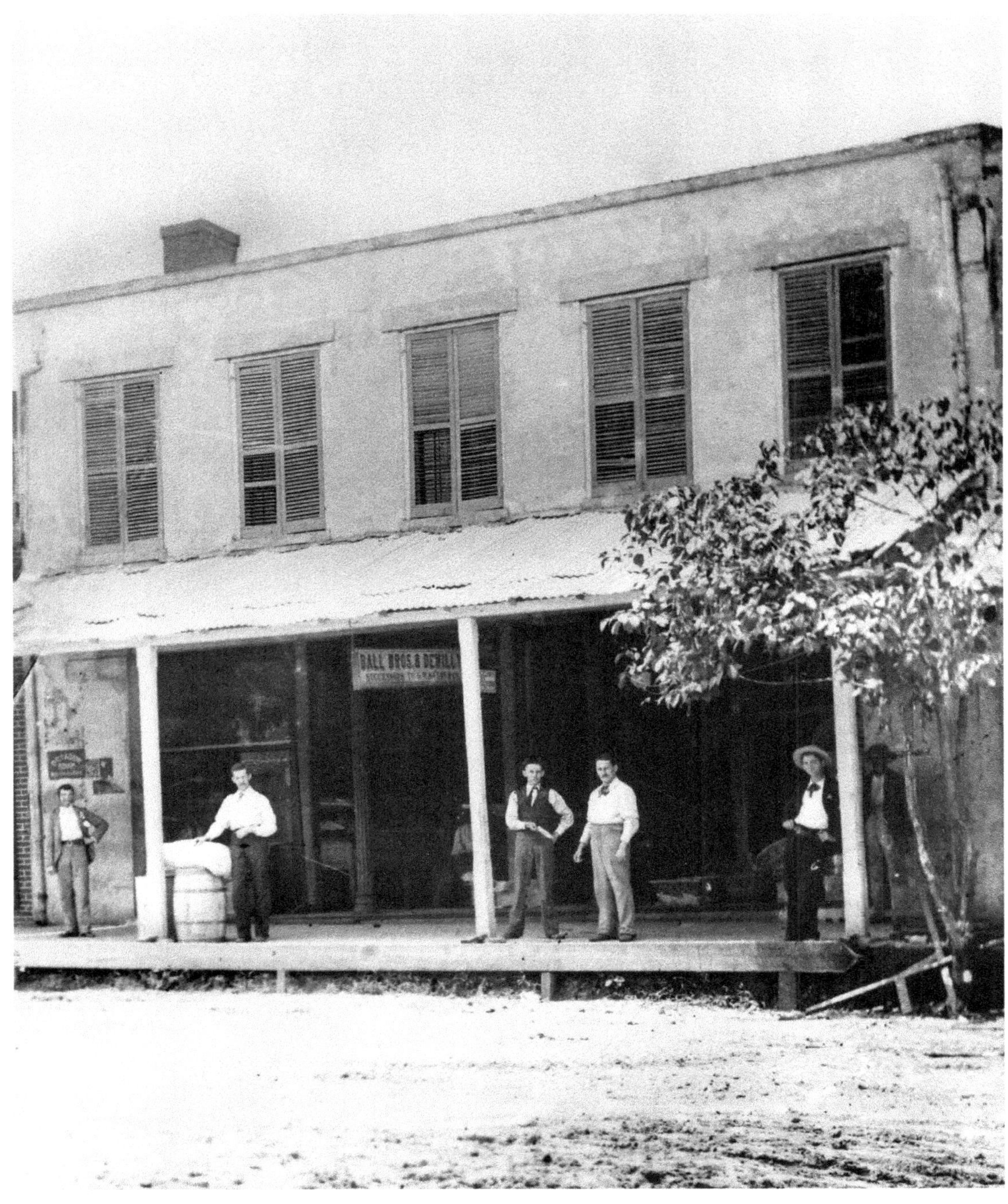

Although it had a rough appearance, Ball Bros. and DeMilly general store was at the center of Tallahassee's business district on Monroe Street in the 1890s. The DeMilly family is one of Tallahassee's oldest, tracing its lineage back to Charles DeMilly, a soldier in the Napoleonic wars who immigrated to Tallahassee in 1828.

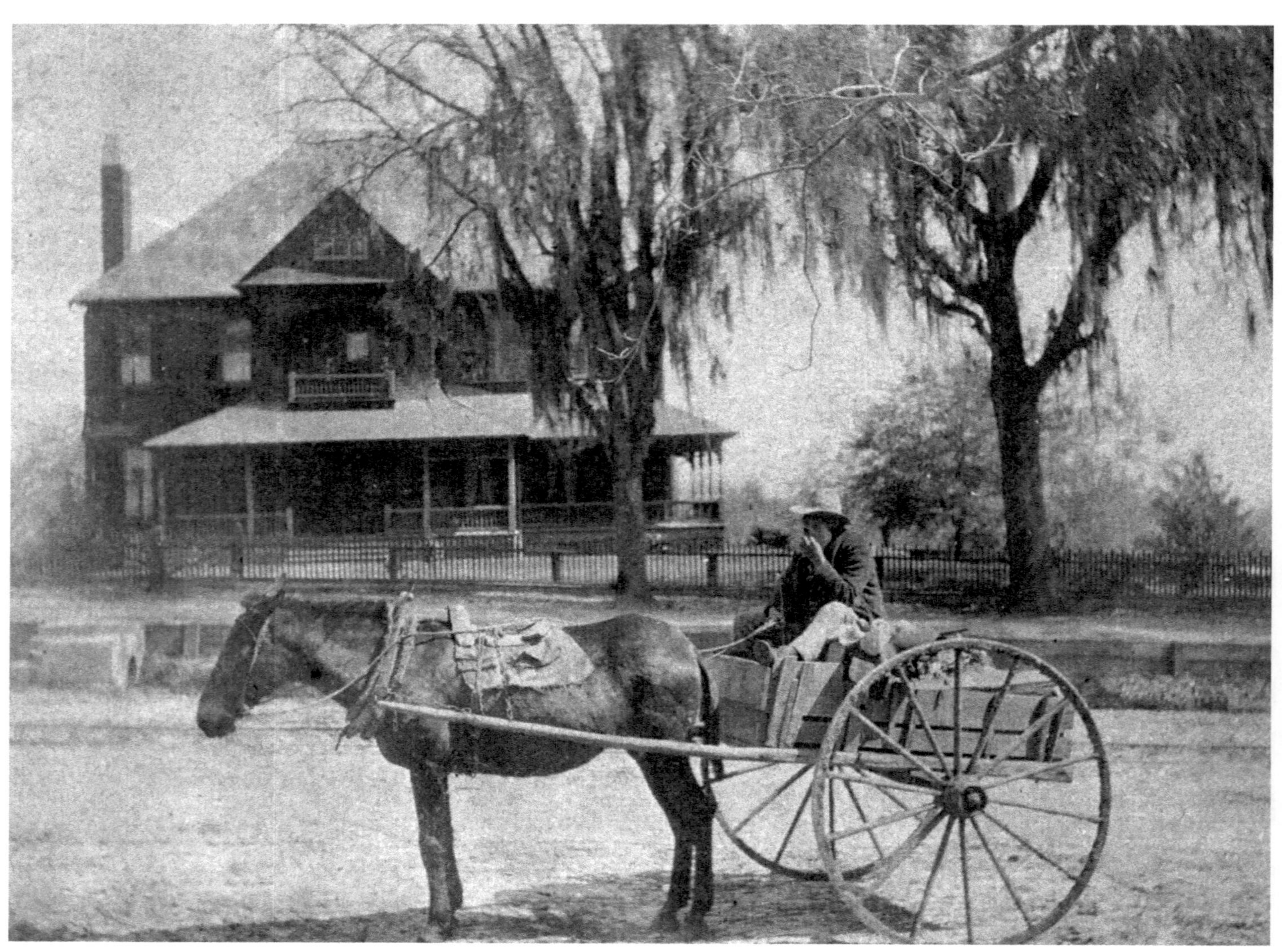

A horse cart and driver pull up in front of the Winthrop home at 610 North Monroe. John L. Winthrop and his wife, Lilia Chouteau, had this elegant house built in 1890. It had sixteen rooms, paneled in oak and cherry. It was appointed with elaborate chandeliers and mirrors, and stained-glass windows.

A source of community pride, the Tallahassee Railroad Company's mule-drawn trolley operated from 1889 to 1896. Two small red mules, Napoleon and Bucephalus, seen with a horse, had to be unhitched and hooked up to the opposite end of the car to begin its return run. The drivers would often wait for patrons to do their shopping.

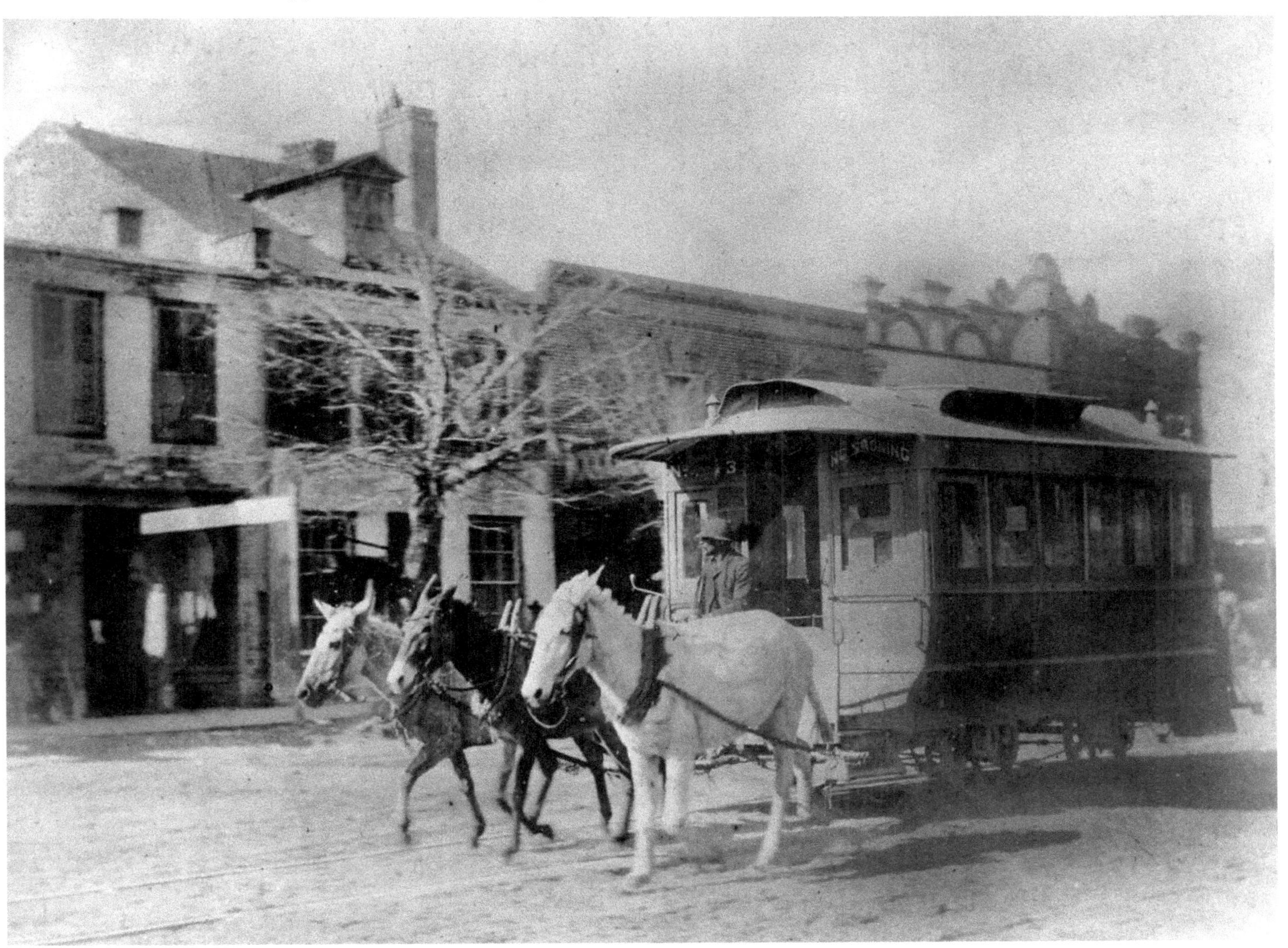

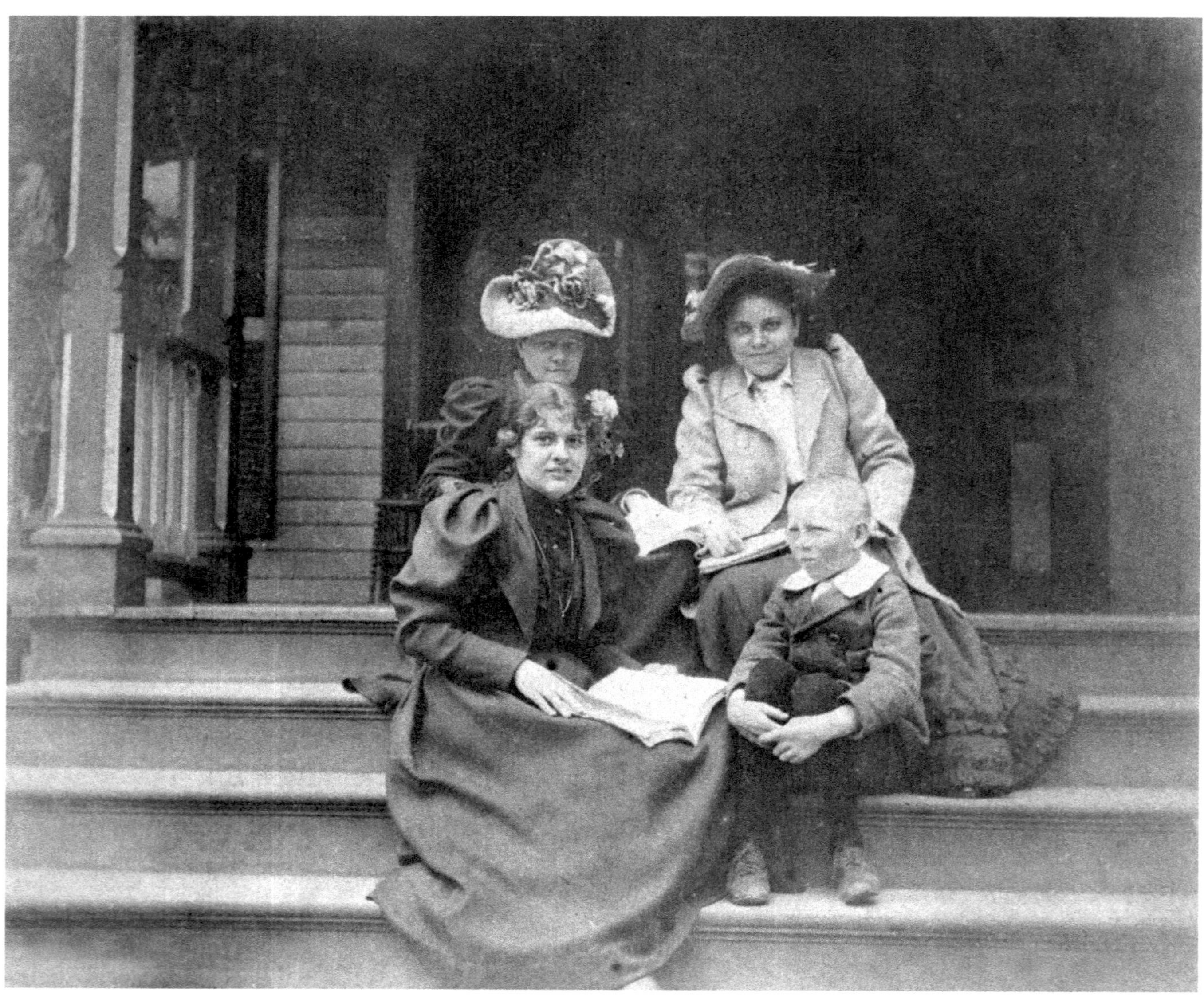

Mrs. Henry Beadel, back left, and Genevieve Dillon, front left, of Tall Timbers plantation, visit Dick and Bernette Long, probably on the porch of the Long House. The Longs were related to Ellen Call Long, daughter of the first territorial governor.

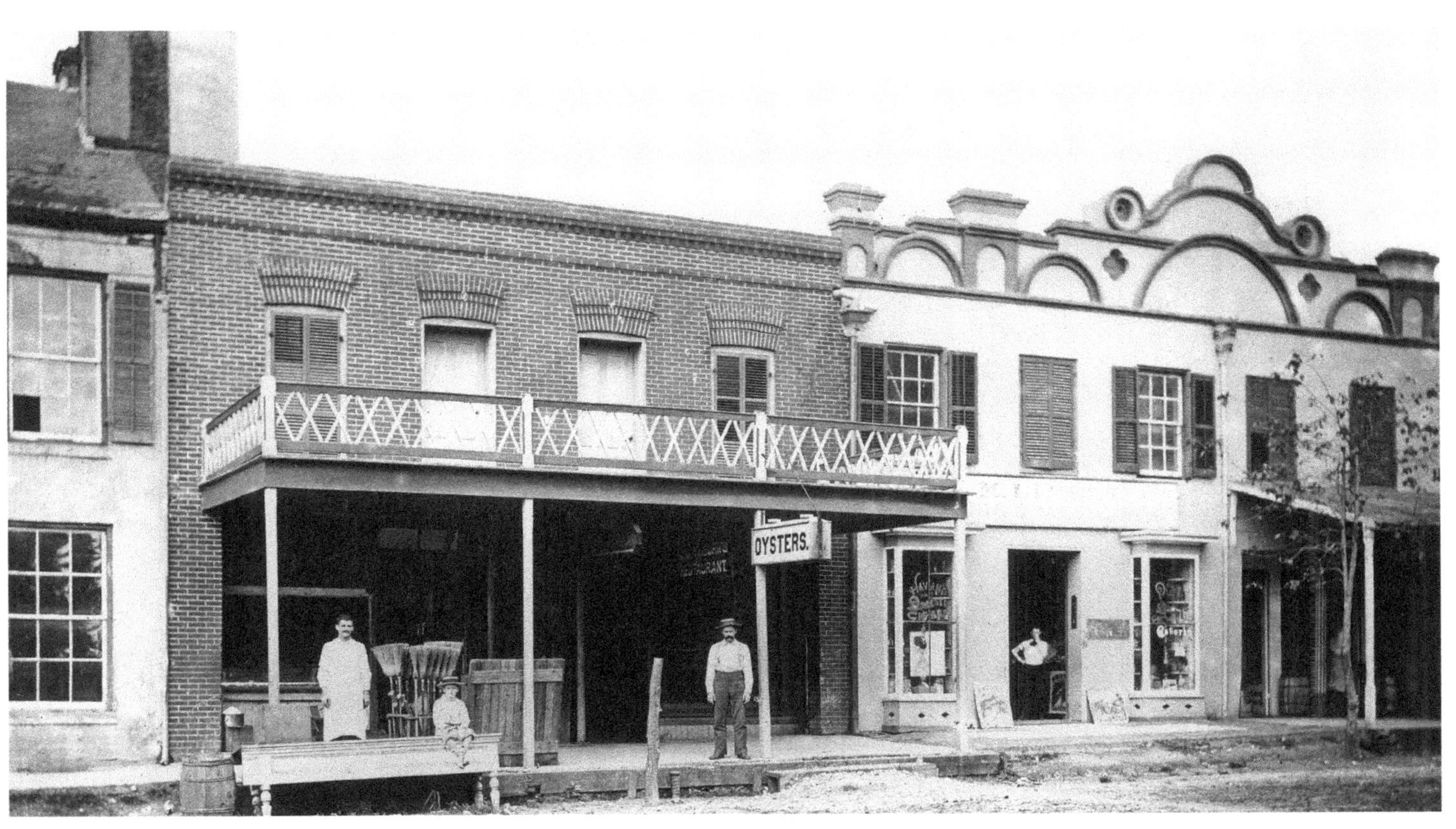

Winburn's Restaurant advertises "Oysters" beside the ornate M. Lively drugstore on Monroe Street in 1894. Sidewalks were a constant problem. Many complained about stores blocking sidewalks with displays of merchandise. The U.S. Postal Service refused service until "good sidewalks were provided."

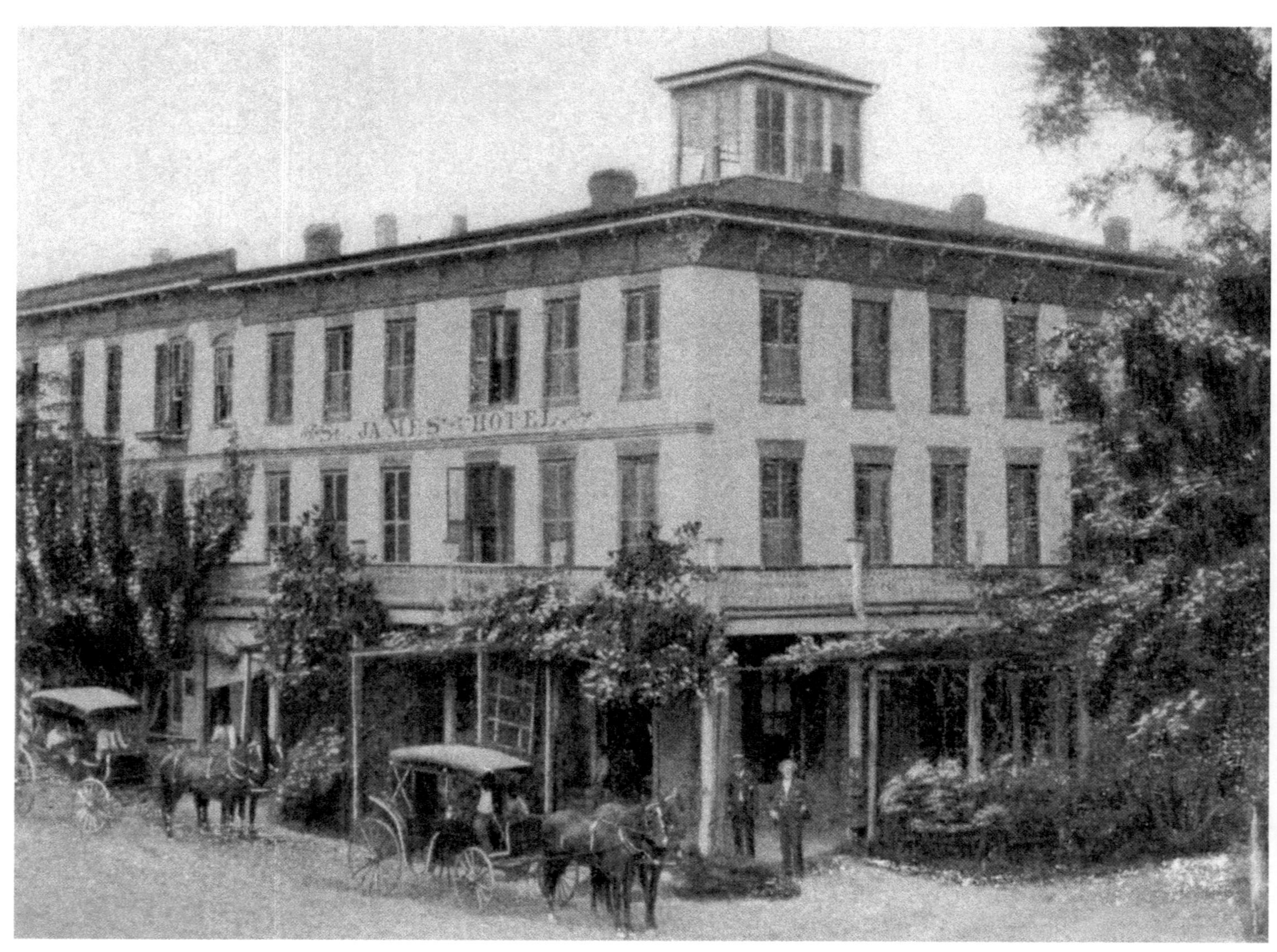

The St. James Hotel, constructed in 1883, was remodeled and renamed the Bloxham in 1908, then demolished in 1913 for the Lewis State Bank building. Three stories tall and topped with an "observatory," it provided a fine view of the countryside. Its restaurant and saloon were frequented by employees from the nearby courthouse.

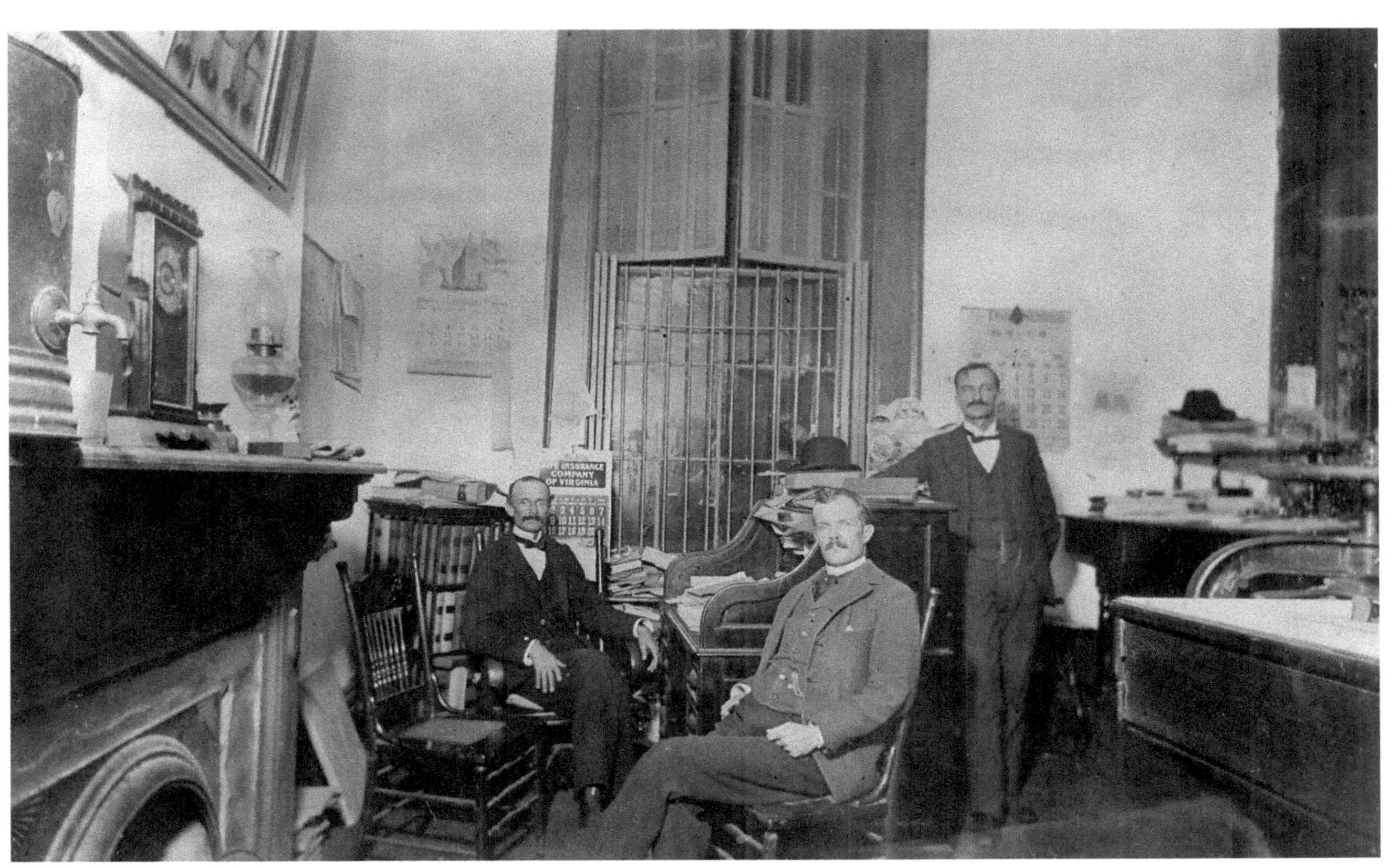

State Treasurer James B. Whitfield sits behind his desk at the capitol, probably with his office staff. He later served as State Attorney General, then on the Supreme Court bench for almost forty years as one of Florida's most distinguished justices. The fireplace was sealed over in 1902 and used as a support for the new capitol dome.

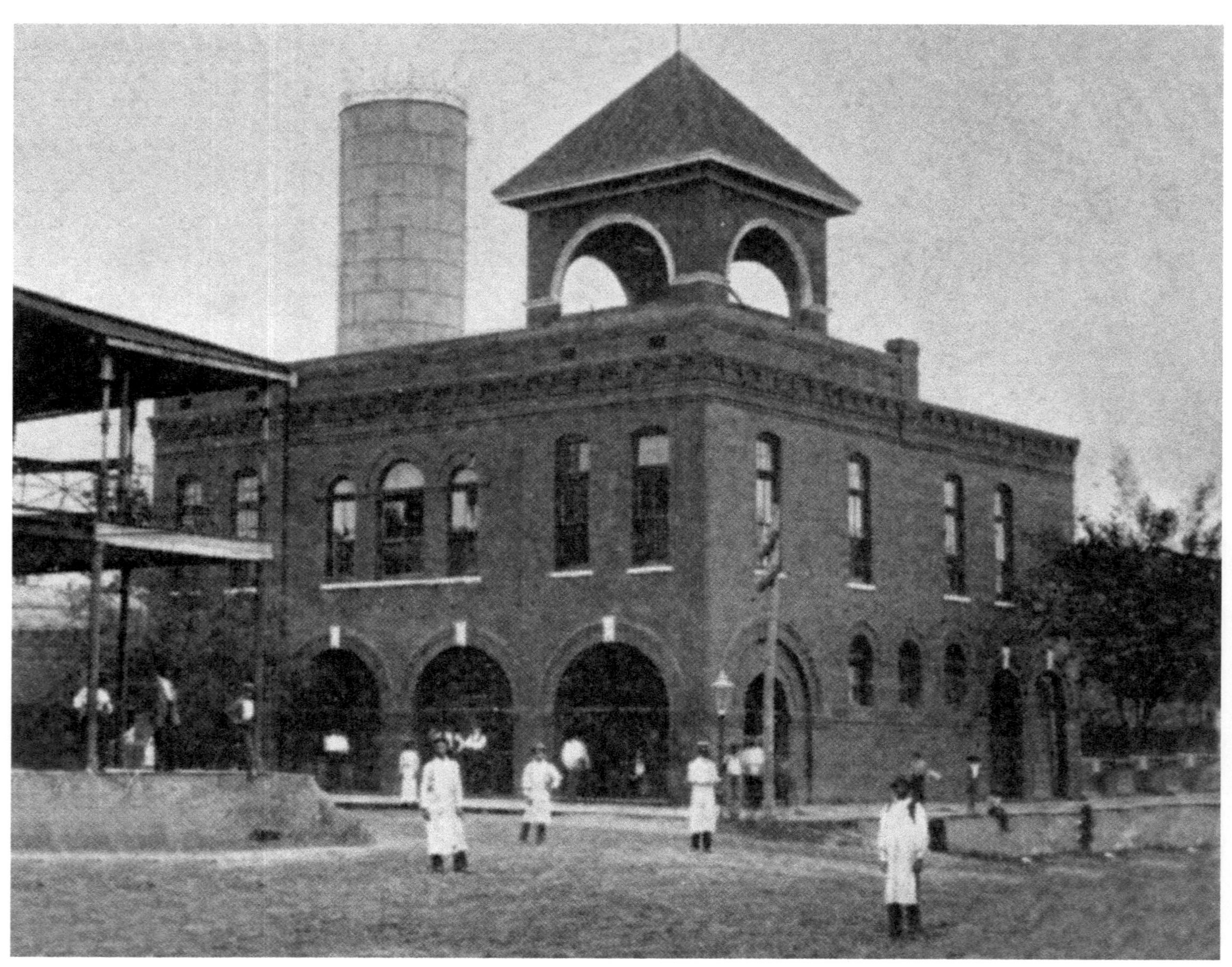

A combined Market and City Hall building was constructed in the 1880s on the southeast corner of Jefferson and Adams, opposite the Opera house, far left. By 1929, the fire department was also located there. The building was leveled in 1966. The city's water tower is visible in the background.

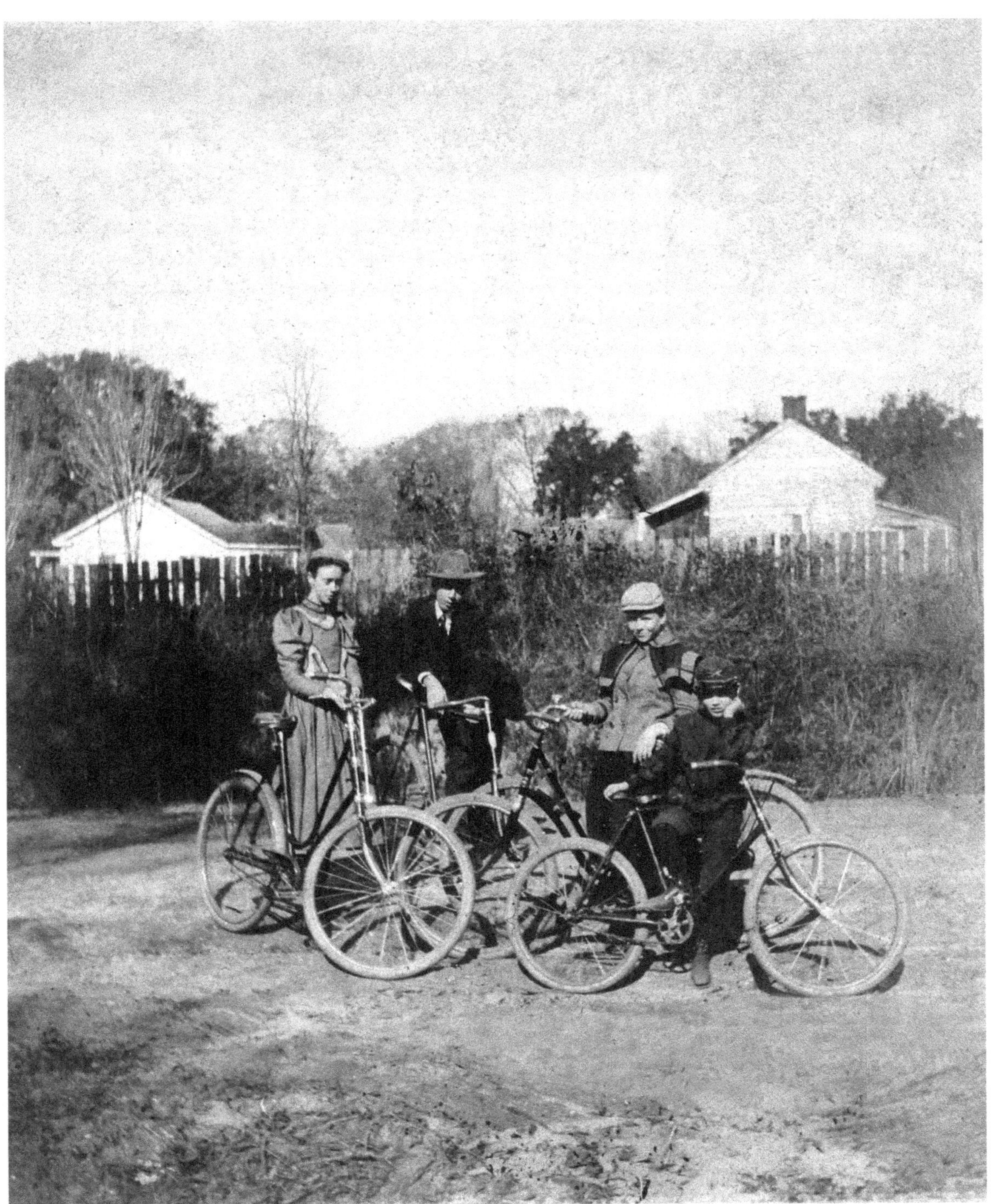

Young cyclists stop to pose for their photograph in December 1898. The smaller-wheeled bicycles were much easier to control than the high-wheeled penny-farthings.

Alvan S. Harper, in customary hat, long-sleeve shirt, and boots, attempts to photograph two dogs in a horse-drawn cart with, it appears, an early hand-held camera. Question is, who is photographing the photographer? The open longleaf pine and wiregrass habitat is typical of the area surrounding and to the north of Tallahassee.

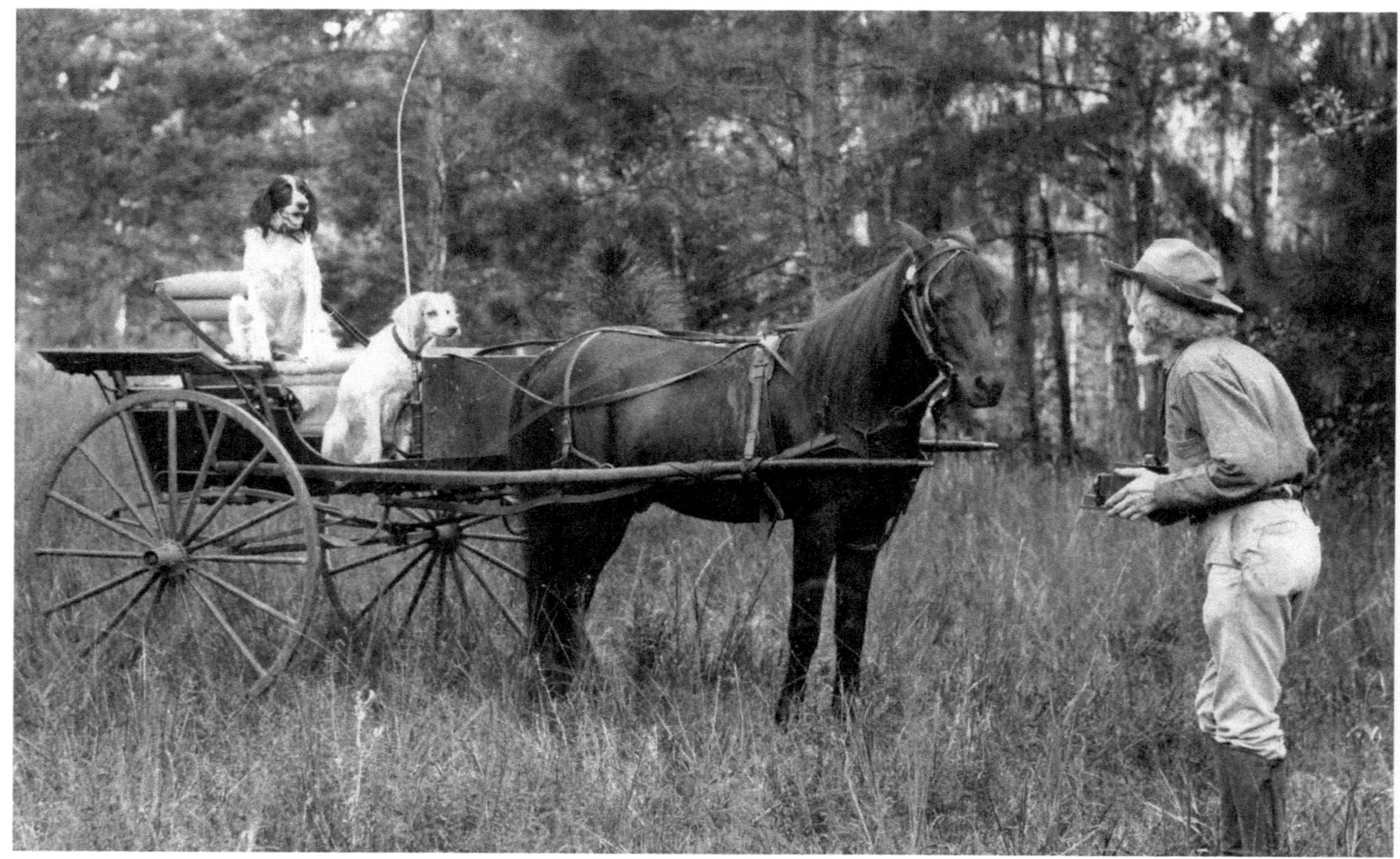

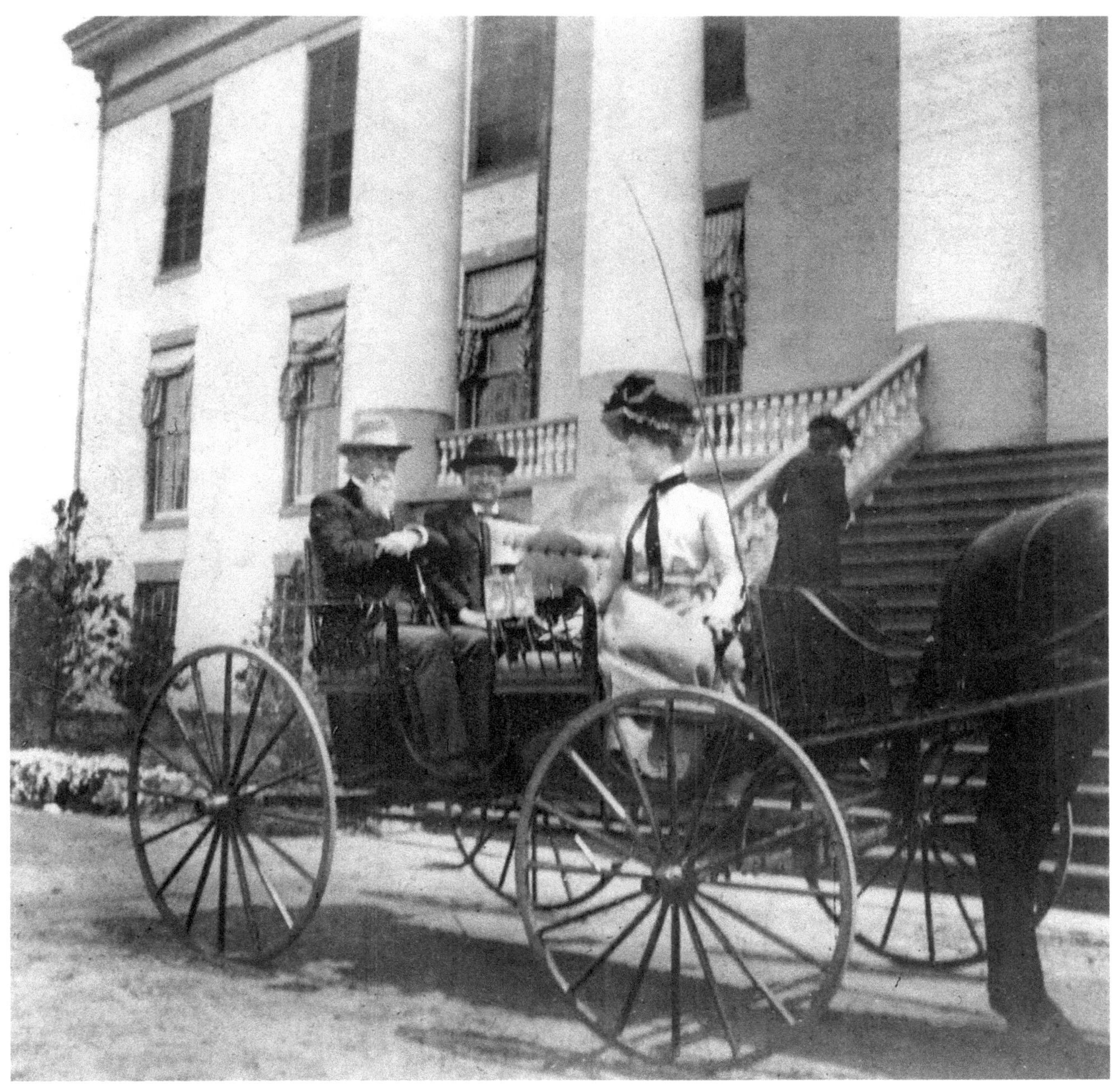

Governor Bloxham in carriage, second from left, pauses at the steps of the old capitol. He served twice as governor, from 1881 to 1885 and from 1897 until 1901. Behind the carriage on the middle floor were the Supreme Court chambers and, directly above, the Senate chamber.

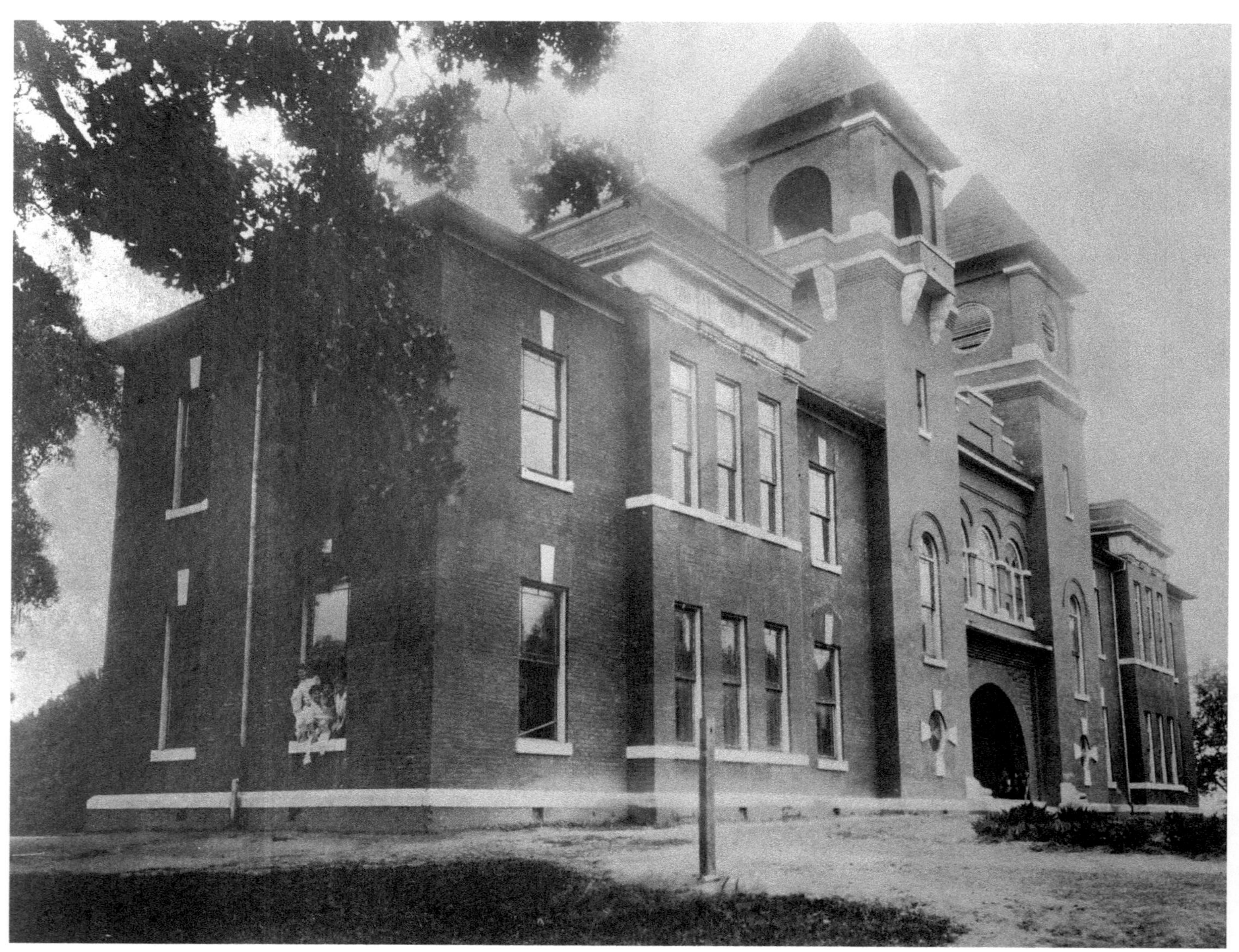

College Hall was constructed in 1891 then replaced with the Westcott building in 1909. The school held several names in the span of a few years, from West Florida Seminary to Florida State College in 1901, Florida Female College in 1905, and Florida State College for Women in 1909.

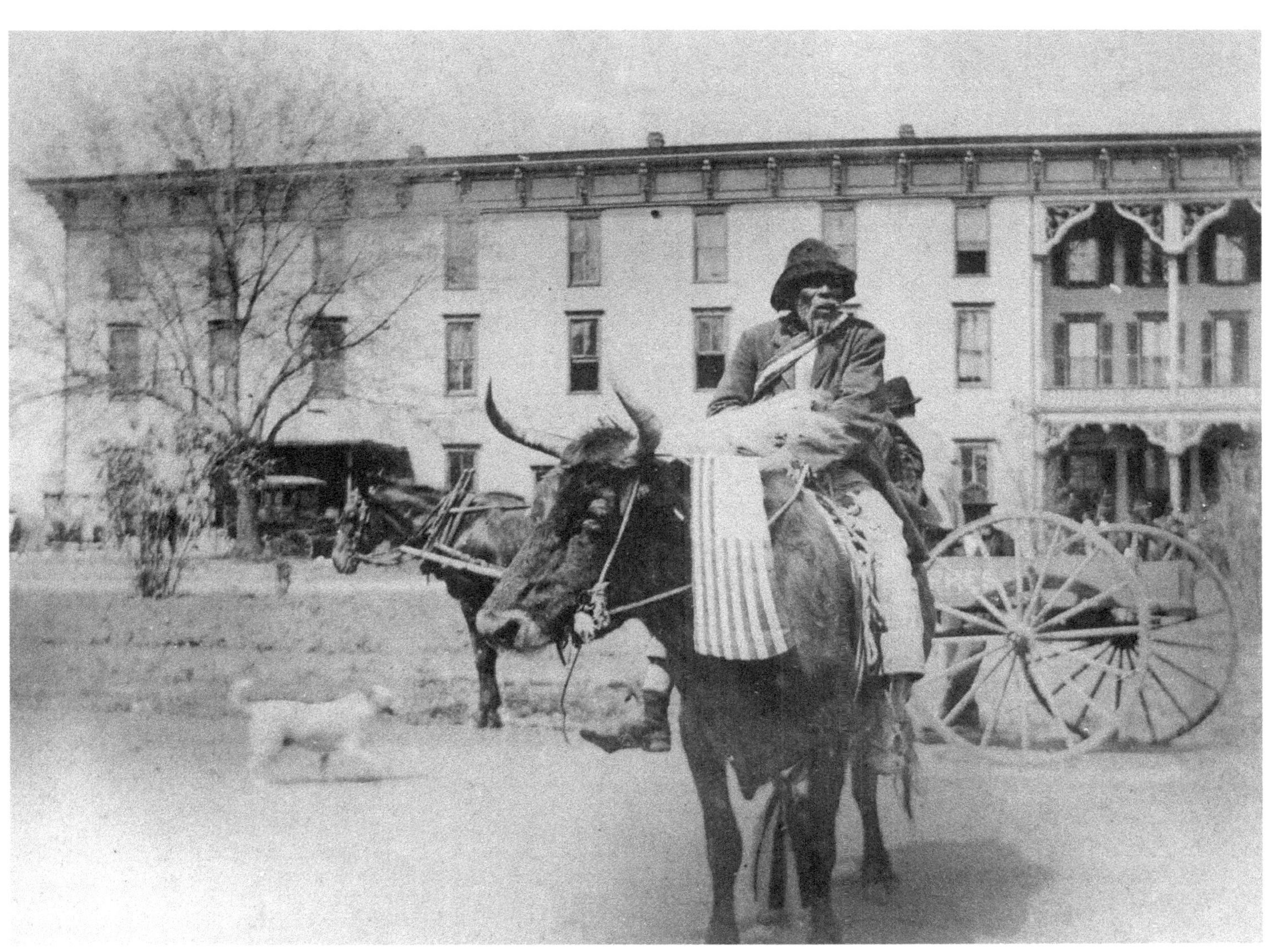

Most of Tallahassee turned out to see and greet President McKinley and the First Lady during their visit in 1899, including "Dirty Smith" riding on an ox. Presidents Nixon, Carter, Clinton, and George H. W. Bush have also paid formal visits to the state capital.

Using locally grown tobacco, the Wanish Cigar Factory employed Cuban-born cigar maker Manuel Roffe, at far-left, to train the other workers. The cigar factory closed around the time the city went "dry," leading to rumors that the employees would not work in a town without liquor.

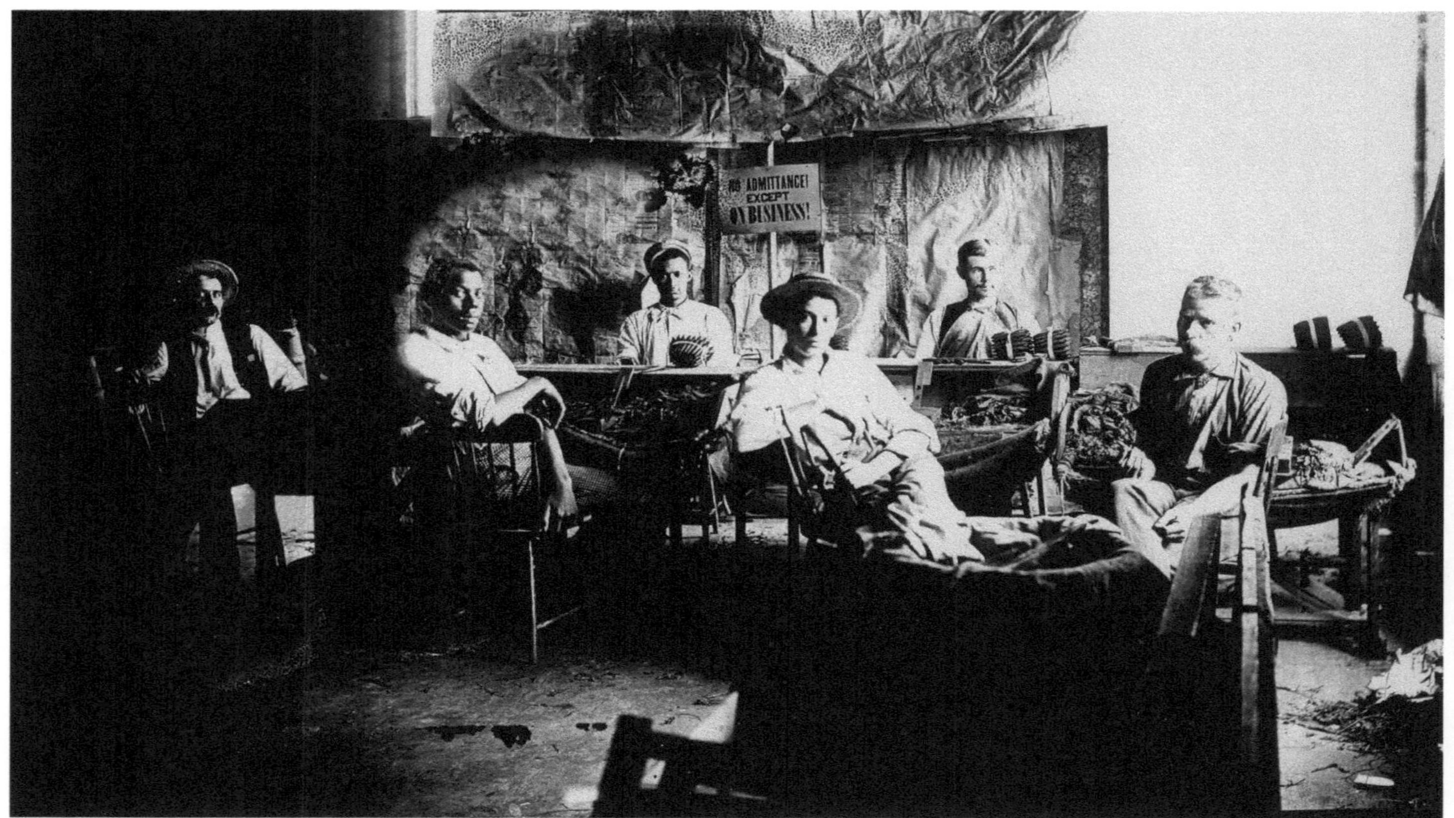

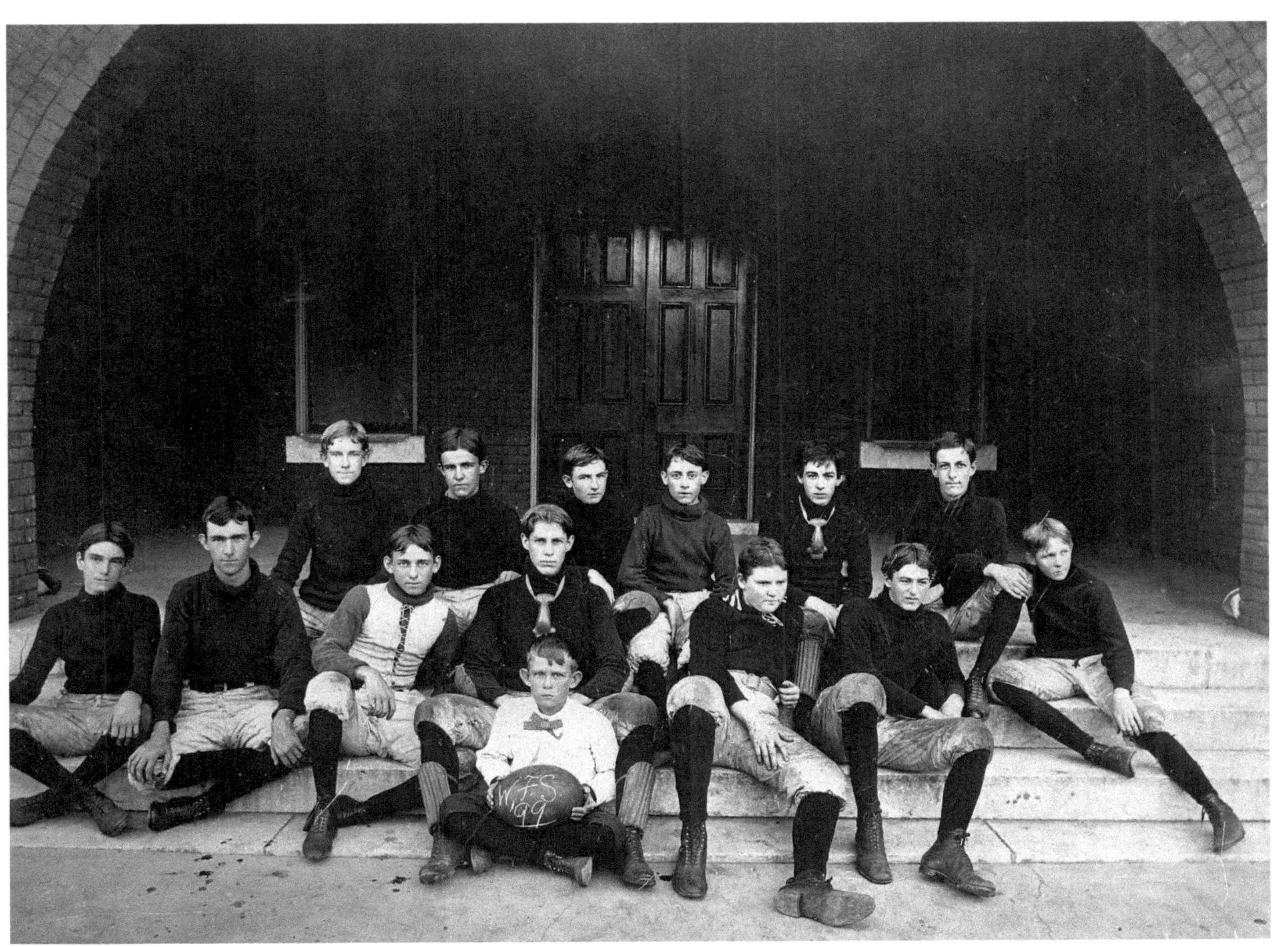

The West Florida Seminary football team of 1899 poses at College Hall. The school continued playing football after becoming Florida State College in 1901. F.S.C. won state championships in 1904 and 1905, coached by college president Albert Murphree. The college team wore purple and gold uniforms.

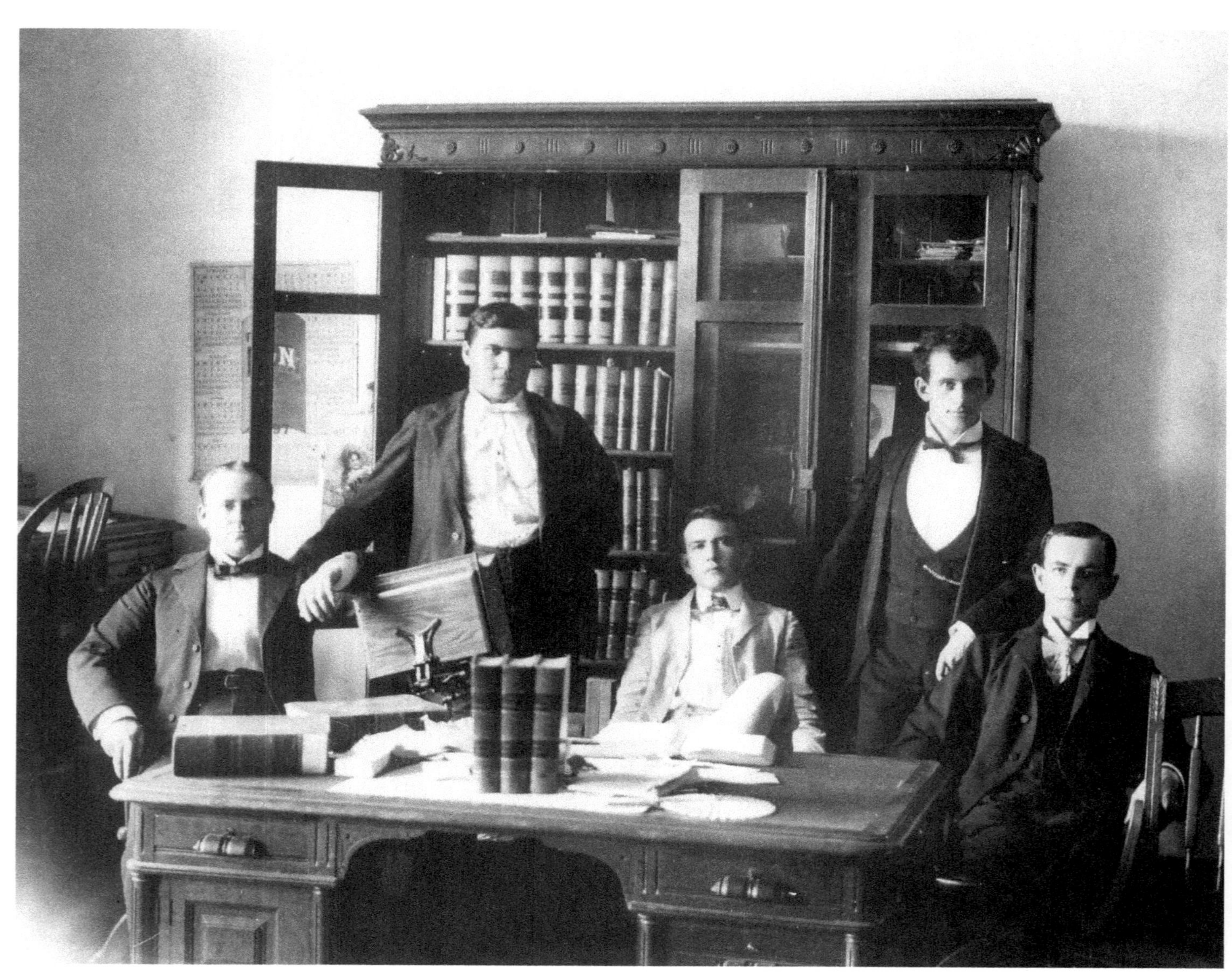

William Cabot Hodges, standing at right, served in the Florida Senate from 1922 to 1940 and was elected Senate President in 1935. "Homestead Bill" supported a homestead tax exemption amendment, aid for the blind, welfare for children, and pensions for the aged. His Tallahassee home, Goodwood Plantation, is now a museum.

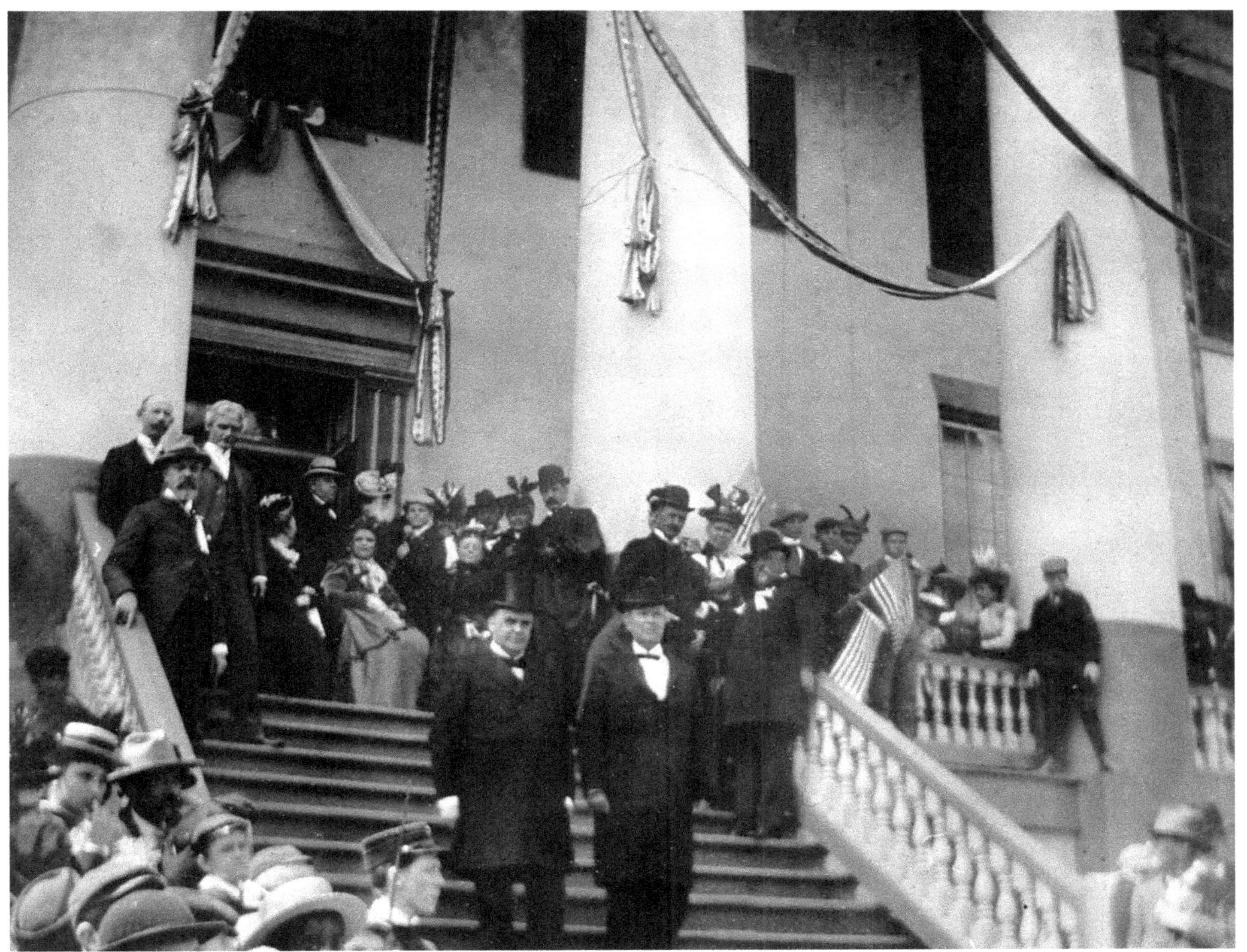

President McKinley, on the steps at front-left, was the first sitting United States president to visit Tallahassee. He was the guest of Governor Bloxham, front-right, at the Capitol on March 24, 1899. Mrs. McKinley, in the light-colored dress, looks on from the top of the staircase. The crush of the throng caused her to faint during the reception.

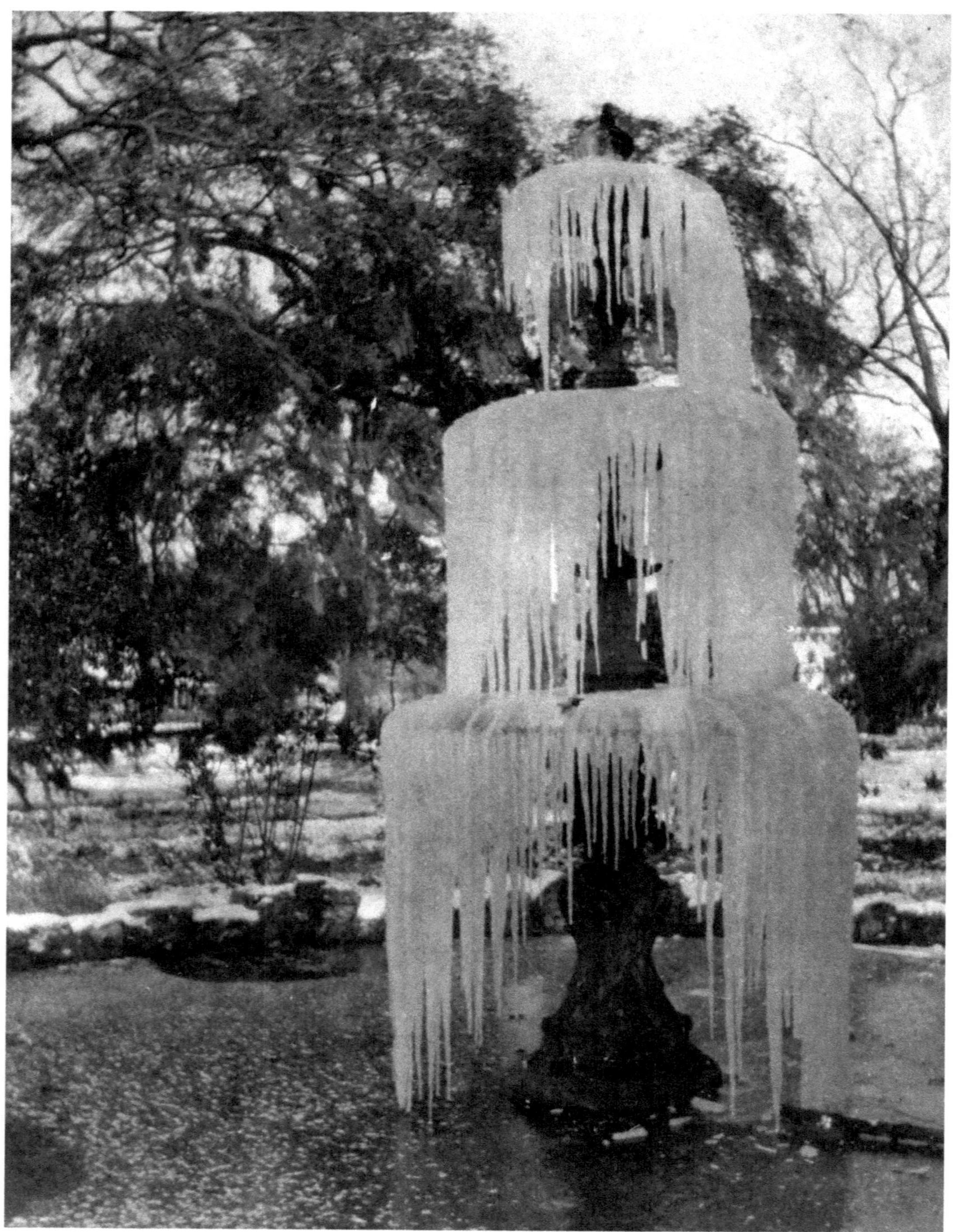

On February 13, 1899, the frozen fountain on the capitol grounds attested to the coldest temperature in Florida's history, at two degrees Fahrenheit below zero. It has snowed only 32 times in Tallahassee since 1891, with a one-day record of 2.8 inches on February 12, 1958. The area averages 35 days a year with minimum temperatures at, or below, freezing.

A Capitol Idea

(1901–1920)

The little capital town of Tallahassee met the new century with a population of only 3,000. Economically it remained a small rural agricultural town. By the end of the First World War, the town had almost doubled in size owing to new agricultural products, with better transportation, and increases in education and state government. Along with this growth came civic improvements.

Still searching for new agricultural markets, small farmers and tenant farmers successfully turned to dairy and livestock. Perhaps the most noticeable and lasting agricultural change came when the old cotton plantations converted to quail hunting preserves, attracting wealthy Northerners. The Florida, Georgia and Alabama Railroad provided the first North-South railway connection and opened new markets for the timber industry. Sawmills and distilleries used the extensive pine forests, producing lumber, naval stores, and turpentine. Large industrial plants were not attracted to the area; the only industries of any sort were the railroad shop facilities, a cigar-maker, and a winery.

The 1905 Buckman Act changed Florida State College to an all-female school. The Florida State College for Women developed under strong leadership into one of the South's premier educational institutions for women. The act also stipulated that the only higher education institution for African Americans in Florida, the State Normal and Industrial College for Colored Students, should remain in Tallahassee.

A statewide election in 1900 to change the location of the state capital failed, and Governor Jennings obtained the funds for the first extensive additions to the old 1845 capitol building. Tallahasseans pointed with pride to the newly remodeled capitol, resplendent with a large dome, electroliers, granite steps, new wings, and stained-glass skylight.

Civic improvements included new inventions and marvels of the new century, like electric street-lamps and an electric power plant. Other improvements included a sewer system and a permanent fire department. Automobiles, at first a rare sight, became common. Dealerships provided cars, leading to brick-paved streets. The new Capitol City Bank prospered, helping to finance the town's growth. Entertainment consisted of steamboat excursions, the town's first movie theater, and numerous fairs and pageants. Separate festivals, the May Day for the white community, and Emancipation Day for the black community, marked the state's segregation laws.

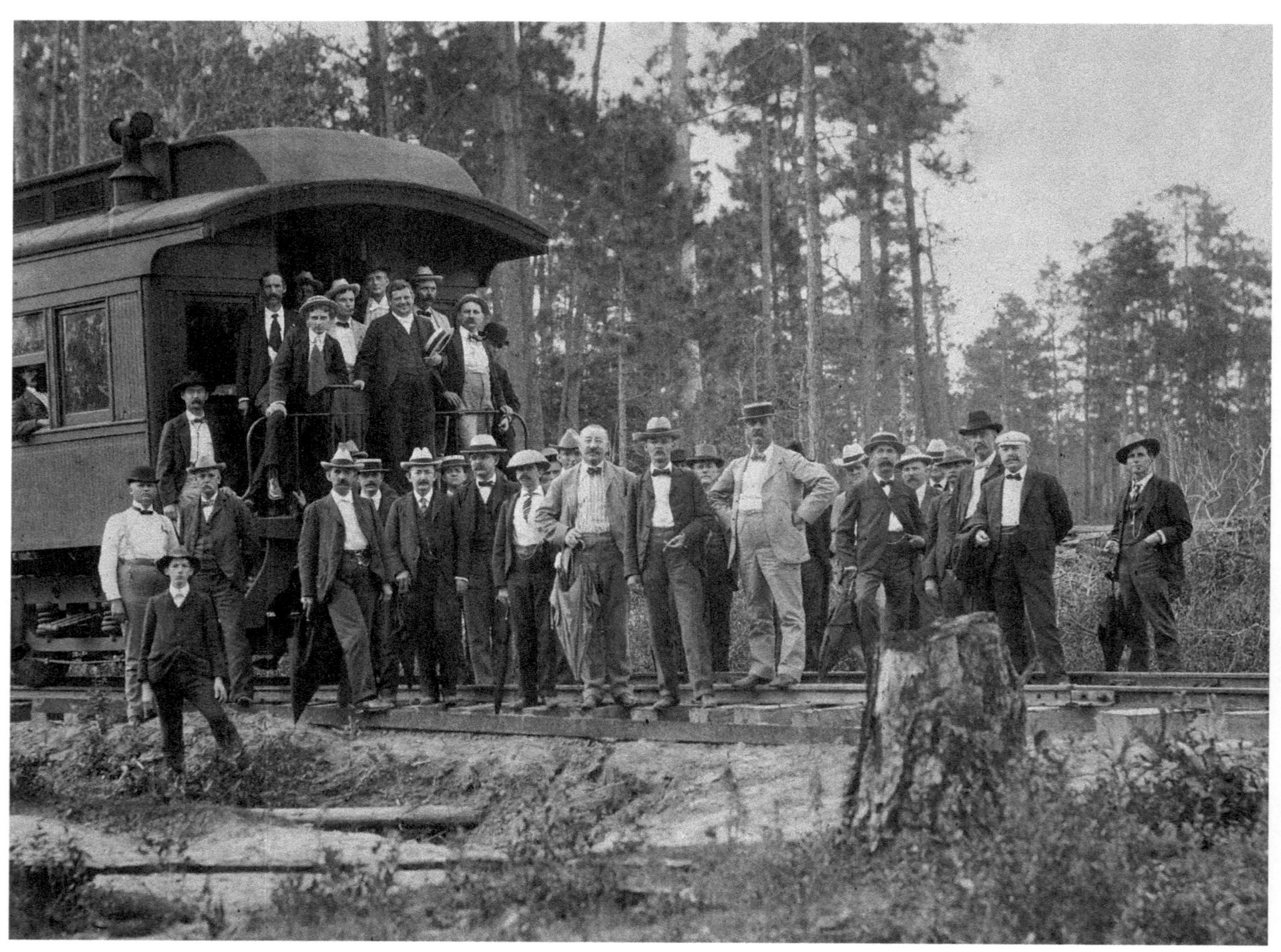

Known locally as "Gophers, Frogs, and Alligators," the Georgia, Florida & Alabama Railway ran 180 miles from Richland, Georgia, through Tallahassee to the Gulf Coast. During World War II it transported thousands of soldiers to Camp Gordon Johnson at Carrabelle. The Seaboard Air Line Railway took control of the line in 1928.

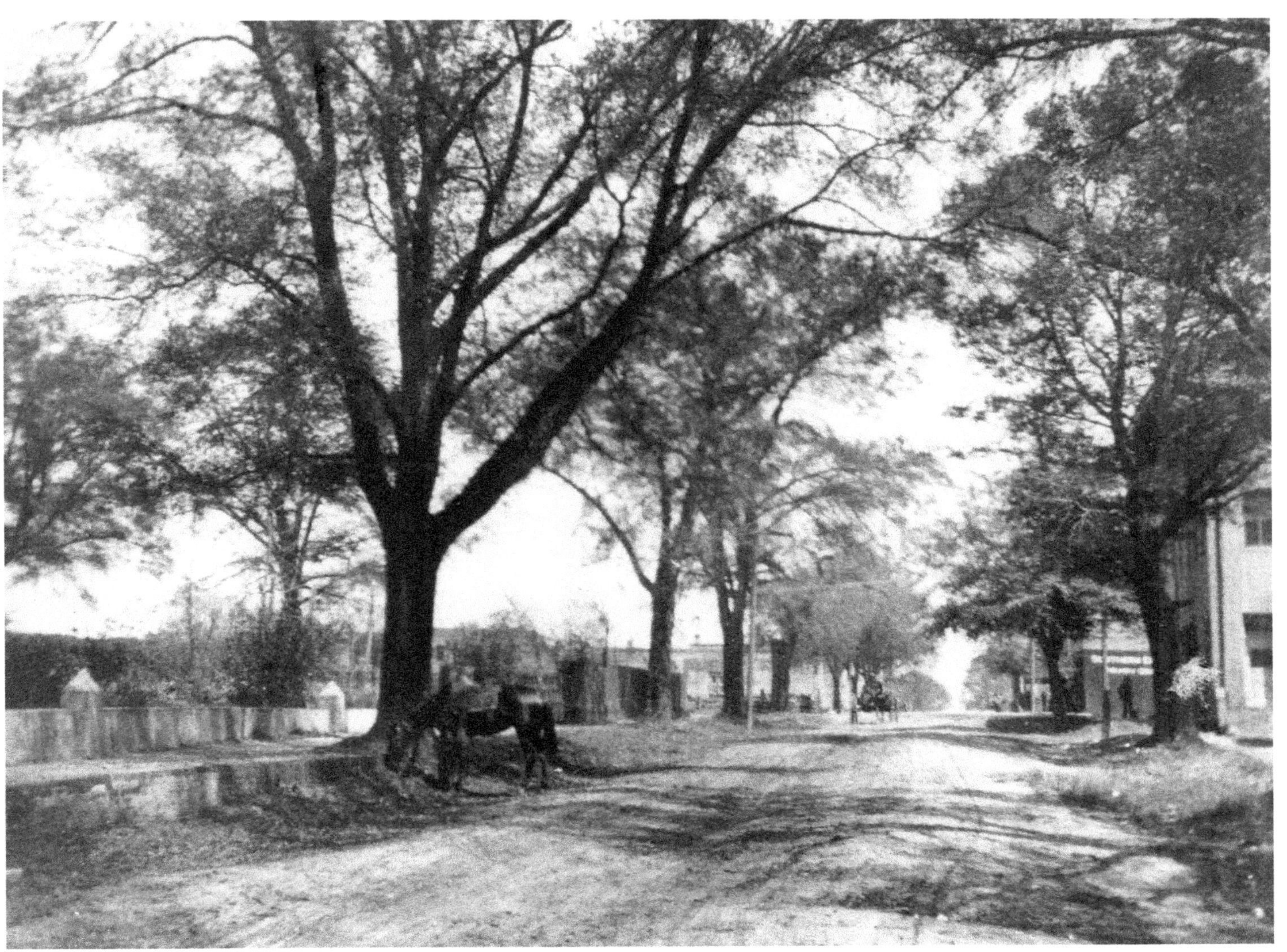

This view faces toward the West Florida Seminary on Clinton Street, later renamed College Avenue. Just a block from the Monroe Street business district, this residential area grew as Tallahassee's population expanded by 45 percent from 1870 to 1880.

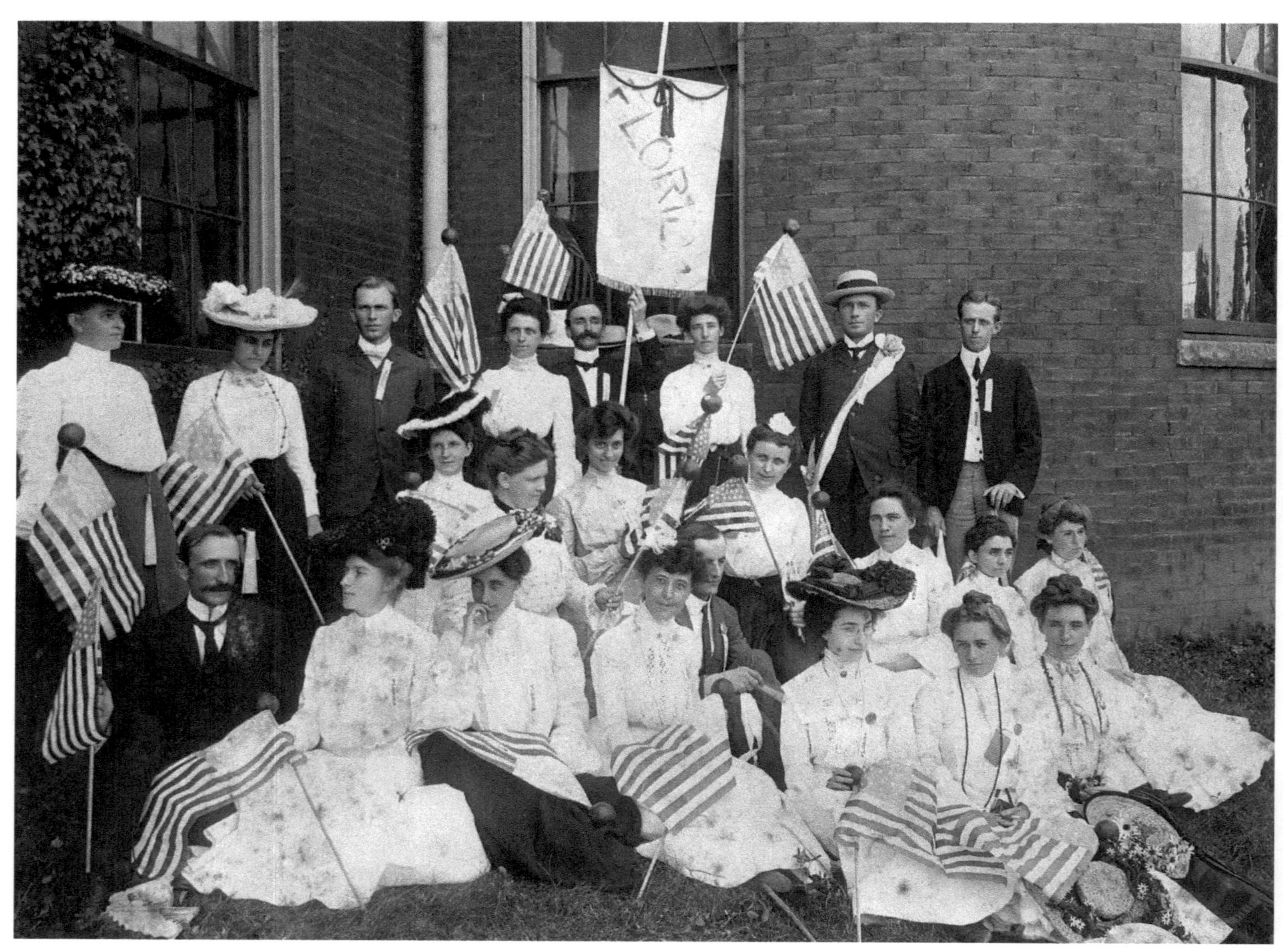

Mary Shutan, a 1902 Florida State College graduate, is fifth from the left in the front row in this "School of the South" class portrait from ca. 1900. In 1902 the co-ed student body numbered 252, and the school offered degrees in classical, literary, and scientific studies and a master of arts degree.

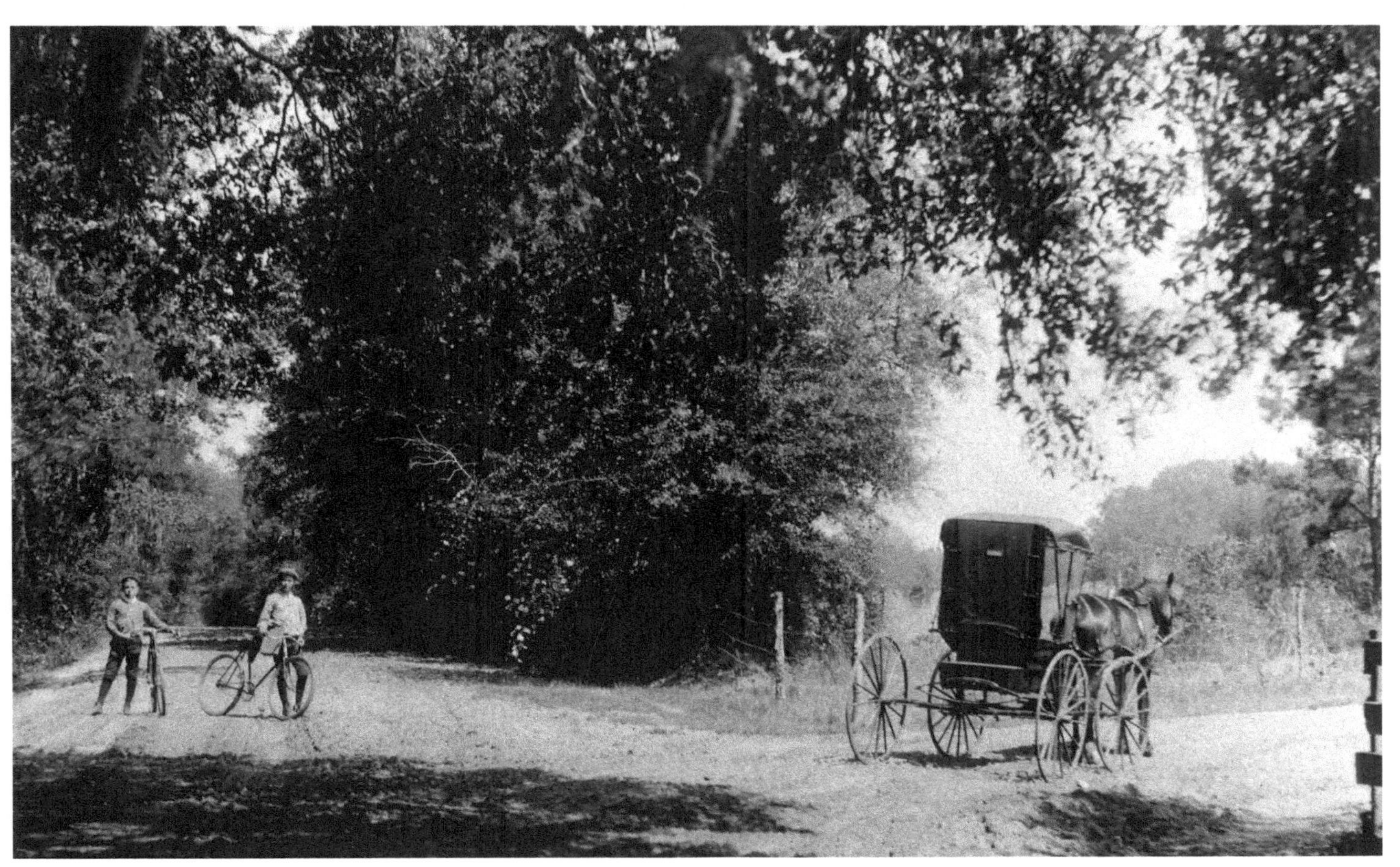

Boys with bikes and a horse-drawn buggy meet at a local crossroads. The canopied roads have shaped Tallahassee's growth and continue to influence the city. Orig nally transportation routes connecting the large plantations to town, the old moss-covered roadways later gave rise to residential and business areas.

This photograph of a Tallahassee bank interior was taken around 1900. Other Tallahassee banks of the time included the Lewis State Bank founded in 1856, the First National Bank located next to the St. James Hotel, and the new Capitol City Bank.

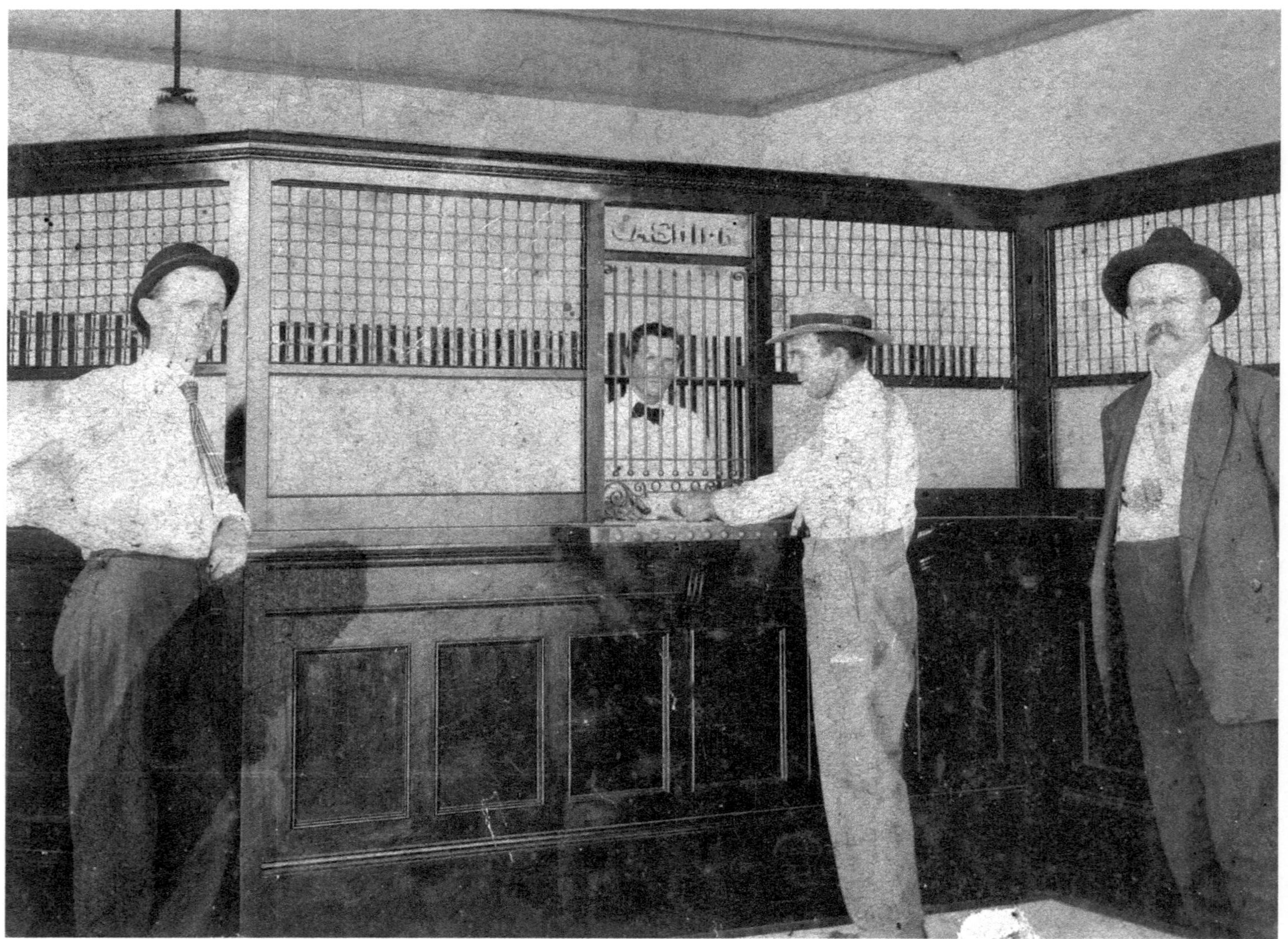

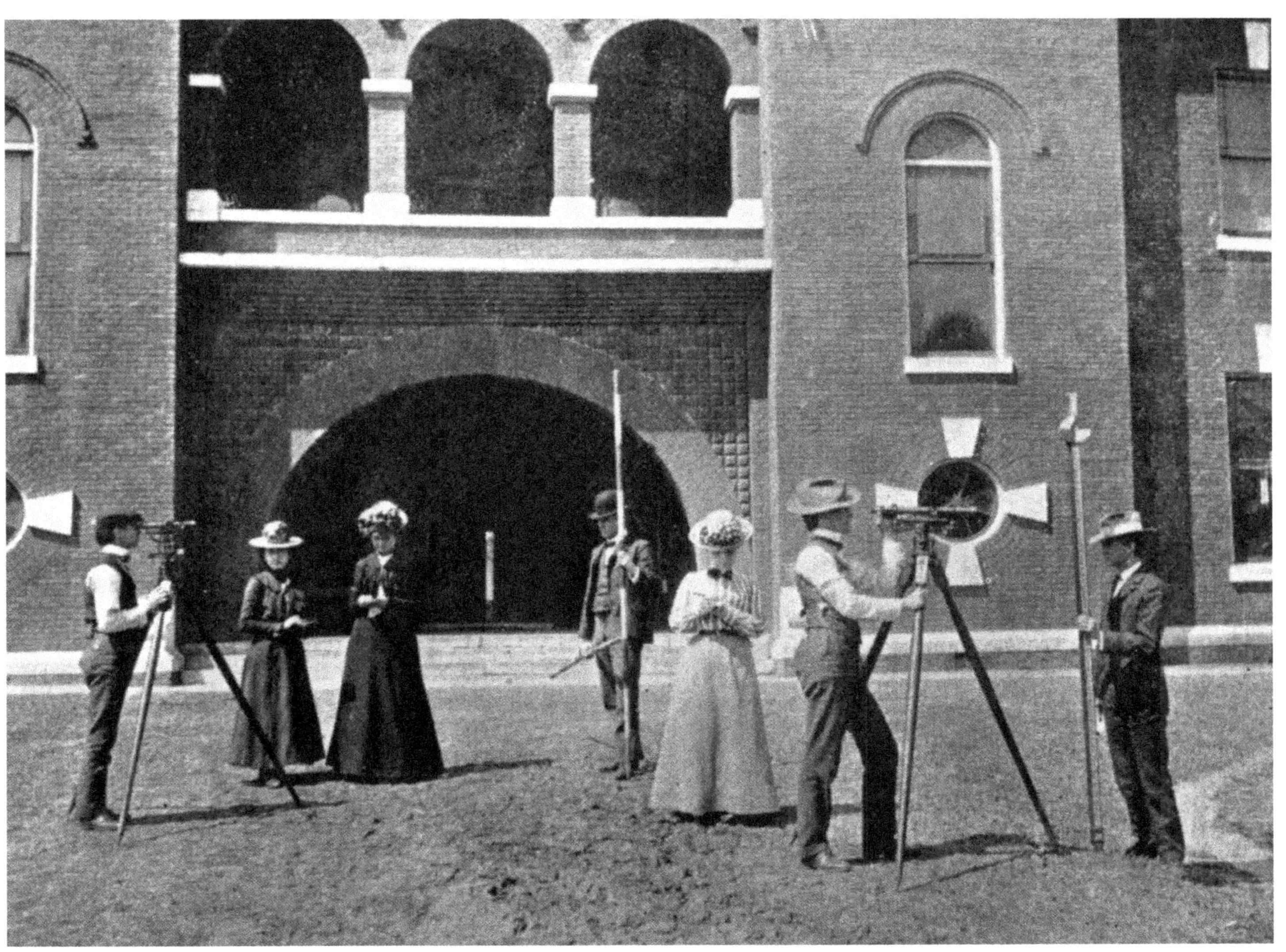

Students practice their field work in a surveying and engineering class in front of College Hall at West Florida Seminary. Renamed Florida State College in 1901, it had four departments: the College, the School for Teachers, the School of Music, and the College Academy.

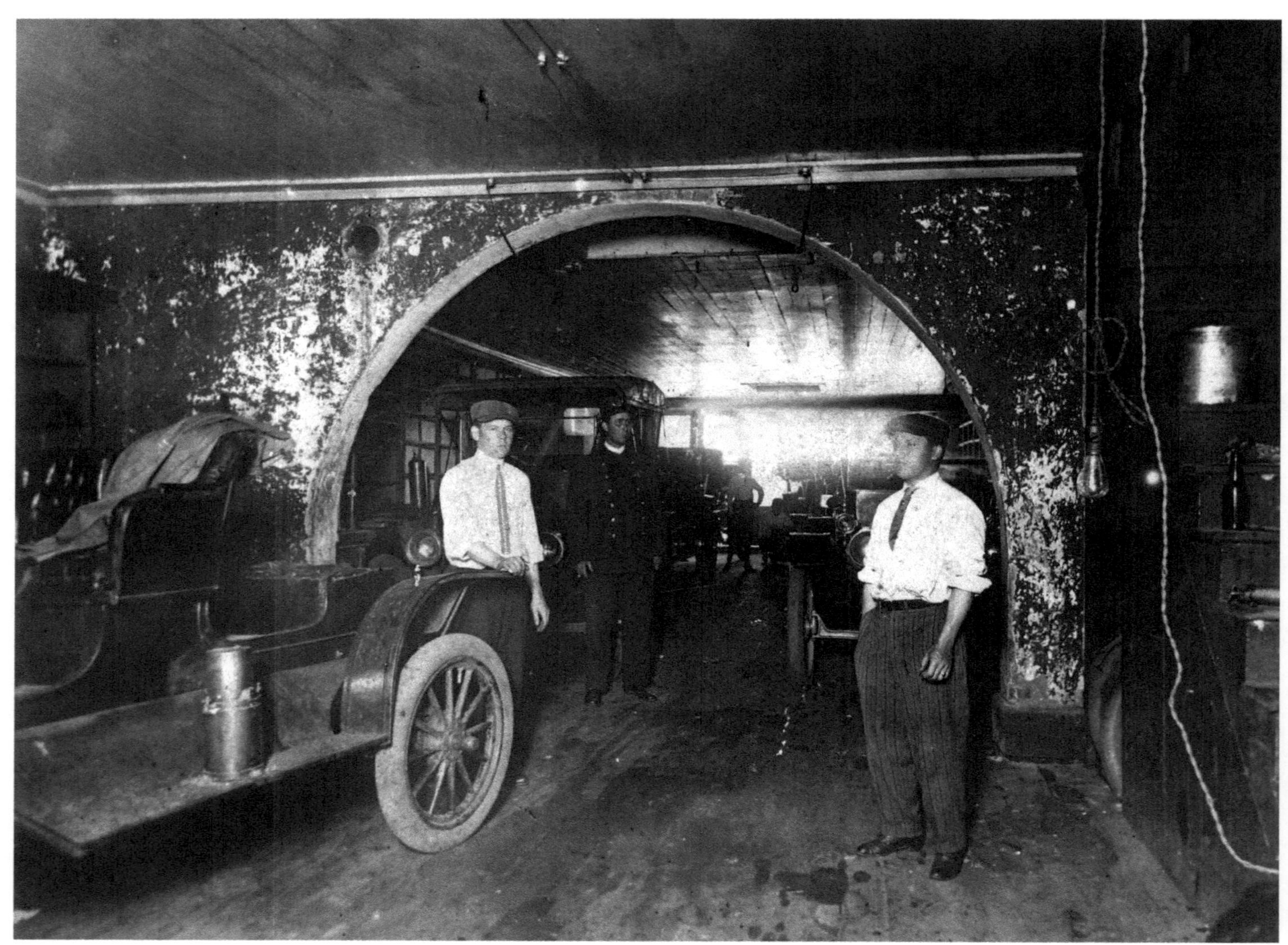

In 1900, the town's first view of an automobile created a great deal of interest. John P. Brown, Sr., on the left next to the automobile, owned this Ford and Overland automobile dealership on Monroe Street, one of the first in town. Baxter Willis Brown, on the right, later operated a Studebaker dealership at the same location.

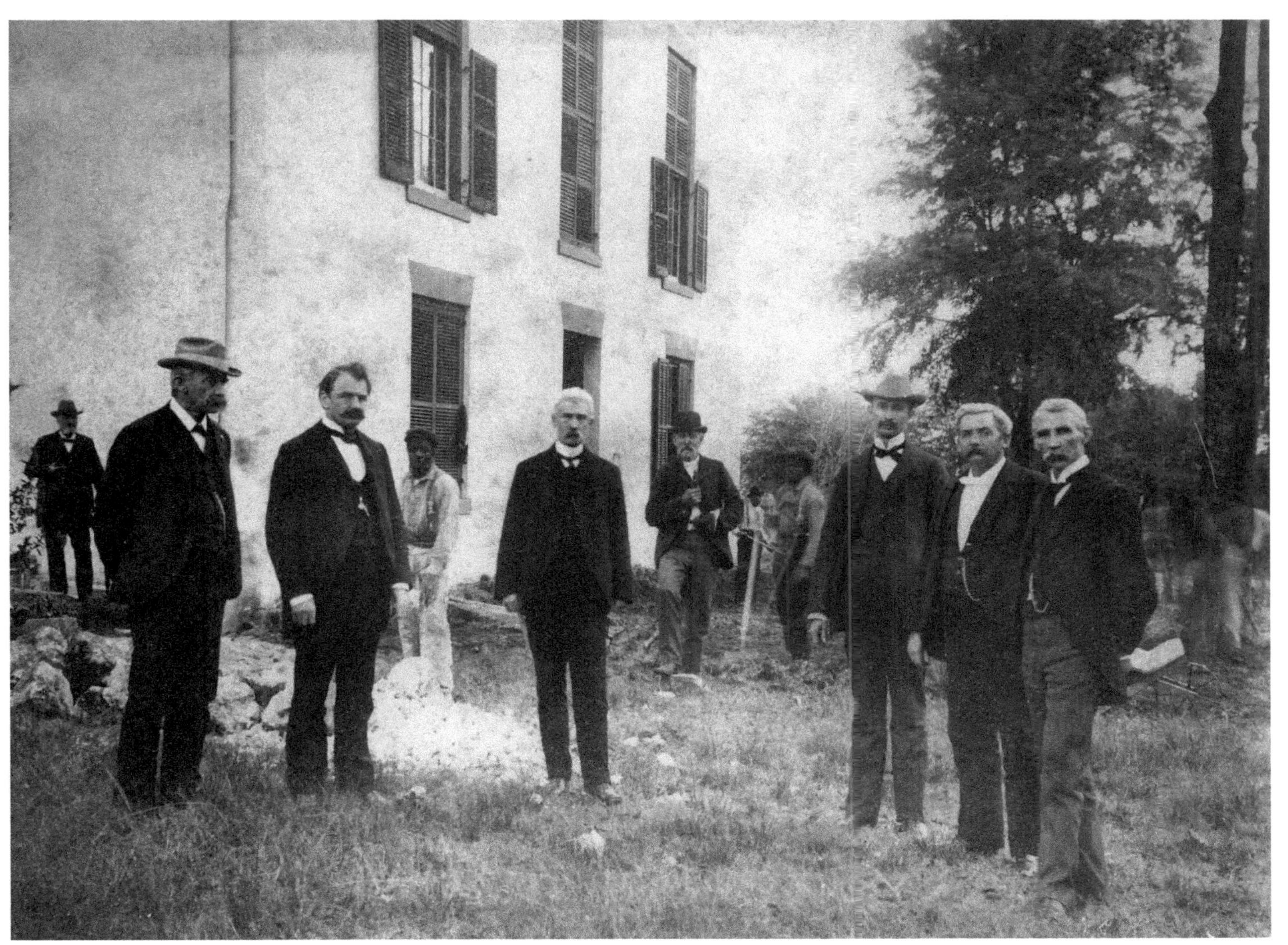

Governor William S. Jennings and cabinet pose at the start of the 1902 Capitol additions. Left to right in the foreground are Comptroller A. C. Croom, Governor Jennings, Attorney General William B. Lamar, Treasurer James B. Whitfield, Superintendent of Public Instruction William N. Sheats, and Agriculture Commissioner Benjamin E. McLin.

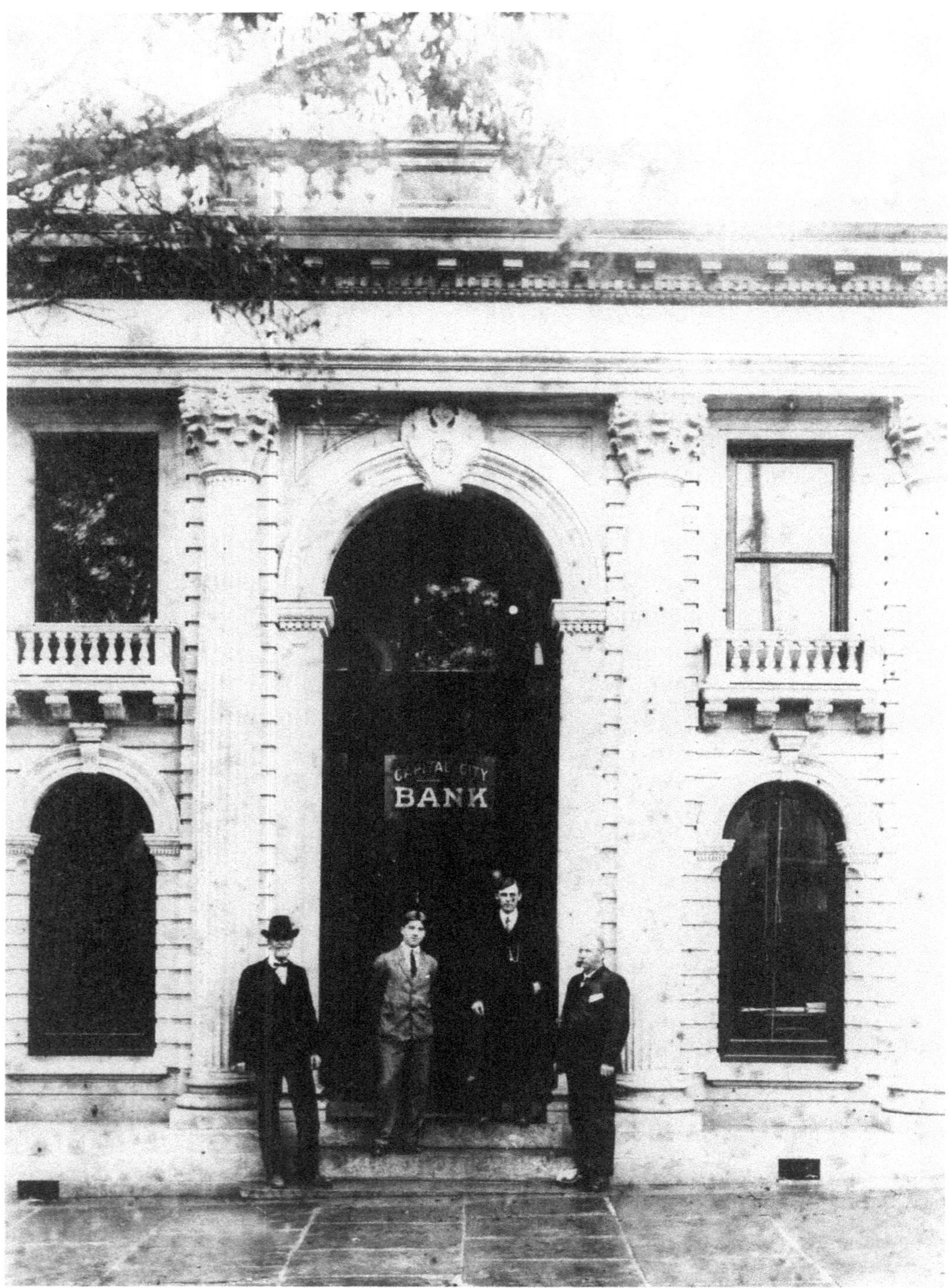

George W. Saxon, left, with hat, decided to switch from dry goods to banking, receiving a charter for the Capital City Bank in 1895. By the end of June, Capital City Bank reported total deposits of $41,000 and total resources of $84,000. In 1917, Capital City Bank approved a loan to the City of Tallahassee for $10,000.

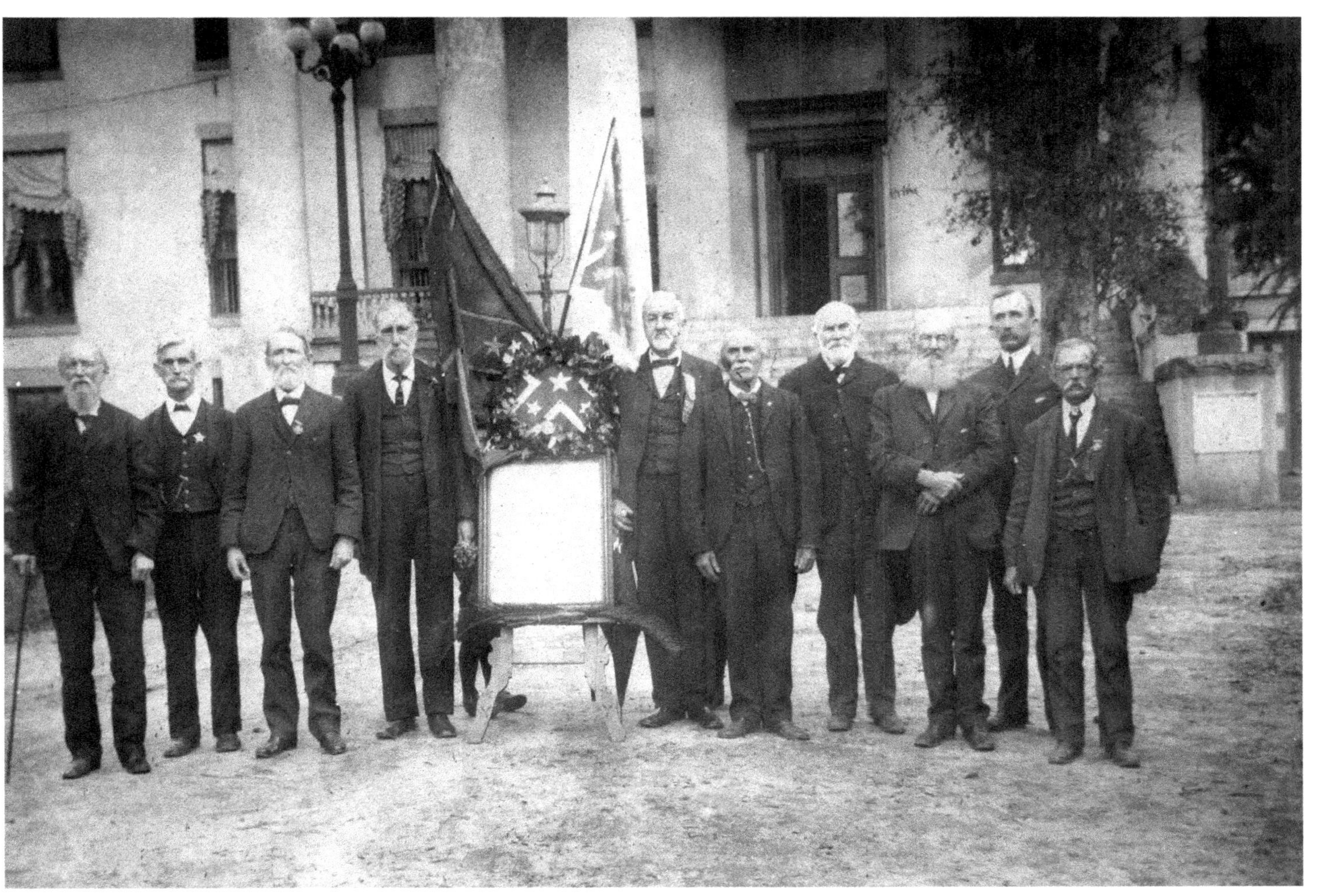

The only Confederate capital east of the Mississippi not captured during the Civil War, Tallahassee joined the South in revering the Confederacy in the early twentieth century. Confederate battle flags were displayed in the capitol, former soldiers and widows were granted pensions, and Confederate veterans were honored.

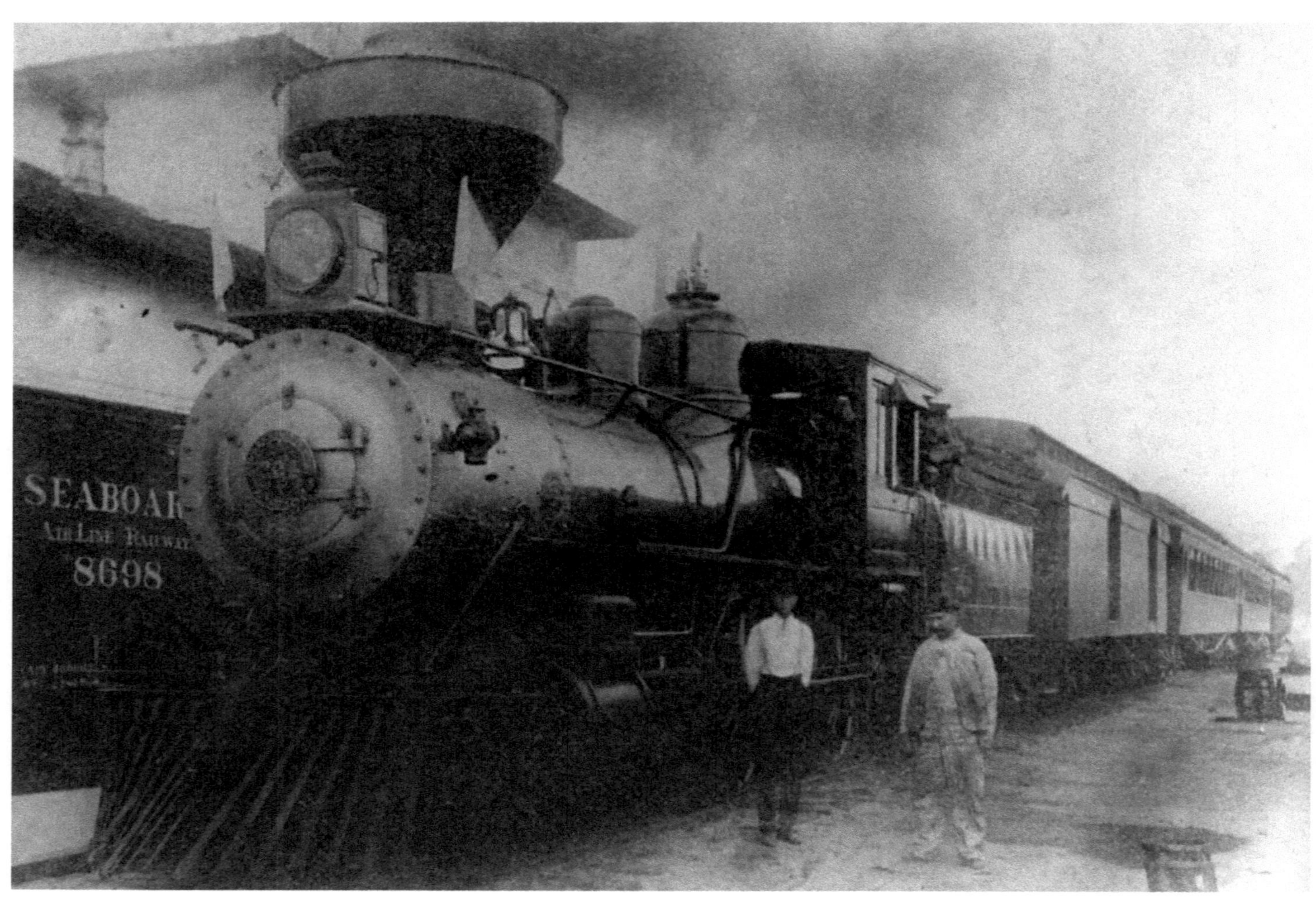

On April 22, 1905, shop foreman J. Williamson, right, and engineer J. O. Loeb, left, pose beside the Seaboard Air Line Railway legislative train. Immediately following the last gavel of the sixty-day legislative session in the spring, there was a rush to the depot as state legislators exited Tallahassee as fast as possible.

Inside the T. B. Byrd grocery store around 1905. Thomas Blake Byrd, fourth from right, and his wife, far right, often held receptions when offering a new line of groceries. Their daughter Kate, the taller girl in the photo, recalled her mother serving olives, pickles, cookies, and coffee, and decorating the store with vines and flowers.

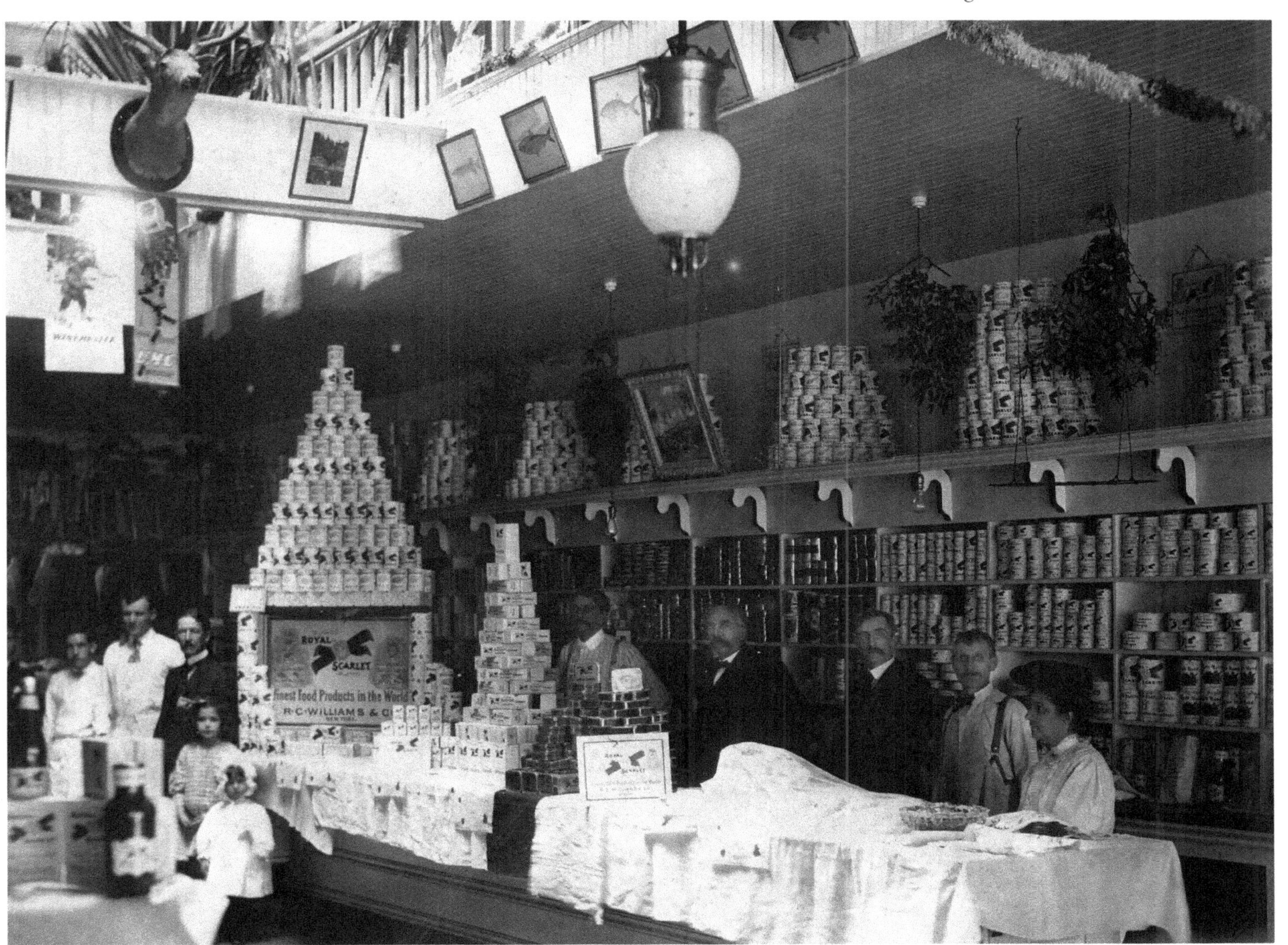

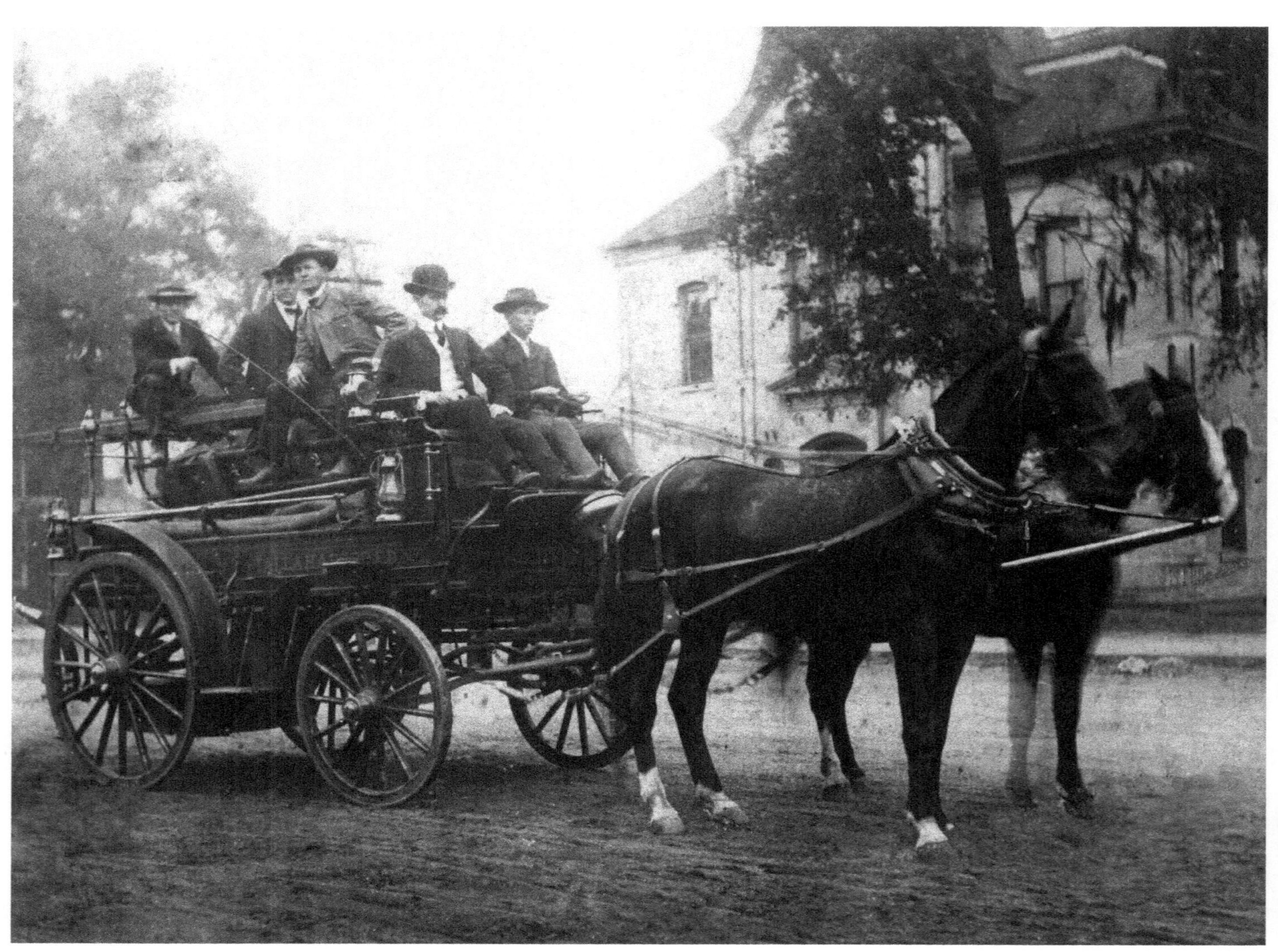

By 1905 Tallahassee had its first fire department. Those aboard the first hose wagon, in front of the Leon County courthouse, include Willie McIntosh, Chief John Hamlin, Assistant Chief W. P. Phillips, and Eugene Levy. Dick and Jake are the horses. Before the department existed, a fire was once put out by two drugstore soda fountains.

The new Leon County courthouse was constructed in 1882 in a new location at Washington Square, three years after the old courthouse burned. The white Italianate structure with tall cupola, accessible tower, and landscaped yard rose proudly over the city. The cupola was removed during remodeling in 1924.

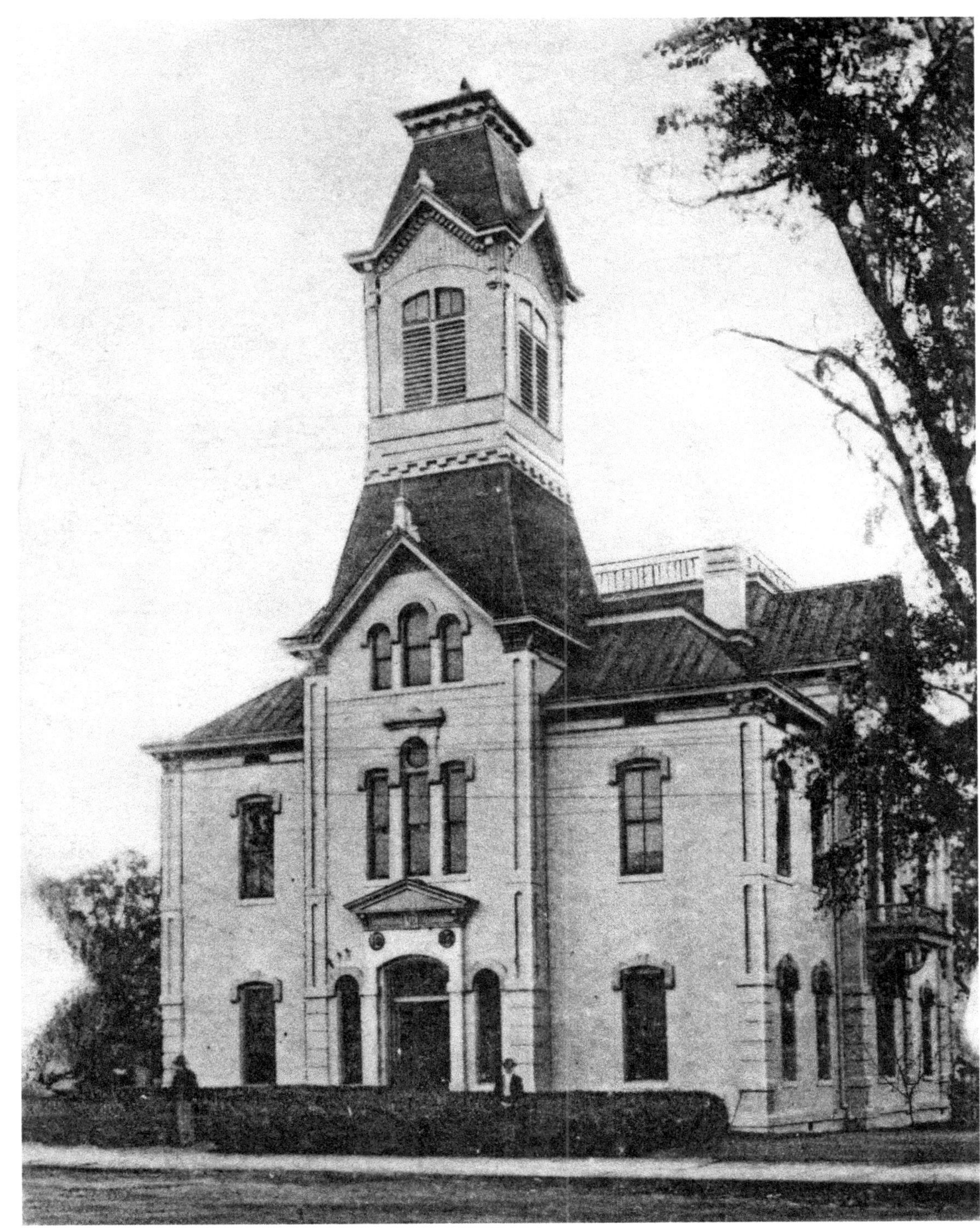

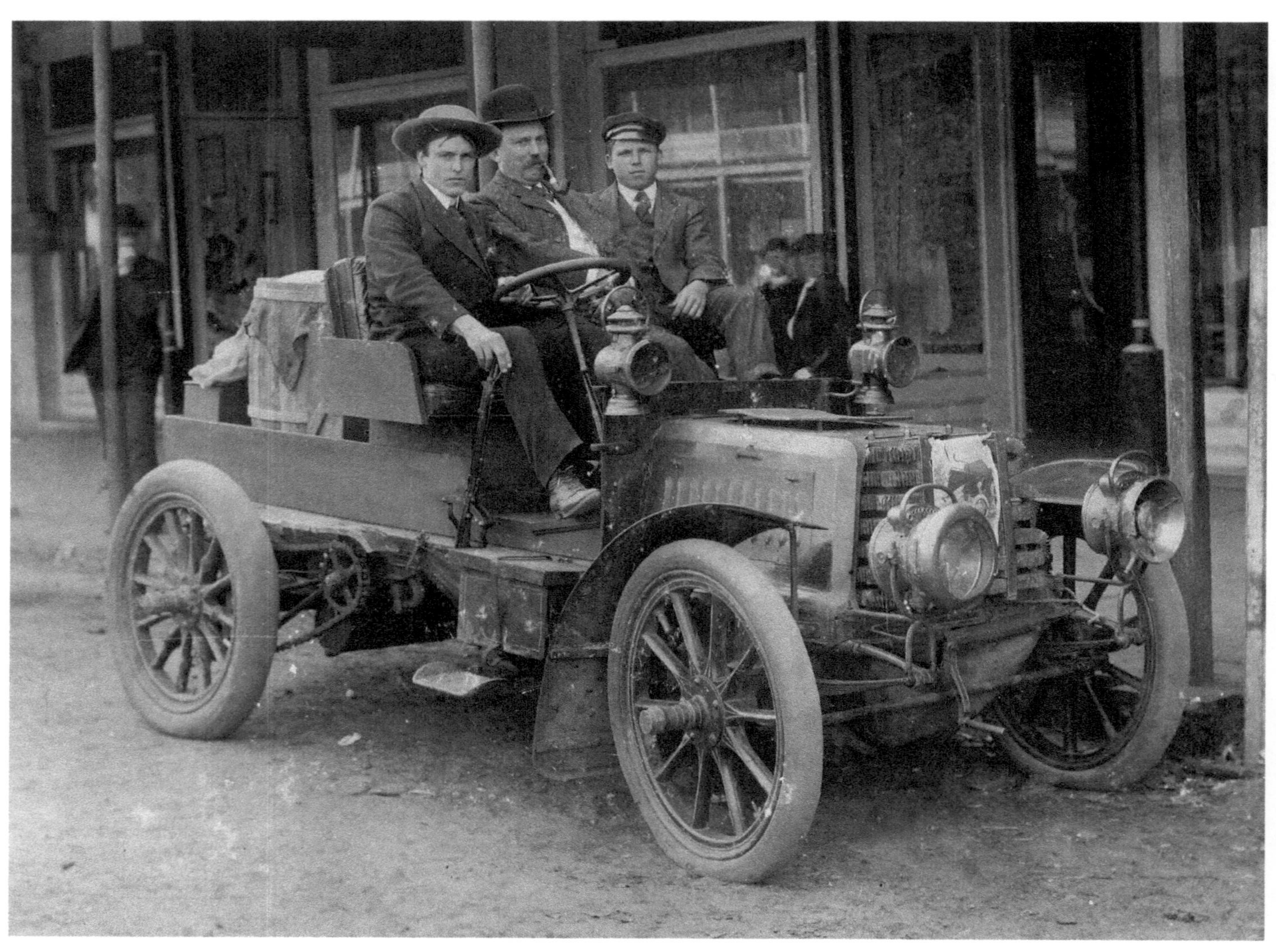

Seated in a 1903 Panhard automobile, not to be mistaken for a Packard, are Zach Fenn, Phelps Wilson, and John P. Brown, Sr. The first cars in Tallahassee were novelty items, attracting attention, and the first city speed limit was 10 m.p.h. One early motorist noted, "To start an auto, the easiest thing was to get a group of people to push it for you and 'pop' the clutch."

The Florida State College graduating class of 1905 was the first class to wear caps and gowns. Also that year, the school became Florida Female College under the Buckman Act, which reorganized Florida's educational system. It would not have another co-ed class until 1947.

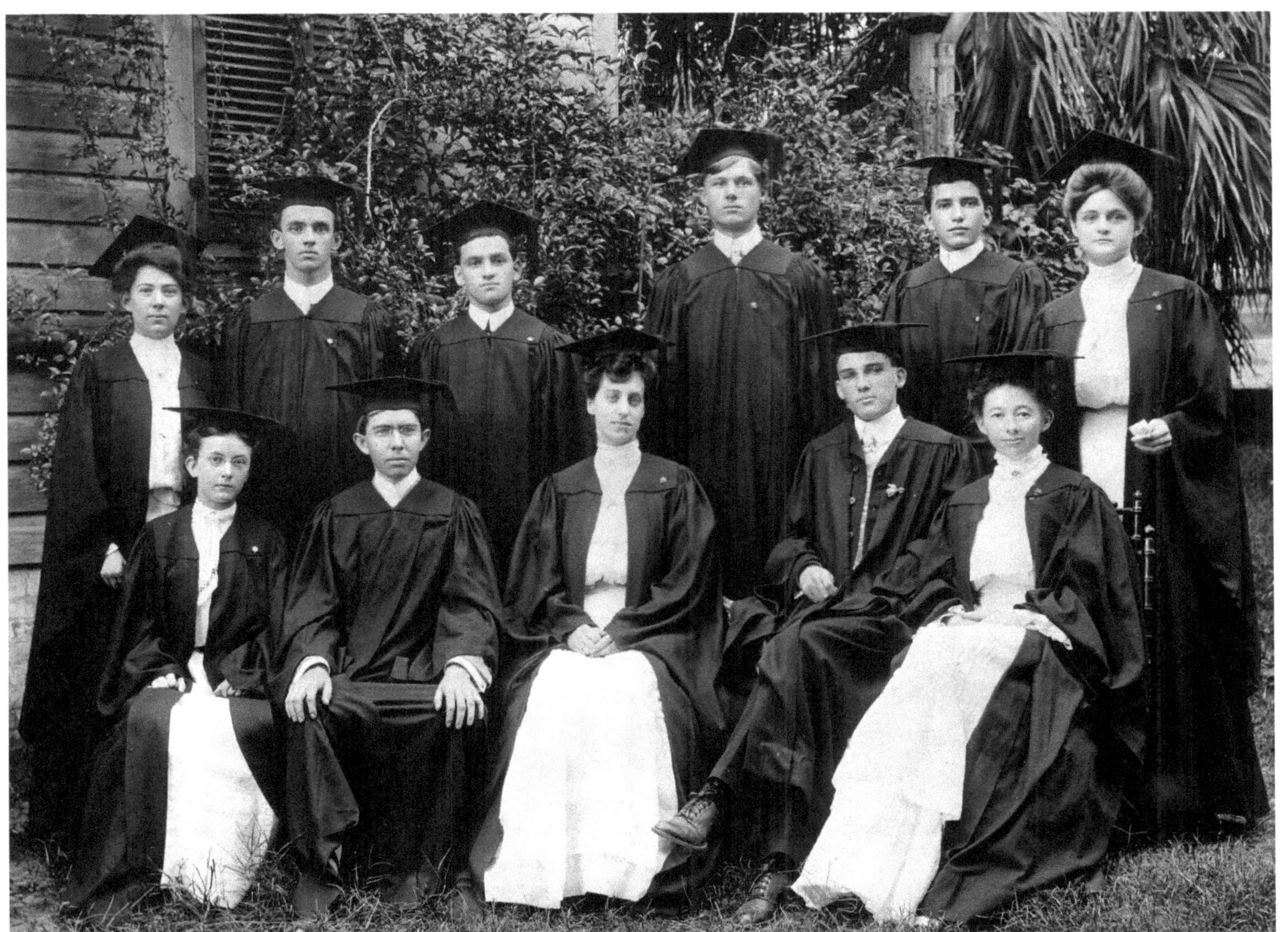

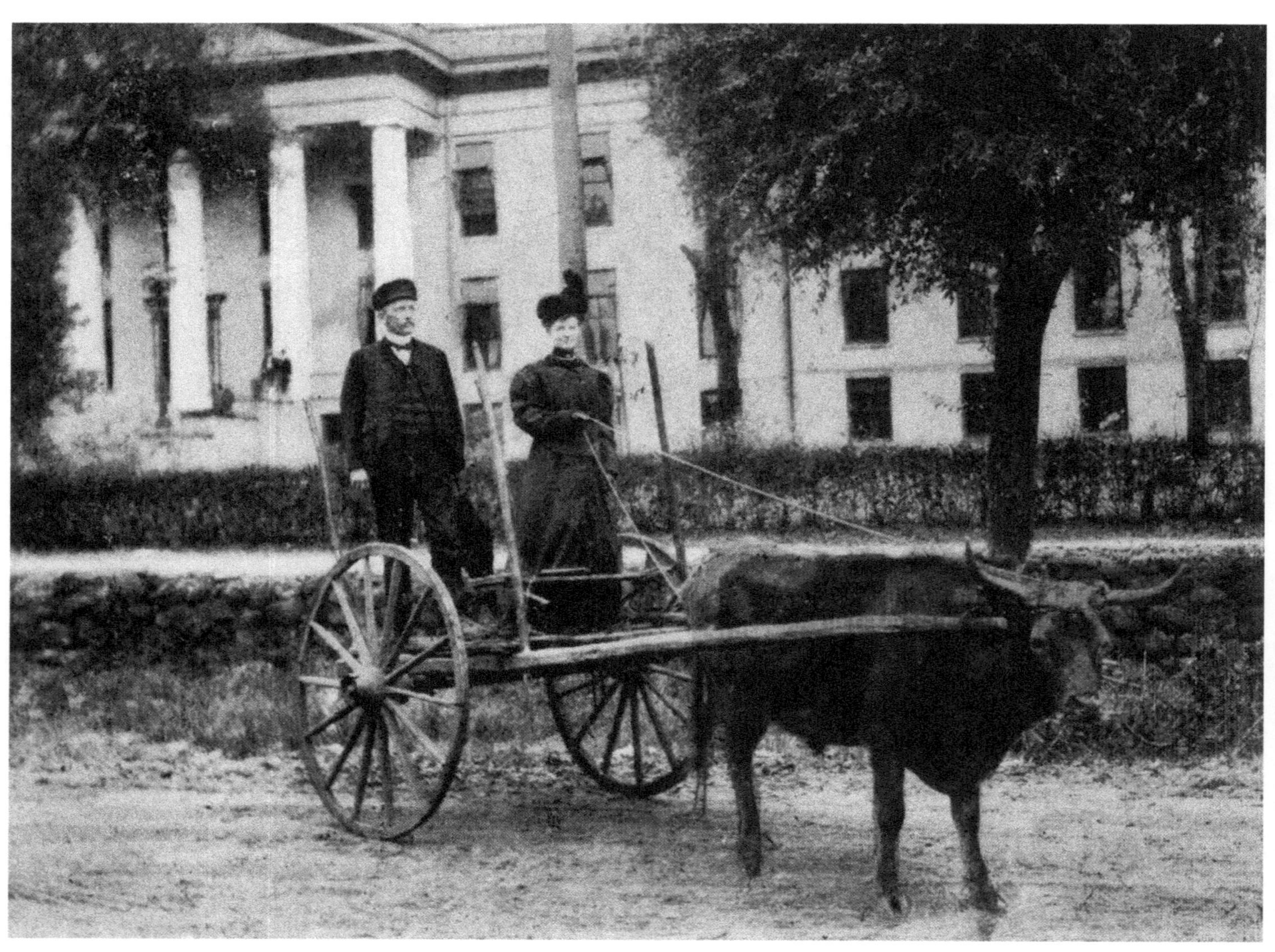

A couple drives an ox-drawn cart on the west side of the Capitol. Under Governor Jennings, the legislature appropriated $75,000 to enlarge the old capitol. Architect Frank Milburn added two wings, the classical dome, stone steps, grand staircase, linoleum floors, and steam heat. It opened to a grand gala in December 1902.

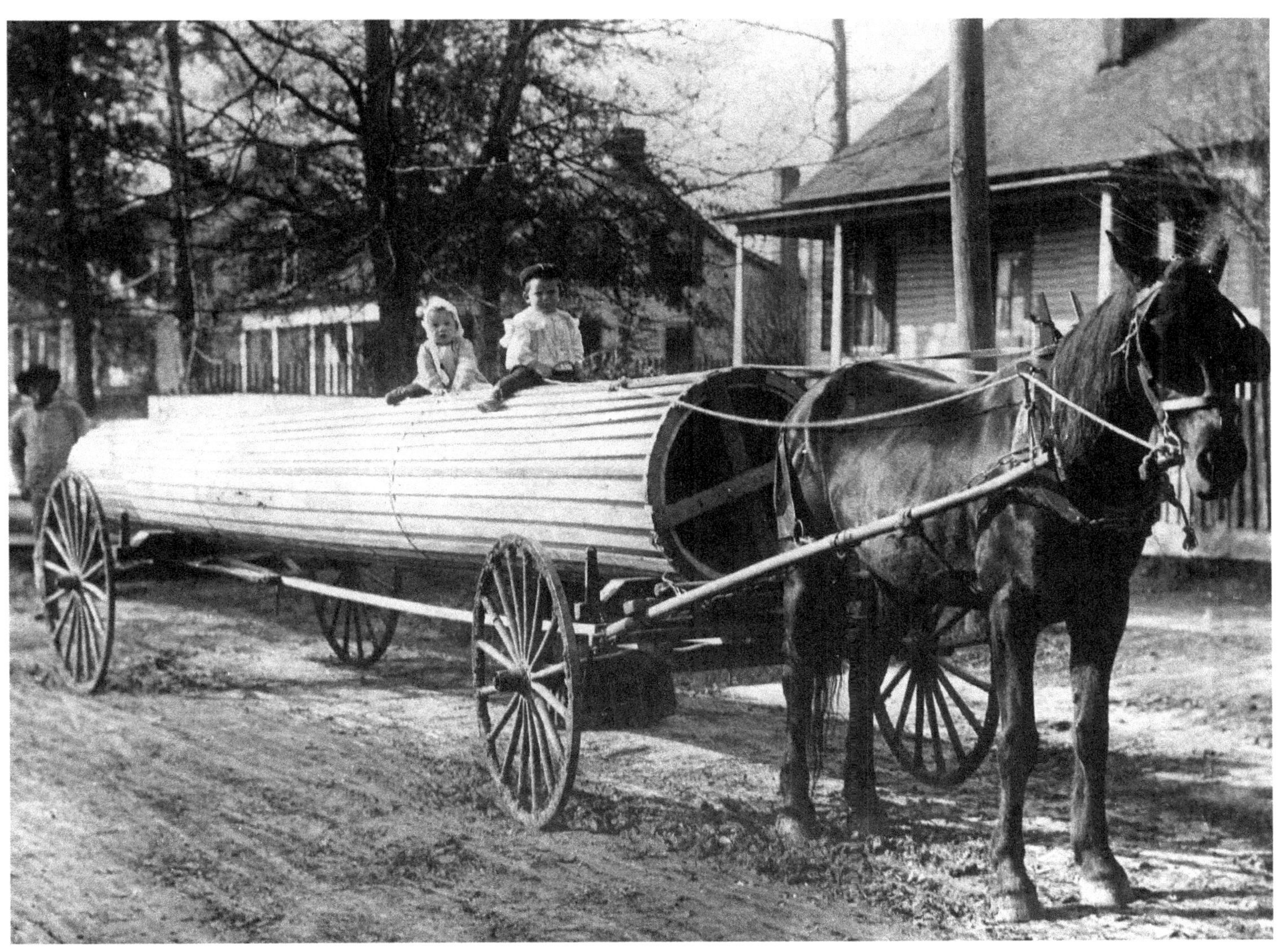

Until 1907 Florida's governors had to purchase or rent a home. Orion C. Parker, Jr., left, and his older brother, Robert C., ride atop a column en route to the site of the first governor's mansion. Built by the boys' father, Orion C. Parker, Sr., at a cost of $25,000 on the plans of Jacksonville architect Henry Klutho, the mansion boasted 24 huge columns.

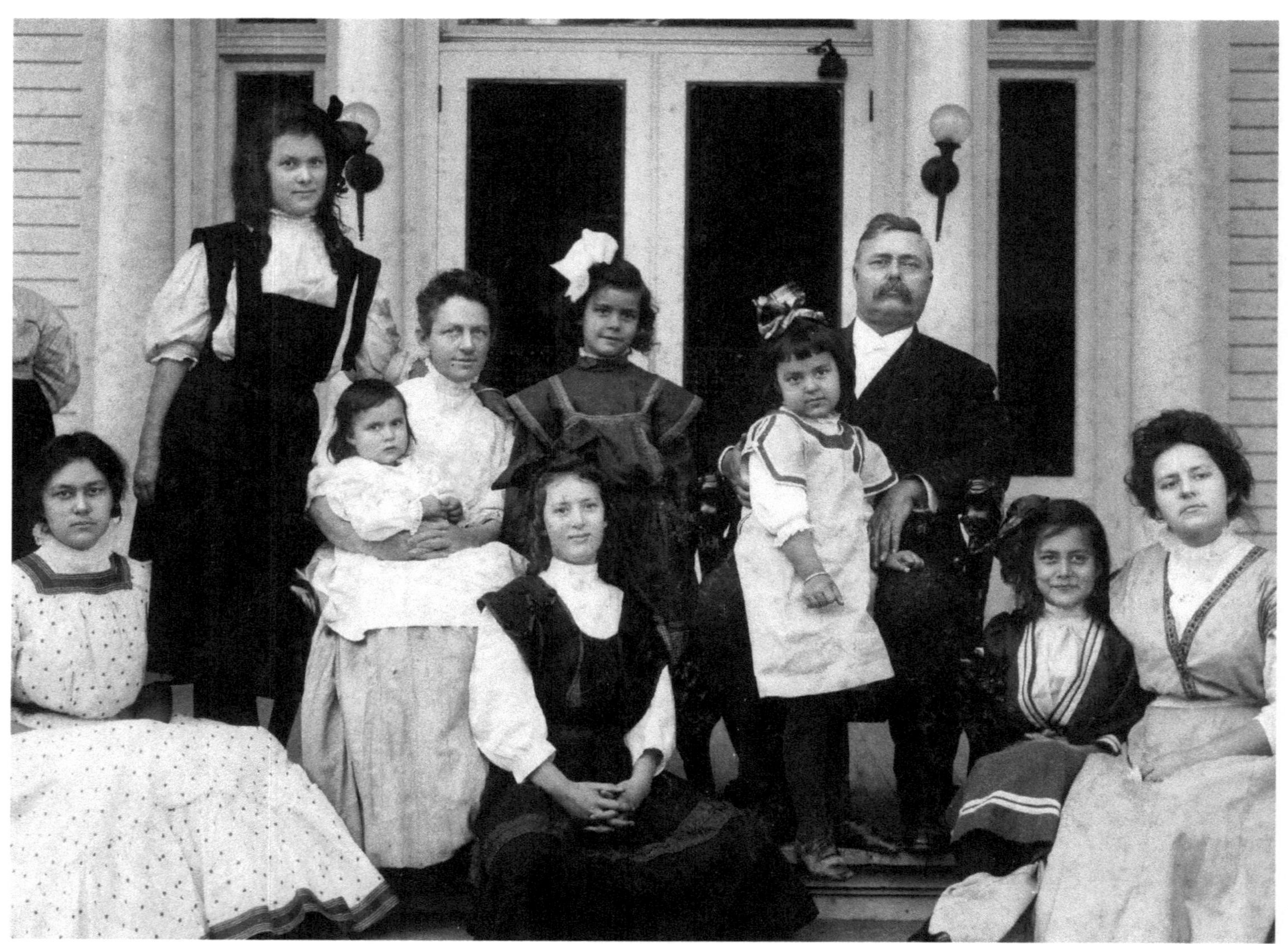

Governor Napoleon B. Broward, his family, and sister-in-law Elsie Douglass, far right, pose on the steps of the new executive mansion. Elizabeth Broward, sitting on her mother's lap, was the first child born to an incumbent governor. Mrs. Broward selected the furnishings at a cost of $4,444.75. The mansion was demolished in 1955.

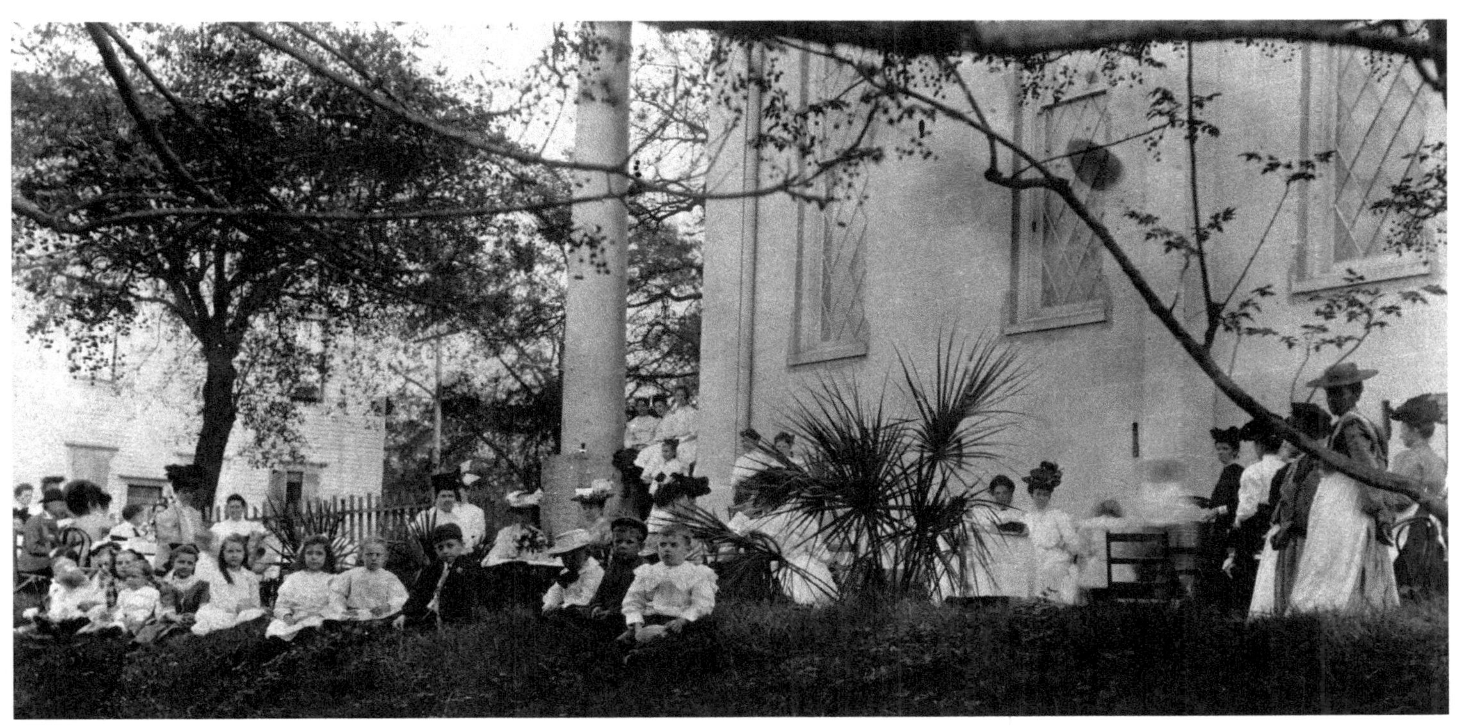

According to local tradition, chicken salad was often served at the many church bazaars and dinners on the grounds of the First Presbyterian church. The recipe has been handed down from Mrs. John Gamble for generations and is known as "Tallahassee Chicken Salad."

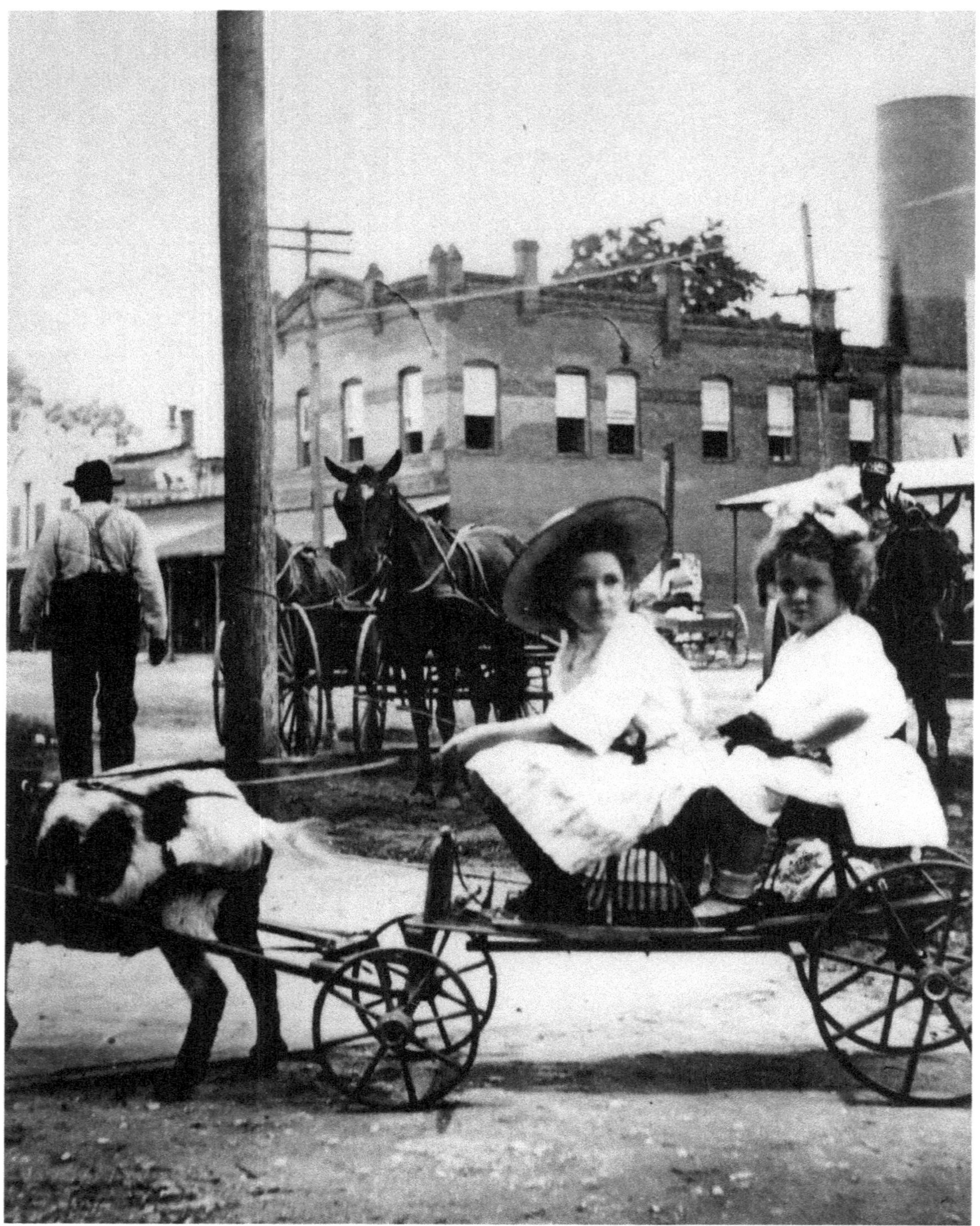

In 1909, two sisters, Mary Louise and Annie Collins Houstoun, drive their own goat cart through the downtown area. Tallahassee's population grew from three thousand to five thousand in the first decade of the twentieth century. Civic improvements included streetlights, electric and telephone service, improved sidewalks, street signs, animal control measures, and a sewage system.

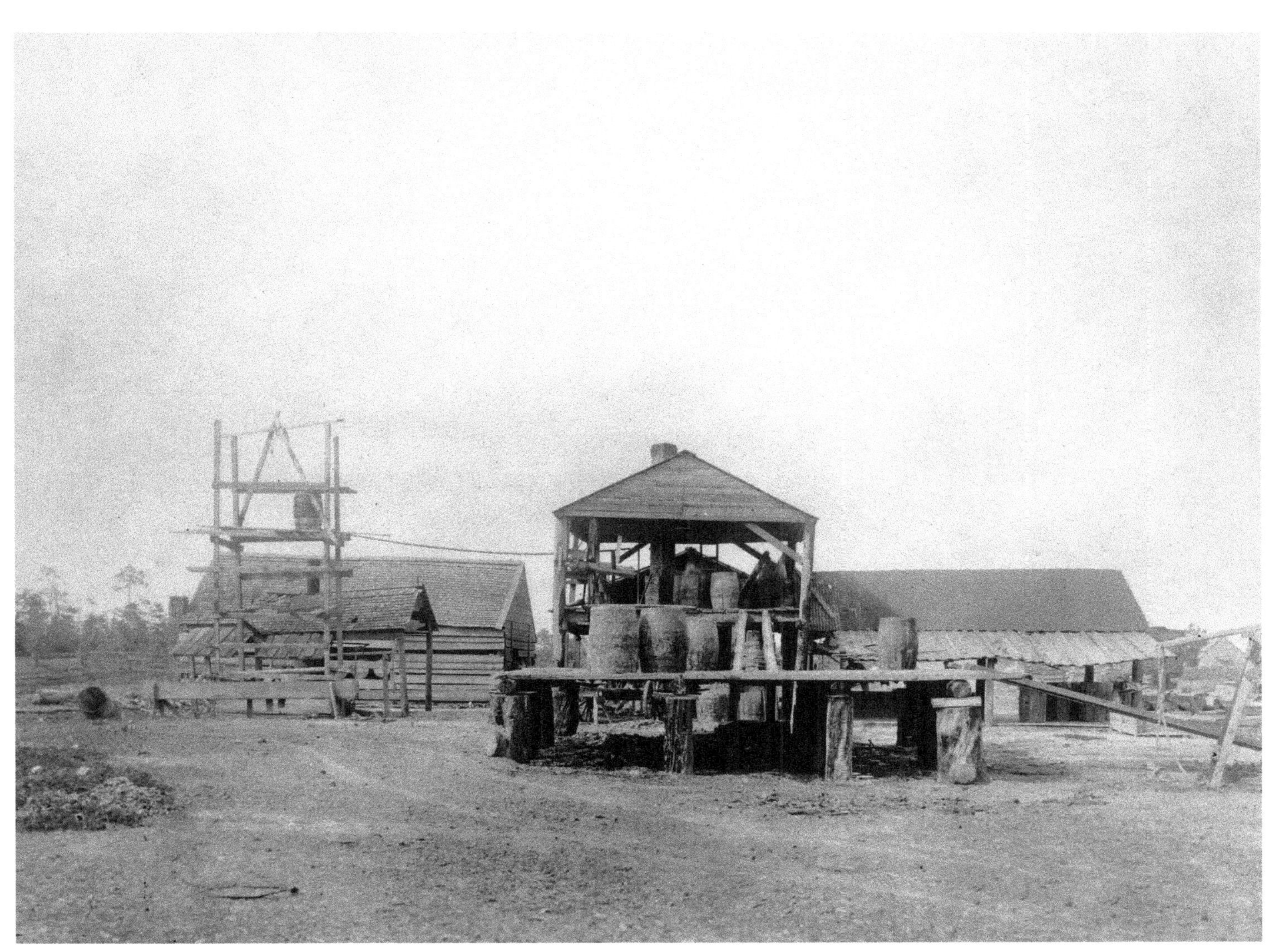

Using the state's large pine forests, the Florida lumber industry produced up to 7,000,000 gallons of turpentine and 800,000 barrels of rosin annually. A turpentine still near Tallahassee distilled turpentine and rosin from the crude gum harvested from pine trees.

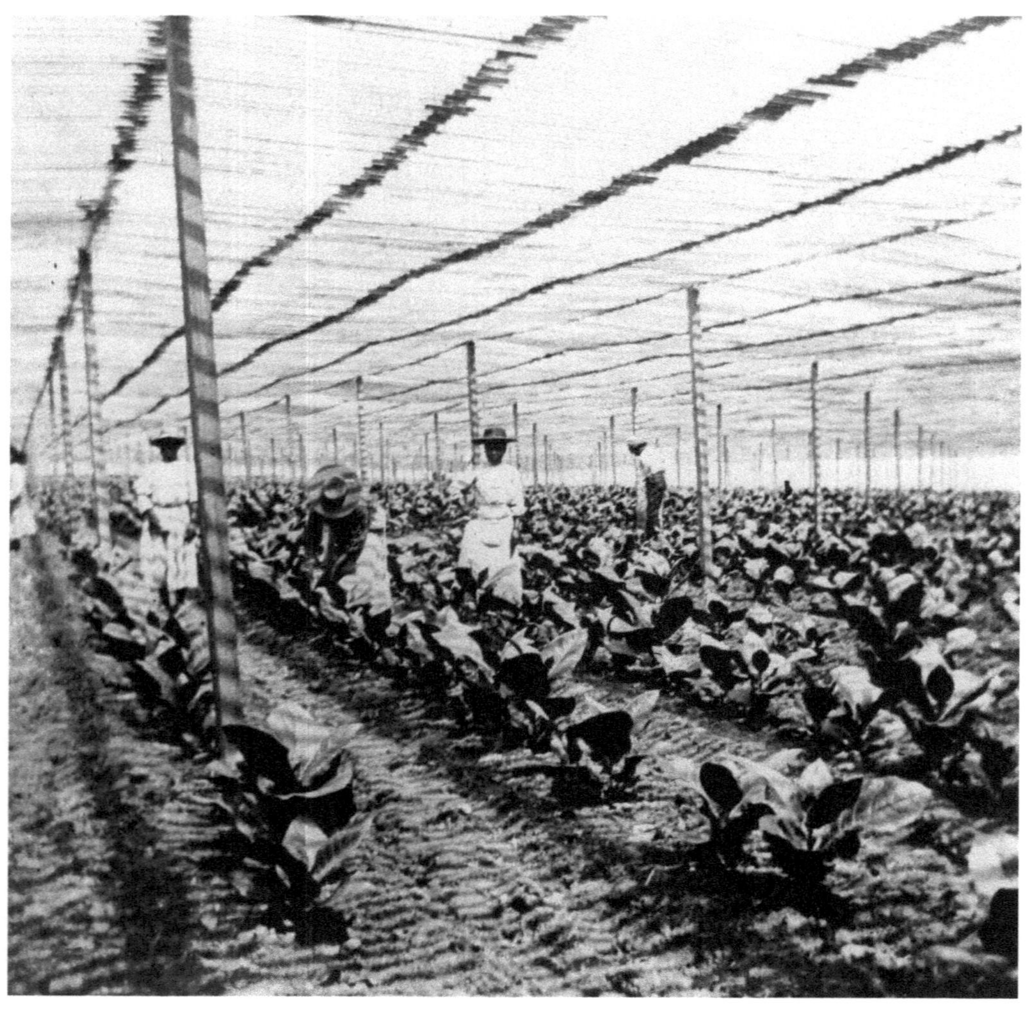

Shown here are workers in the tobacco field beneath the slat-covered shelter at the Johnson-Wolfe Tobacco Company farm. Shade tobacco, used for cigar wrappers, was grown under cotton tents to protect it from the sun. Shade tobacco was once a staple crop, but by the 1930s, most tobacco farms in the area had shifted to other products.

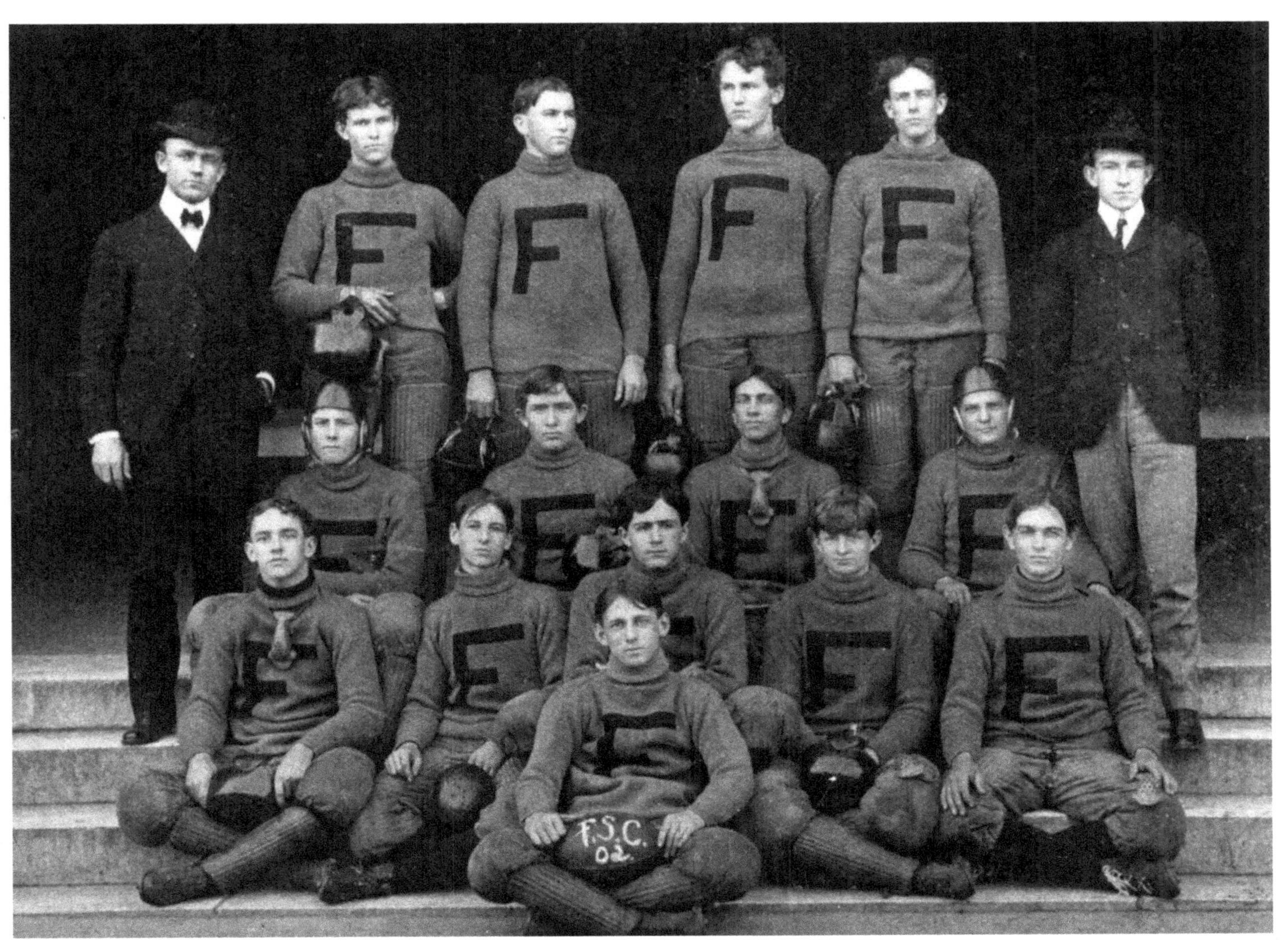

The long-standing Florida State University and University of Florida football rivalry dates to this 1902 team. That year Florida State College, now FSU, twice played Florida Agricultural College, now UF. Each team won on their home field 6-0. On this team is Guyte P. McCord, later clerk of the Florida Supreme Court.

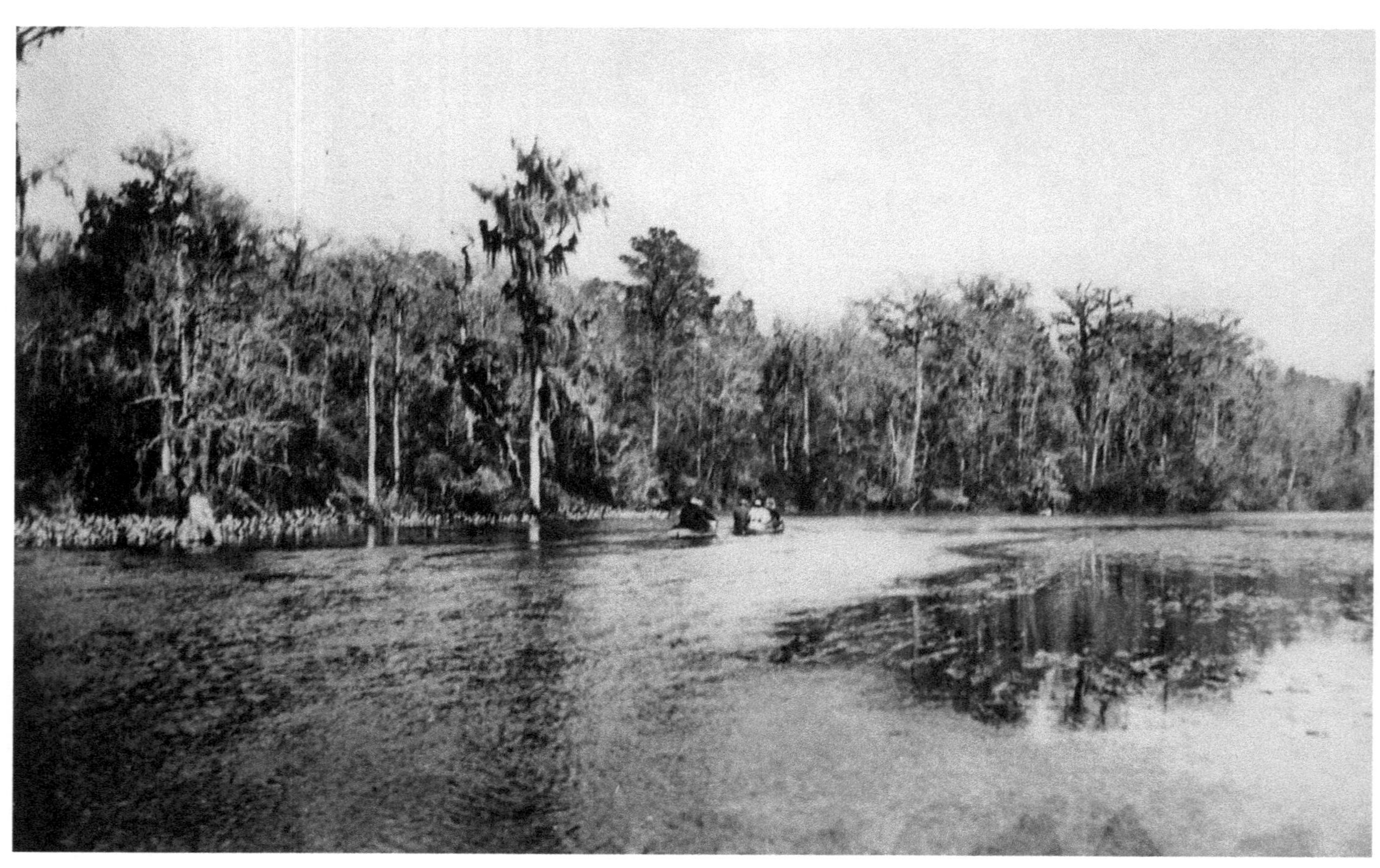

Guests from Goodwood enjoy an outing by canoe at Wakulla Springs, one of the largest and deepest fresh-water springs in the world, and a longtime favorite for health and recreation among Tallahassee residents. A National Natural Landmark, it has offered wildlife viewing, swimming, a guest lodge, boat tours, and mastodon bones.

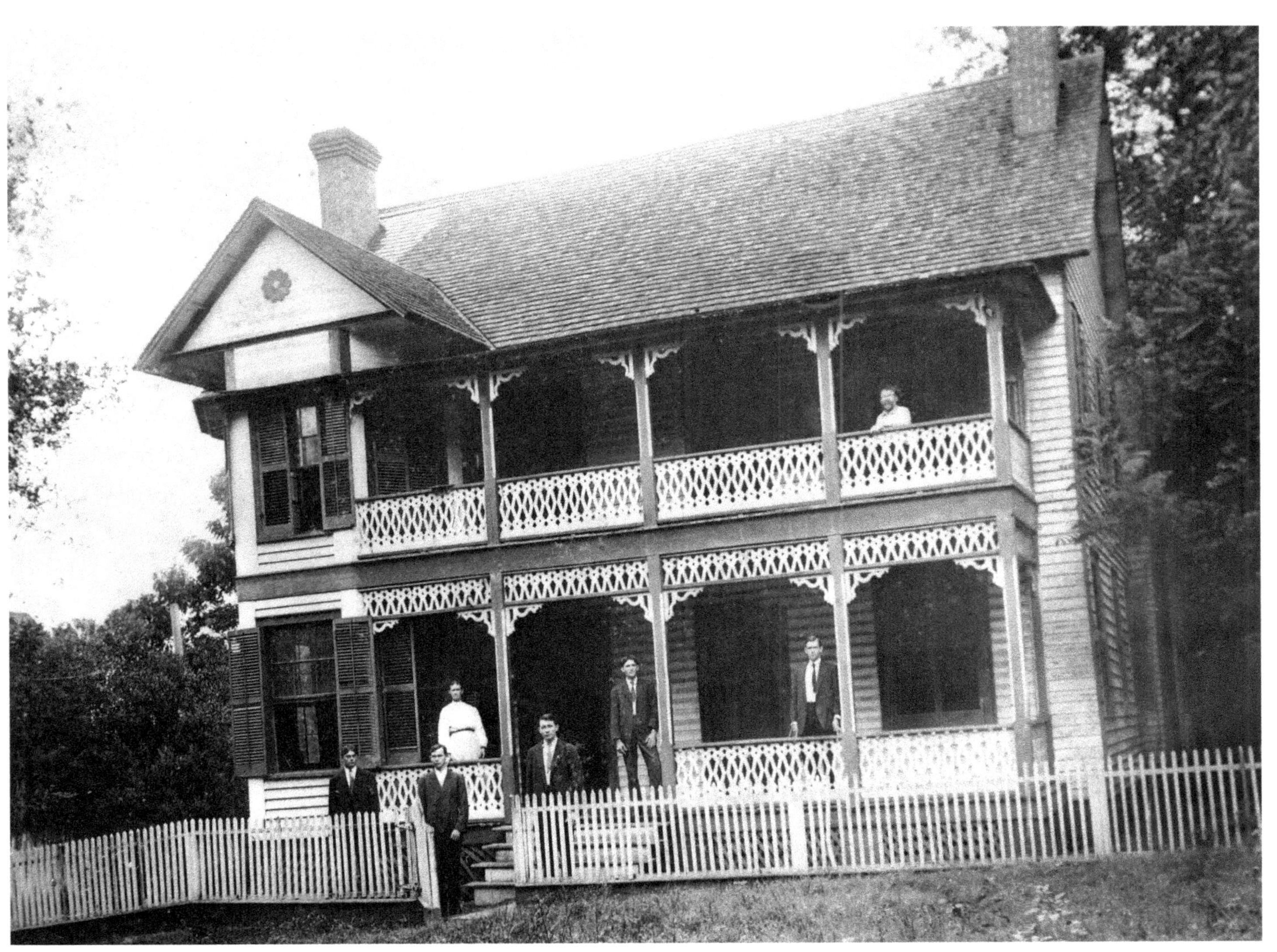

Lizzie Clemons stands on the porch of the Breeze Hotel, a boardinghouse she managed. She later married Madison Leslie, a legislator from Madison who had stayed at the house. While the Florida Legislature was in session, many families turned their large stately homes into boardinghouses.

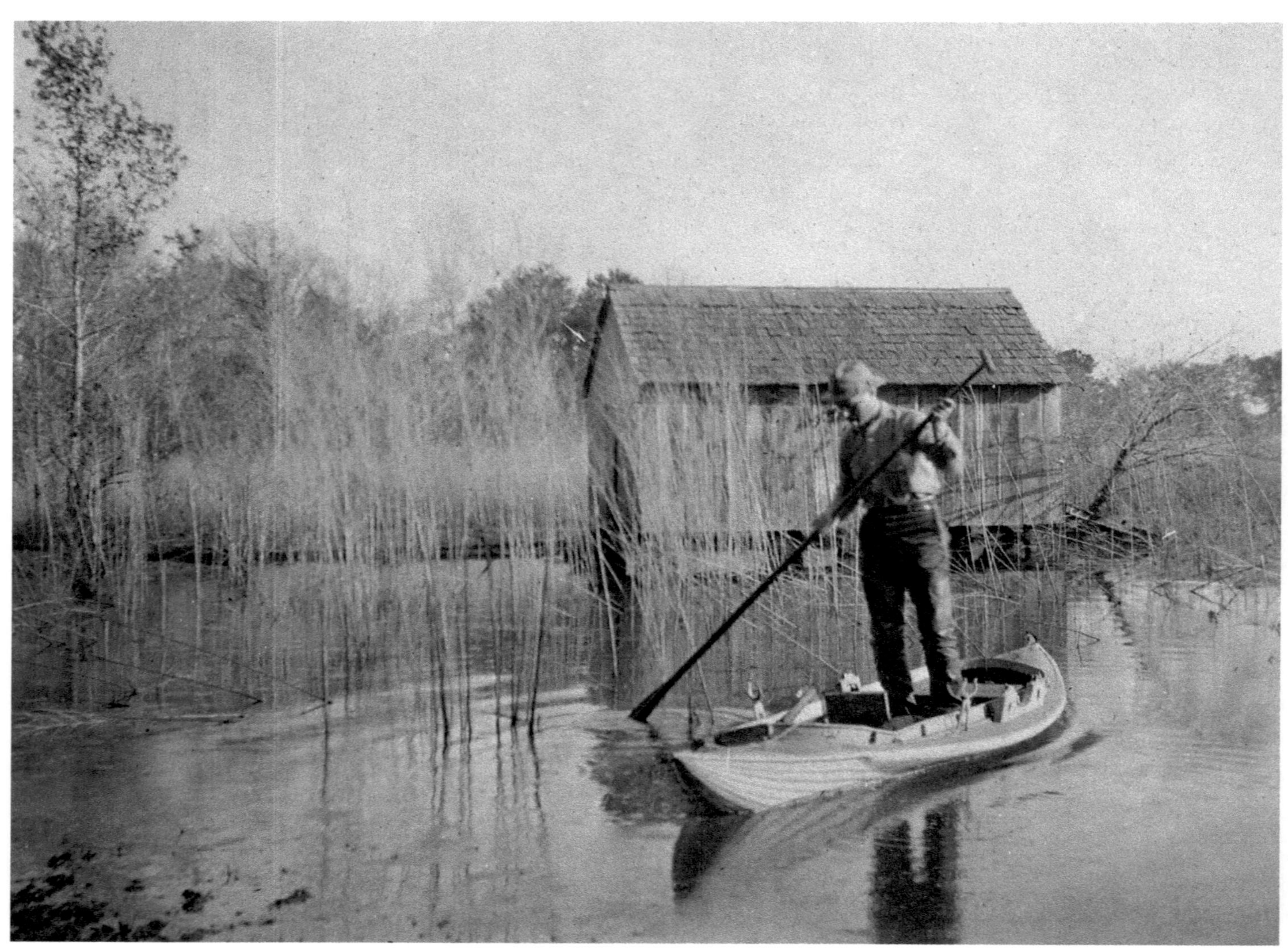

Henry L. Beadel, noted nature photographer and philanthropist, built this handmade tin duck-hunting boat. Tall Timbers Plantation was purchased in 1895 by Edward Beadel and later owned by his nephew, Henry. Devoted to wildlife photography and ecological research, Henry established Tall Timbers Research Station in 1963.

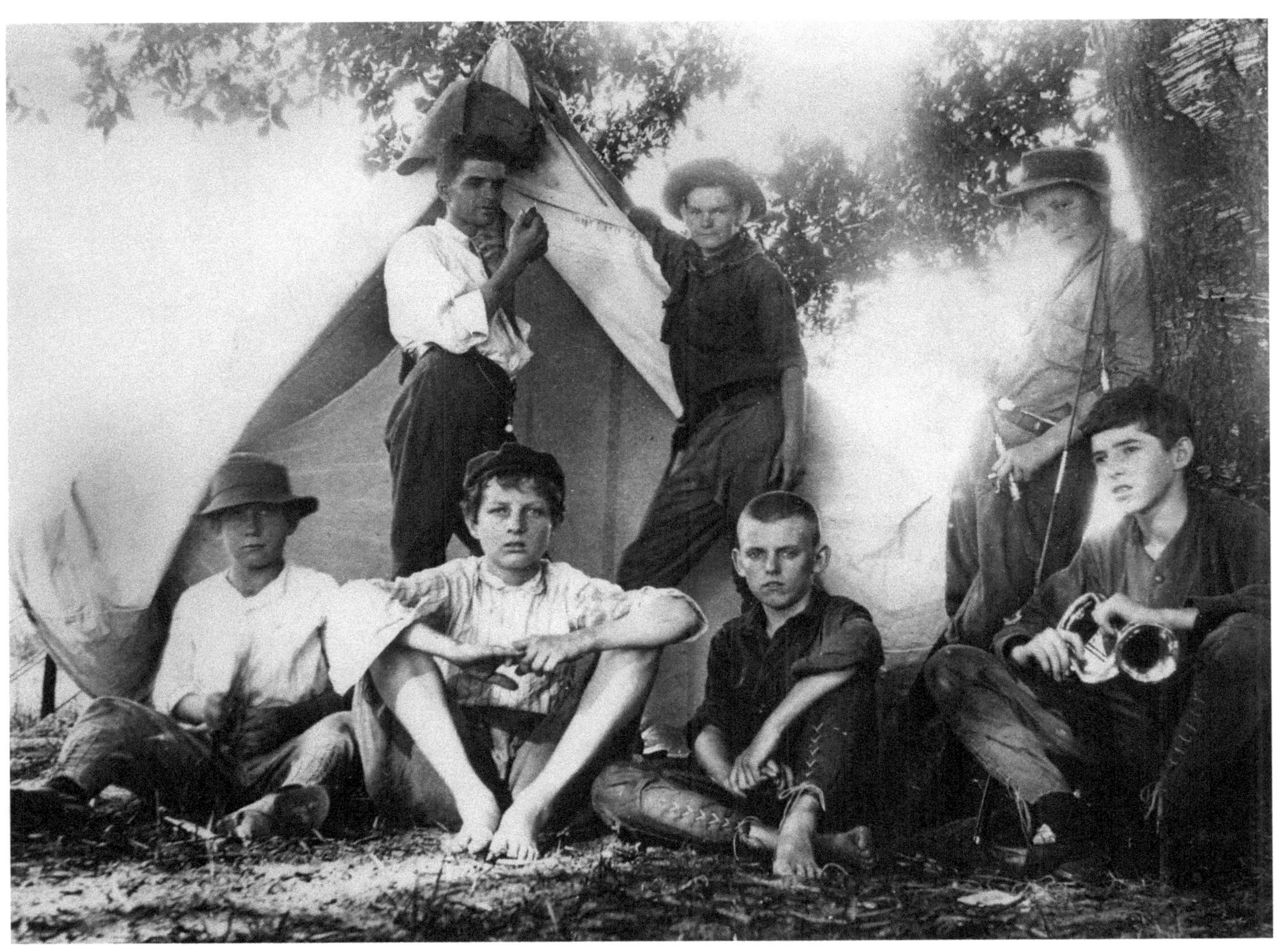

Just two years after the Boy Scouts were founded in the United States, Tallahassee had its own troop. Standing on the left is Scout Master Will Yon. Among the others pictured are, seated second from right, Walter Phillips, and on the far right, John Christian. In 1912 a local paper reported that "the Boy Scout movement in Tallahassee is a sure thing."

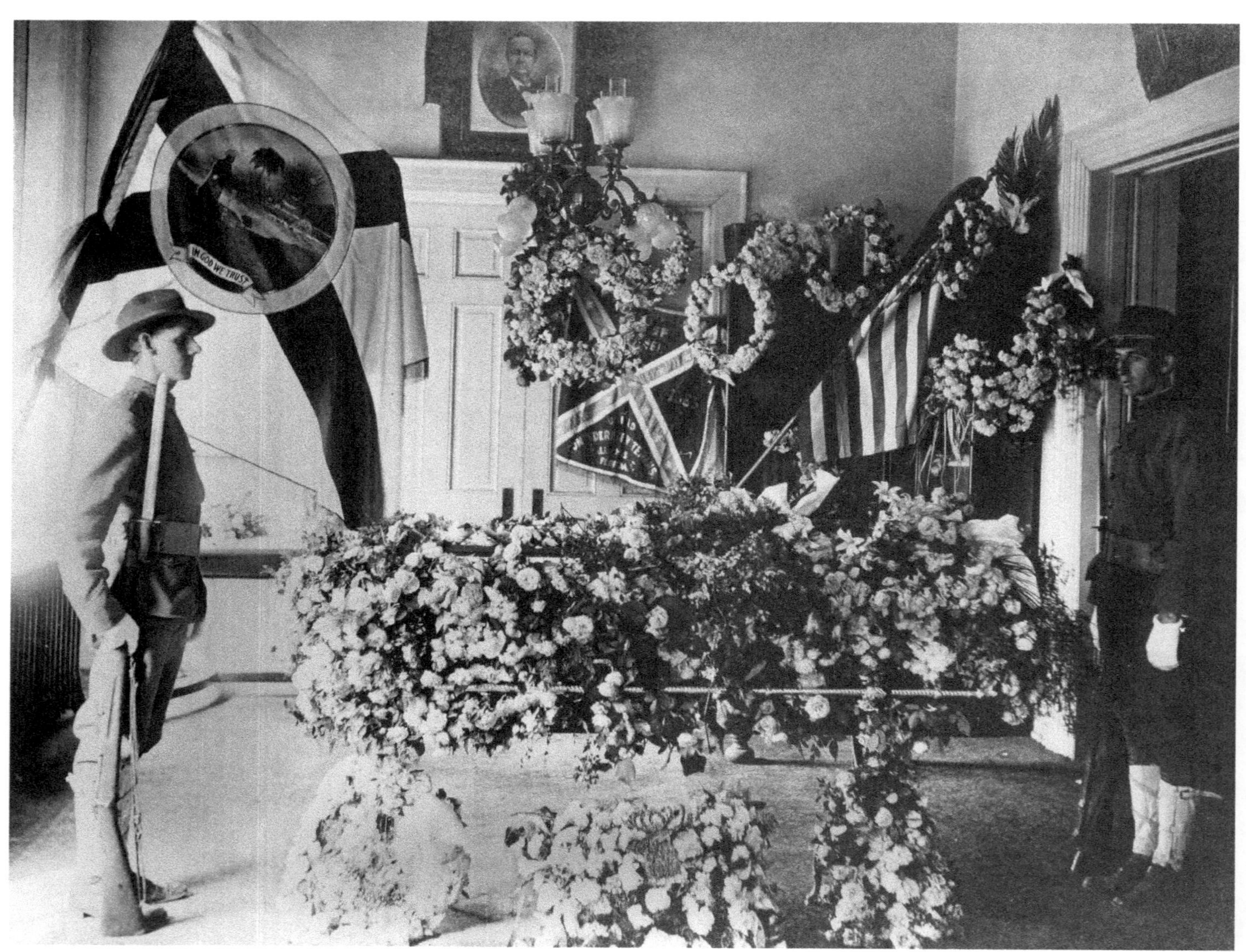

Former governor William D. Bloxham lies in state in the governor's suite at the capitol. He died on March 15, 1911. During the restoration of the governor's suite in the early 1980s, this photograph was sent to the Jet Propulsion Laboratory in California for digital imaging in order to reproduce the carpet seen underneath the casket.

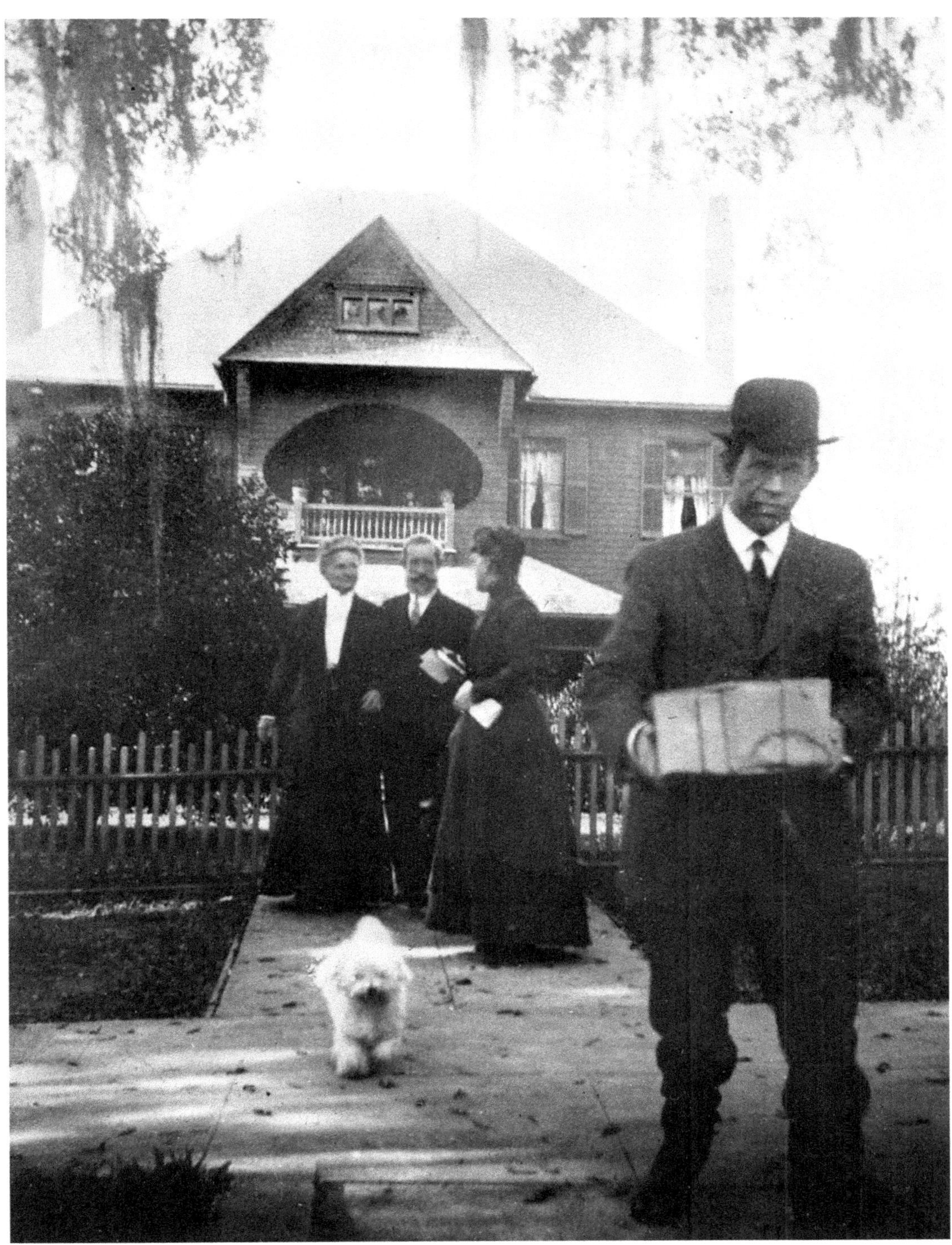

Outside the Winthrop home on January 19, 1913, are Lilia Chouteau Winthrop, John S. Winthrop, Mrs. Long, and Valle Randolph. As a young man John Winthrop received property from the settlement of the Croom Family lawsuit. His estate, Barrow Hill, about 4,000 acres, was divided between two separate tracts of land in the county.

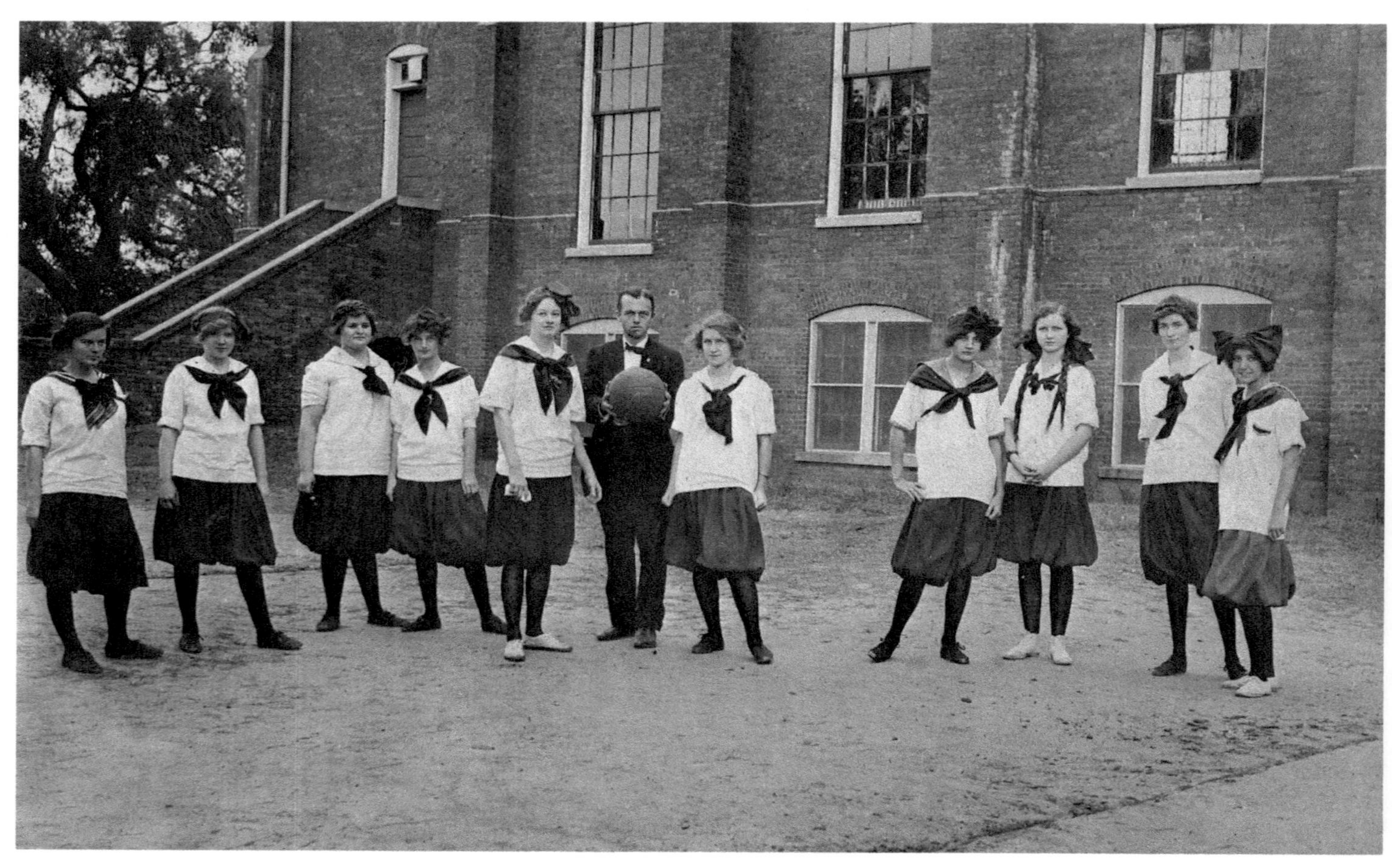

Kate Byrd, far right, is pictured with the Leon Academy girls basketball team in 1914. This is one of a group of photographs documenting her life growing up in Tallahassee. She was born in 1898 to Thomas and Rubie Byrd. Other photographs of her include her father's grocery store, her family's home, a trip to Lake Bradford, and her portrait as Queen of the May Day festival.

Fanny Tiers bought Goodwood in 1911, made changes to the main house, and added the first swimming pool in Tallahassee, which she opened to the community. By 1925 the estate included the main house, seven guest cottages, two stables, a carriage house, skating rink, swimming pool, aviary, greenhouse, and a water tower.

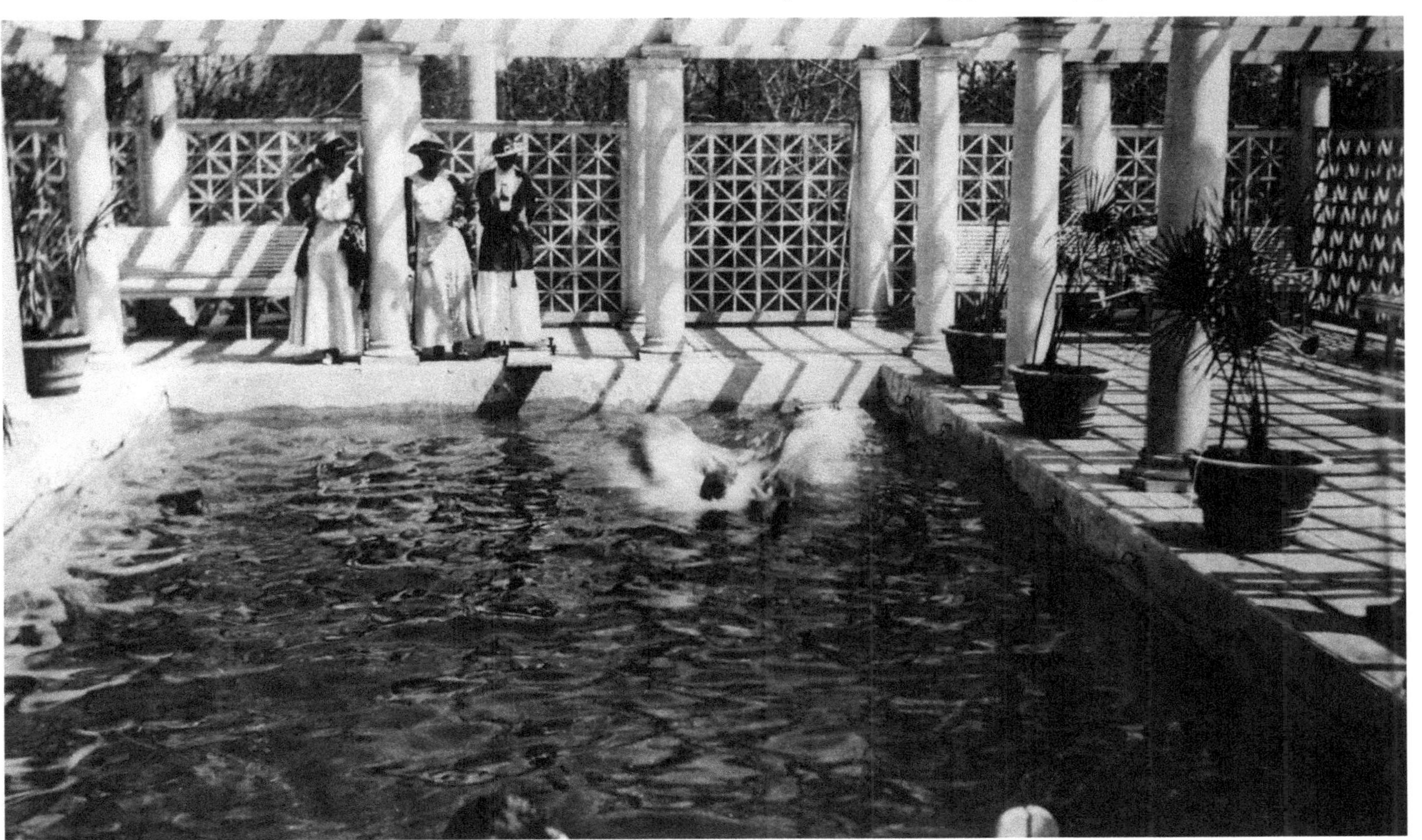

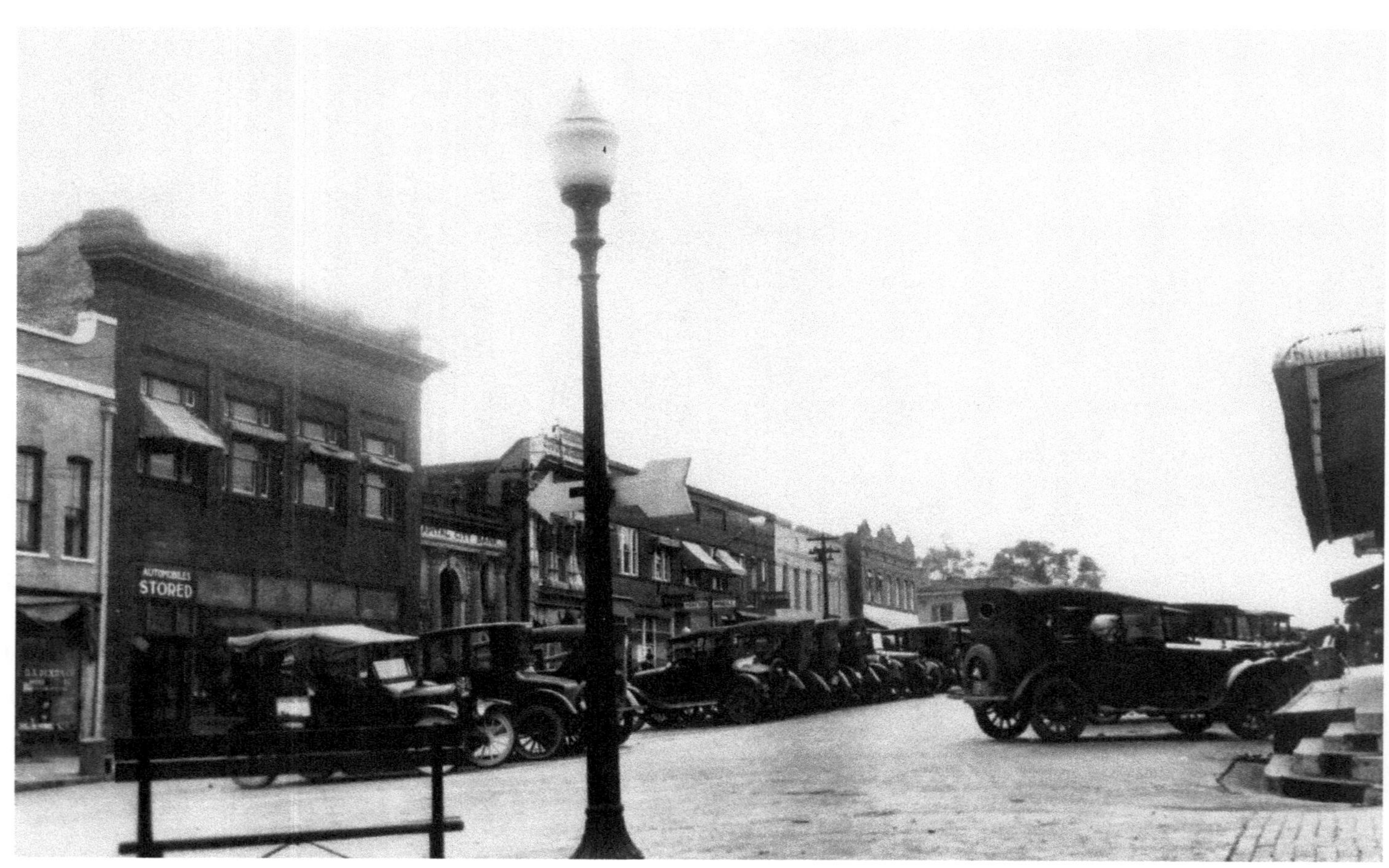

By the 1920s brick streets and automobiles had replaced dirt roads and ox carts along Monroe Street. Electric lamps, benches, and street signs were welcomed improvements. The arrow seems to point to the one-story Capital City Bank. The two buildings on either side of the bank were built after 1900 when the city enjoyed a period of economic growth.

John P. Brown drives Mr. Lewis in a Maxwell touring car, decorated for a parade. They are outside the Ford dealership on Pensacola Street. Two years earlier, in 1912, Tallahassee first paved its streets, which the local paper heralded as "one of the greatest events in the history of Tallahassee."

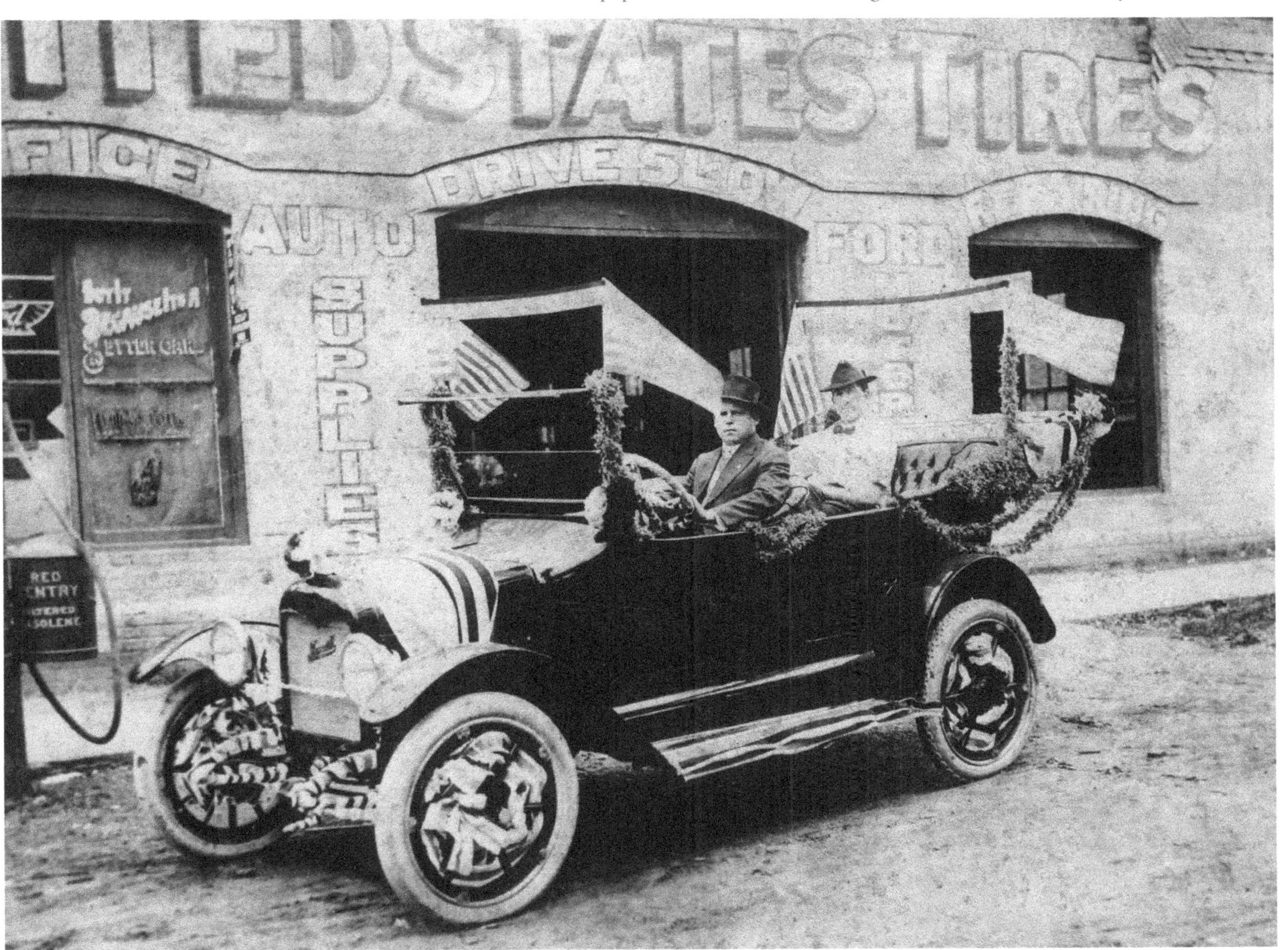

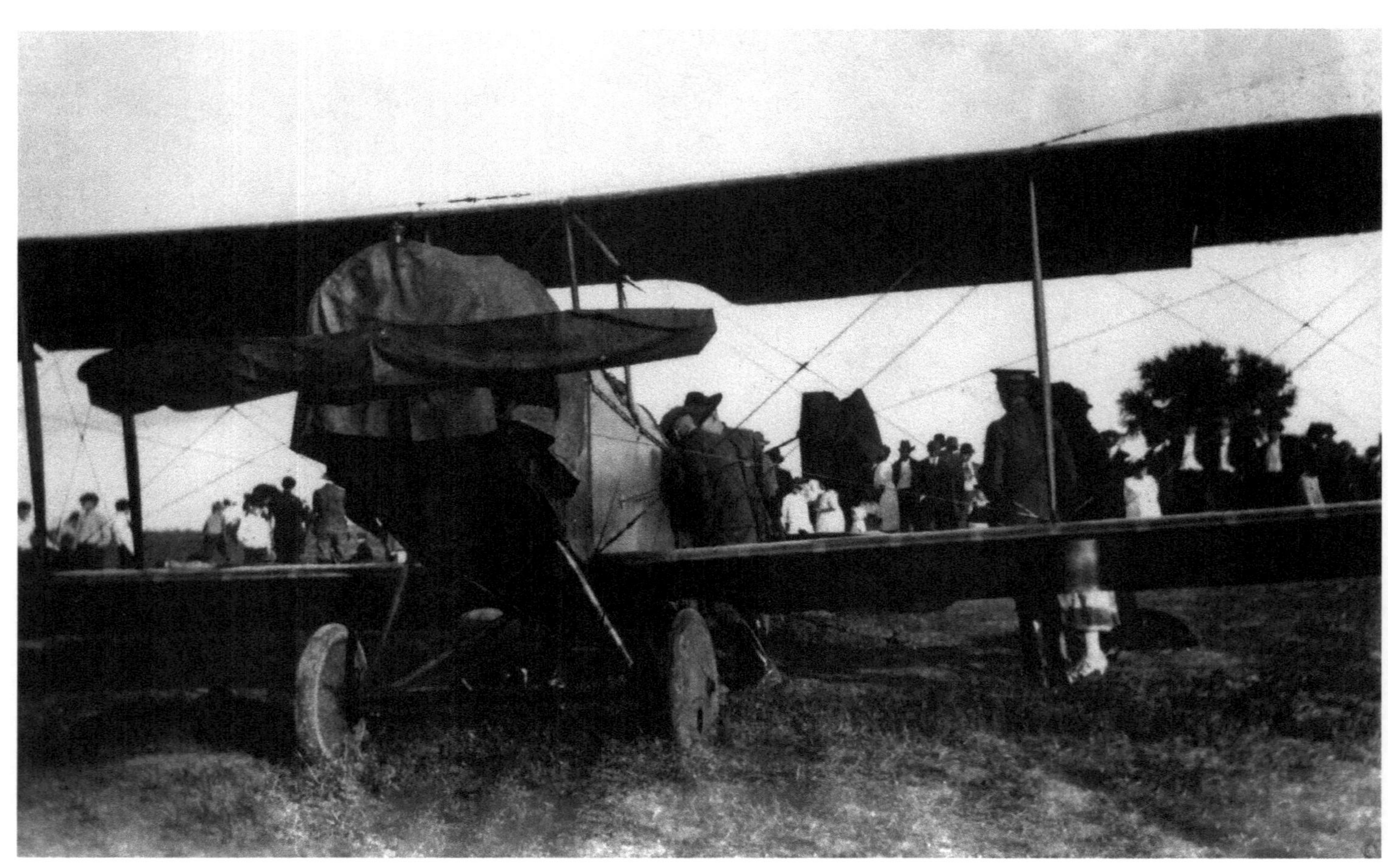

During World War I, thousands of soldiers passed through Tallahassee on trains headed to ports or training camps. This visiting army plane sparked excitement and added to the growing interest in aviation. The first airstrip was Smith field off of St. Augustine Road about a mile from the capitol.

A Capital City

(1921–1940)

Between the wars Tallahassee's economy slowly changed from its predominantly agricultural base in the nineteenth century to a service-oriented economy attuned to the colleges and state government. During this period Tallahassee almost tripled in population, from 6,000 to 16,000, partly attributable to a growing state government fueled by the land boom of the 1920s and the expanding two schools of higher learning. The timber industry and sawmills were still important economic assets to the community, but as the city annexed land, more small landowners turned from farming to working in the city for the government or educational sectors.

The little downtown area gradually changed as many of the residences were torn down and replaced with businesses and public buildings. The Venetia and Busy Bee restaurants and the new Floridan Hotel were some of the new establishments, and New Deal programs subsidized many public buildings including a new U.S. post office and federal courthouse. In the midst of change, there was some effort not to forget the town's past. The first campaign to save the old oak trees was successful in preserving stately live oaks throughout the city.

The two institutions of higher learning both benefited from strong, capable leaders. Under the direction of President Edward Conradi, the Florida State College for Women continued to offer nontraditional courses for women, especially in science and math. Florida A&M, under President John Robert Edward Lee, became accredited as a Class A institution and a member of the Association of American Universities.

Tallahassee's centennial celebration topped social events along with larger inaugural parades and balls. Recreational choices grew even though the popular Daffin movie theater burned. It later reopened as the State Theater. The city's first golf course opened, and fishing or sightseeing excursions to Wakulla Springs, St. Marks, and the Gulf of Mexico became increasingly popular.

As the state's population grew, so did the number of state employees and facilities. The Firestone, Knott, and Martin buildings were constructed, and the Capitol was remodeled twice. In 1923 the building's size was almost doubled and the interior completely remodeled, featuring marble staircases. In 1937, a north wing for the House of Representatives was added. A south wing for the Senate was delayed owing to World War II and not completed until 1947.

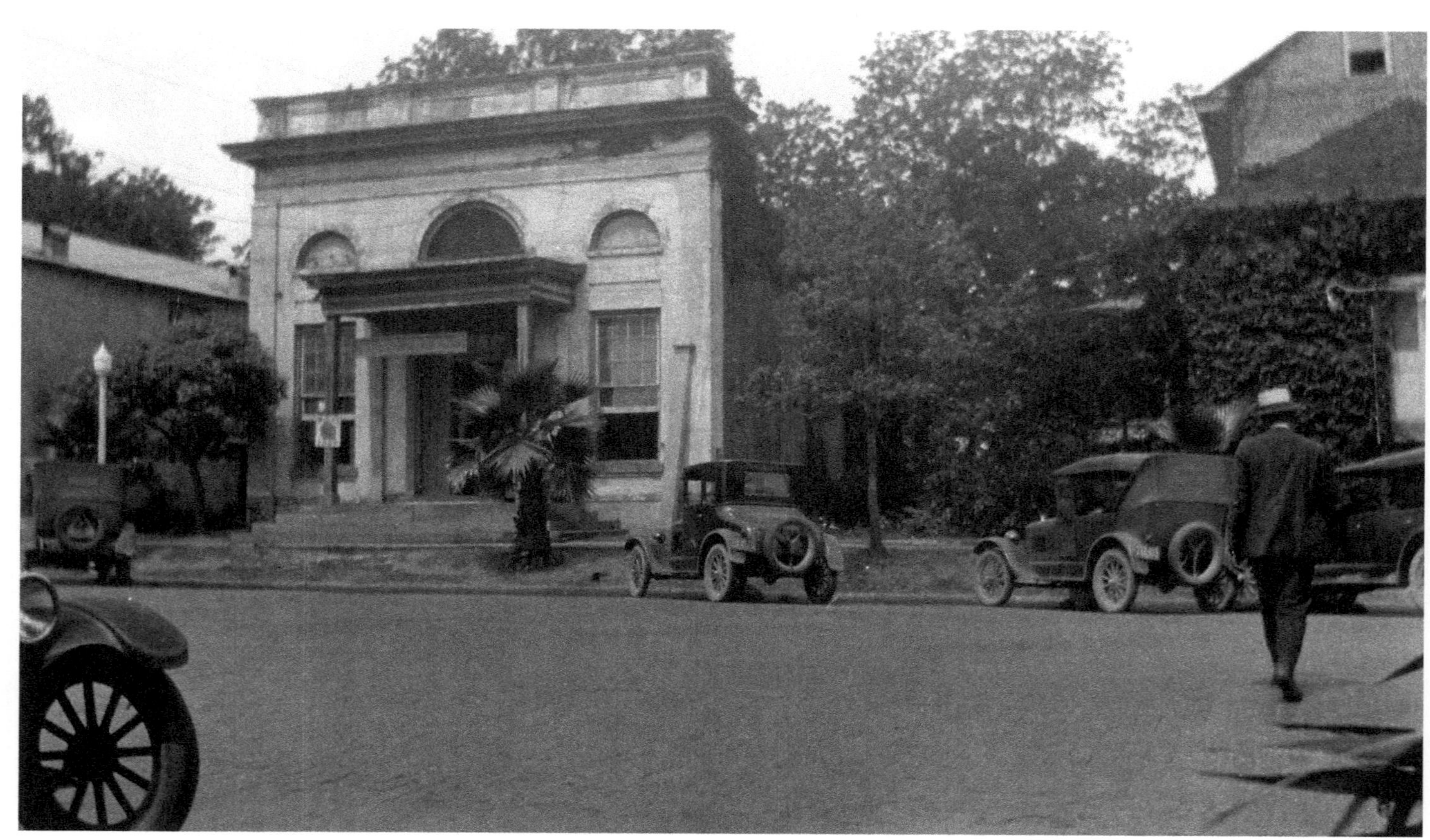

A view of the Union Bank Building at its original location on Adams Street, sometime in the 1920s. Since 1841 the building has been used as a church, feed store, art house, coffeehouse, dance studio, beauty shop, and shoe factory. Moved and restored in 1971, the state's oldest surviving bank building opened as a museum in 1984.

The Hill City Golf Course in 1921 consisted of a few holes on a site southeast of the capitol. Incorporated in 1924 as the Tallahassee Country Club, its wooden clubhouse with one large ballroom was a principal Tallahassee social center, the scene of private parties and receptions and formal balls.

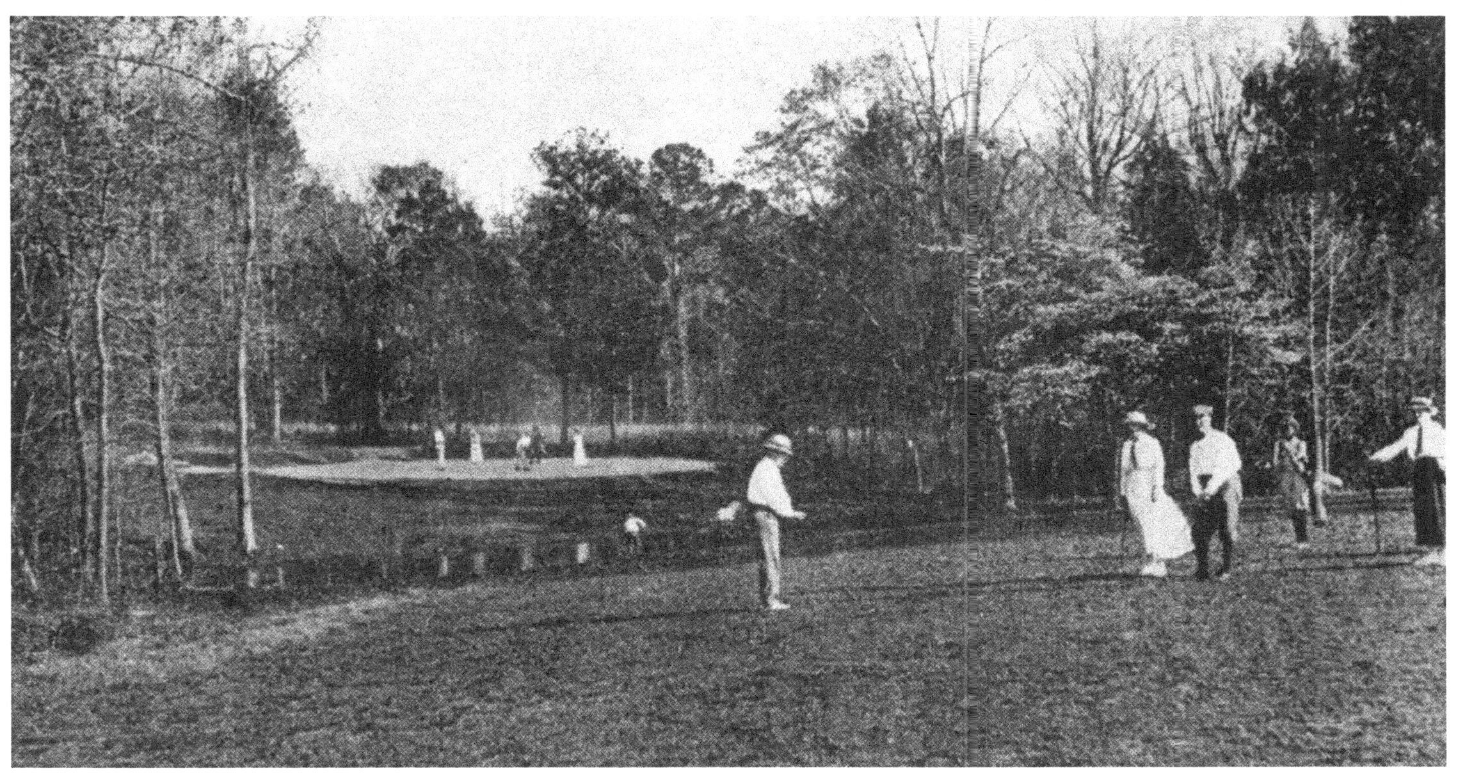

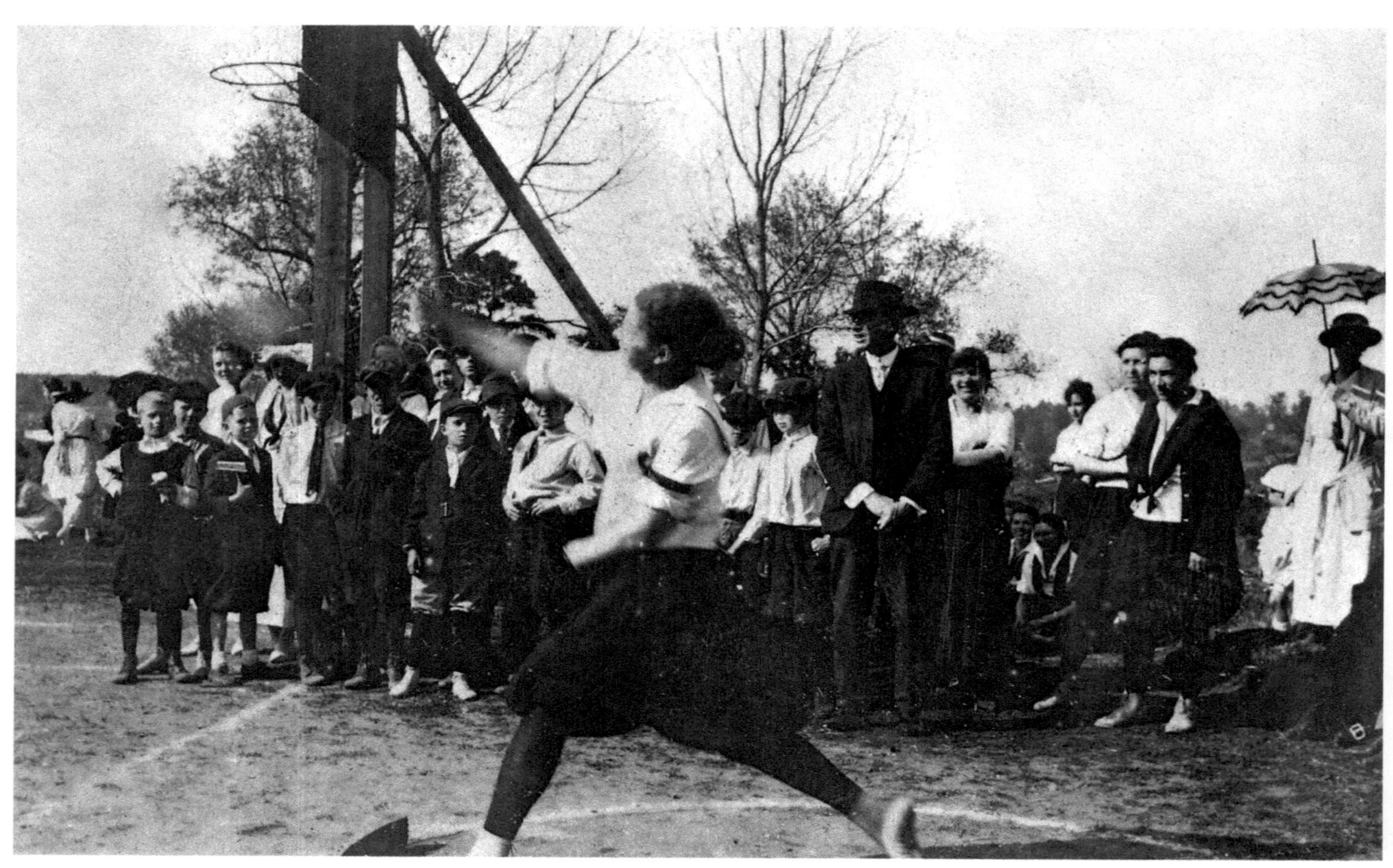

A student competes in the shot put at the 1920 field day at Florida State College for Women. The college divided intramural teams between the "evens" classes graduating in even years, and the "odds" classes graduating in odd years. Events included baseball, basketball, high jump, long jump, hurdles, running, and javelin.

Revenue agent James E. Bowdoin stands beside a Model-T Ford with a confiscated moonshine still in downtown Tallahassee. During the Prohibition era, moonshine stills were abundant in the area west of the city. Bowdoin was shot in West Florida in 1925. Leon County was dry from 1904 to 1967.

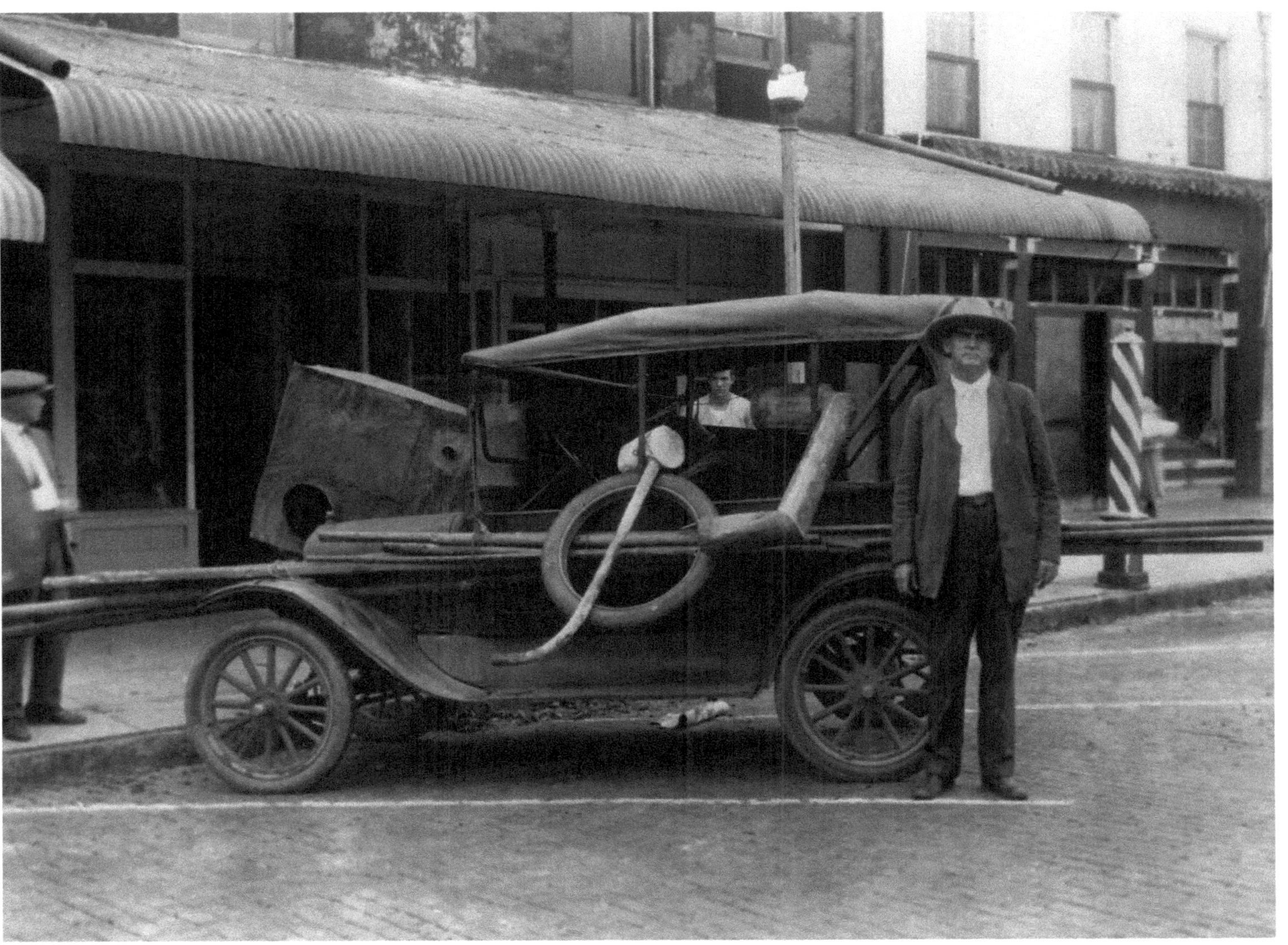

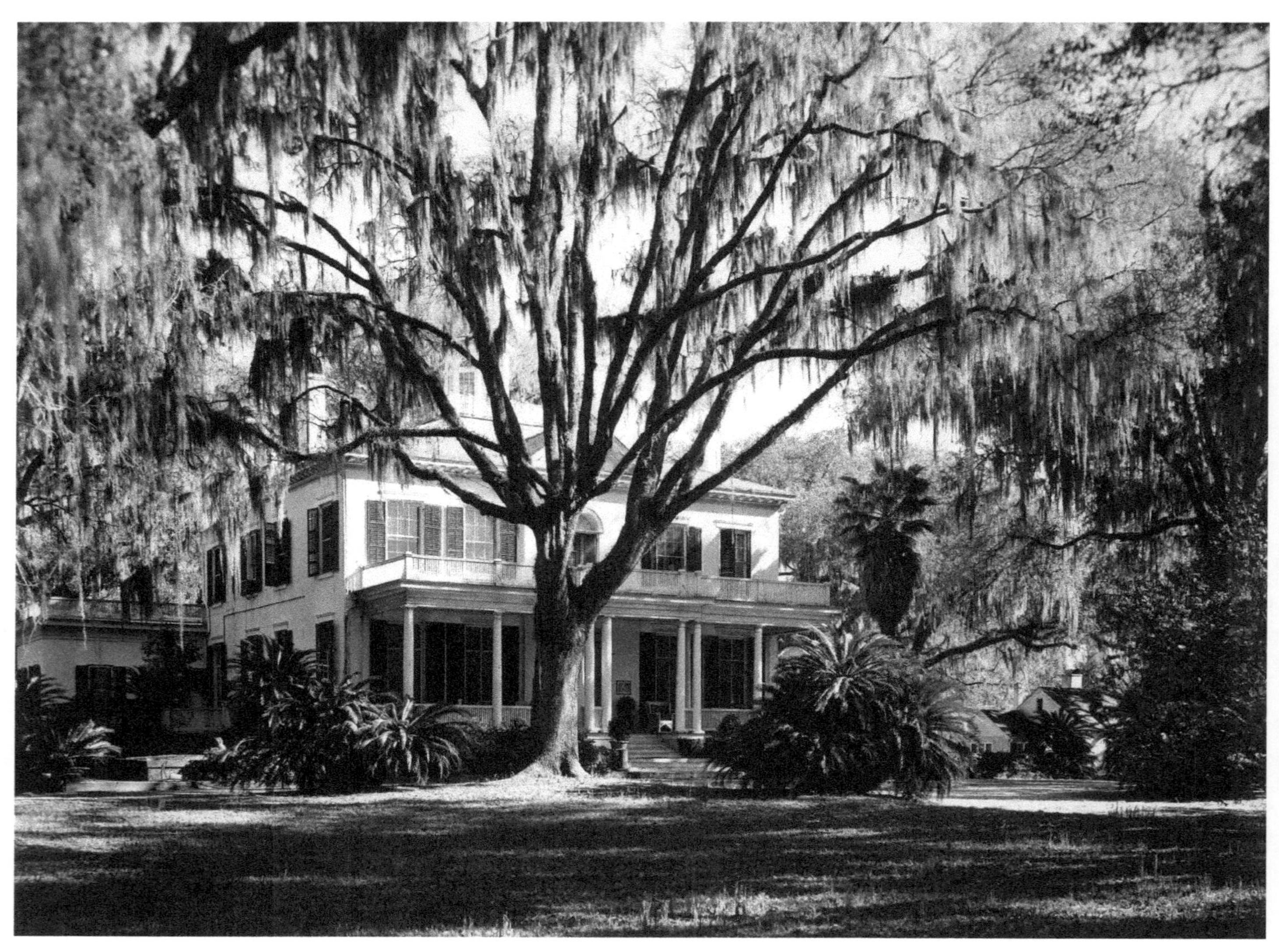

A large oak tree graces the main house at Goodwood Plantation. State senator William Hodges and wife Margaret bought Goodwood in 1925 for $80,000, including 167 acres of land and all the furnishings. After Senator Hodges became the senate president in 1935, Goodwood became a center for political activities.

Tallahassee grandly celebrated its centennial with a week of parades, shows, fireworks, concerts, and exhibits from November 9 to 15, 1924. The Knights of Columbus float participated in the centennial celebration parade on November 11. The "Black Citizens Historical Parade" was held separately.

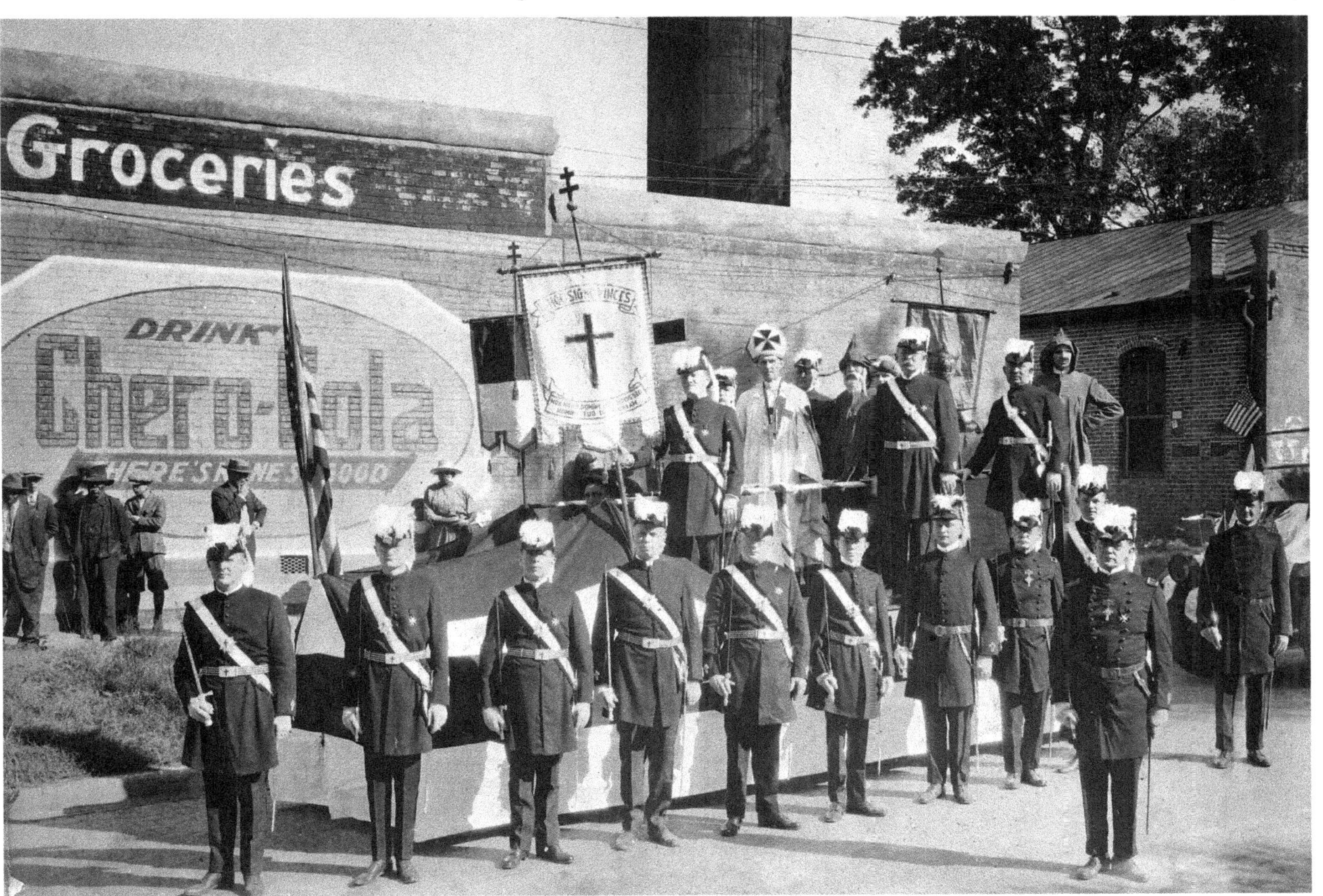

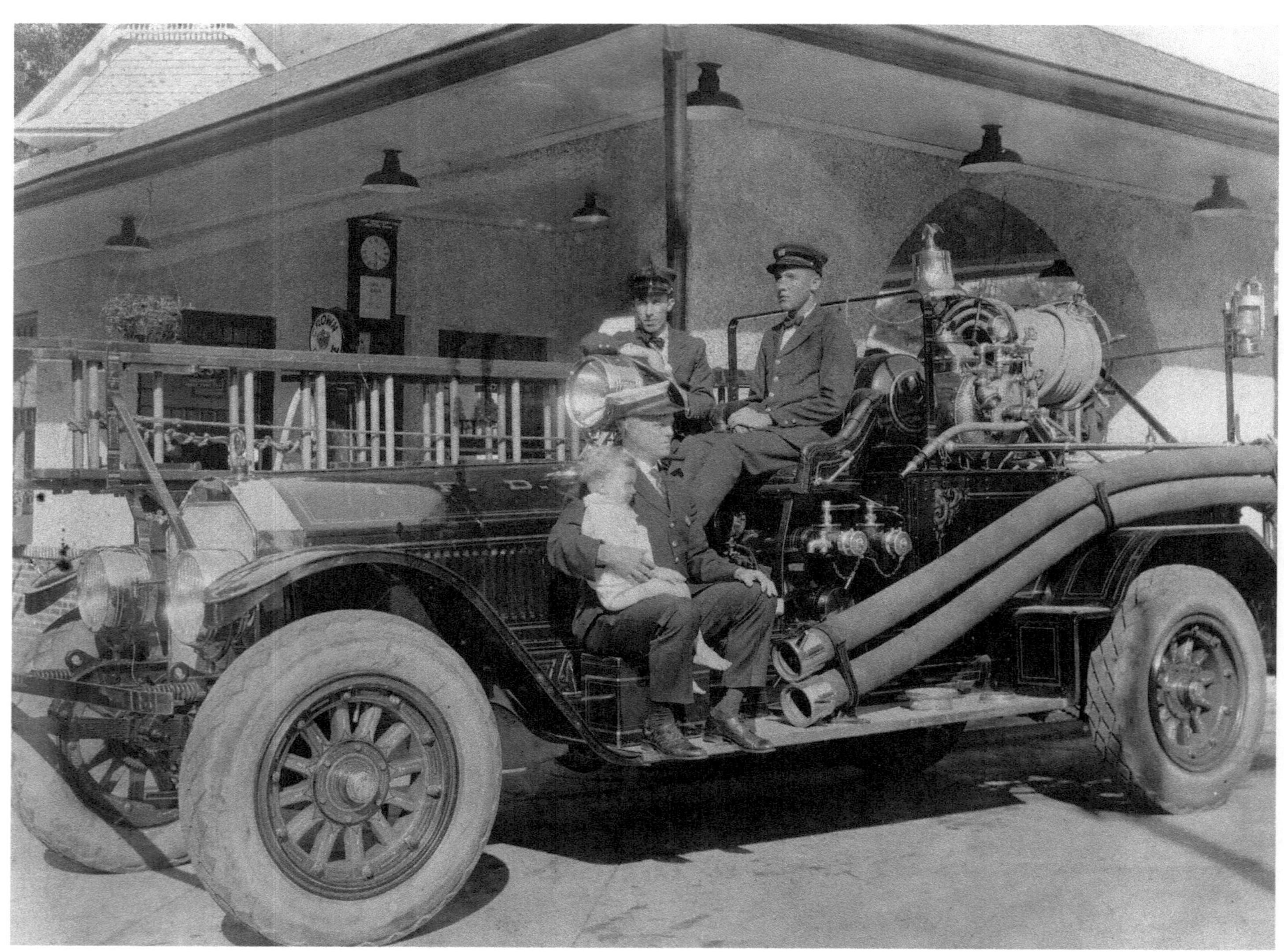

Among the firefighters on the truck at a gas station is Fire Chief Thomas P. Coe holding young Ridgeway Coe. By 1924 Tallahassee's fire department had three paid full-time men and 20 partly paid "volunteers." The equipment consisted of two triple combination motor-driven pumpers carrying 1,200 feet of hose.

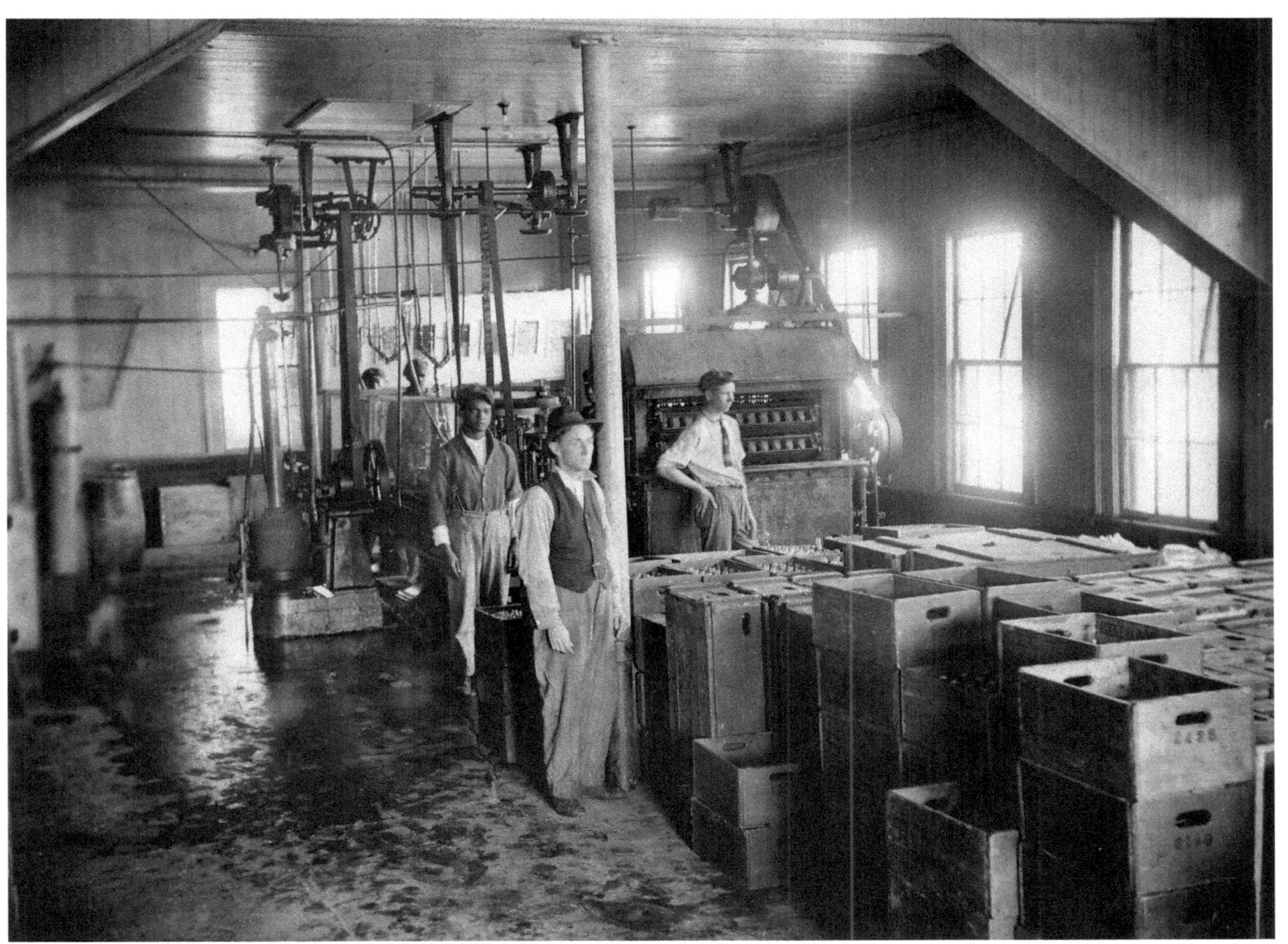

The Middle Florida Ice Company was located near Gaines Street and next to the railroad to allow freight needing refrigeration to be quickly unloaded and stored in special coolers. Although electric service was available in 1908, as of the 1920s few Tallahassee residents had electric refrigerators and the ice man was still a familiar figure.

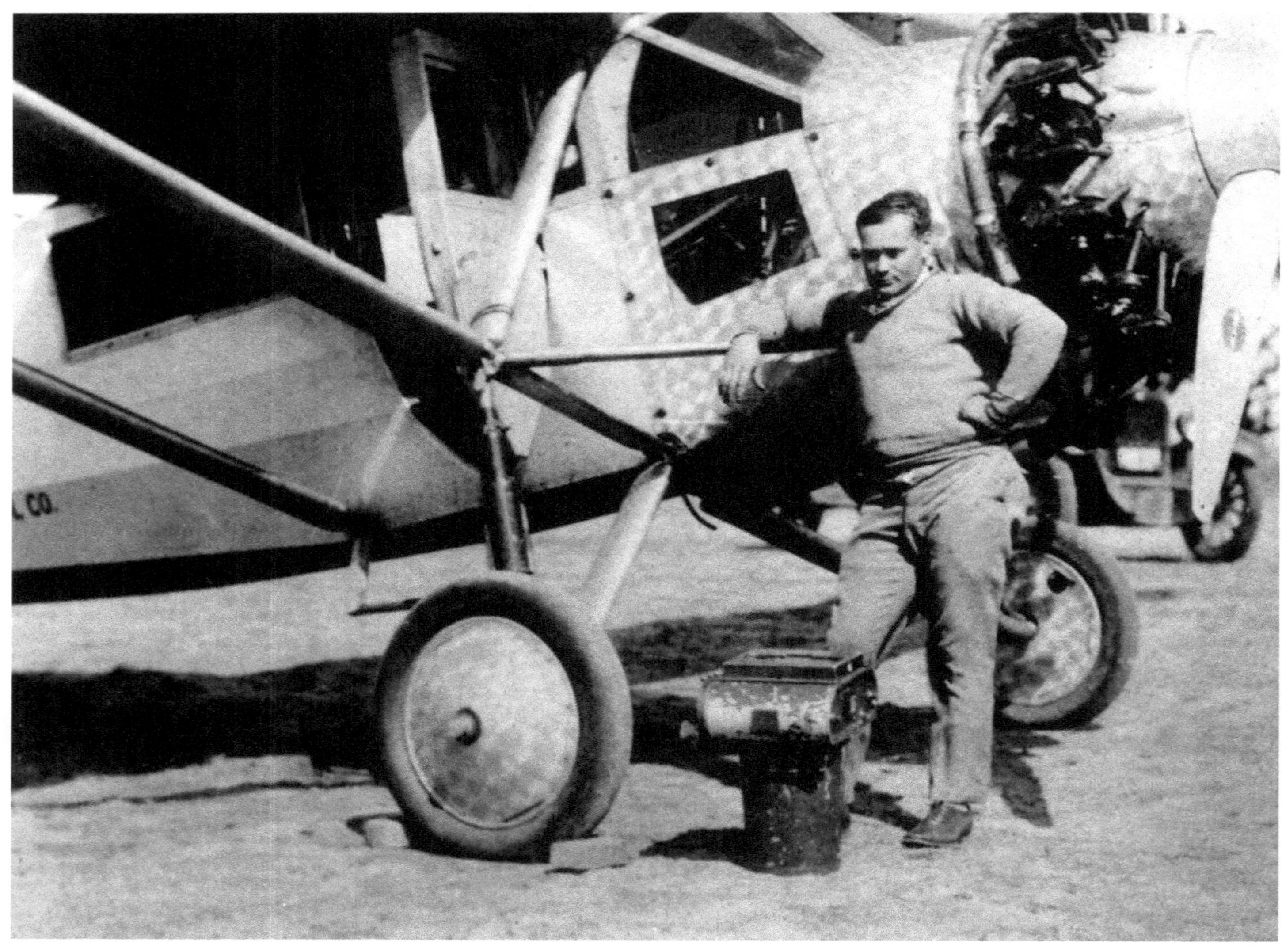

This Ryan Monoplane, sister ship to Charles Lindbergh's *Spirit of St. Louis,* carried an aerial camera, sighted through the floor of the plane, to make surveys of Leon County. As aviation became more popular, V. H. Smith, owner of the only landing strip, wanted his land back, forcing the city to devise plans for a real airport.

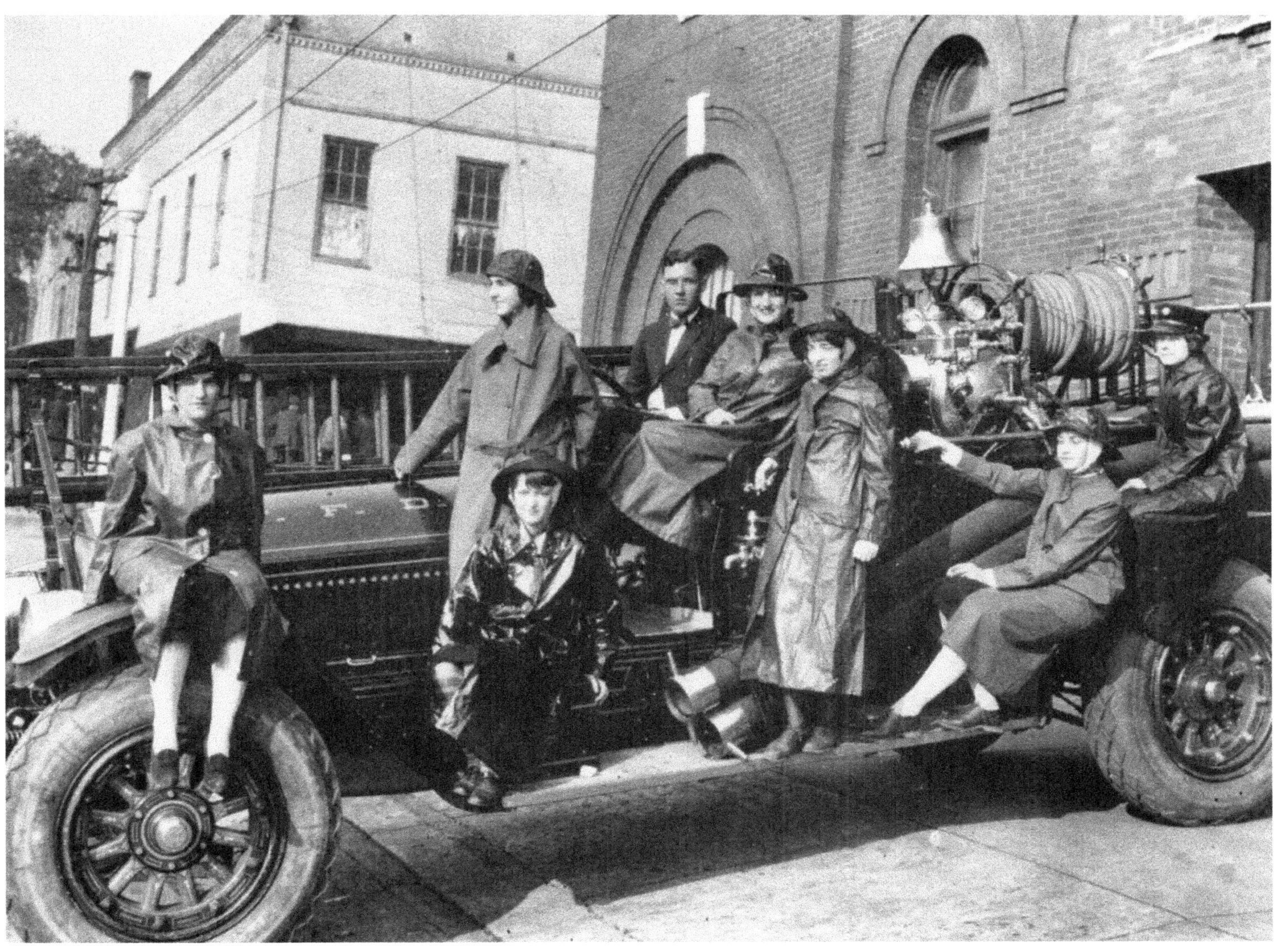

Students at Florida State College for Women pose as firemen on a fire truck at the Tallahassee Fire Department. The photograph was taken around 1925 at the fire department located in the City Hall building. Just five years earlier, a Sunday morning fire destroyed East Hall at the college.

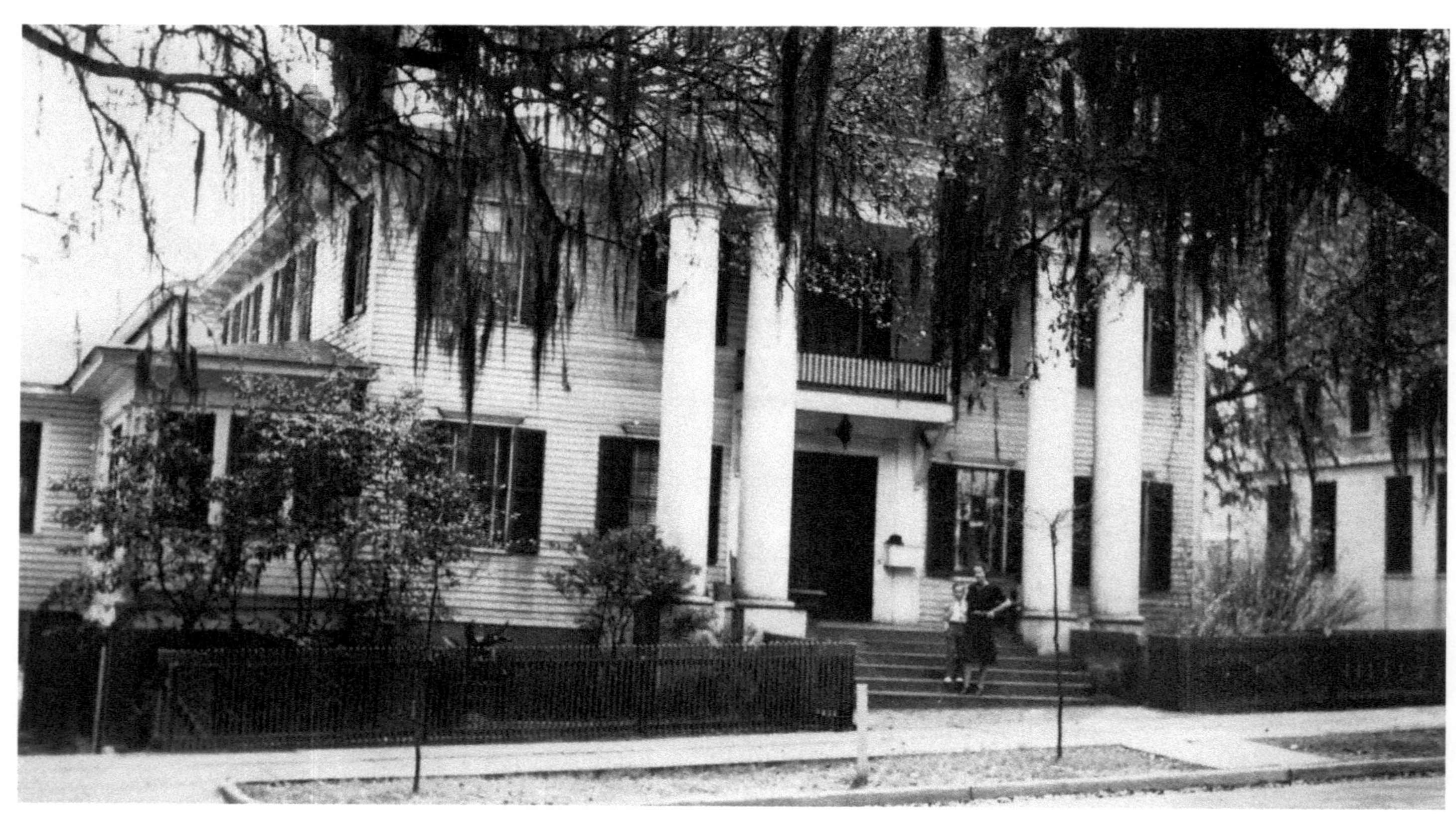

Built in 1843 for Thomas Hagner, the Knott House became Union Army Headquarters in 1865, where the Emancipation Proclamation was read. Acquired by State Treasurer William Knott in 1928, his wife Luella attached verses to its furnishings. "The House That Rhymes" opened to the public in 1992 as the Knott House Museum.

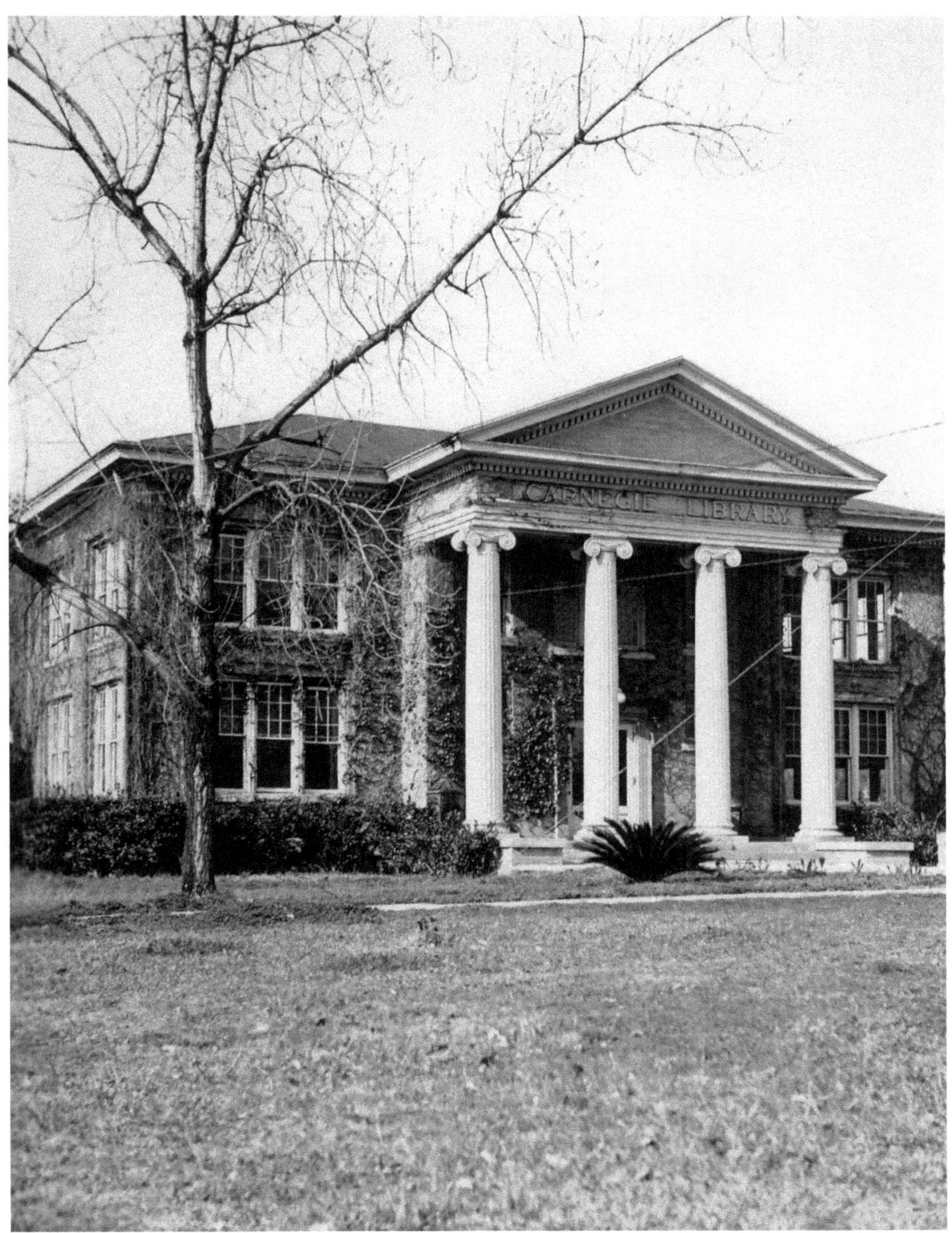

The Carnegie Library building is currently the oldest building at Florida A&M University and houses the Black Archives Research Center and Museum. Financed with the assistance of a $10,000 grant from philanthropist Andrew Carnegie and completed in 1907, it was the first library funded by Carnegie on a black university campus.

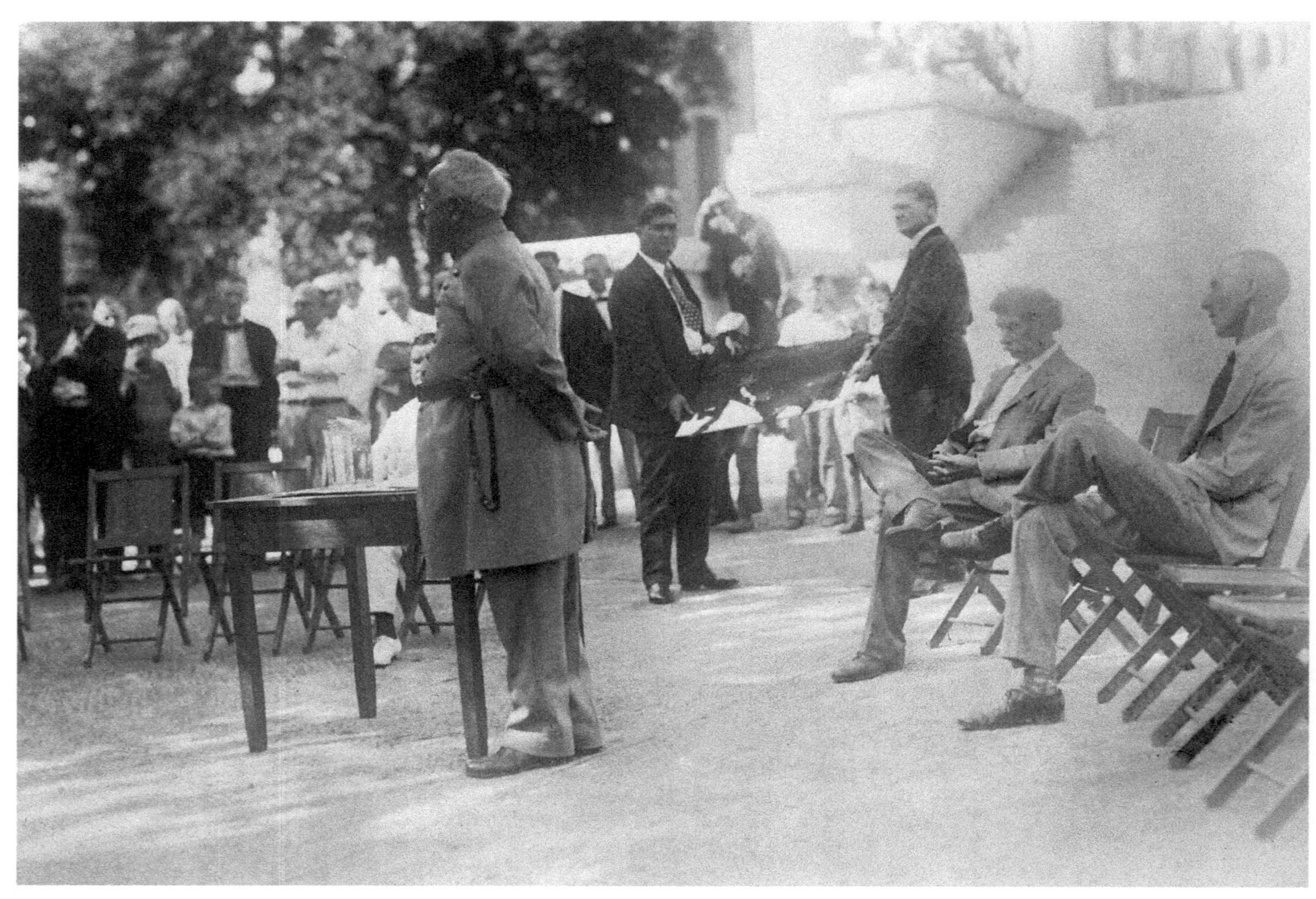

Colonel Thomas Jefferson Appleyard, veteran of the Confederate Navy, speaks during the ceremony for the return of the regimental colors of the 4th Florida Infantry in September 1927. The flag was captured at the Battle of Franklin, Tennessee, November 30, 1864, by Charles McCleary of the 111th Ohio Volunteer Infantry.

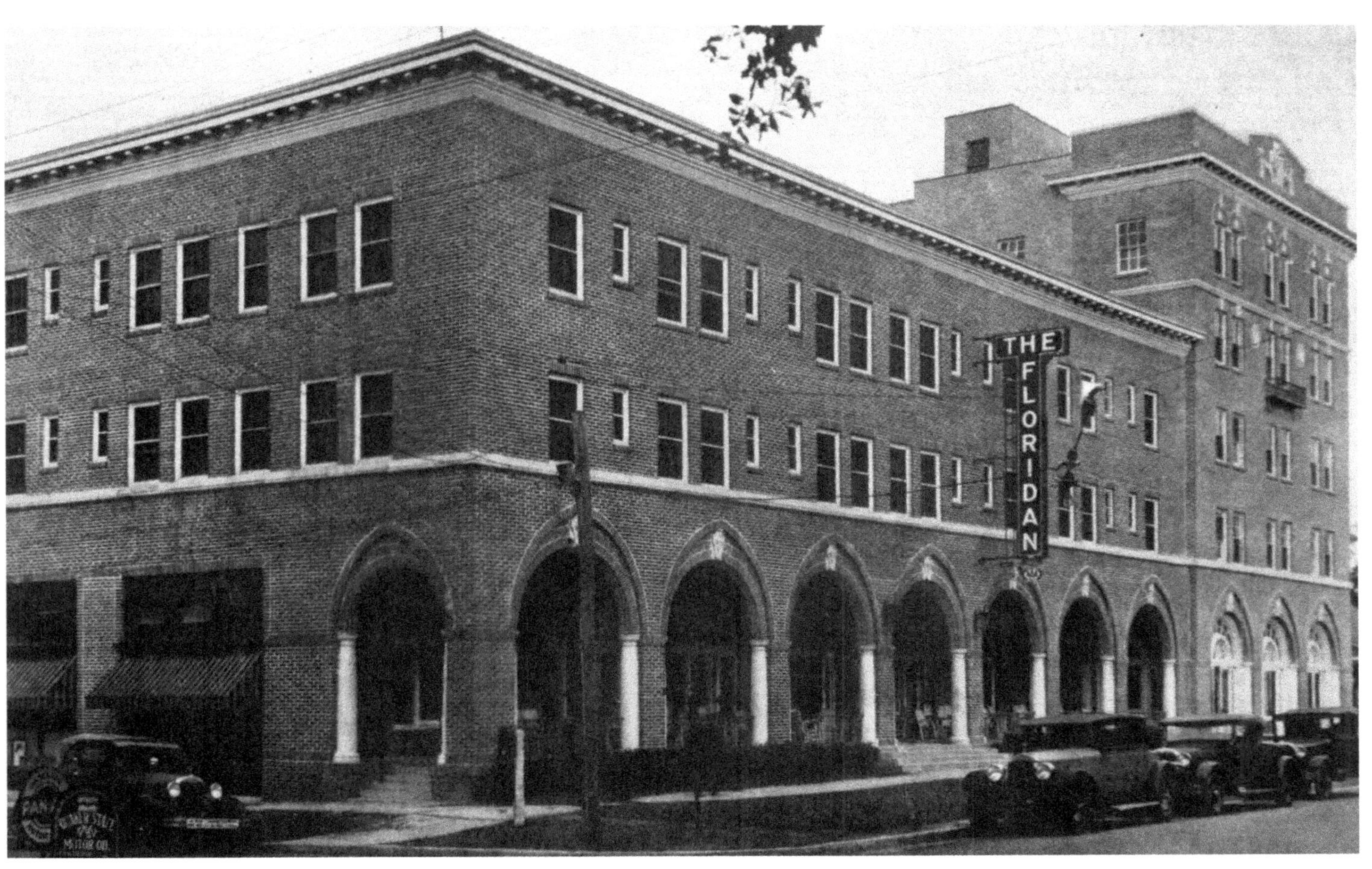

The Floridan Hotel on the northwest corner of Monroe and Call opened on May 2, 1927, and became a Tallahassee landmark. Ruby Diamond, local philanthropist, lived there for nearly fifty years. In 1945 Lord Halifax, ambassador to the United States from Great Britain, visited there. It closed in 1978 and was demolished in 1985.

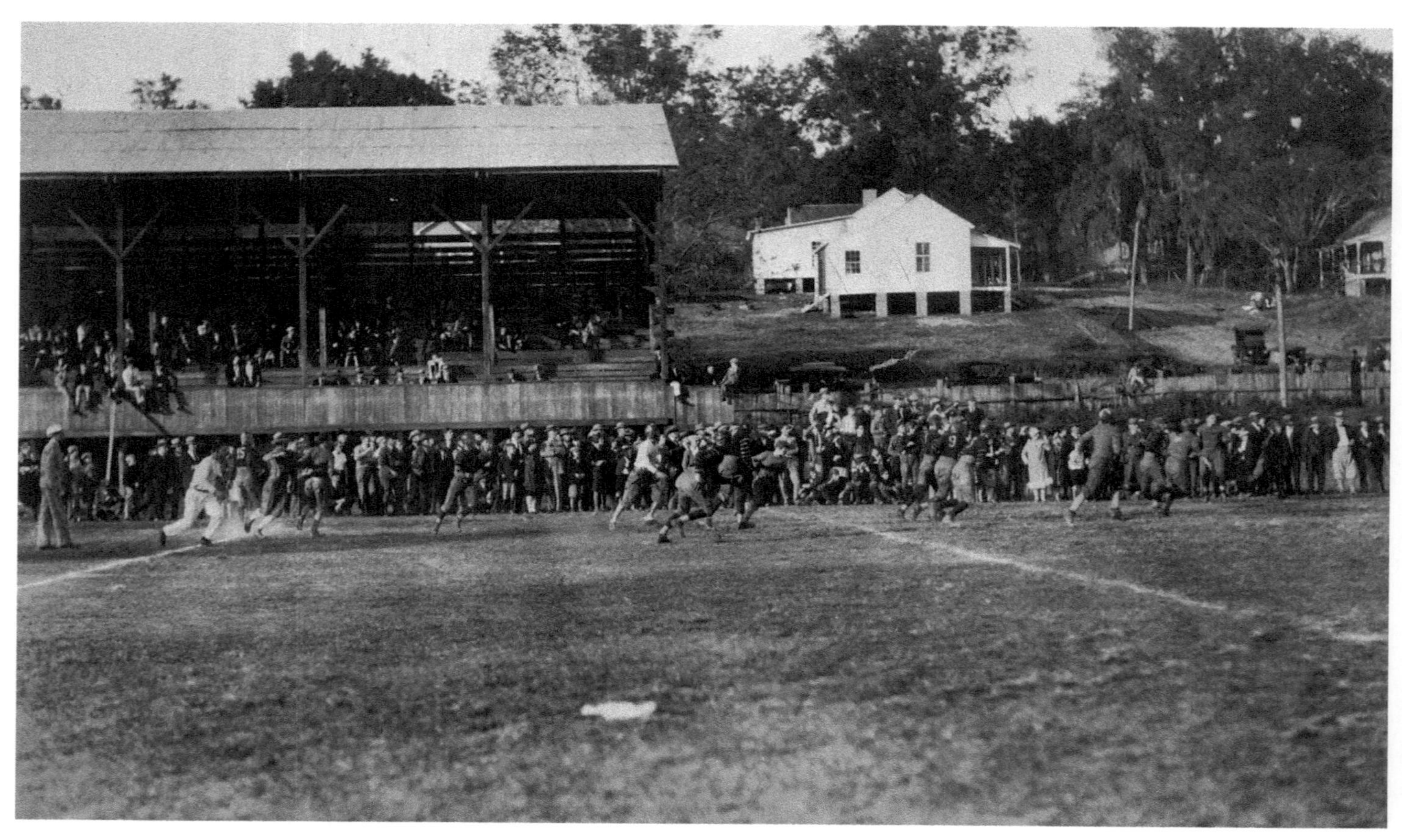

A 1920s Leon High School football team plays at Centennial Field on South Monroe. Started in 1916, Leon Football was the winningest high school program in Florida in the twentieth century, with 535 wins, 61 winning seasons, 3 state championships, 3 state runner-ups, and 12 national high school records.

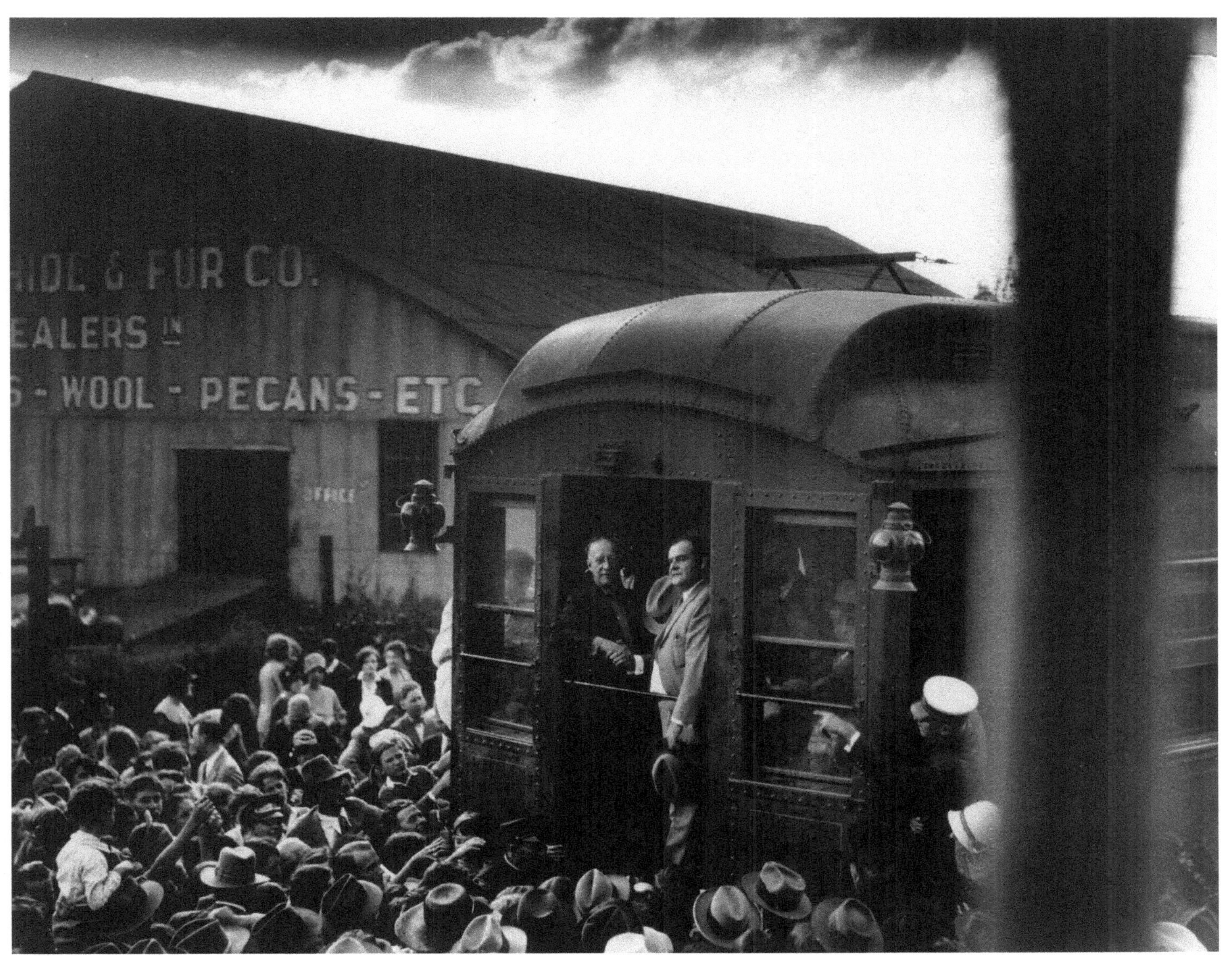

Florida's Democratic governor John W. Martin, on the right holding his hat, greets New York's governor Al Smith, the 1928 Democratic candidate for President. Smith did not carry Florida in the election, for several reasons. He opposed Prohibition and Republican Herbert Hoover was popular in Florida for his humanitarian work following two major hurricanes.

In 1913, the Florida Supreme Court moved into a new building, where it shared space with the Railroad Commission. When the court moved to its own building in 1949, the building was renamed the Whitfield. The court furniture, saved when the Whitfield Building was leveled in the 1970s, was placed back inside the Old Capitol.

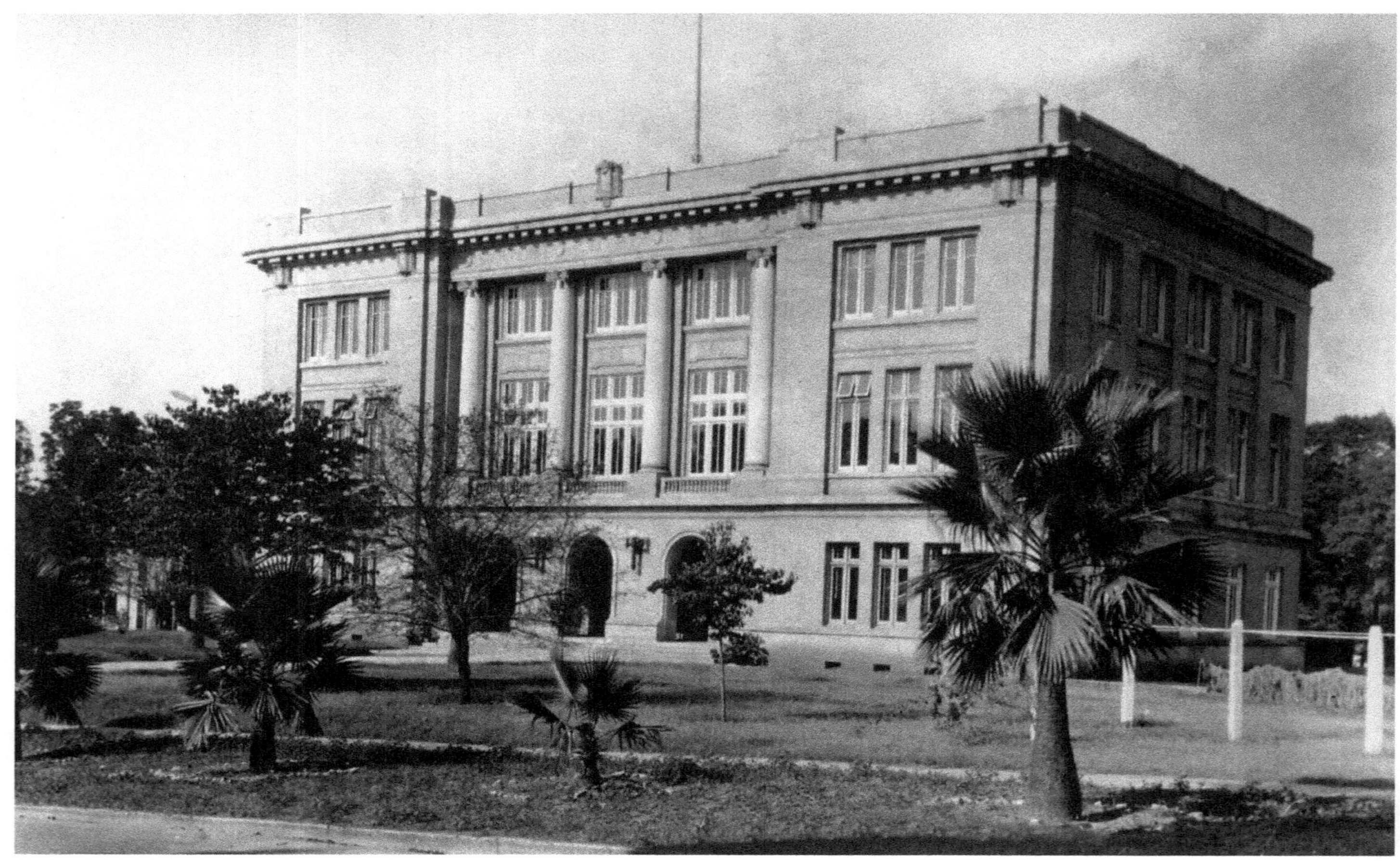

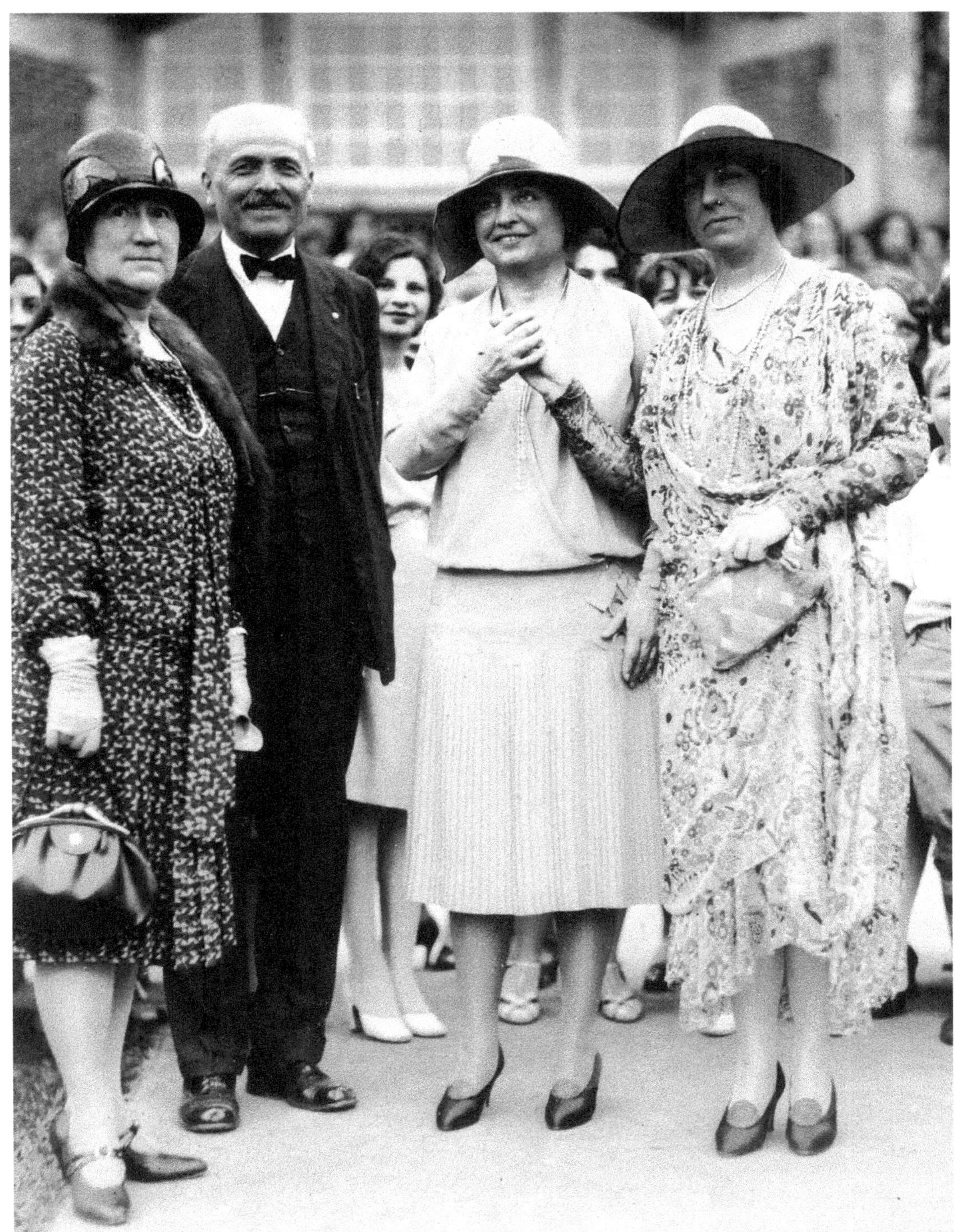

President and Mrs. Conradi greet Helen Keller. Edward Conradi, president of the Florida State College for Women from 1909 until 1941, worked tirelessly to improve the institution. In 1924, F.S.C.W. became the first state woman's college in the South approved by the Association of American Universities.

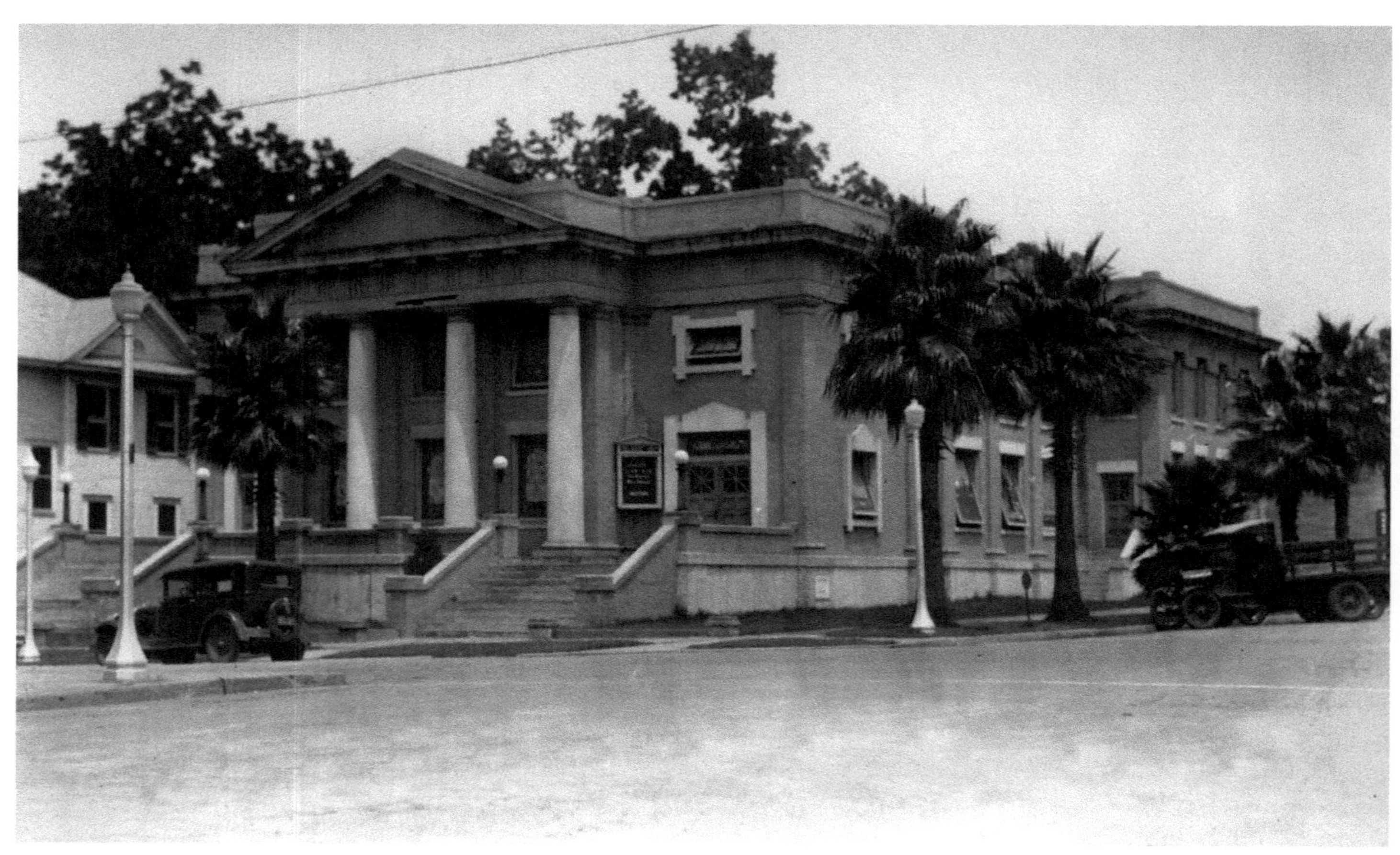

Organized before the Civil War, the First Baptist Church of Tallahassee dedicated its second building in November 1915. Under pastor-builder J. Dean Adcock, the church purchased a lot on the northeast corner of Adams Street and College Avenue for $5,000 and built this new church, seating 350.

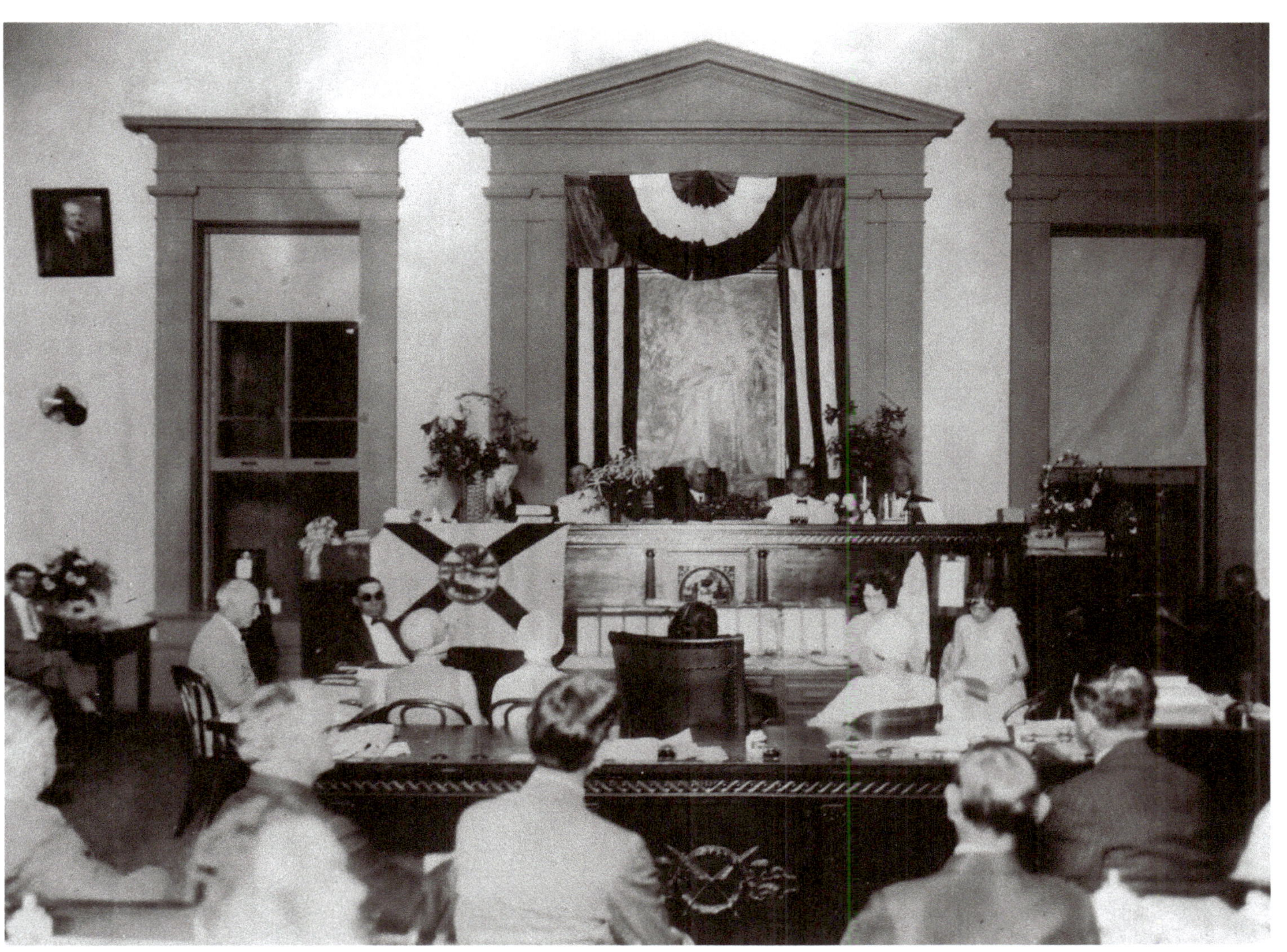

A portrait of Andrew Jackson is unveiled at the Florida Senate chamber on April 9, 1929. The plaque reads "Andrew Jackson, First Territorial Governor of Florida, painted by Frank Townsend Hutchens after Thomas Sulley." It hung in the Senate chamber until 1977 and is currently housed in the old capitol.

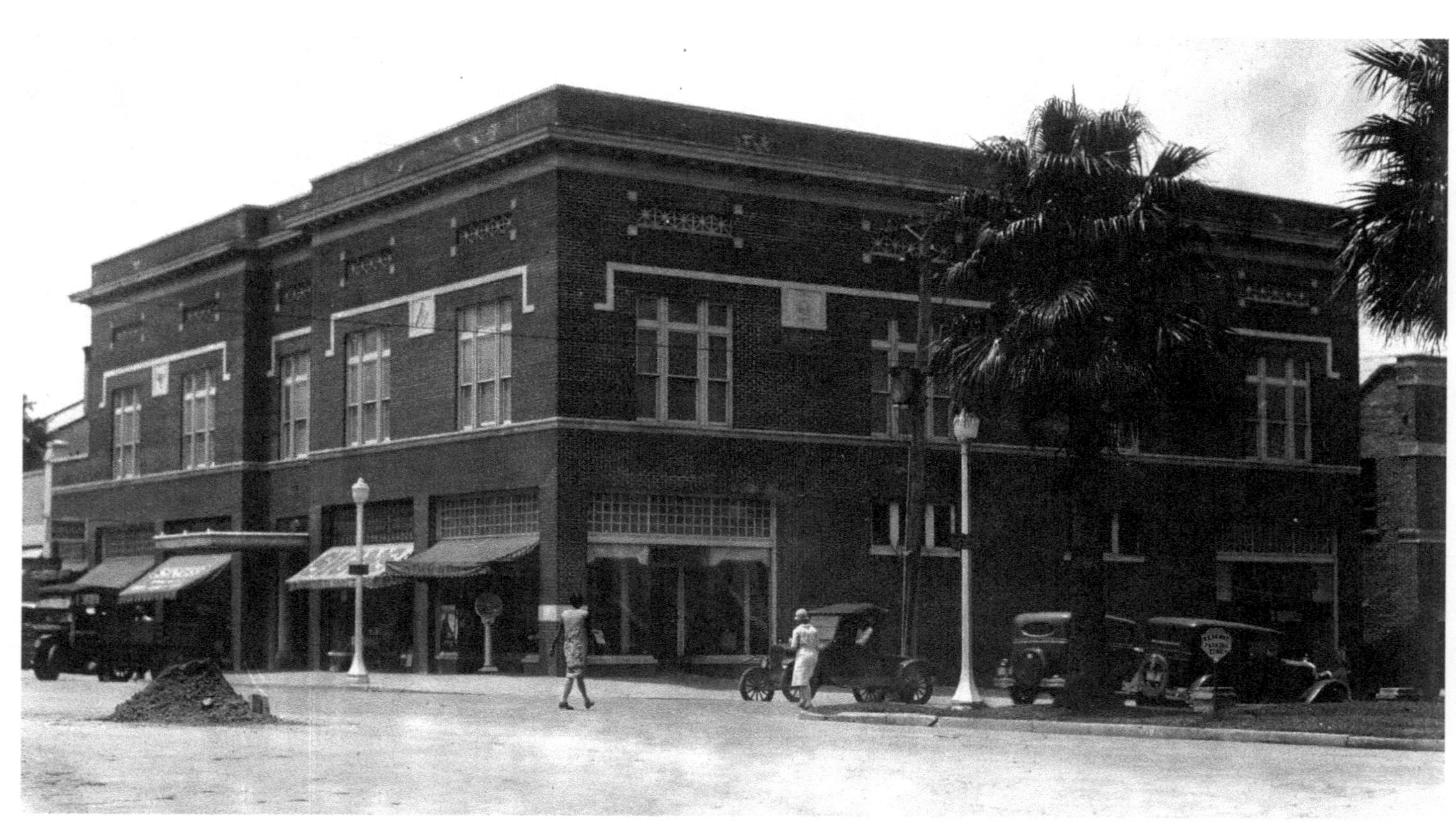

The first Masonic lodge was built on this site in 1854 and was replaced with this Masonic Hall in 1929. It was used until the 1970s when it became the Governor's Club. As Florida's first Masonic lodge, the lodge performed the cornerstone ceremonies for the 1845 State Capitol building.

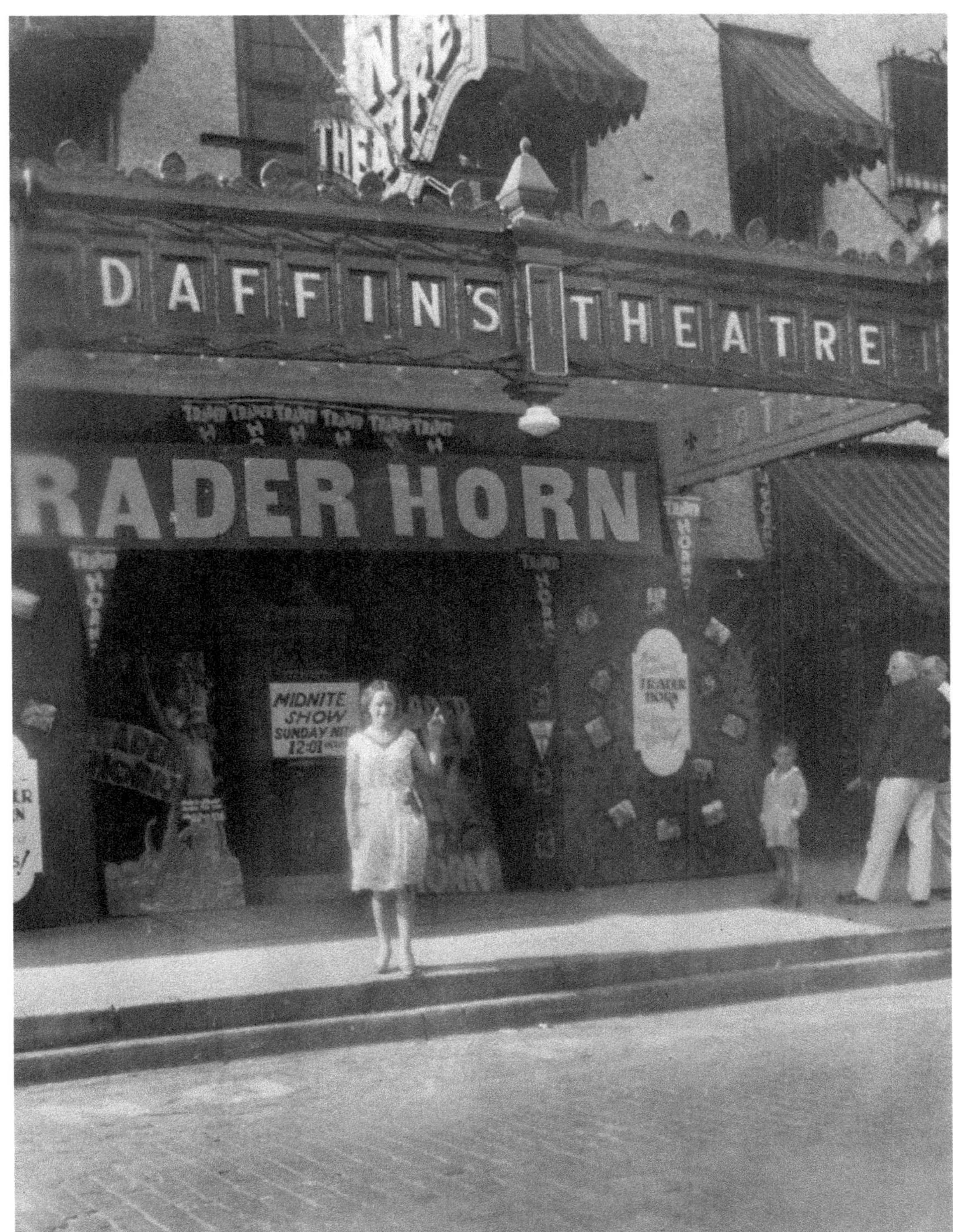

The Daffin Theatre on College Avenue opened in 1910 in a remodeled livery stable and operated as the Capitol City, the Daffin, and the State Theatre before it burned in 1933. The little boy at right, Ernest Daffin, was later a stand-in for "Boy" in a Johnny Weissmuller Tarzan movie filmed at Wakulla Springs.

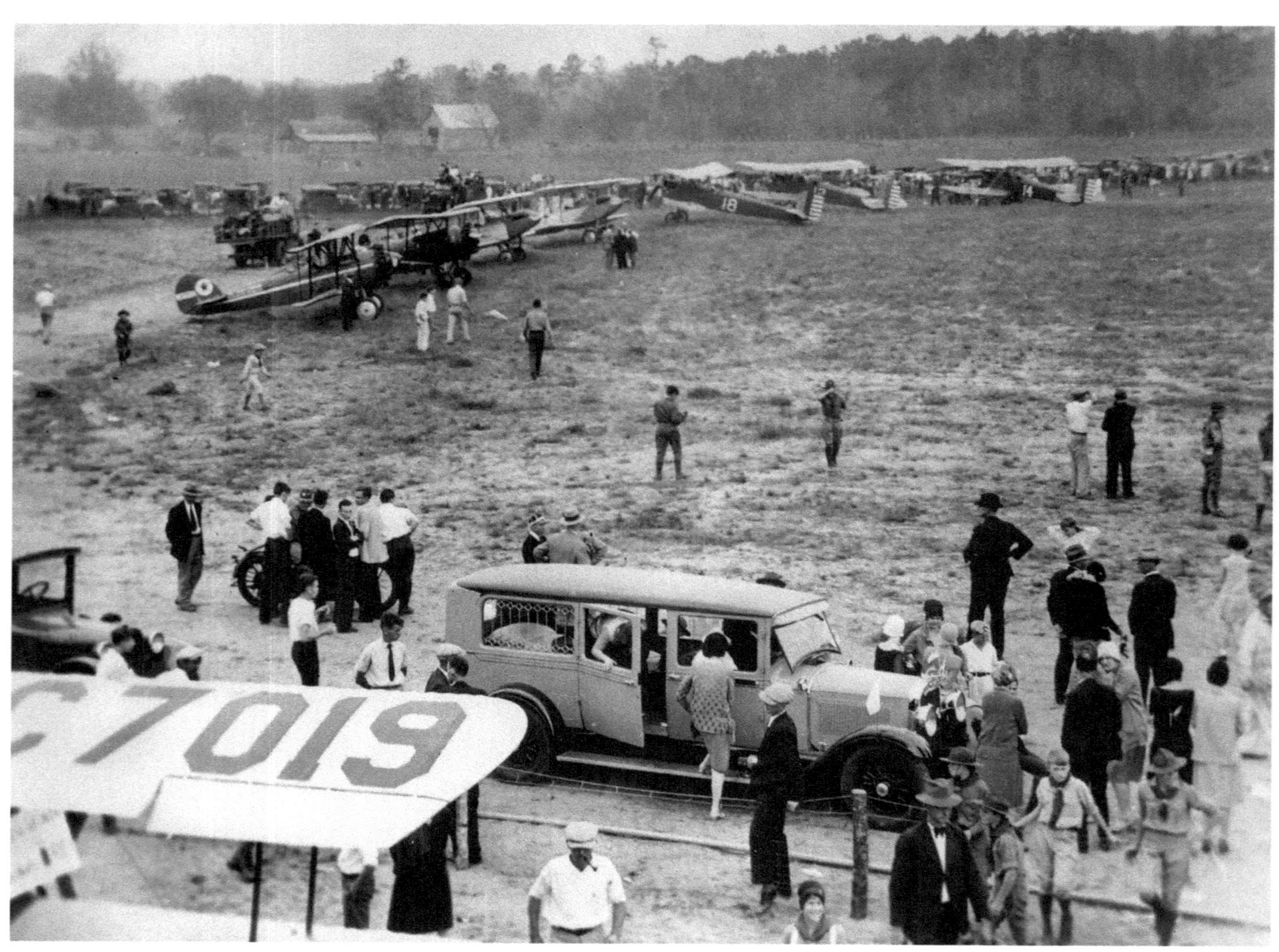

The dedication ceremonies of Dale Mabry Municipal Airport lasted two days, November 10-11, 1929. Governor Doyle Carlton dedicated the town's first airport, complete with a hangar, gas service station, and lighting system. The field was named for Dale Mabry, a World War I aviator killed in a dirigible crash in 1922.

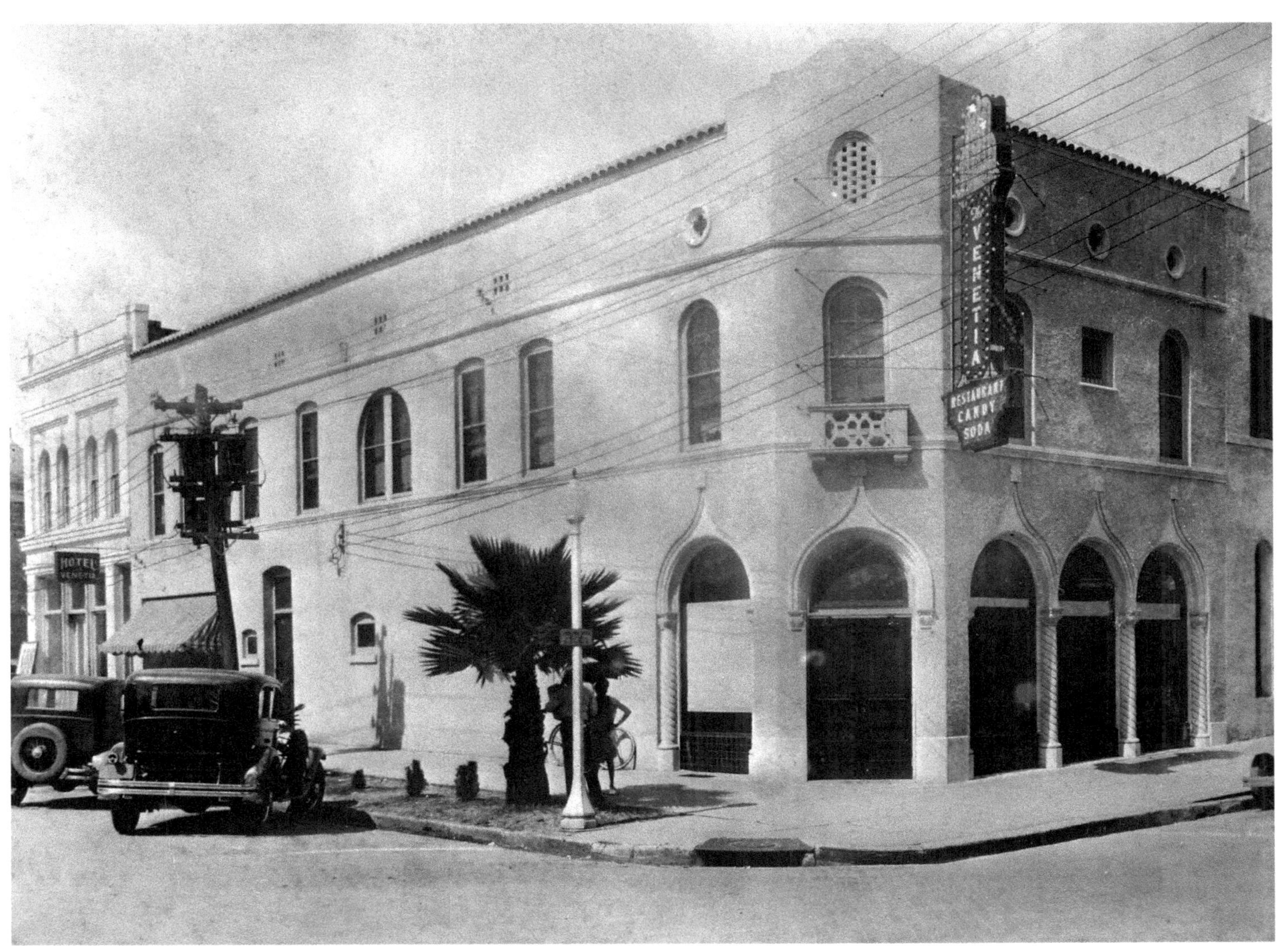

Victor and John Camechis owned and operated the Venetia Restaurant and Hotel located on the northeast corner of Adams Street and College Avenue. Opened in 1929 the business burned December 6, 1933. John Camechis, from the island of Patmos, was the first known immigrant of Greek heritage living in Tallahassee.

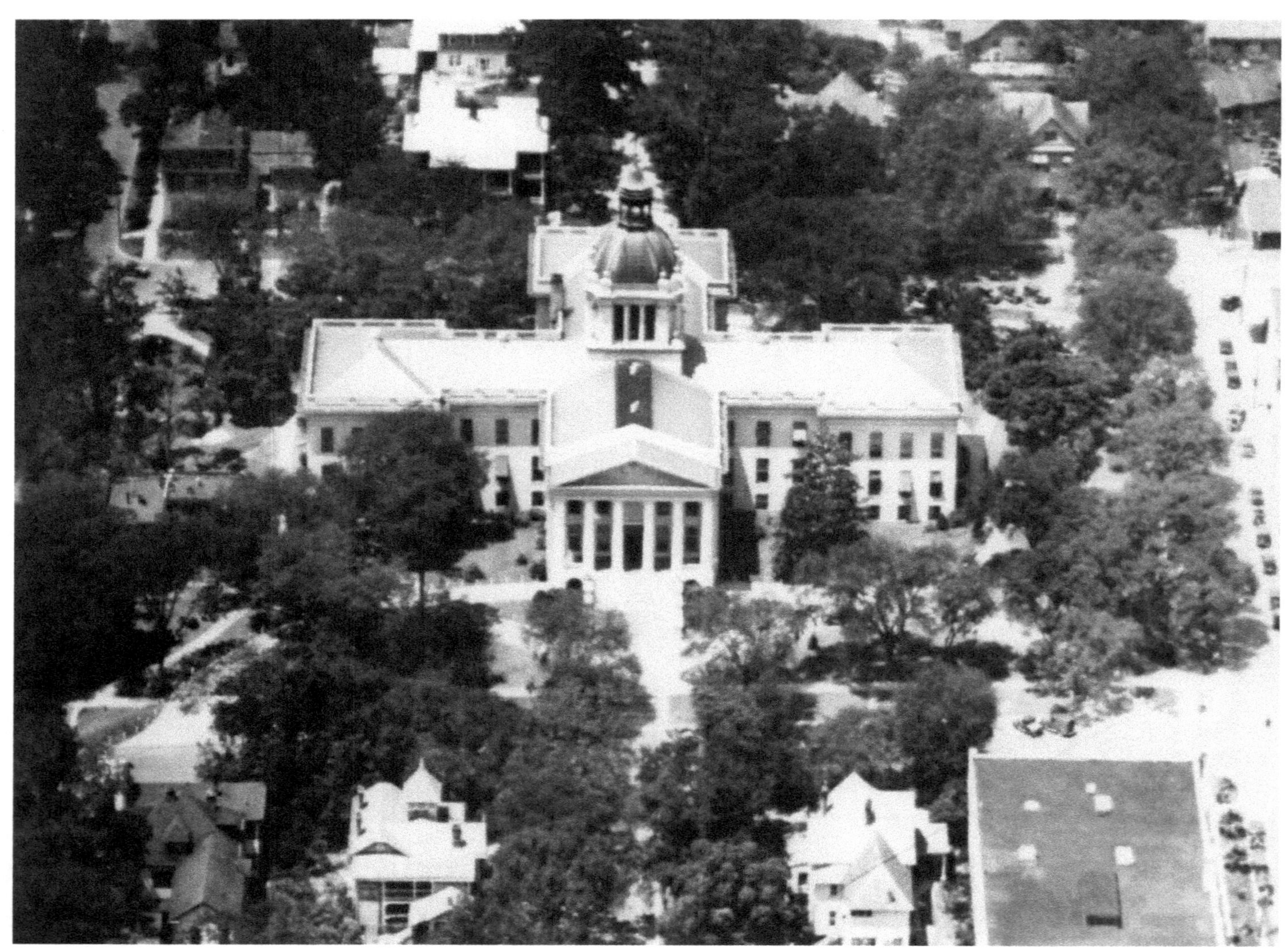

This aerial view shows the state capitol after the 1923 additions by architect Henry Klutho of Jacksonville. The 1920s land boom increased the state's population, and the growing government required additional space. Klutho's design added a west and east wing, almost doubling the size, and included a remodeled interior with marble halls and staircase.

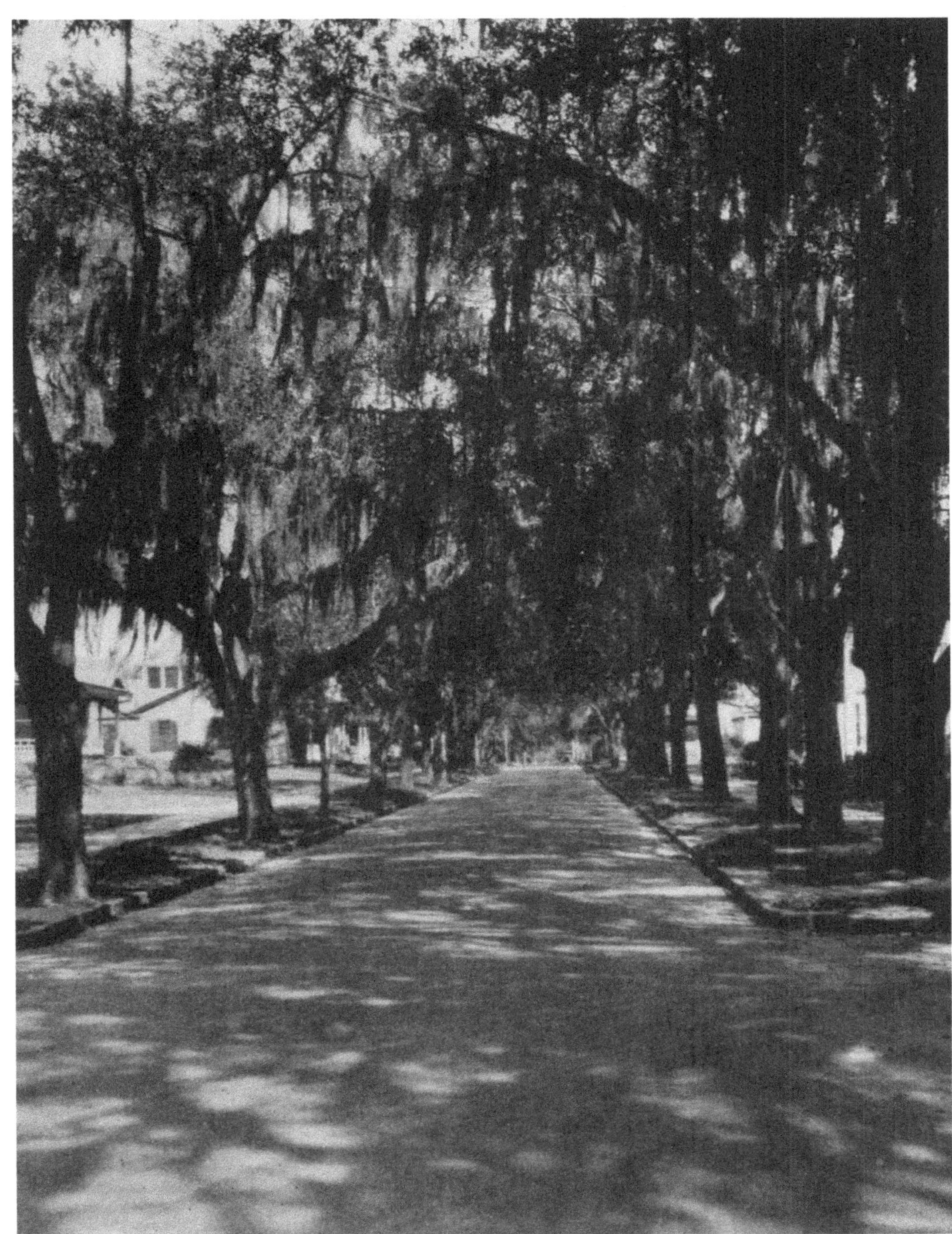

Calhoun Street was nicknamed "Gold Dust Street" for its wealthy residents and grand homes built by governors, planters, and bankers. Threatened by a road-widening project in the 1940s, these old live oak trees were saved by local citizens. The Calhoun Street Historic District is now listed on the National Register.

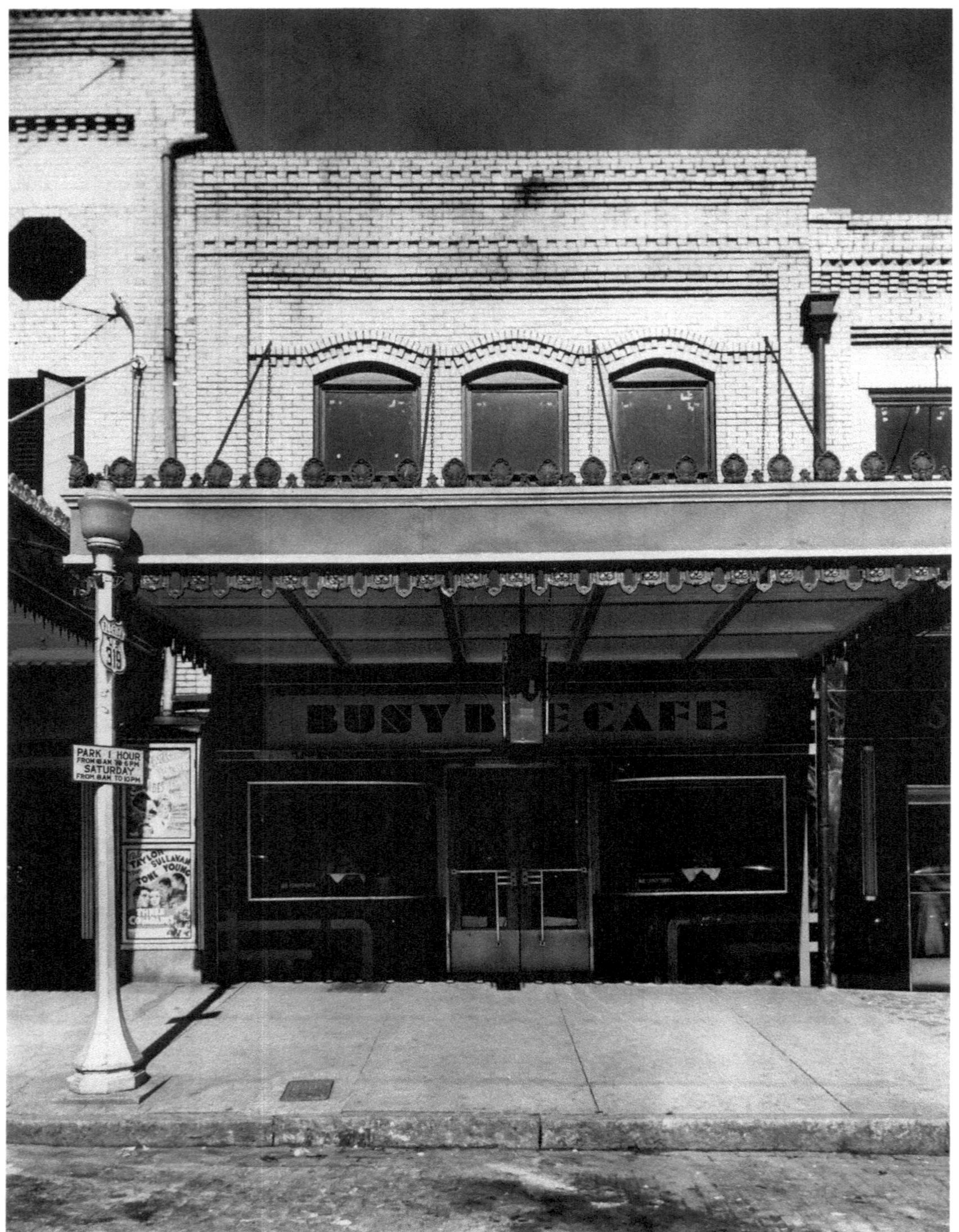

A popular restaurant on West Monroe, the Busy Bee Cafe served politicians and the public from 1925 to the 1950s. At one time associated with John Camechis and the Venetia Hotel, the menu included locally favorite fish—pompano, Spanish mackerel, mullet, and snapper. Diners could order oysters fried, raw, broiled, or in a stew.

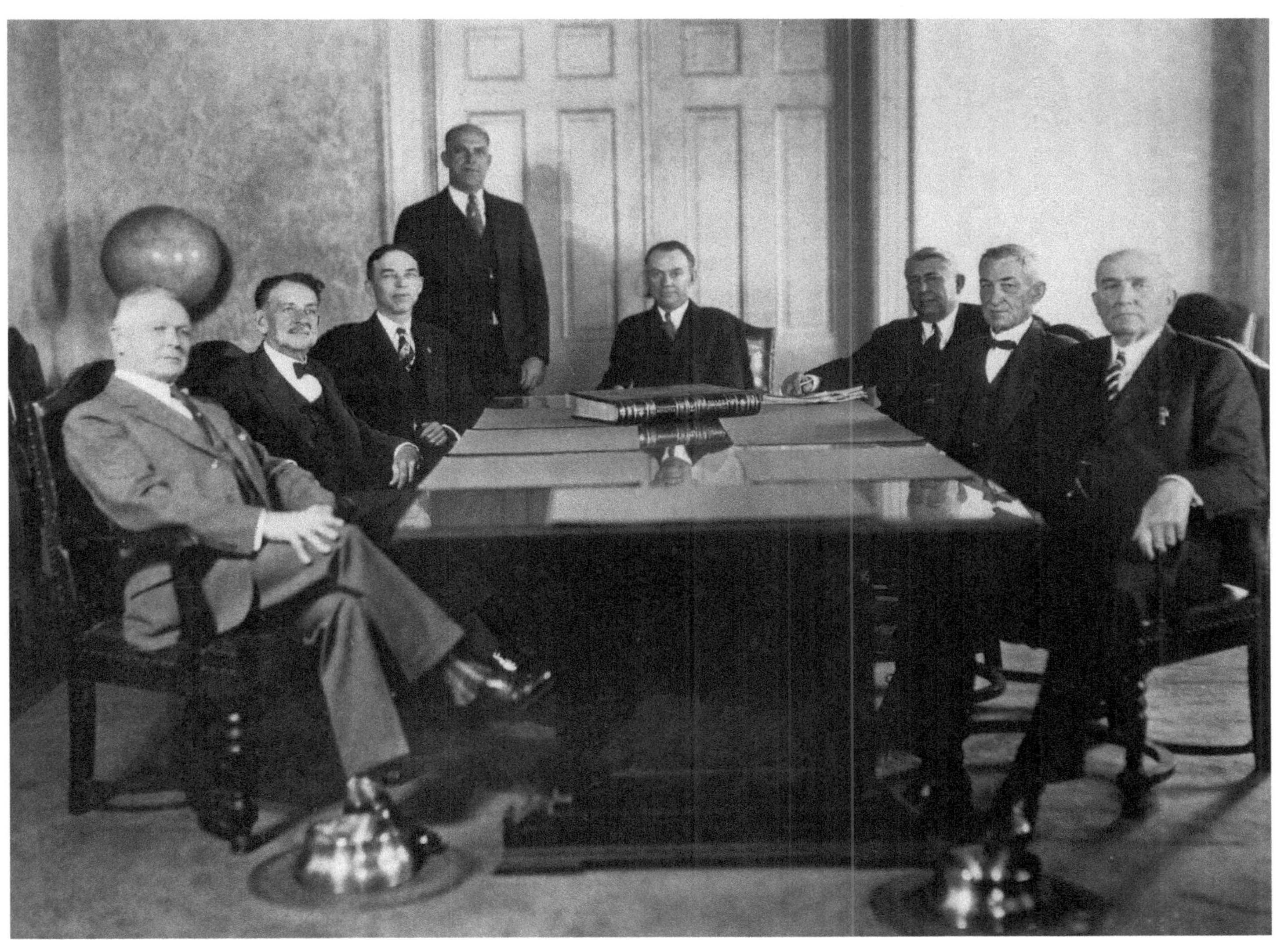

Florida's 25th governor, Doyle E. Carlton, and members of his cabinet sit for the photographer in a meeting room at the state capitol. During Carlton's administration, 1929 to 1933, Florida faced four disasters: collapse of the state's land boom, a violent hurricane, Mediterranean fruitfly infestation, and the national Depression.

The Elberta Crate and Box Company Mill in Tallahassee was a large employer in 1933. Another group of products from the vast timber forests around Tallahassee was the crates and pallets produced at this mill from 1922 to 1977. During World War II the labor force at the mill included prisoners of war.

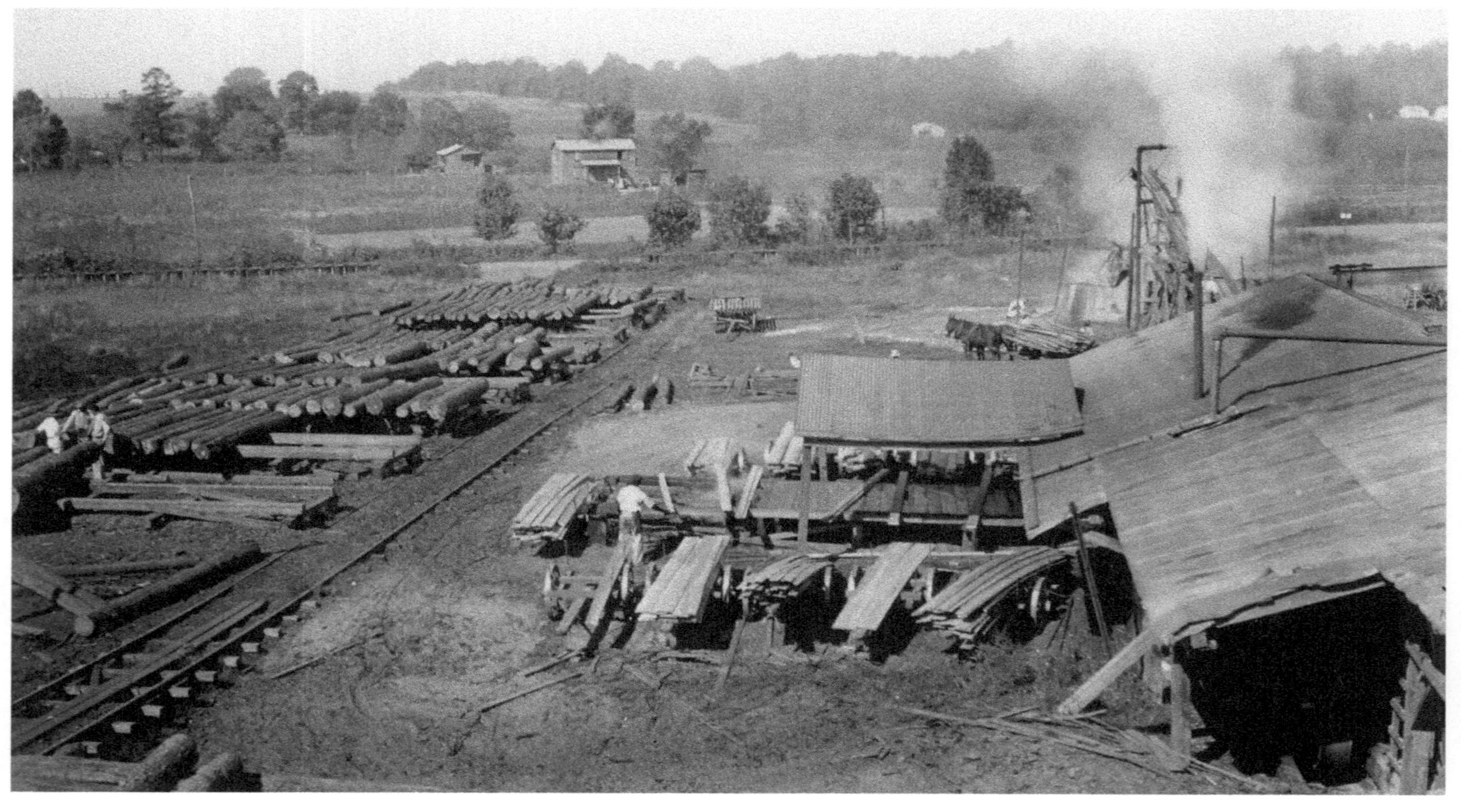

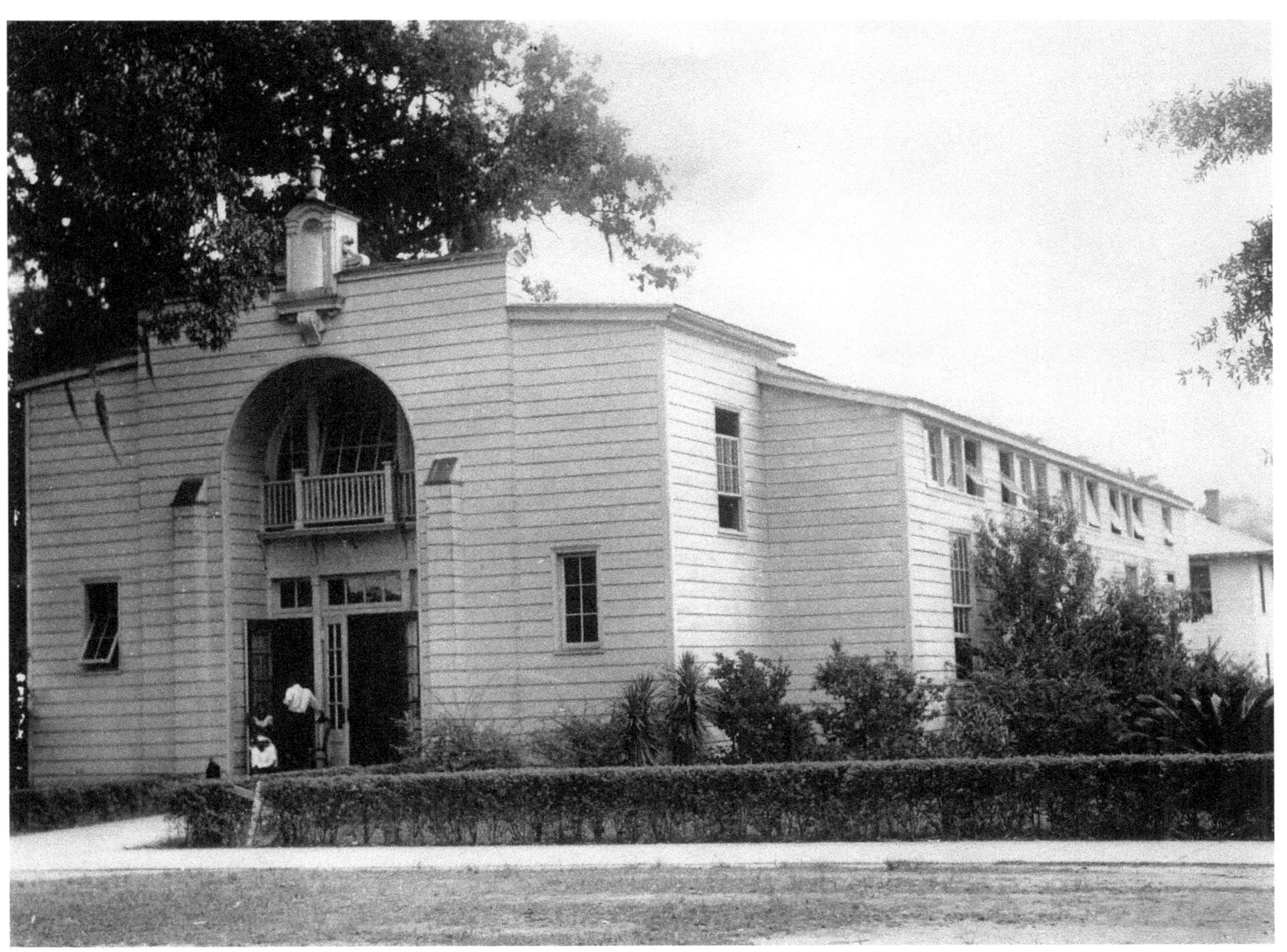

This gymnasium building at Florida Agricultural and Mechanical College for Negroes was a project of the Federal Emergency Relief Administration, a New Deal program. Founded in 1887, this historically black school became Florida Agricultural and Mechanical University in 1953.

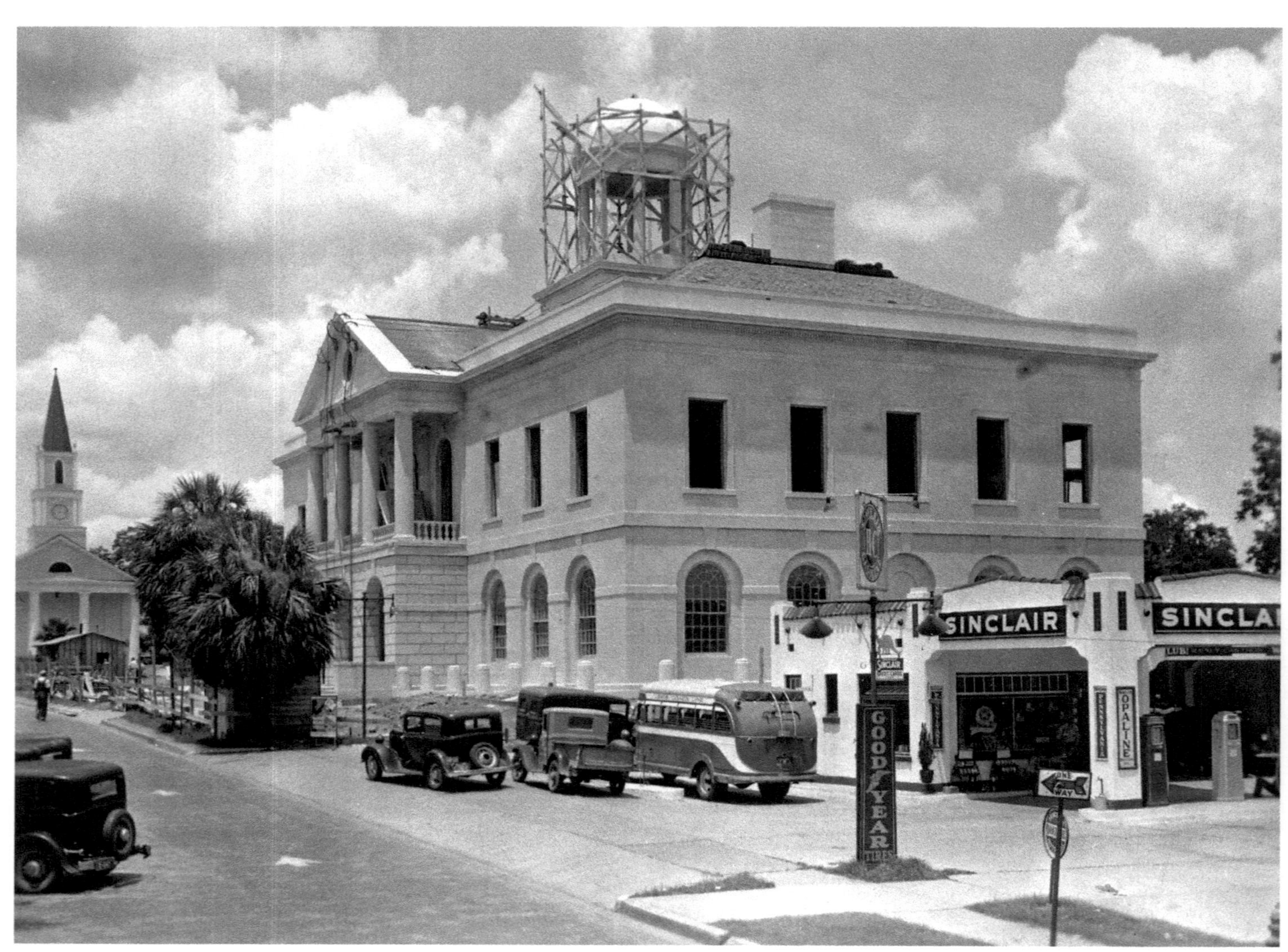

Beers Construction Company built the U.S. Post Office and Federal Courthouse at a cost of $300,000. A Works Progress Administration project, it opened January 14, 1937, on Park Avenue at the old Leon Hotel site. Edward Buk Ulreich, a Hungarian-born artist, painted the murals in the lobby depicting the history of Florida.

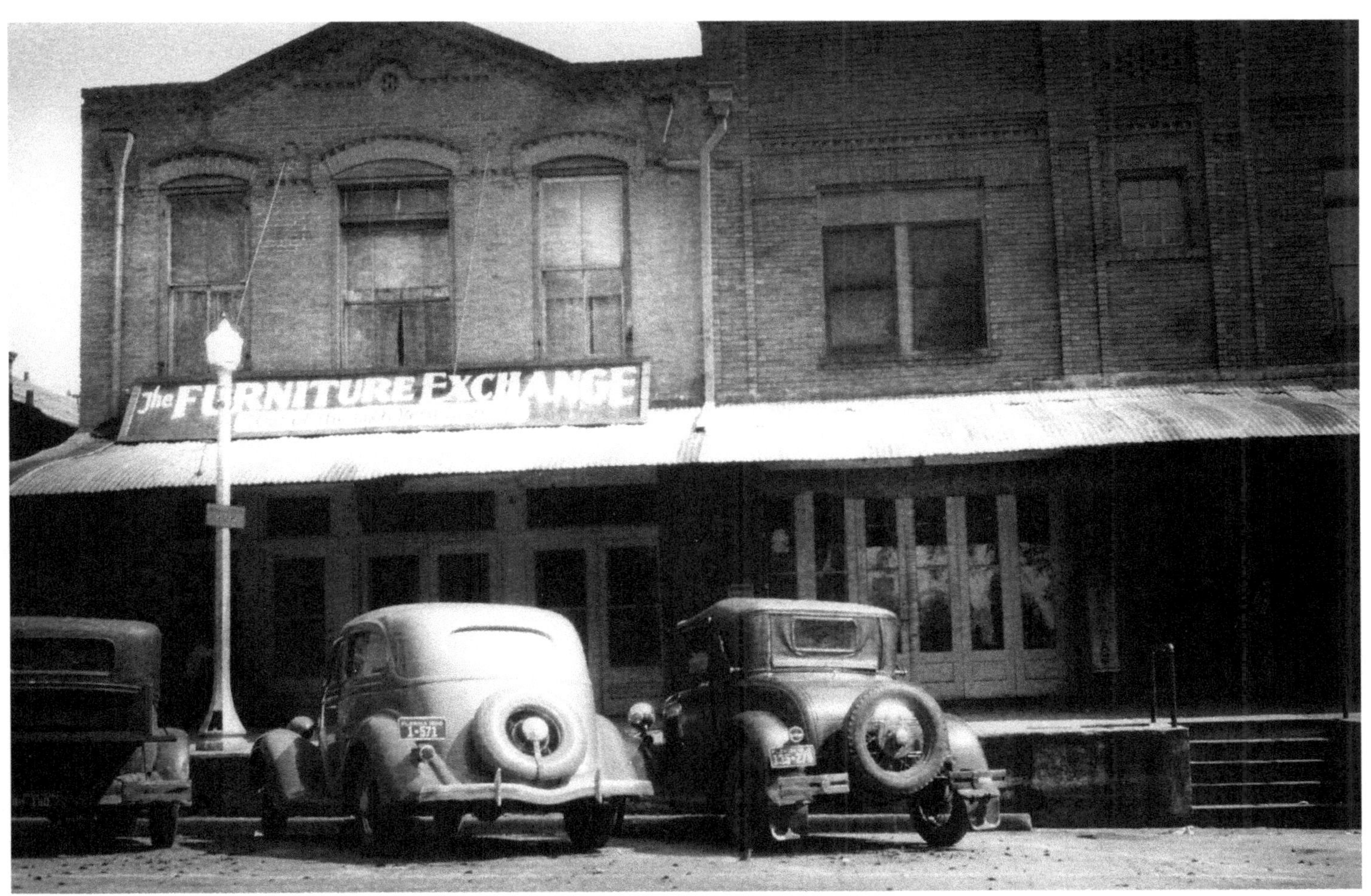

The national crime wave of the 1930s struck Tallahassee on January 29, 1934, when Sheriff Frank Stoutamire, tipped off about a bank robbery, pursued two suspects in a sedan onto Adams Street. Racing past the Furniture Exchange, officer Barney Gatlin shot out the tire of the fleeing car. One of the suspects was wounded during the arrest.

This typical 1930s grocery store, owned by John L. Jordan, at right, was at 519 Gaines Street just a few blocks from the train station. Once a mixed residential neighborhood, the city voted in 1925 to allow businesses to locate near the train depot without the consent of area residents.

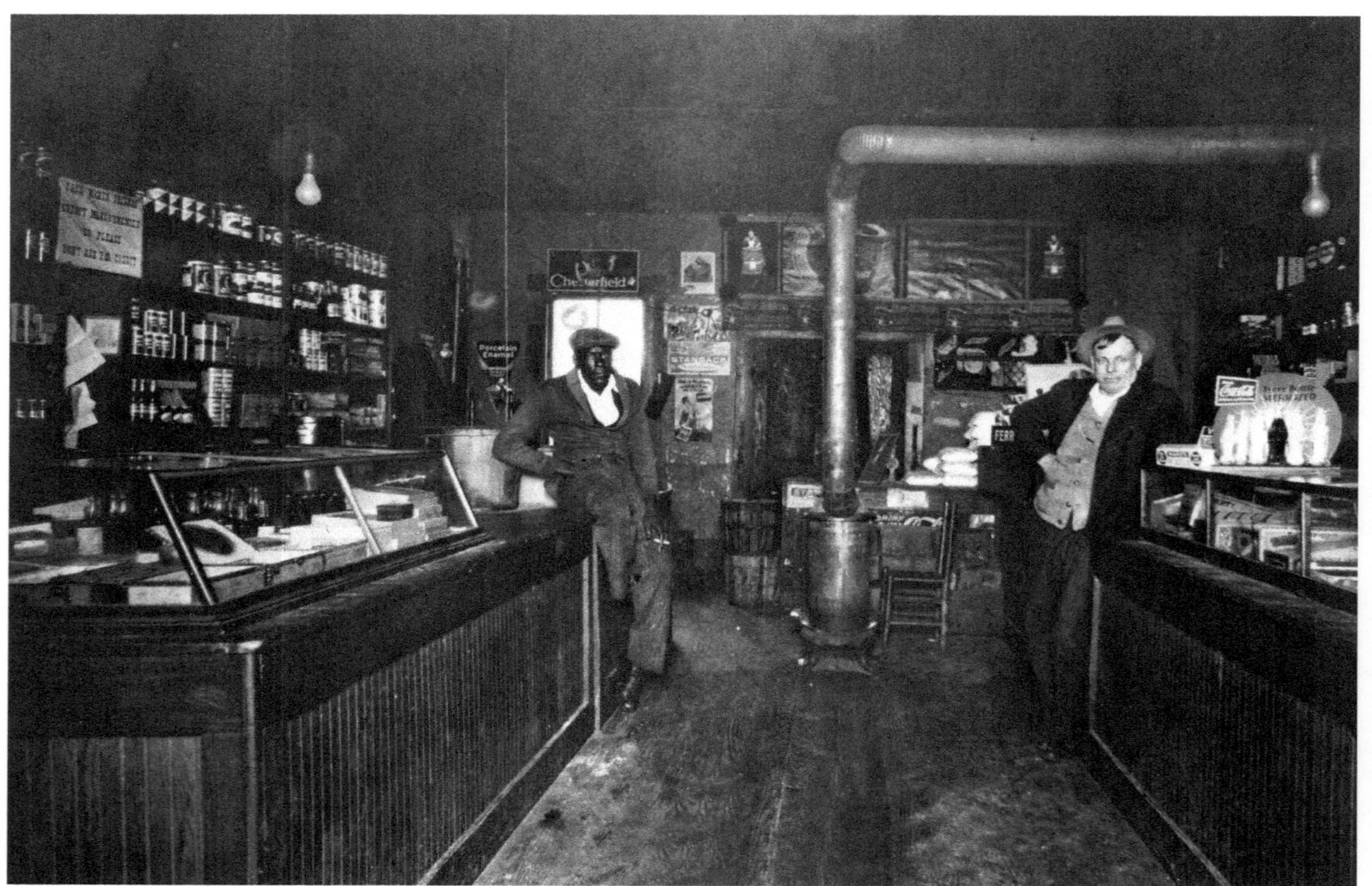

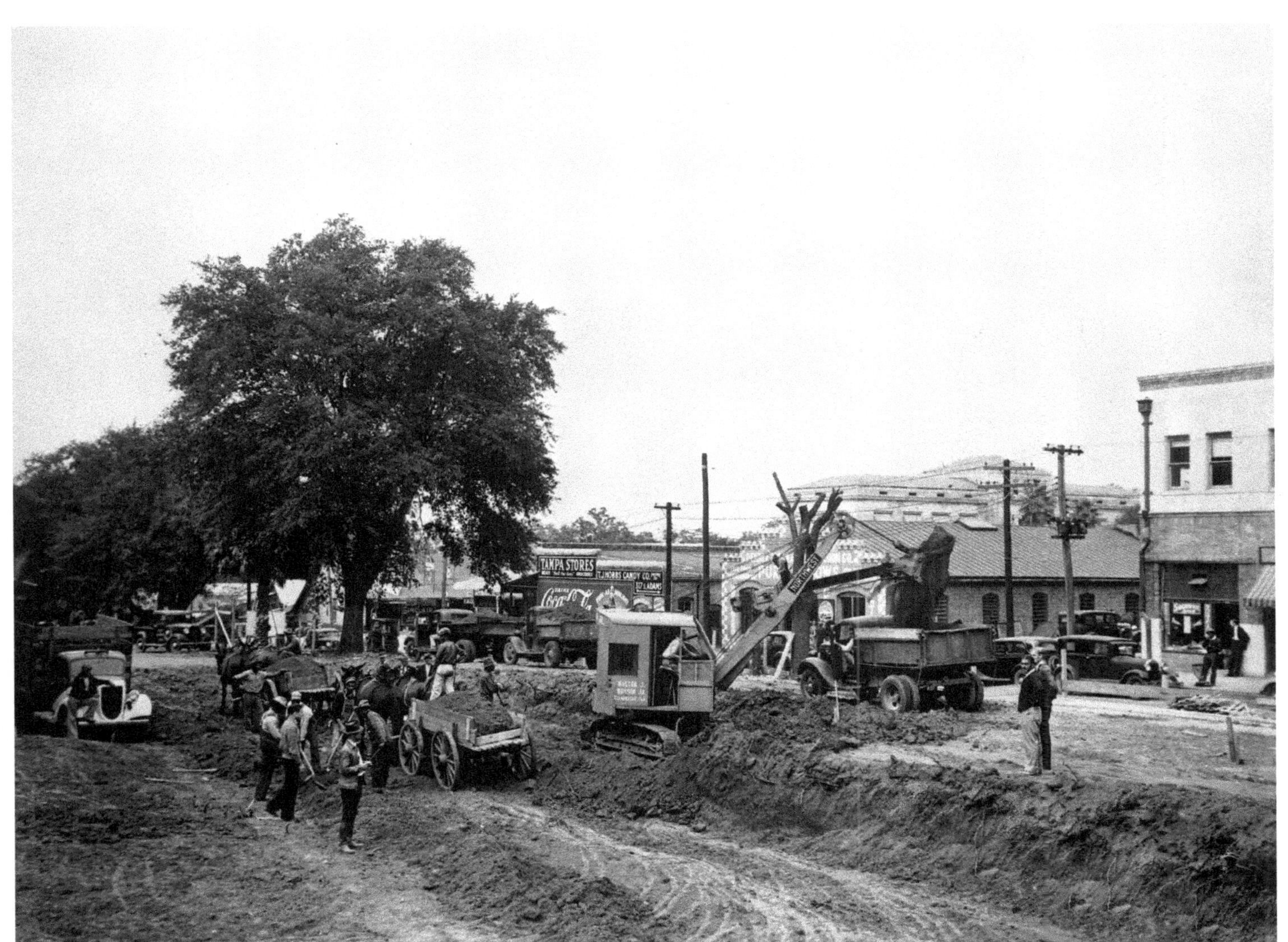

Architect M. Leo Elliot designed, and the Beers Construction Company built, two new wings to the state capitol. Construction started in 1936 on the north chamber, for the House of Representatives, and was finished the next year. The south wing, for the Senate, was delayed by World War II and not completed until 1947.

The Tallahassee Flyer, a streamlined motor coach owned by the Seaboard Air Line Railway, stops on its inaugural run from Jacksonville. Greeting it are Governor David Sholtz, several justices of the Supreme Court, and the state railroad commissioner. Mrs. Sholtz, with the flowers, christened the train with a bottle of wine.

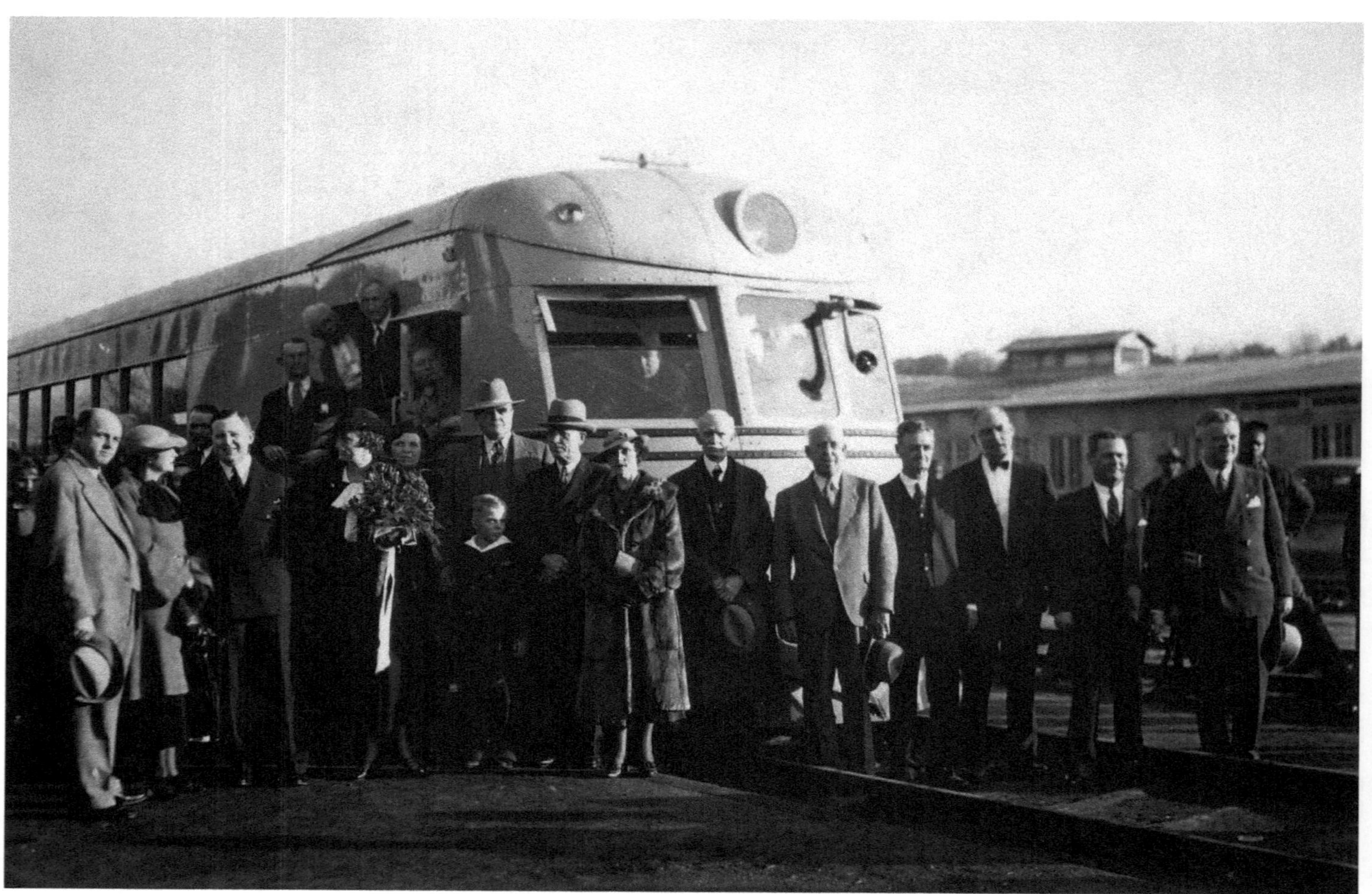

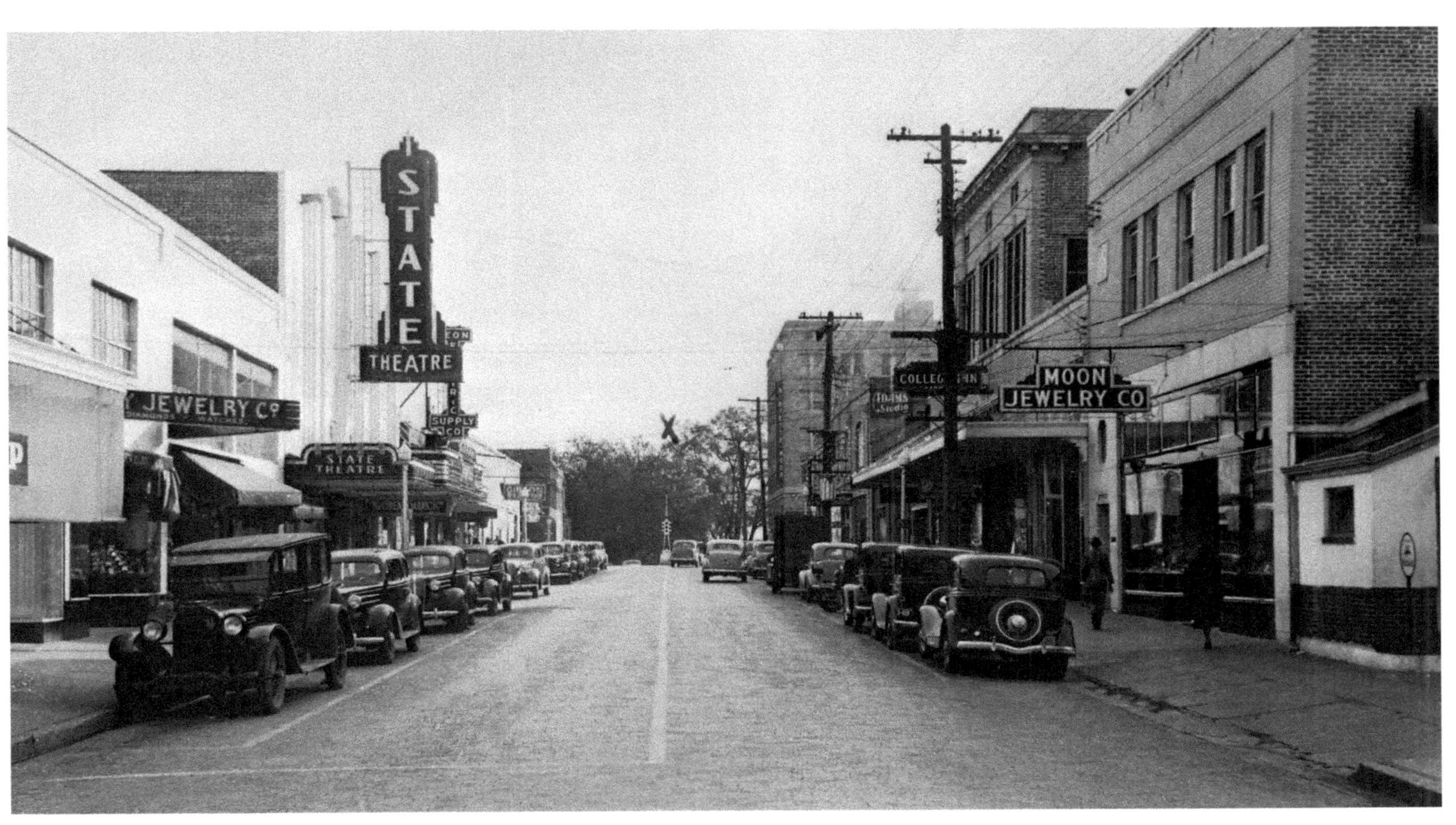

A new and larger State Theatre opened on College Avenue less than a year after the original burned in 1933. The art deco theater included a marquee that reached across the entire front of the building, and a two-story-tall vertical sign. It closed in 1971 and was demolished in 1988.

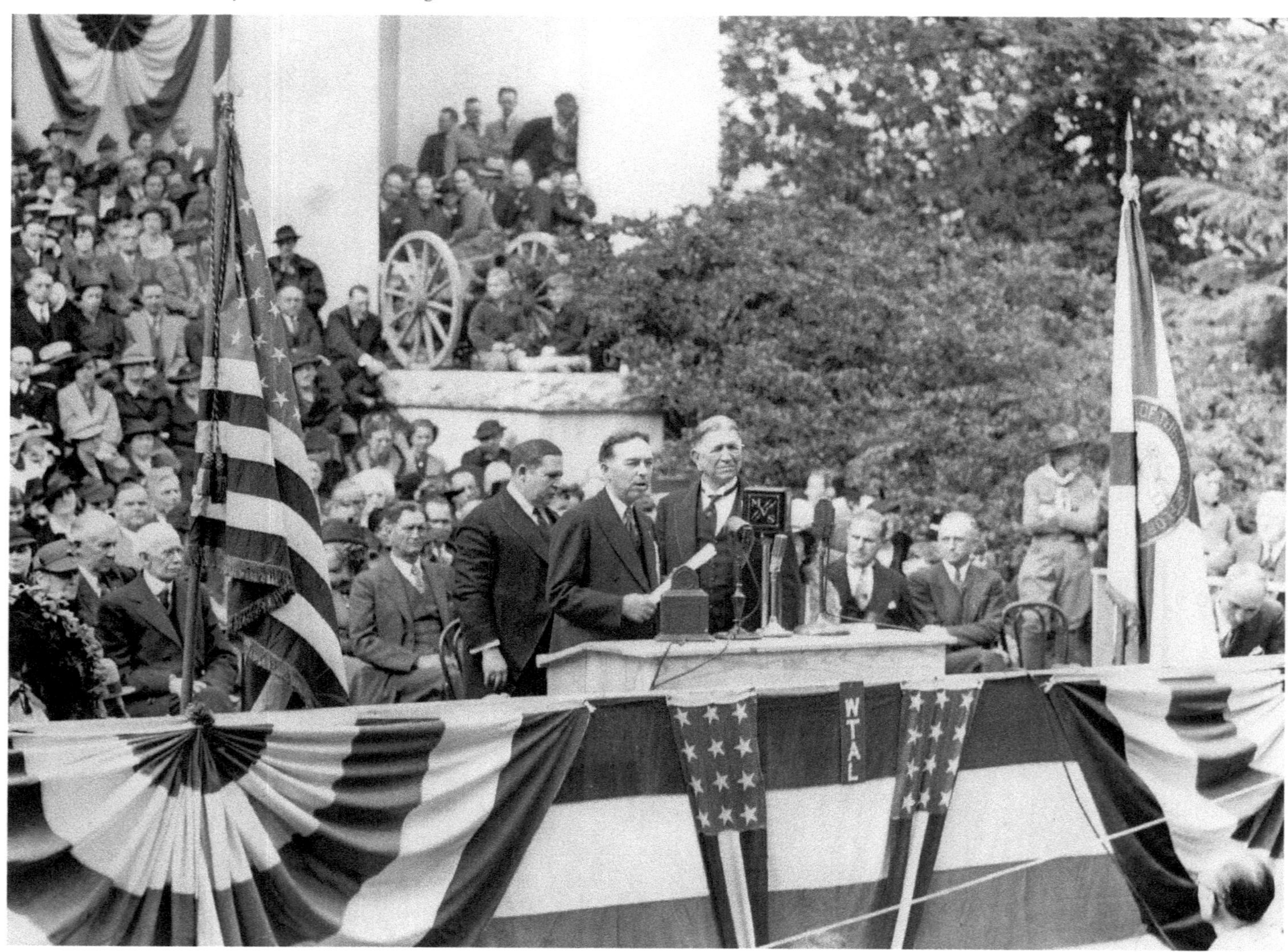

The inauguration of Governor Frederick Preston Cone takes place on the steps of the Capitol on January 5, 1937. On the podium is Secretary of State Robert A. Gray holding a document, Governor Cone, and behind them former governor Dave Sholtz. Chief Justice James B. Whitfield, seated directly behind the U.S. flag, administered the oath.

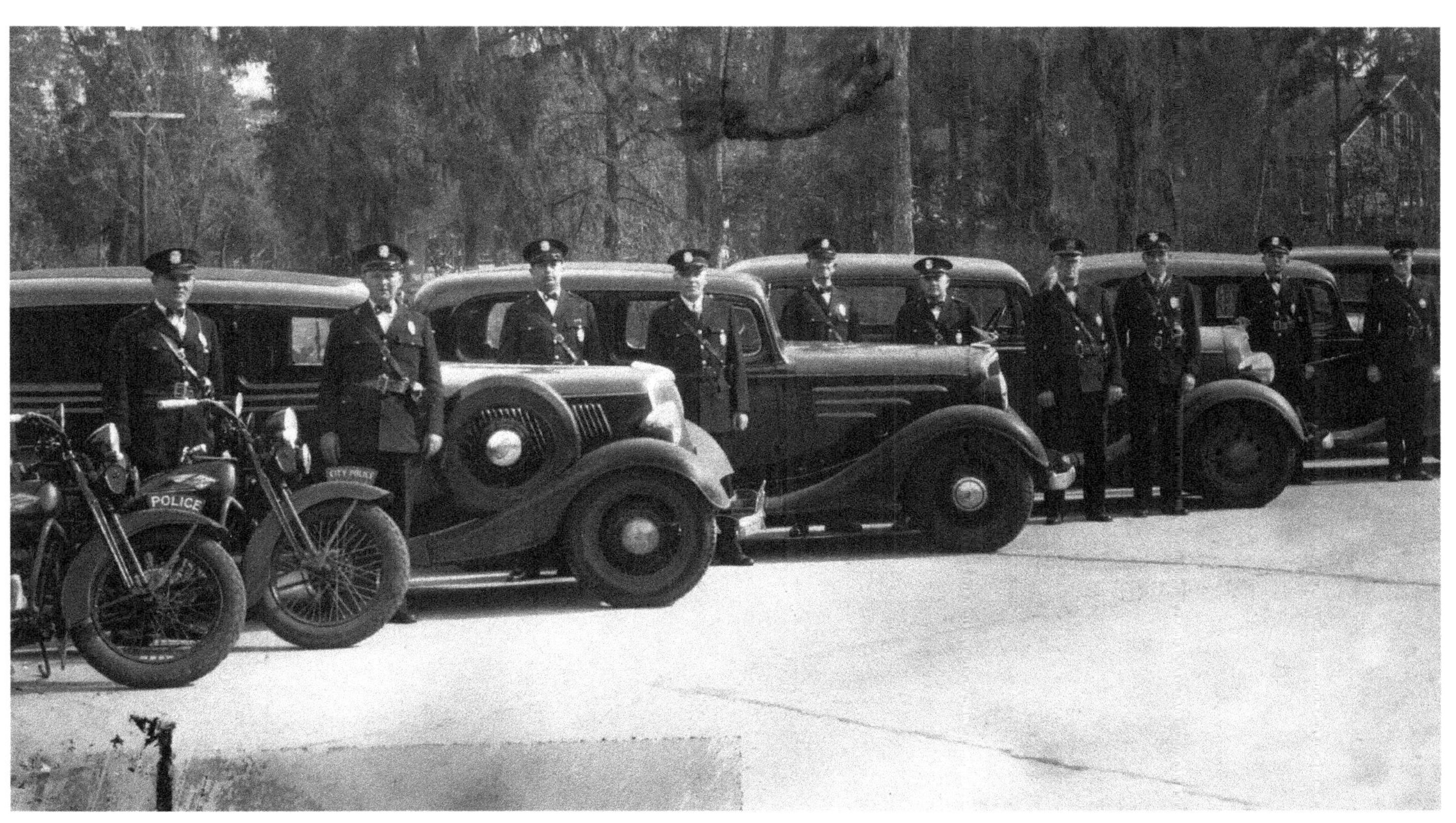

Proud members of the Tallahassee Police Department stand beside their vehicles around 1937. Established in 1841, it is the oldest police department in the South, third oldest police department in the nation, and the third-longest accredited law enforcement agency in the United States.

Present on October 10, 1938, at the first scheduled Eastern Airlines flight from Tallahassee, are Mayor J. R. Jinks, second from left, and president of Eastern Airlines, Captain Eddie Rickenbacker, fourth from left. Eastern Airlines offered four daily flights from Tallahassee to Memphis, Tennessee, Birmingham, and Montgomery, Alabama.

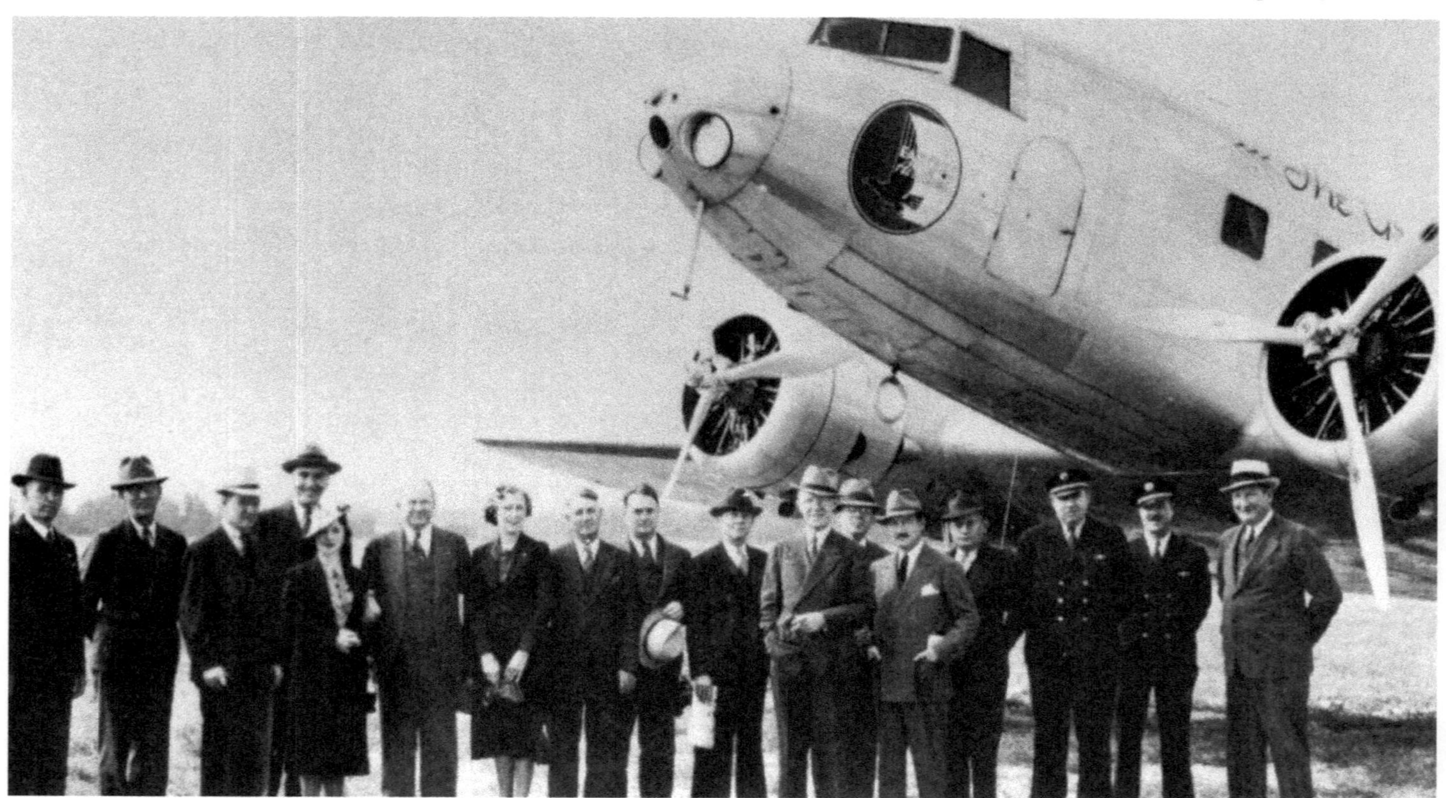

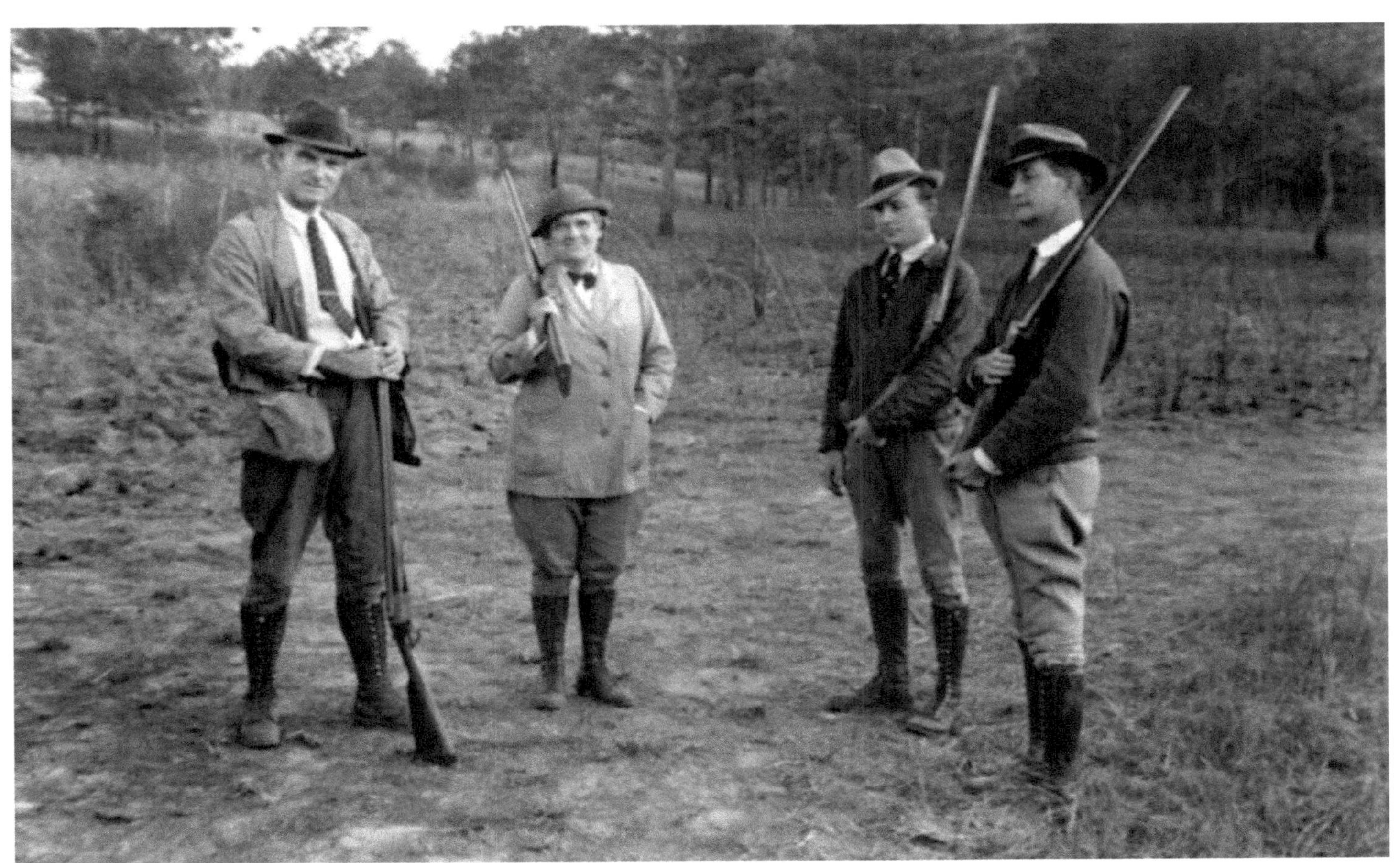

Genevieve Beadel and party are ready for a dove shoot at Tall Timbers Plantation in January 1938. A 1931 report of research on the effects of fire on wildlife at Tall Timbers established that annual controlled fires were critical for clearing the underbrush and maintaining the quail population.

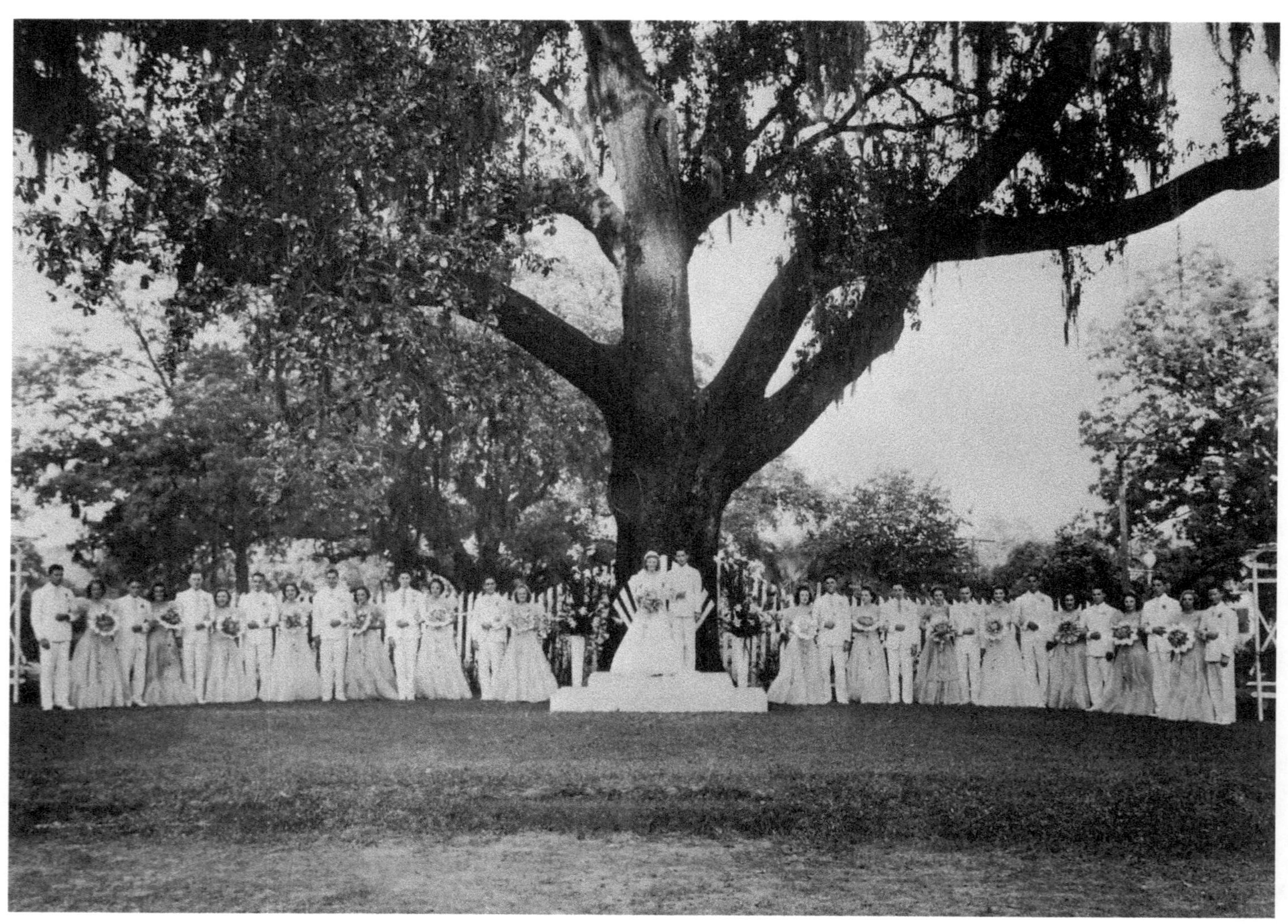

The 1939 May Day Queen and King pose with their court under the majestic May Oak in Lewis Park. One of the oldest festivals in the South, more than 130 May Queens were crowned in this annual pageant, the last one in 1974. For years, the May Queen and her court changed into their costumes at the Knott House. The May Oak collapsed in August 1986.

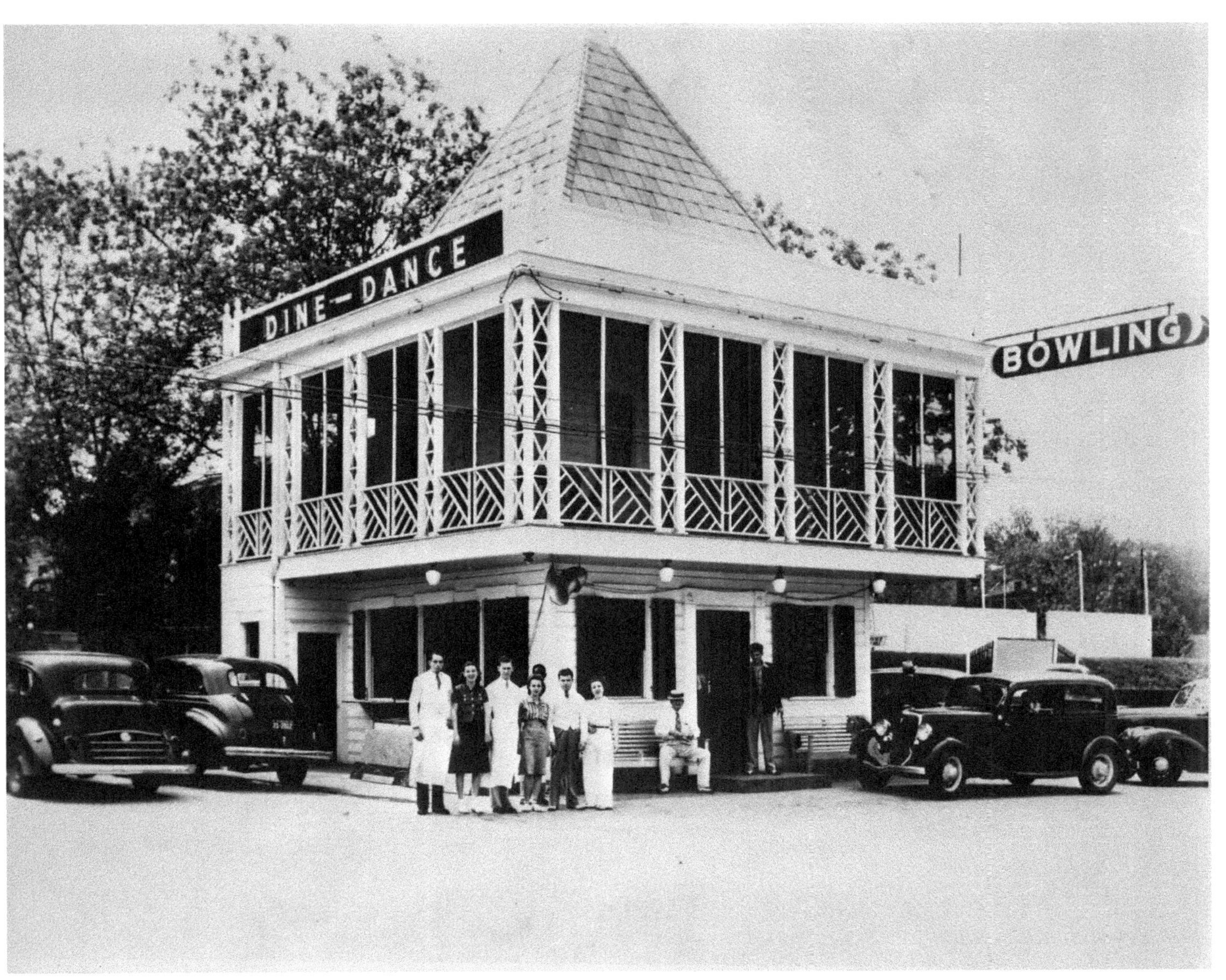

Popular in the 1930s, the Green Derby nightclub and restaurant operated until the 1950s, later becoming the Country Flower Shop. It literally sits on the other side of the tracks, just south of the Monroe Street railroad overpass. In 2006 a church purchased the property and started remodeling it as an office and coffeehouse.

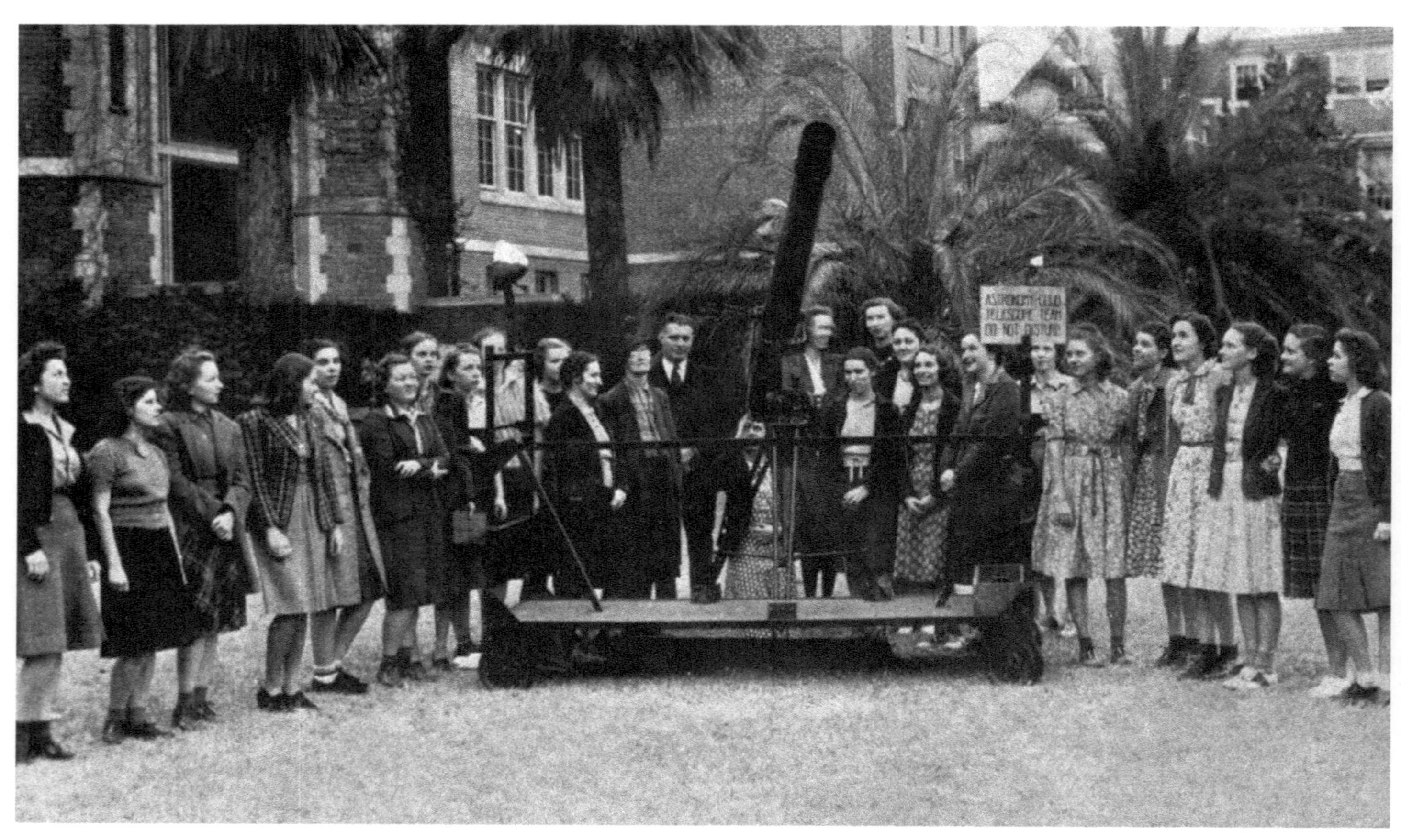

Members of Florida State College for Women Astronomy Club assemble for a portrait around 1940. With a number of excellent professors on the science and math faculties, the science department at F.S.C.W. boasted four science laboratories: biology, chemistry, physics, and psychology.

A Capital Complex
(1941–1970)

Florida historians quip that "no one lived here before air conditioning," referring to statistics like Tallahassee's 350 percent population growth from 1940 to 1970. World War II was another factor, adding military training bases throughout Florida. Dale Mabry Air Field aided Tallahassee's growth by constructing new facilities that provided jobs. The buildings were later turned over to the city. The city supported the training base with dances, parties, and entertainment. Many young G.I.'s married local girls and others later returned

The city faced profound social changes as the civil rights movement confronted Tallahassee's segregation laws. Throughout the 1950s and 1960s state and local officials fought against the U.S. Supreme Court's desegregation rulings. Led by C. K. Steele, the Tallahassee bus boycotts successfully ended segregation on the city's buses. Later, Florida A&M University students led peaceful boycotts and picketing of downtown Tallahassee stores. By 1970, the county's all-black schools were closed and the school system was integrated.

Downtown businesses continued to prosper and new business districts opened alongside expanding residential areas. Residents also enjoyed the new and enhanced parks of Lake Ella, Myers Park, and McClay Gardens State Park. Although restaurants like the Silver Slipper had found ways around the city's liquor laws, Tallahassee, officially "dry" since 1904, changed its local ordinance and became "wet" in 1967.

While the two schools of higher learning grew academically, the athletic programs at both schools achieved national attention. Florida A&M College for Negroes became Florida Agricultural and Mechanical University, home to the world famous "Marching100" band and legendary football coach Jake Gaither. Florida State College for Women became co-ed, becoming Florida State University in 1947 and Coach Bill "Pete" Peterson built the Seminole football program, giving it national recognition.

State government had a great impact on Tallahassee, enlarging state facilities and payroll. In 1949 a new Supreme Court building was completed and in 1955 the first governor's mansion was replaced with a new one, modeled after Andrew Jackson's home in Nashville, the Hermitage. The Carlton, Collins, and Mayo office buildings were part of major state construction projects. After 120 years of remodeling and additions to the old capitol, construction began on a new capitol building in 1970.

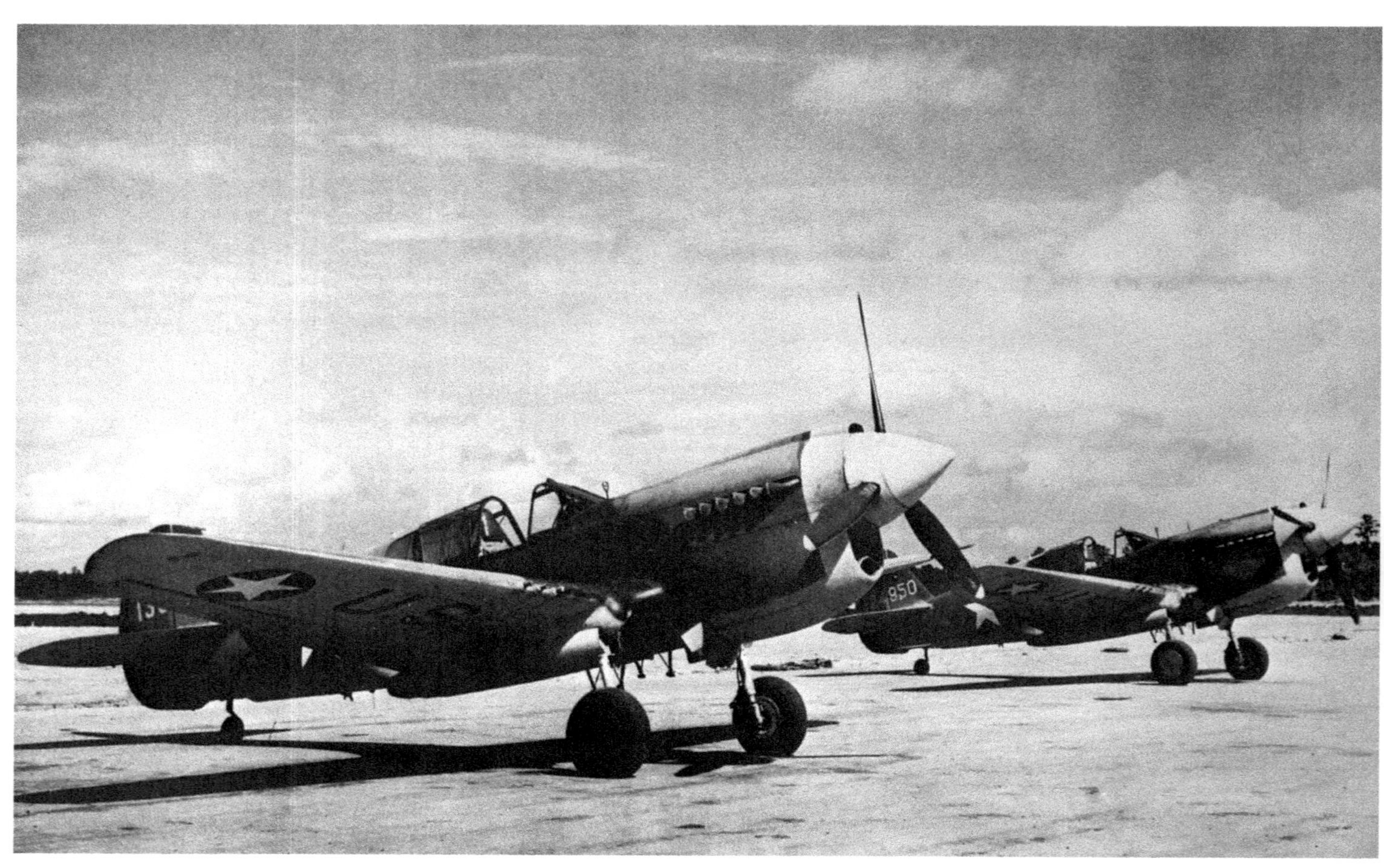

The Army Air Corps leased Dale Mabry Field from the city in 1941 for a training base. Barracks, repair shops, warehouse, and a hospital were added. More than seven thousand men trained at the base, including Filipino, British, Chinese, French, and Brazilian airmen. After the base closed in late 1945, the city retained all of the base facilities.

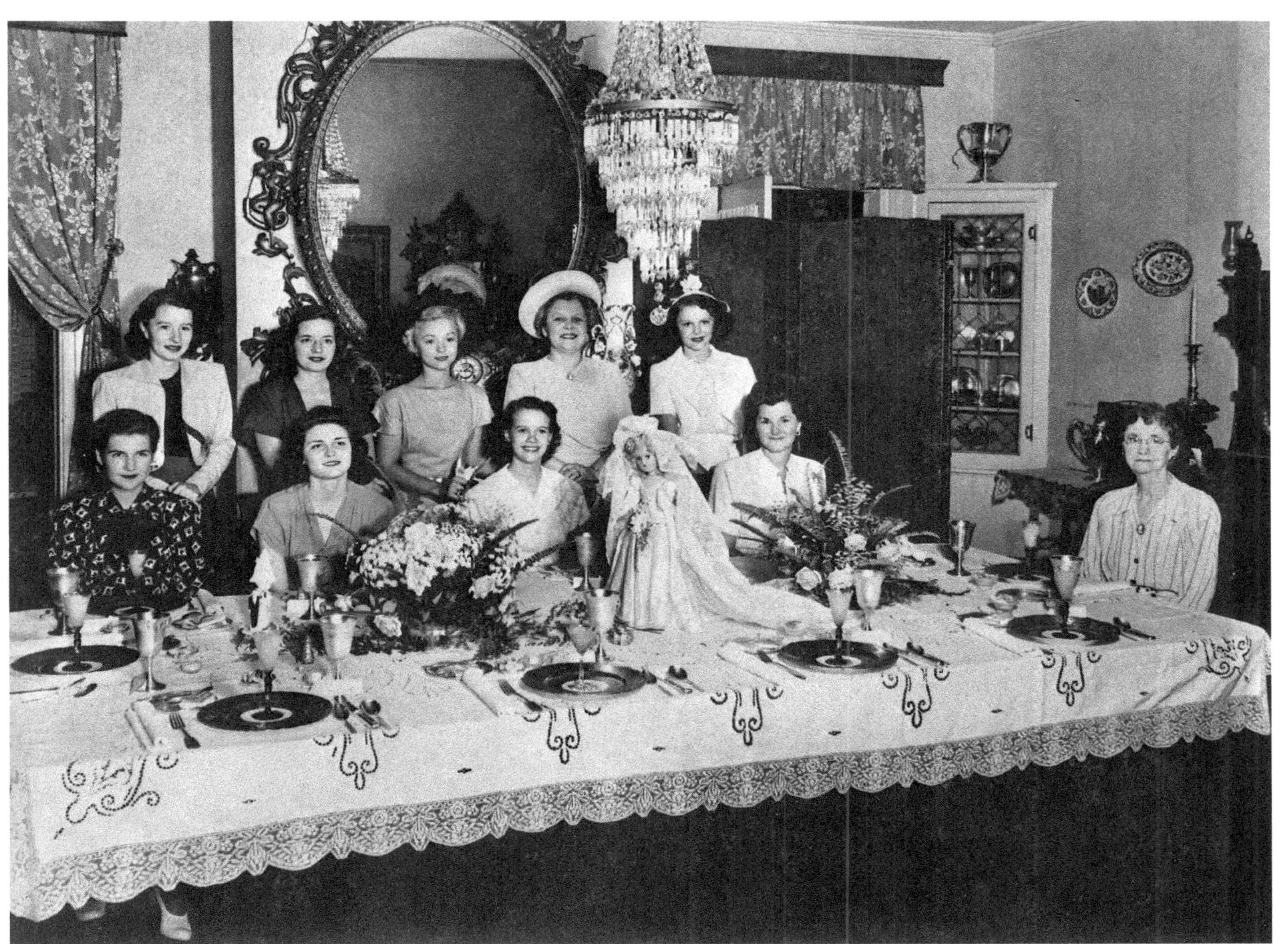

Luella Knott, sitting to the far right, hosts a bridal luncheon in her dining room in 1948. The dining room has changed very little—visitors to the Knott House museum can see the same table, chandelier, and mirrors, even the very china and tablecloth.

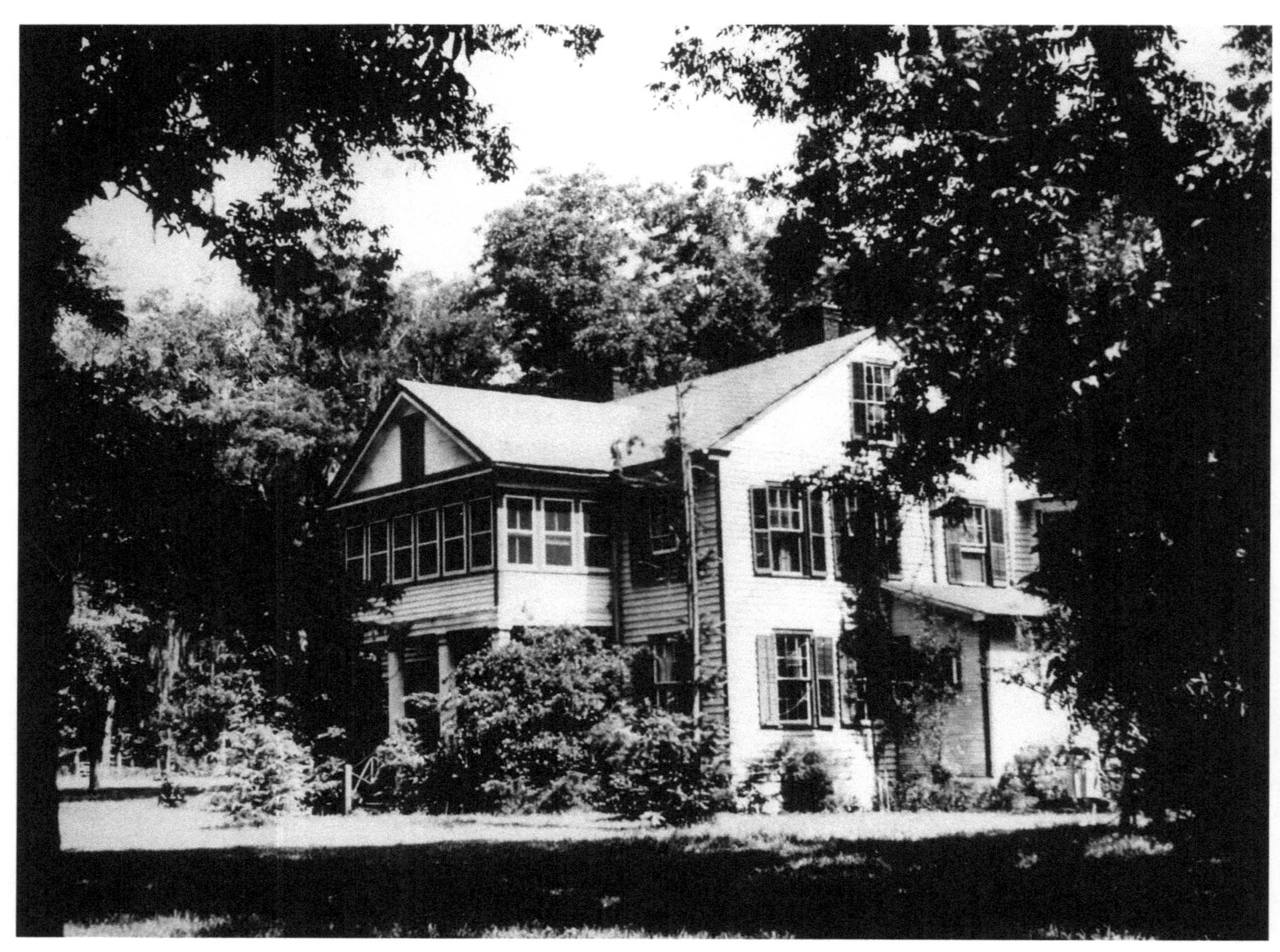

The Johnson-Butler-Caldwell House, home to Governor Millard Fillmore Caldwell, was built about 1850 by George C. Johnson, and purchased in 1867 by Doctor Robert Butler. Governor Caldwell bought it in the 1940s. Located on Old Bainbridge Road, it was moved to the Florida State University Law School Green in 1986.

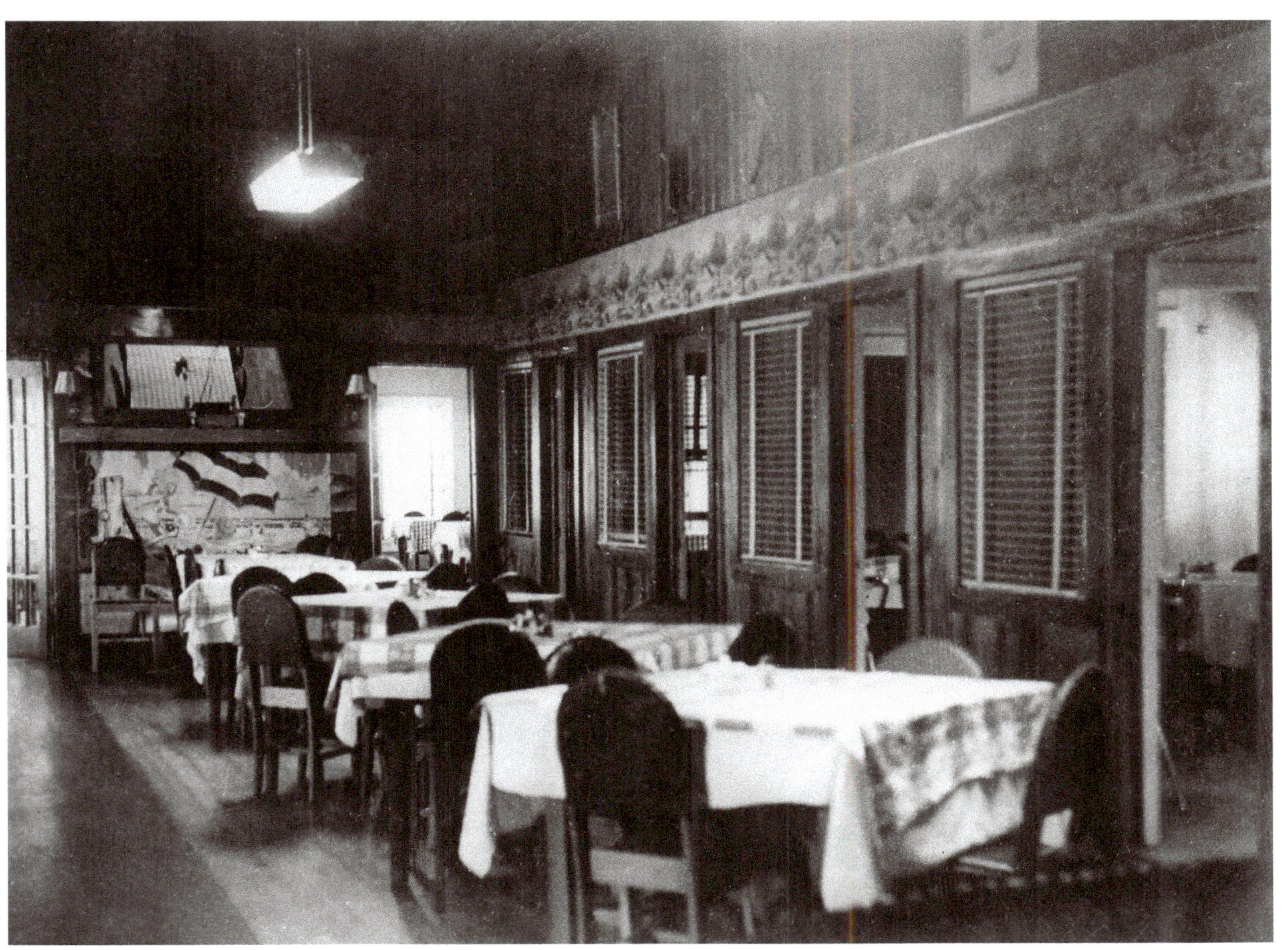

The Silver Slipper, a Tallahassee dining legend since 1947, was licensed only to sell beer and wine. Patrons desiring stronger drinks brought their own bottles in a brown paper bag into private dining rooms. Governors and legislators frequented the Slipper as well as four U.S. presidents, a former U.N. secretary general, and many movie stars.

Couples say goodnight in front of Bryan Hall at Florida State College for Women. The city provided chaperoned dances and parties with food and entertainment for the soldiers from Dale Mabry Air Field. The Victorettes, the Bombadiers, the Girls Defense Club, and other clubs were formed to provide dates and dance partners.

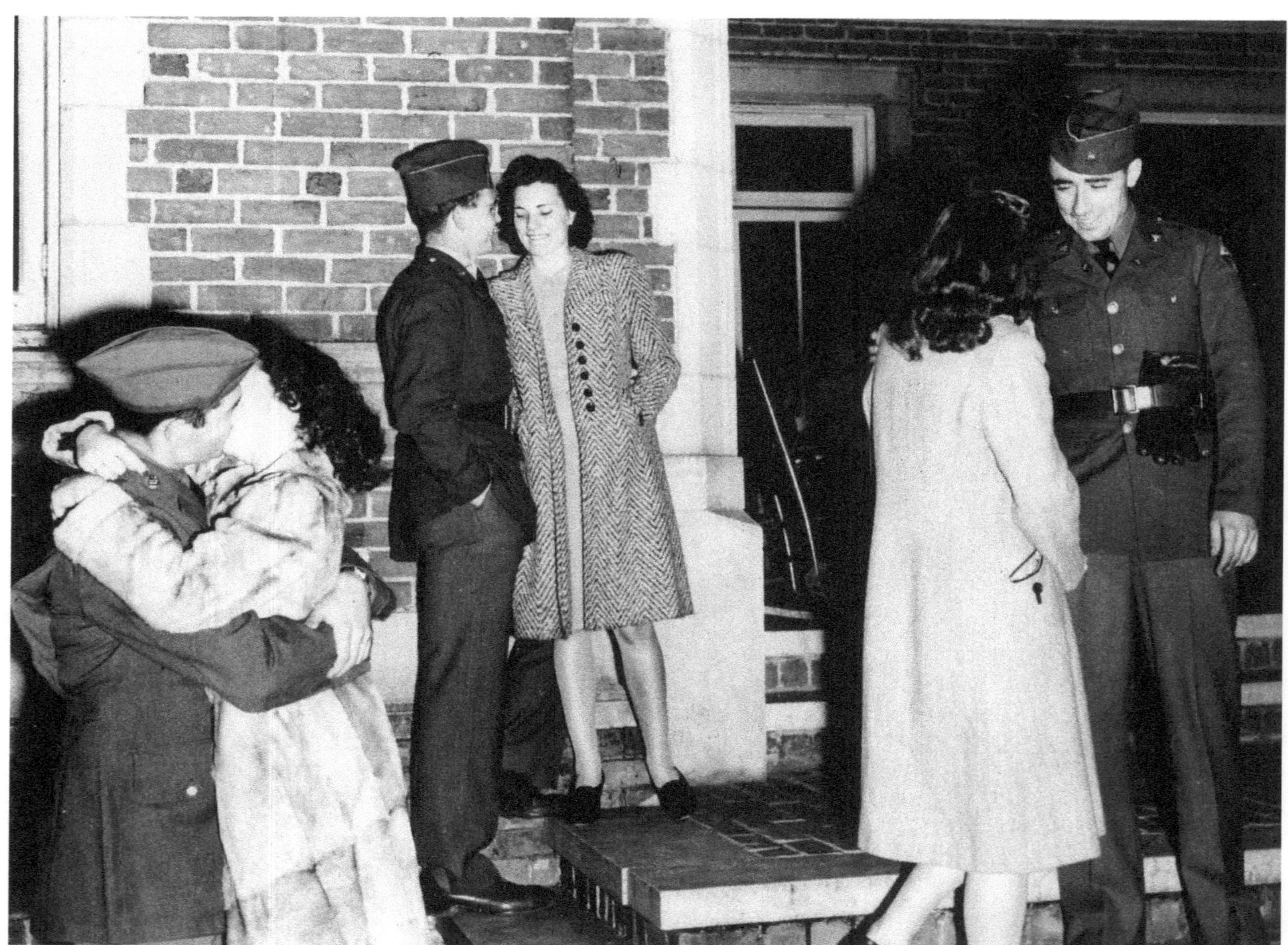

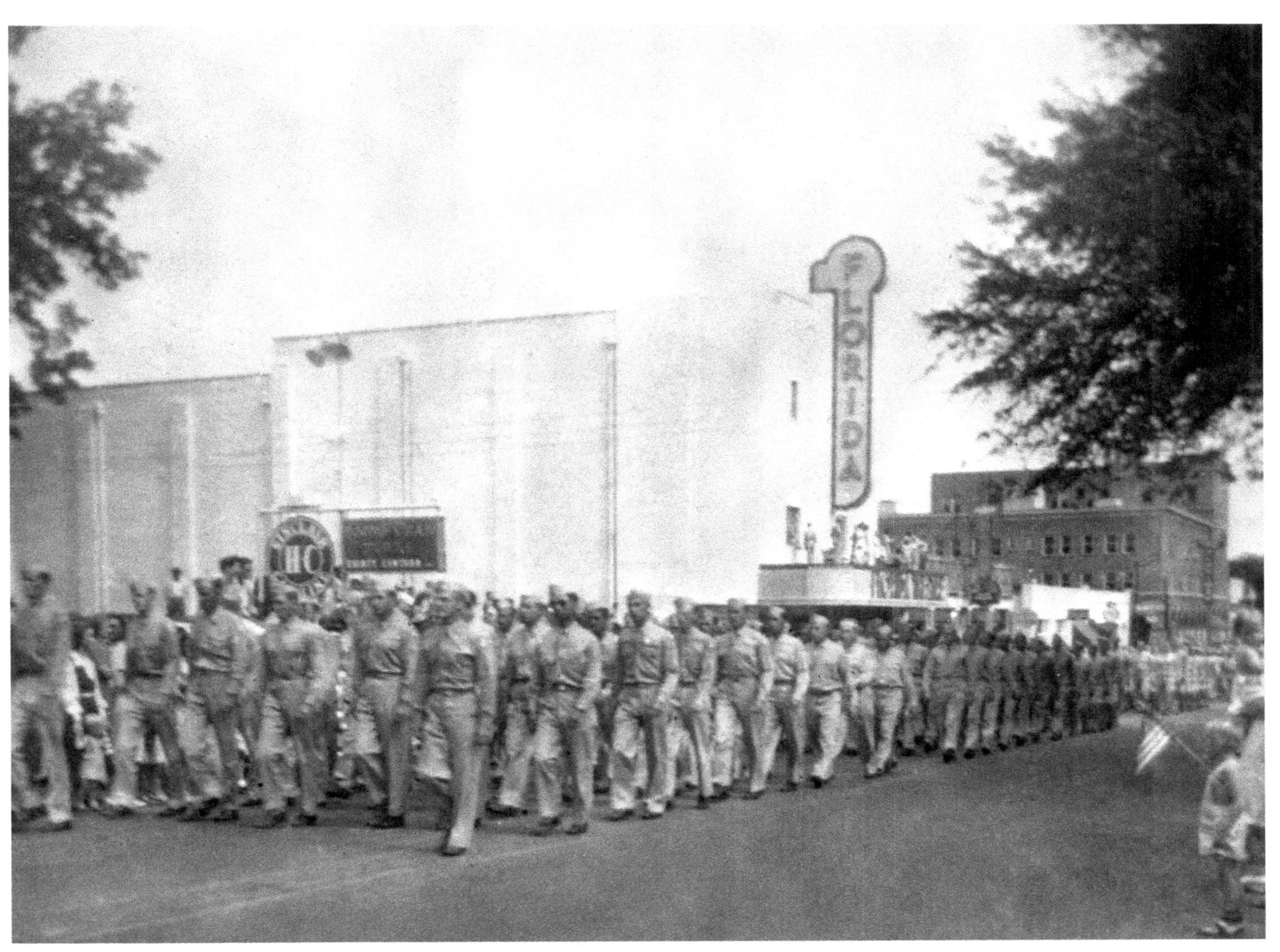

Servicemen from Dale Mabry Airfield march past the Florida Theater as Tallahassee celebrates victory over Japan, August 15, 1945. More than 250,000 Floridians served in the military. Because of its warm climate and vacant land, Florida became home to 170 military training bases, located throughout the state.

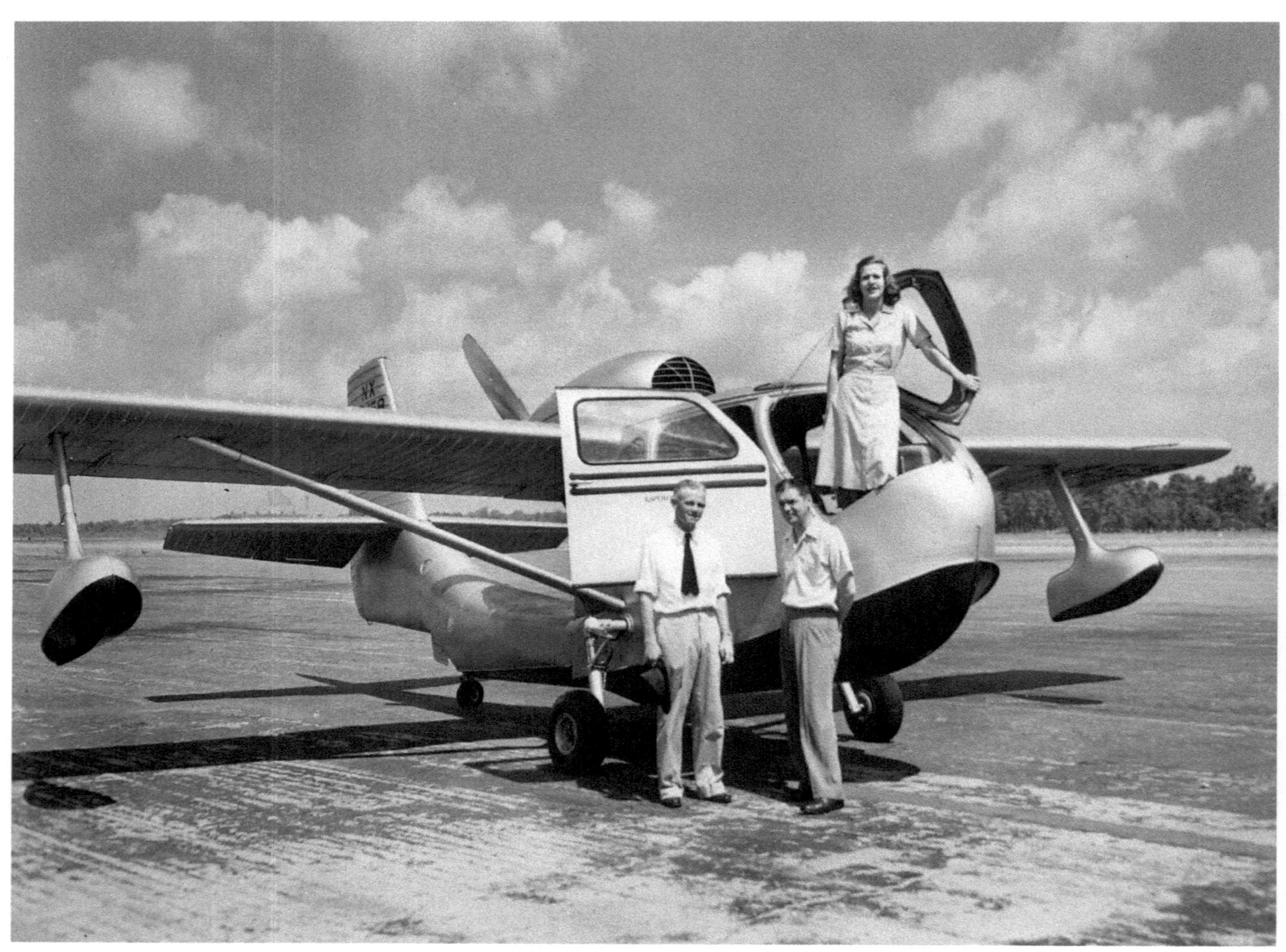

Ivan Munroe, "the father of aviation in Tallahassee," stands beside the door of an experimental seaplane at the city airport in 1946. Munroe, the airport manager, later provided flight training, aerial photography, and charter services. Surviving six crashes, he was quoted as saying, "In my day the men were made of steel and the planes were made of wood."

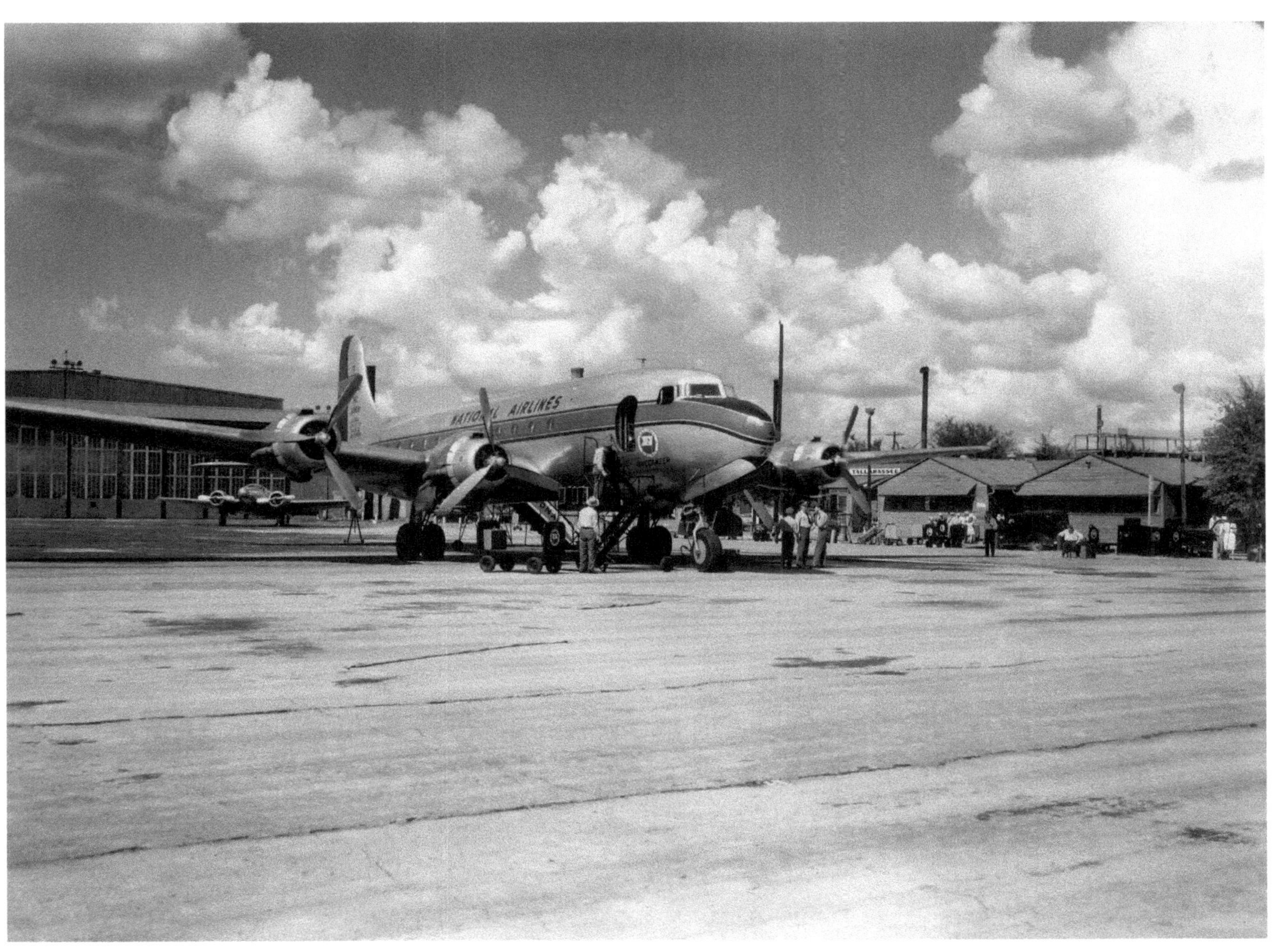

A National Airlines DC-6 is being serviced at the Tallahassee airport on September 1, 1947. With the departure of the Army air base, civilian air traffic reopened after the war. National Airlines provided service to Jacksonville, Pensacola, Mobile, and New Orleans. National's slogan was "the Buccaneer Route."

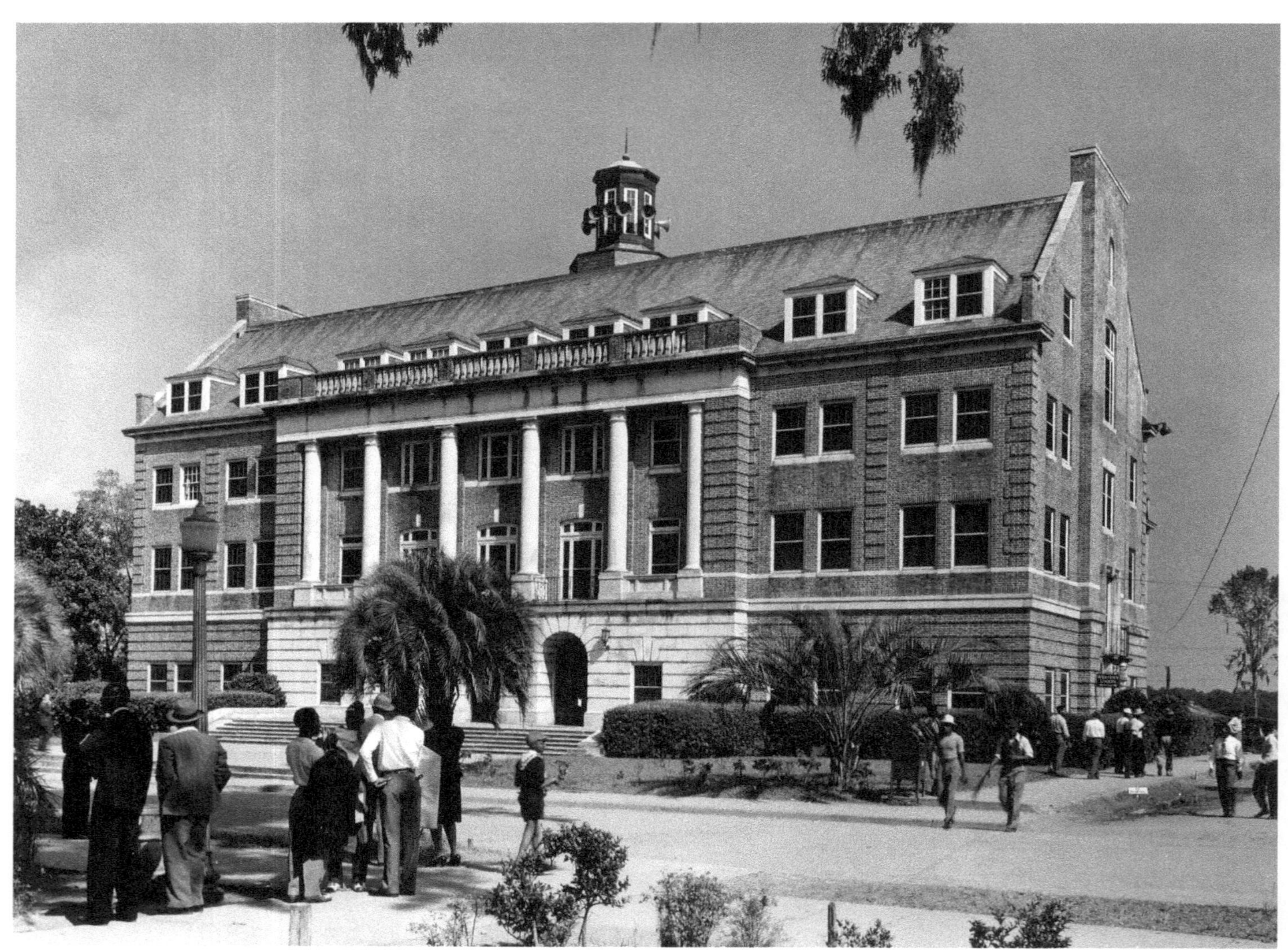

Lee Hall, the administration building at Florida A&M University, was named in honor of President John Robert Edward Lee, Sr. During his administration, from 1924 to 1944, President Lee expanded the physical plant, built a stronger faculty, and extended services. Florida A&M is home to the world-famous "Marching 100" band.

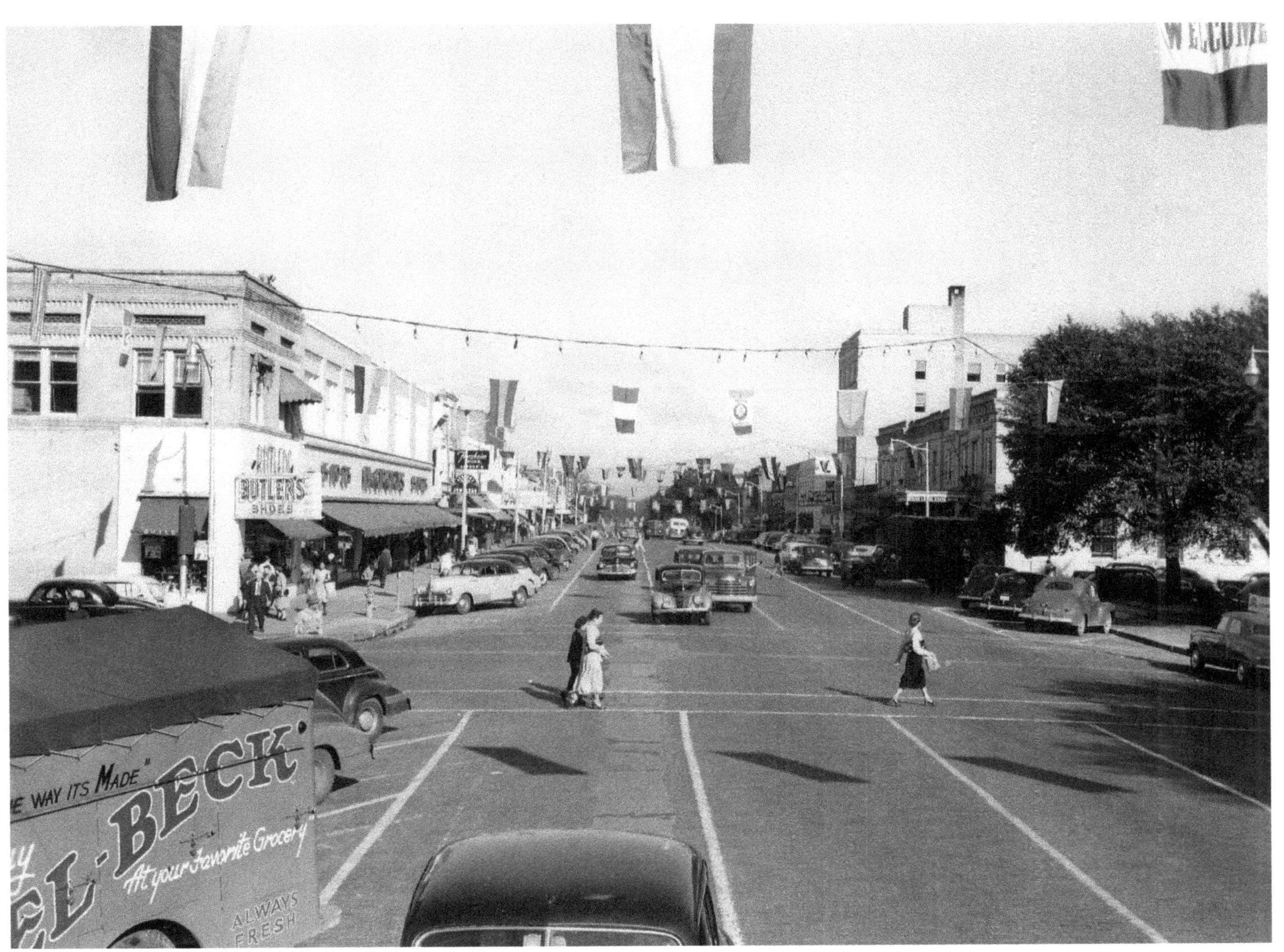

Tallahassee experienced a boom after World War II, the population growing almost 70 percent by 1950. In view here, facing north on Monroe Street, is the central business district. Butler's shoes is on the left, the 1928 Exchange Bank building is in back at right, and the trees on the right stand in front of the Leon County courthouse.

Florida governor Millard Caldwell greets General Jonathan Wainwright, May 30, 1947. General Wainwright was forced to surrender U.S. forces in the Philippines to Japan in 1941. He was a prisoner of war until 1945, when he returned home to a hero's welcome and was awarded the Medal of Honor. He retired from active duty in August 1947.

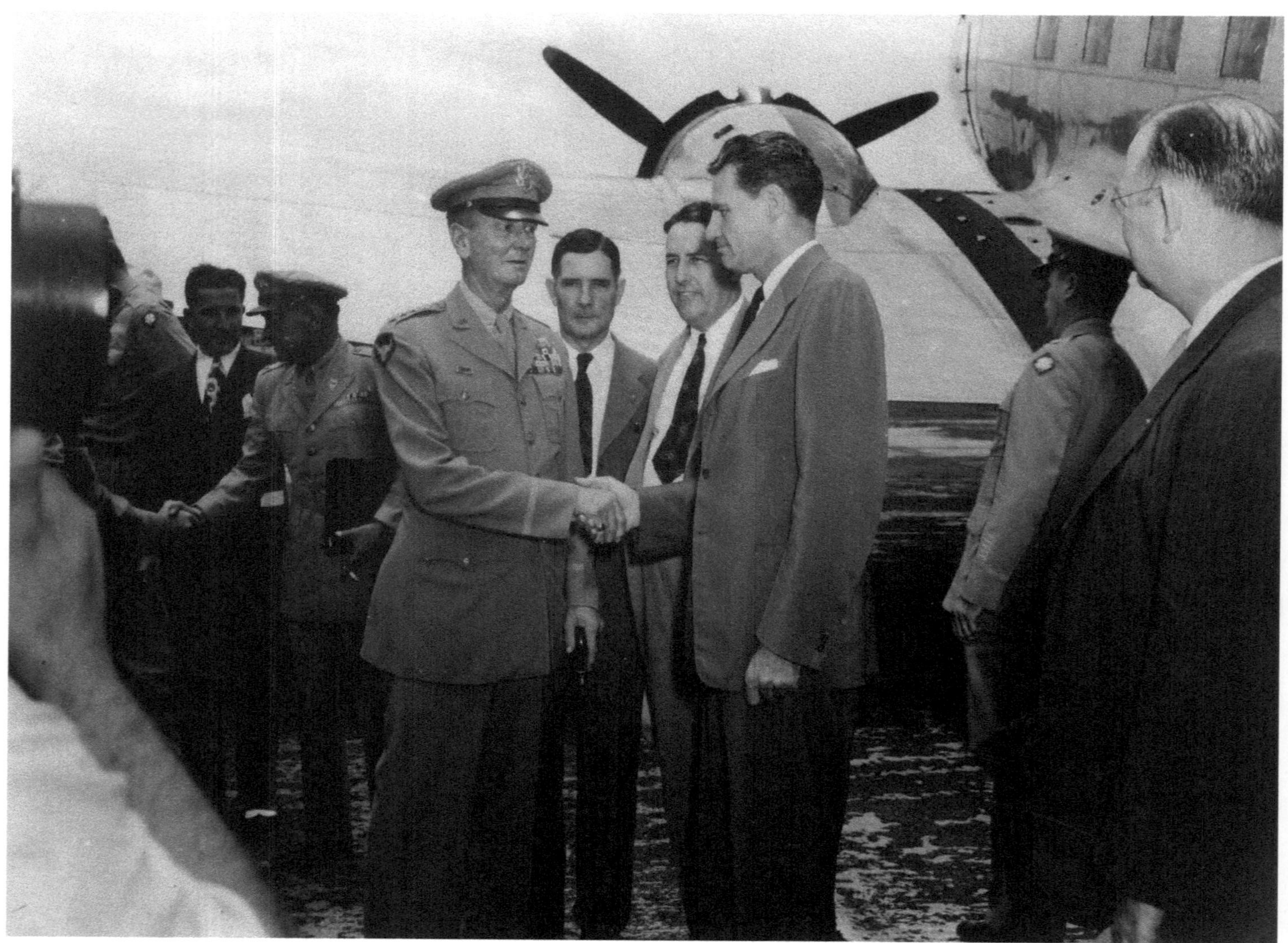

A Southeastern Telephone Company traffic operating room as seen in 1949, with long-distance switchboards on the left and local lines on the right. The first telephone exchange opened in Tallahassee in 1896 with 65 subscribers. Operators had to be unmarried women between 17 and 26, and able to reach the top of the switchboard.

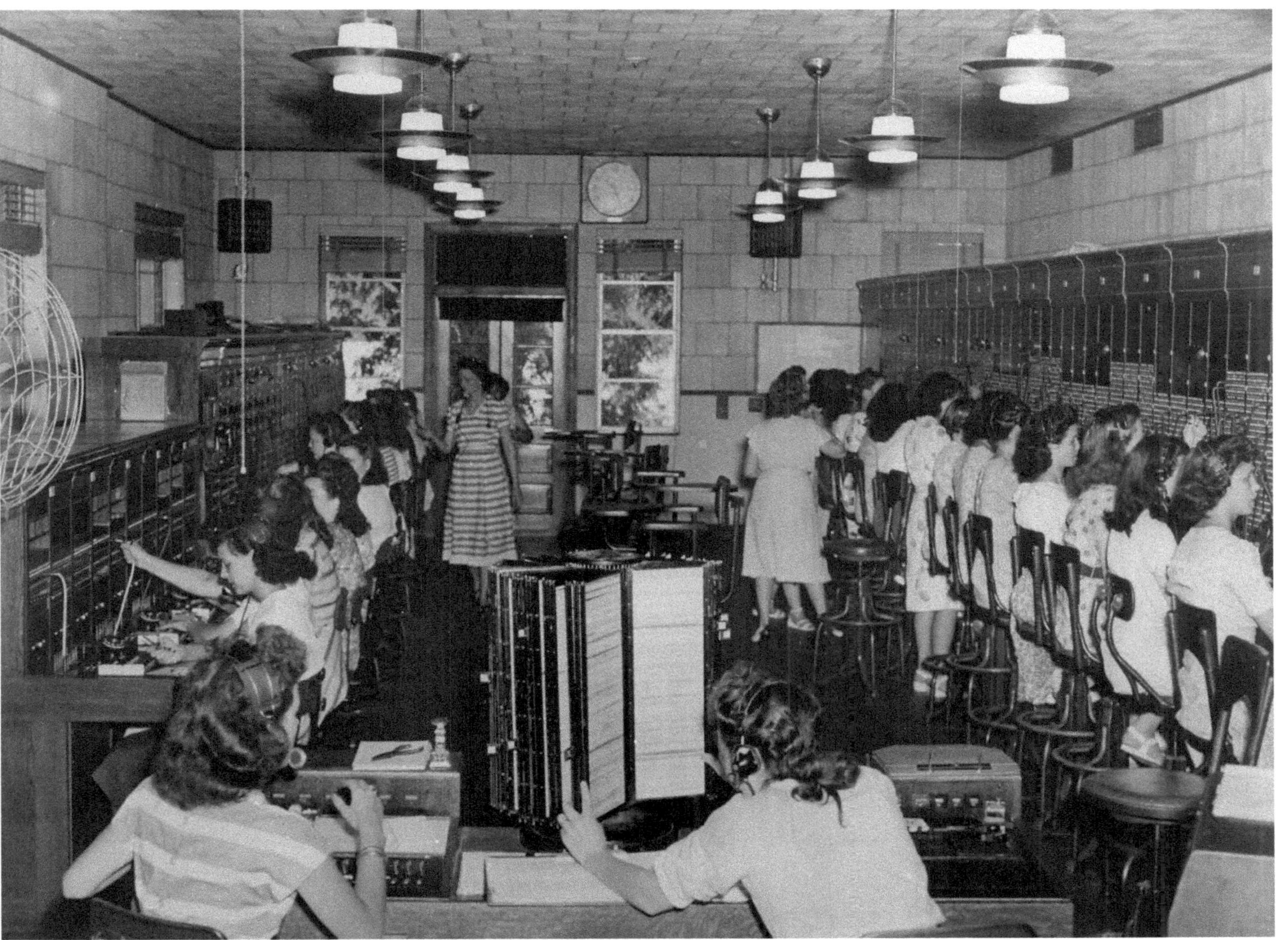

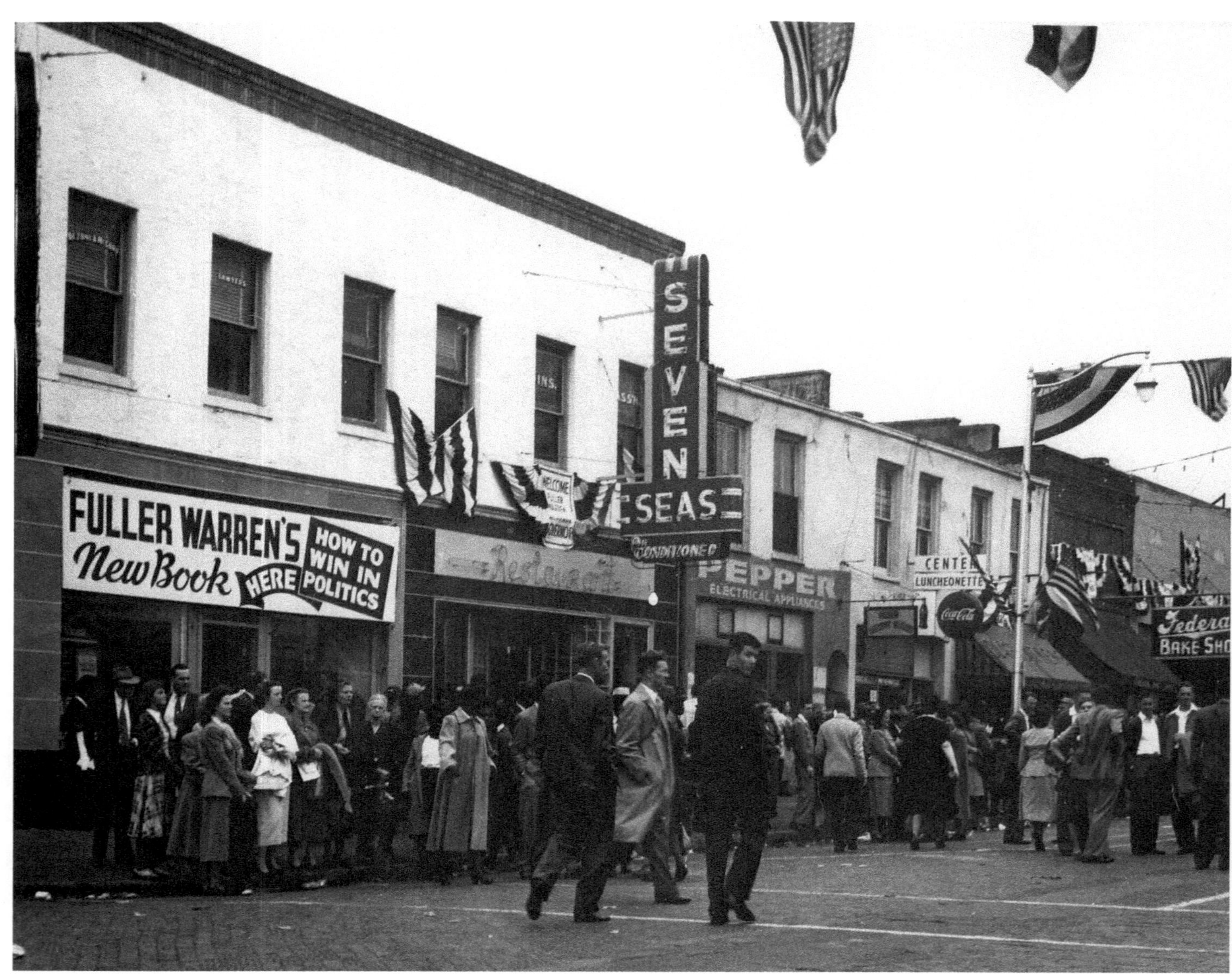

On January 4, 1949, crowds gather in front of the Seven Seas restaurant on Monroe Street for Fuller Warren's inauguration day activities. A large parade was followed by the swearing-in ceremonies, then a picnic on the capitol grounds with 28,000 plates of barbecue, and finally an inaugural ball in the evening.

In the 1950s Monroe Street remained the central business district. From the left are Fain drugstore, Gulf Life Insurance Company, the Book Corner, and Jenkins Music Company. From 1910 to 1950, Fain's drugstore was informally known as the "information" center of Tallahassee.

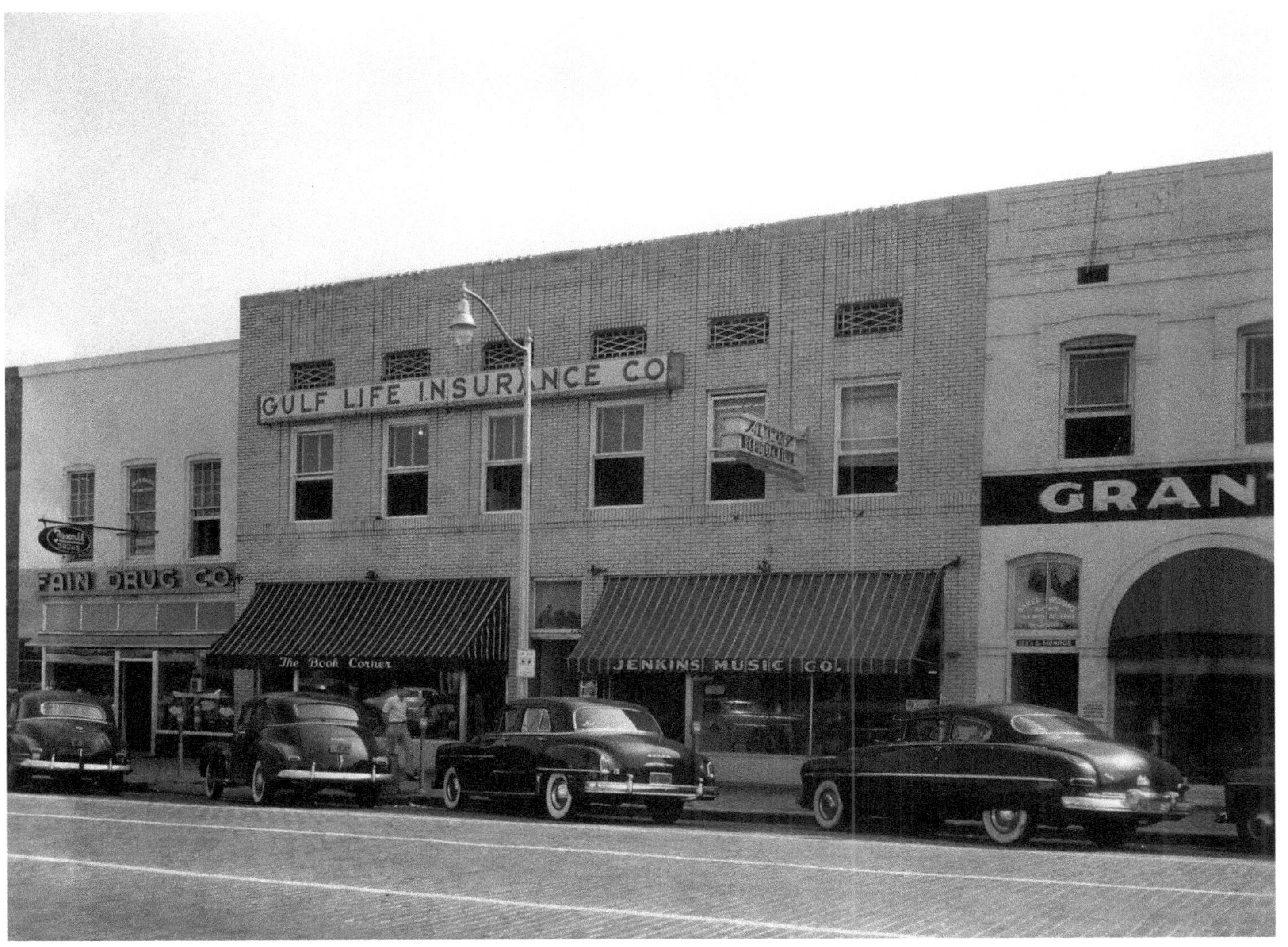

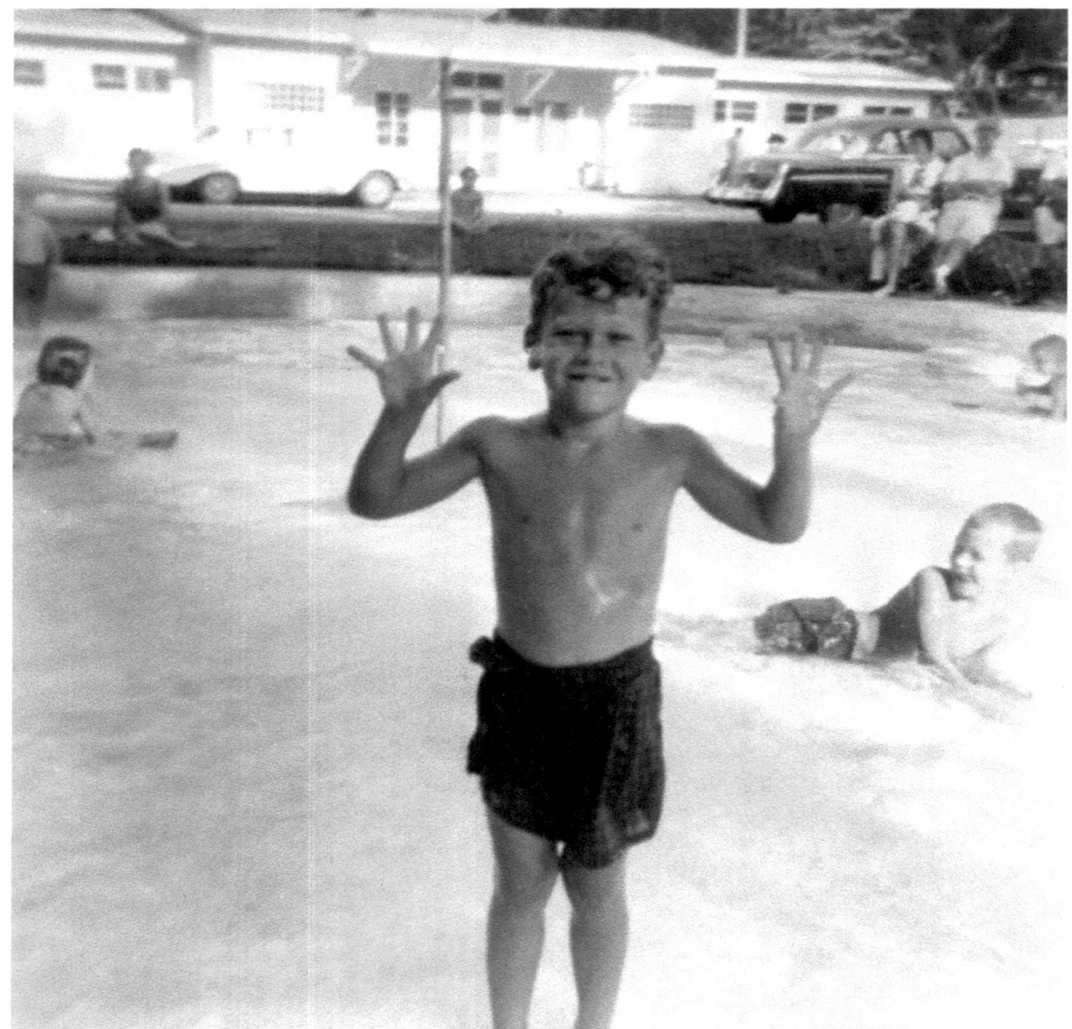

Andy Edel relaxes at right, while brother Thomas shows off for the camera during a family outing to Myers Park in 1959. One of the oldest parks in Tallahassee, Myers rests on the former site of an Apalachee Indian village, Spanish explorer Hernando DeSoto's camp, a Spanish mission, Governor Duval's home, and Lakeland Plantation.

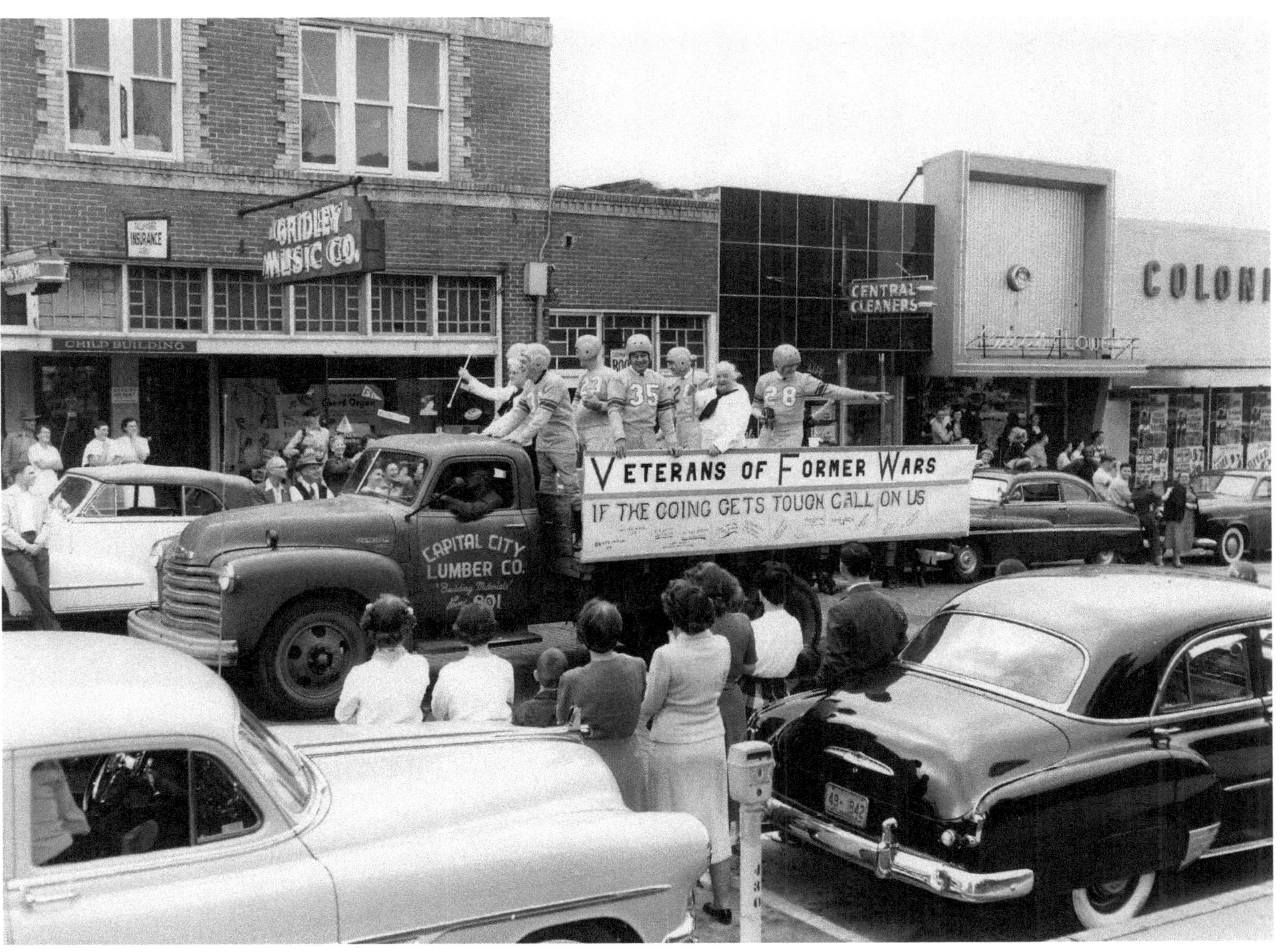

After World War II the impact of veterans applying to colleges on the G.I. bill was a leading factor in Florida State College for Women becoming co-ed as Florida State University in 1947. Participating in the 1950 FSU homecoming parade, the "Veterans of Former Wars" are alumni of the 1902–1905 Florida State College football team.

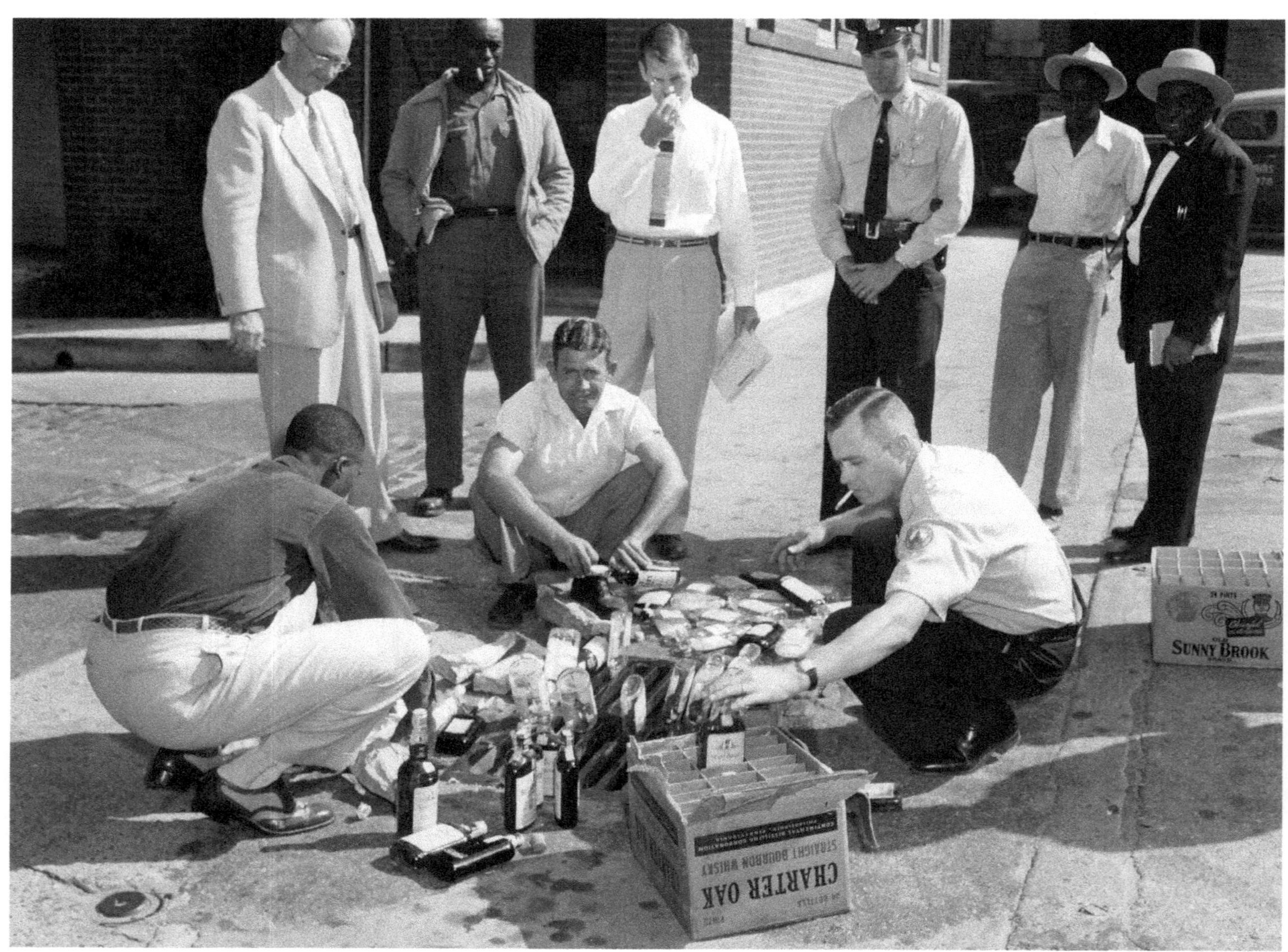

Although national prohibition ended in 1933, Leon County continued to be a "dry" county, prohibiting anything stronger than beer and wine until 1967. With many legislators coming from "wet" counties, Tallahasseans found ways to oblige them. In 1953 beverage agents in Tallahassee inspect confiscated bottles.

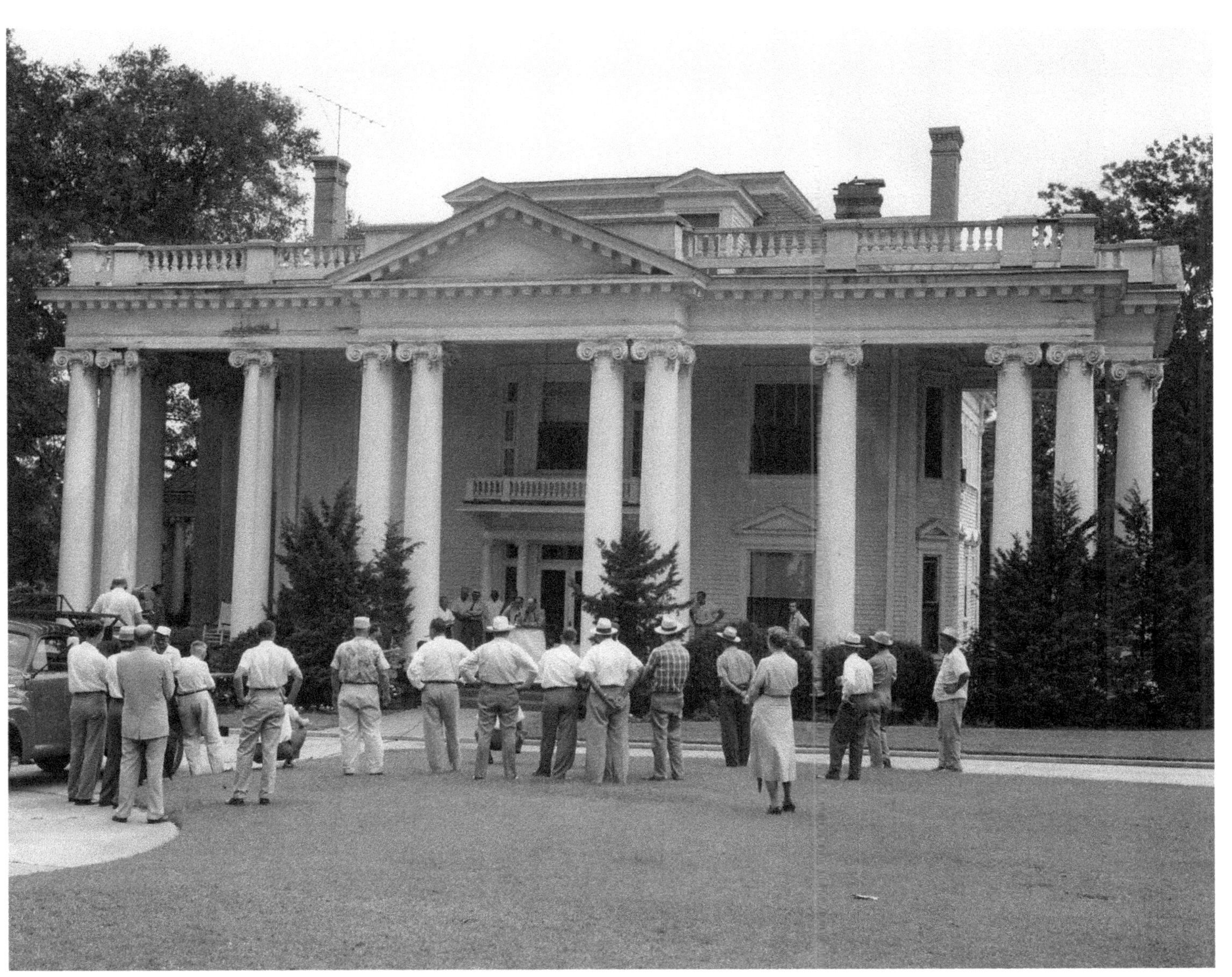

By 1955, the Florida Governor's Mansion on Adams Street had developed severe structural problems and was scheduled for demolition. On July 28, a large crowd was on hand for the start of the Executive Mansion's auction, led by auctioneer Howard Cranston. It was announced that "the auction will go on until everything is sold."

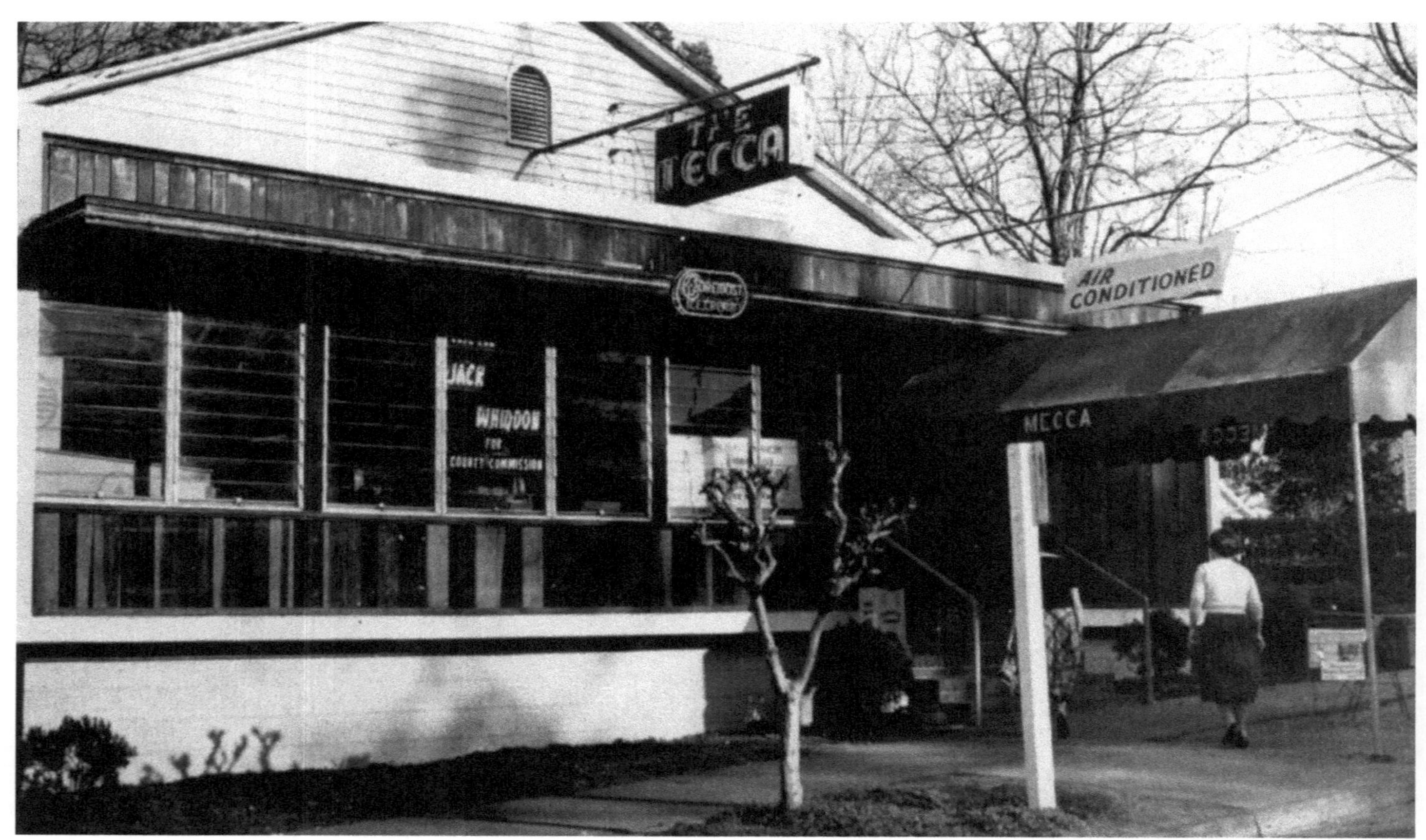

By the 1950s and 1960s the civil rights movement in Tallahassee had started protests and boycotts in attempts to end the segregation laws in place since the early twentieth century. On March 16, 1960, civil rights protesters attempted a boycott against the Mecca, a popular diner across from Florida State University.

Acting governor Charley E. Johns, fourth from left, meets with the cabinet. Governor Dan McCarty had died after less than a year in office. Senate president Charley Johns then became acting governor. The constitution required another election for the remainder of McCarty's term. Johns lost that election to LeRoy Collins in 1955.

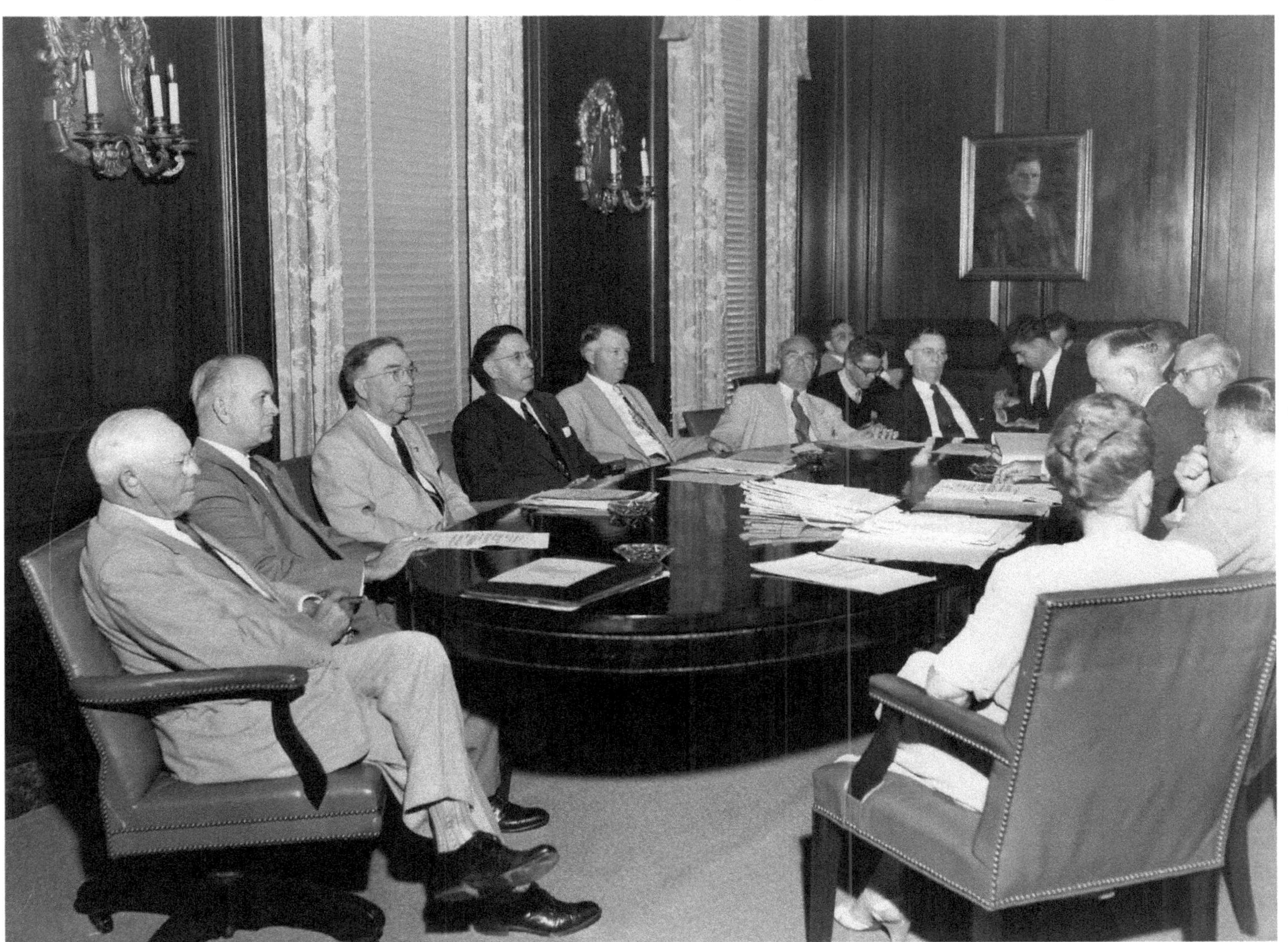

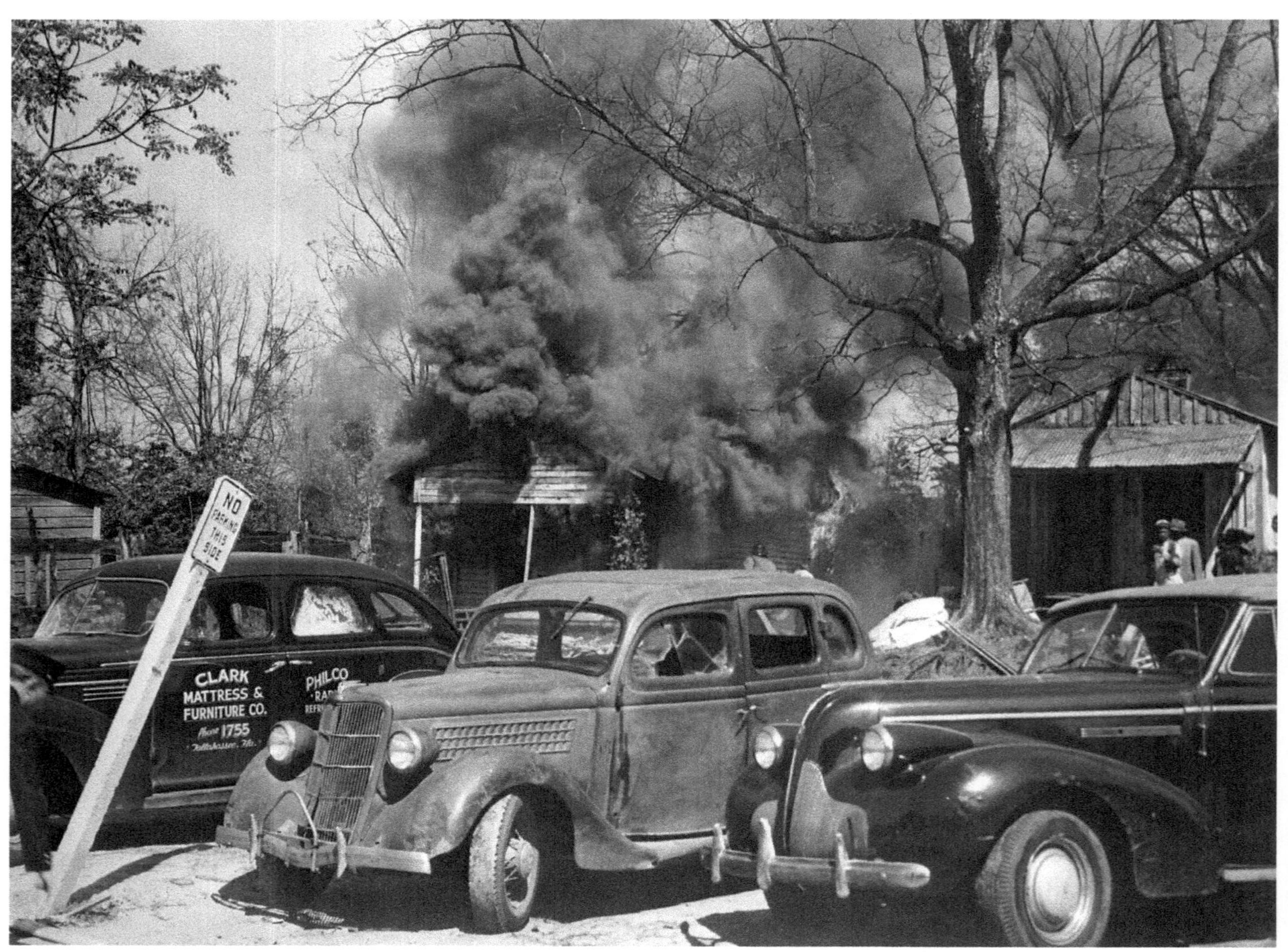

A fire destroys a Frenchtown home in the 1950s. An older neighborhood, by the 1920s Frenchtown was established as a thriving African American community. Before integration, many visiting musicians, such as Ray Charles, played at Frenchtown's cafes or stayed at its hotels while working the "Chitlin' Circuit."

A man and three boys stop along a garden walk at McClay Gardens. In 1923 Alfred McClay purchased the site, and started an extensive ornamental garden featuring camellias, azaleas, dogwoods, a secret garden, and a reflecting pool. His widow donated it to the state in 1953. In 1965 the garden were renamed in McClay's honor.

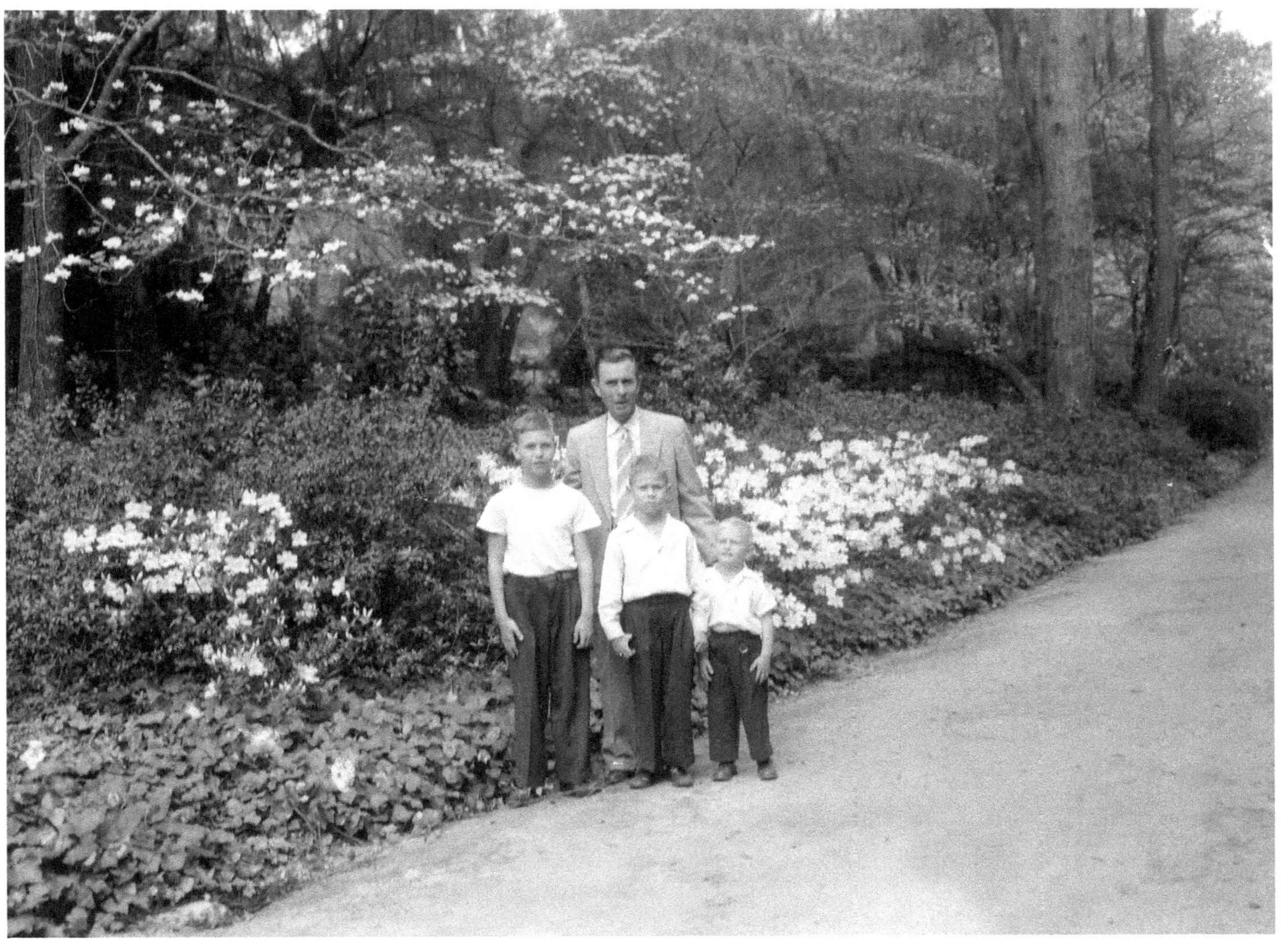

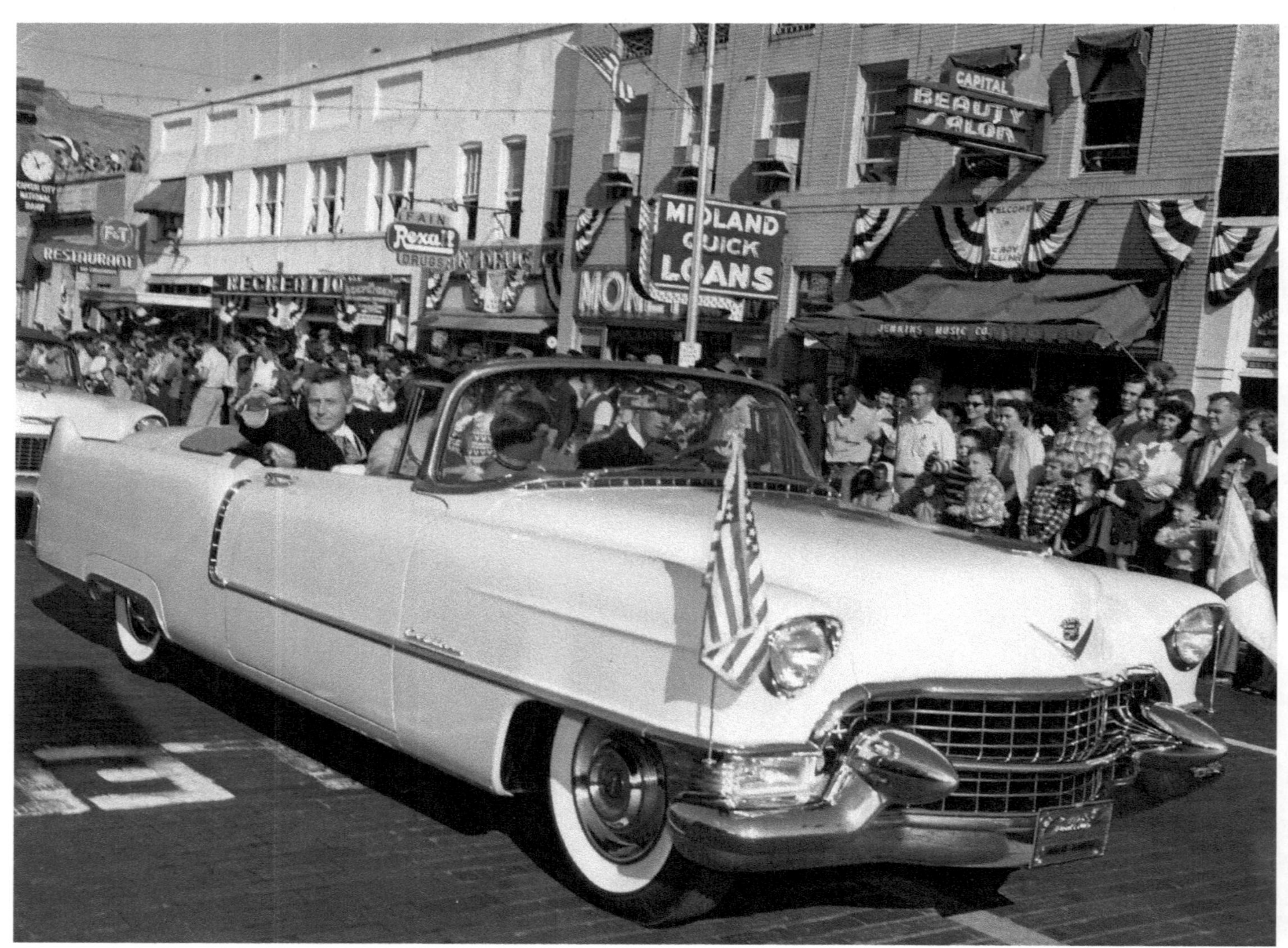

Inaugural parades traditionally came down Monroe Street to the capitol. On his way to the reviewing stand, Governor Collins waves to the crowds on January 4, 1955. Governor Collins' moderate positions on racial issues slowly led the state toward integration and he strengthened Florida's educational system.

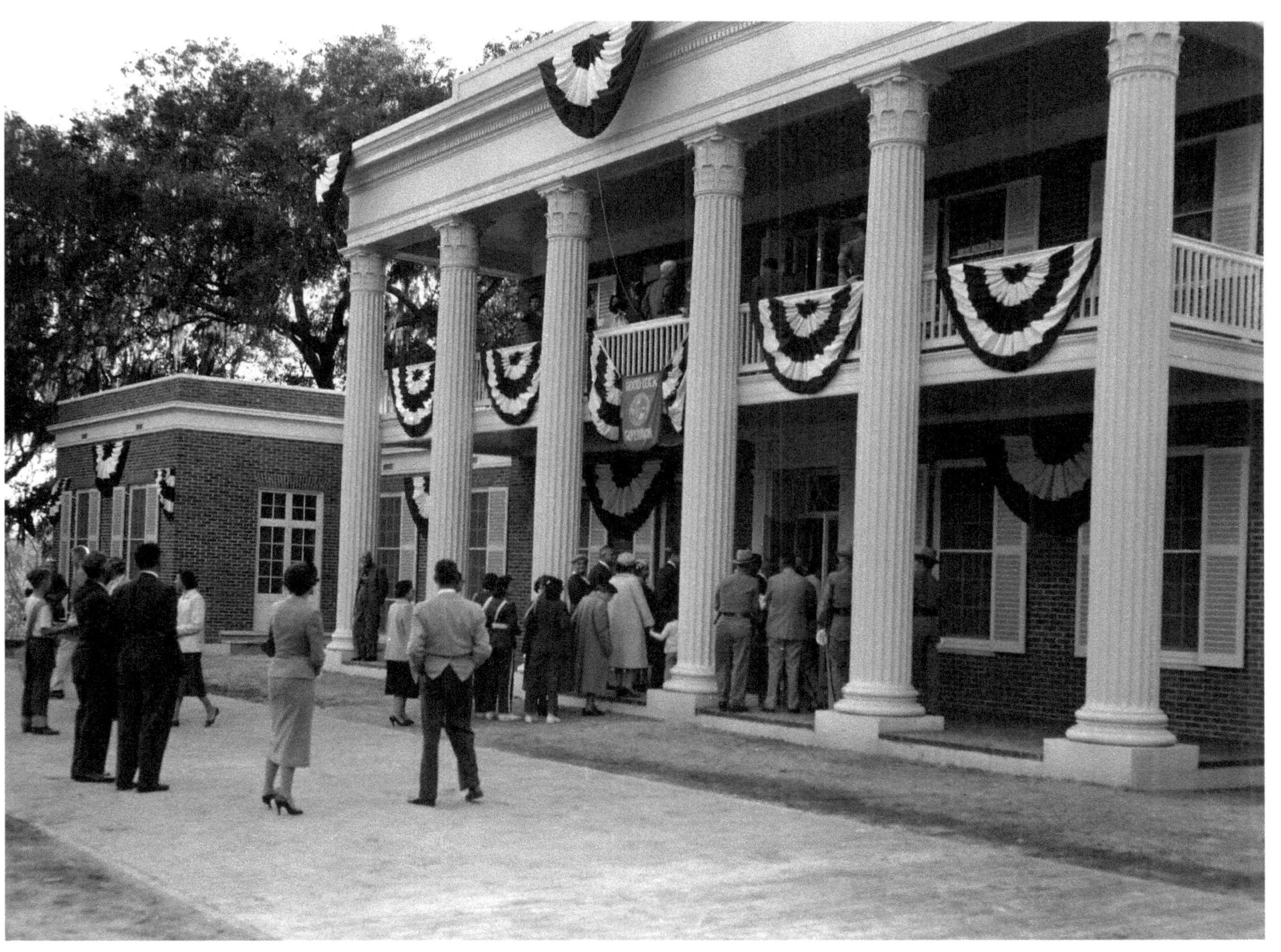

Guests tour the recently completed Governor's Mansion during the 1957 inauguration ceremonies. Work commenced in 1955 on the new mansion, designed after Andrew Jackson's home in Nashville, the Hermitage. During construction, Governor Collins moved next door to "the Grove," his wife's family home since territorial days.

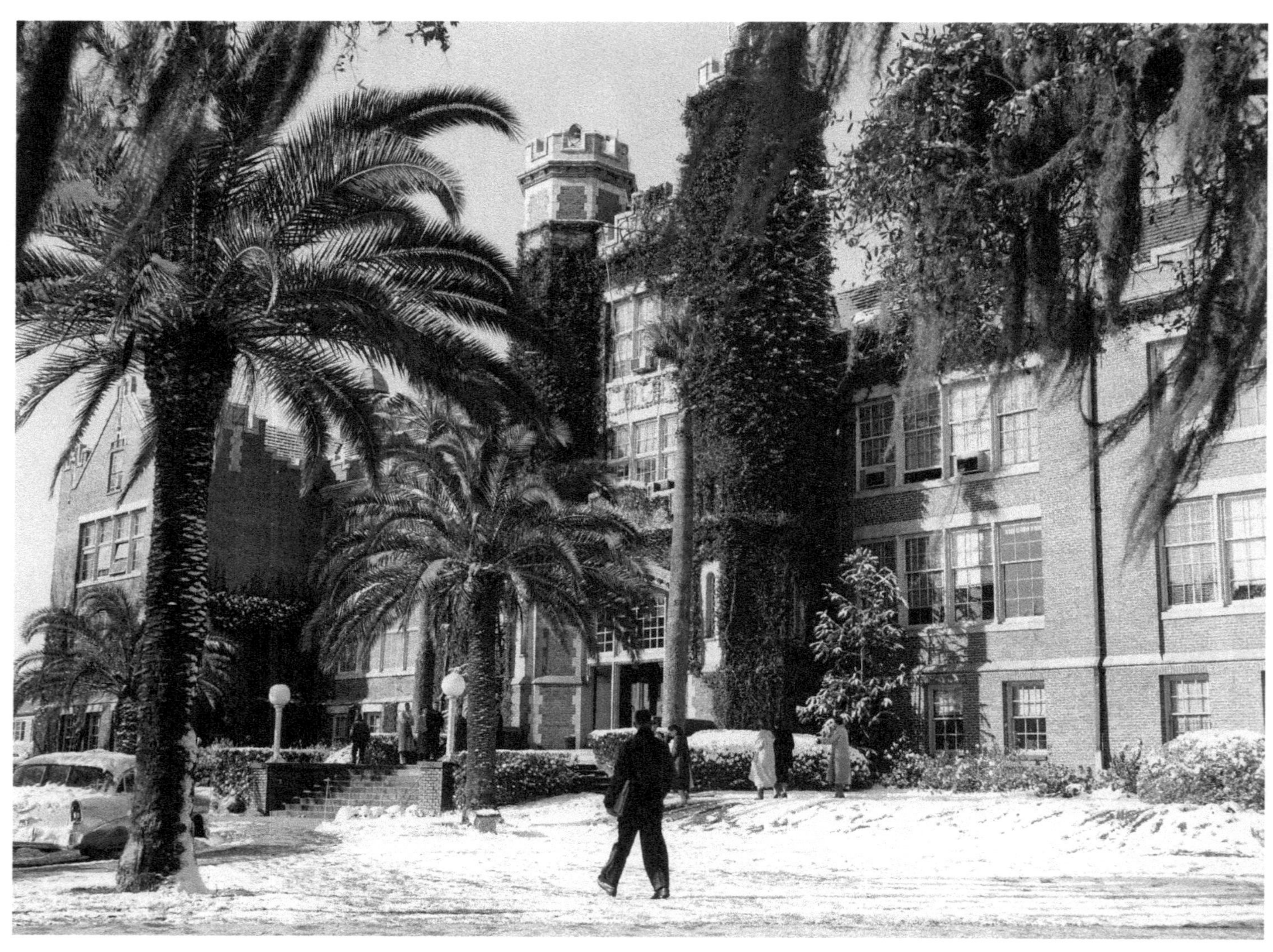

Florida State University students walking to classes view snow on the palm trees, Spanish moss, and the old Westcott building, an unusual sight. On February 12-13, 1958, Tallahassee was hit with the heaviest snowfall on record in a 24-hour period—2.8 inches. It has snowed only 32 times in Tallahassee since 1891.

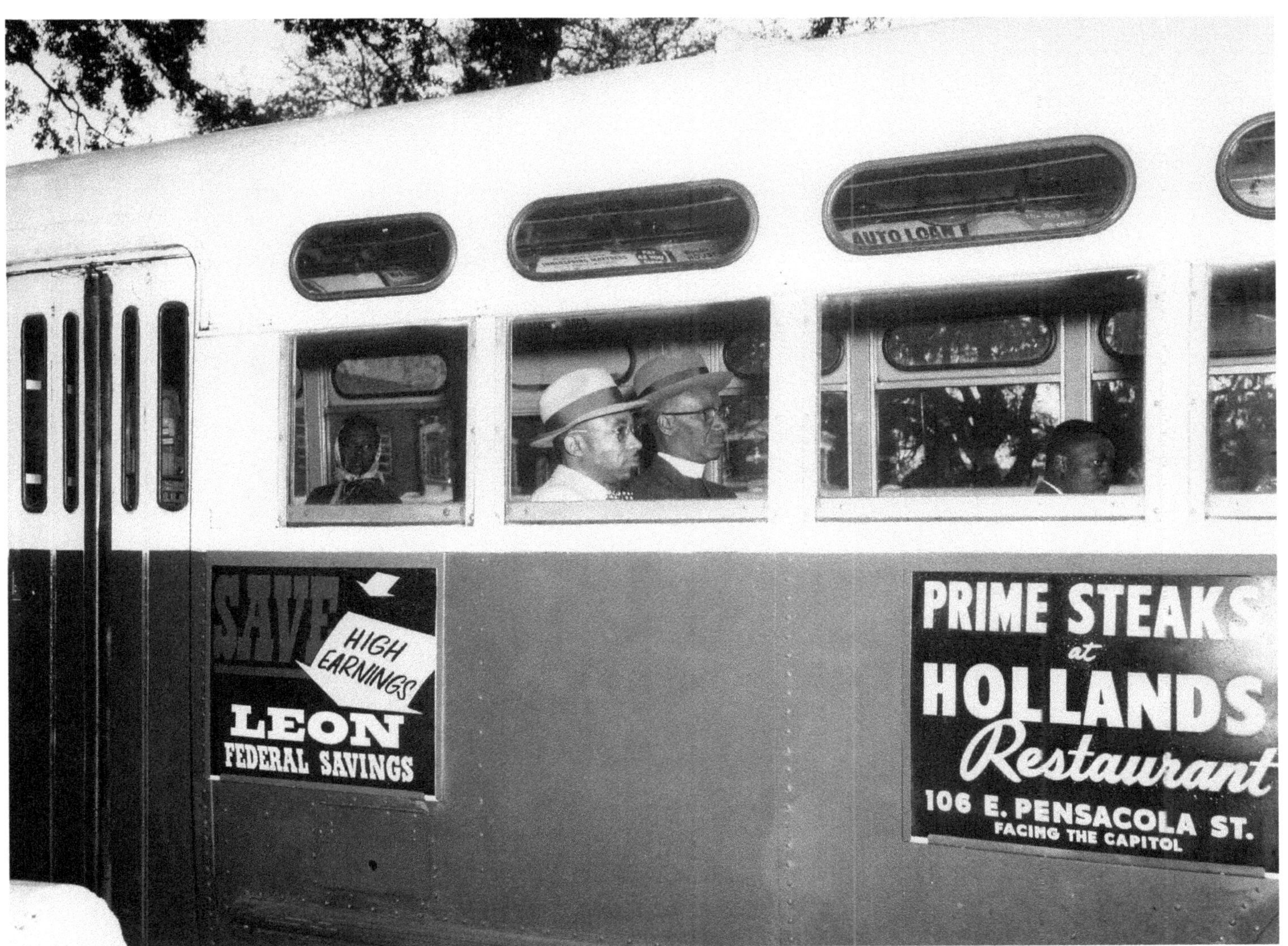

On May 26, 1956, two Florida A&M University students refused to give up their bus seats and were arrested. African Americans then started a bus boycott. On December 24, C. K. Steele and Dan Speed rode in the "white" section of a Tallahassee bus, ending the boycott. On January 7, 1957, the city repealed the bus segregation regulation.

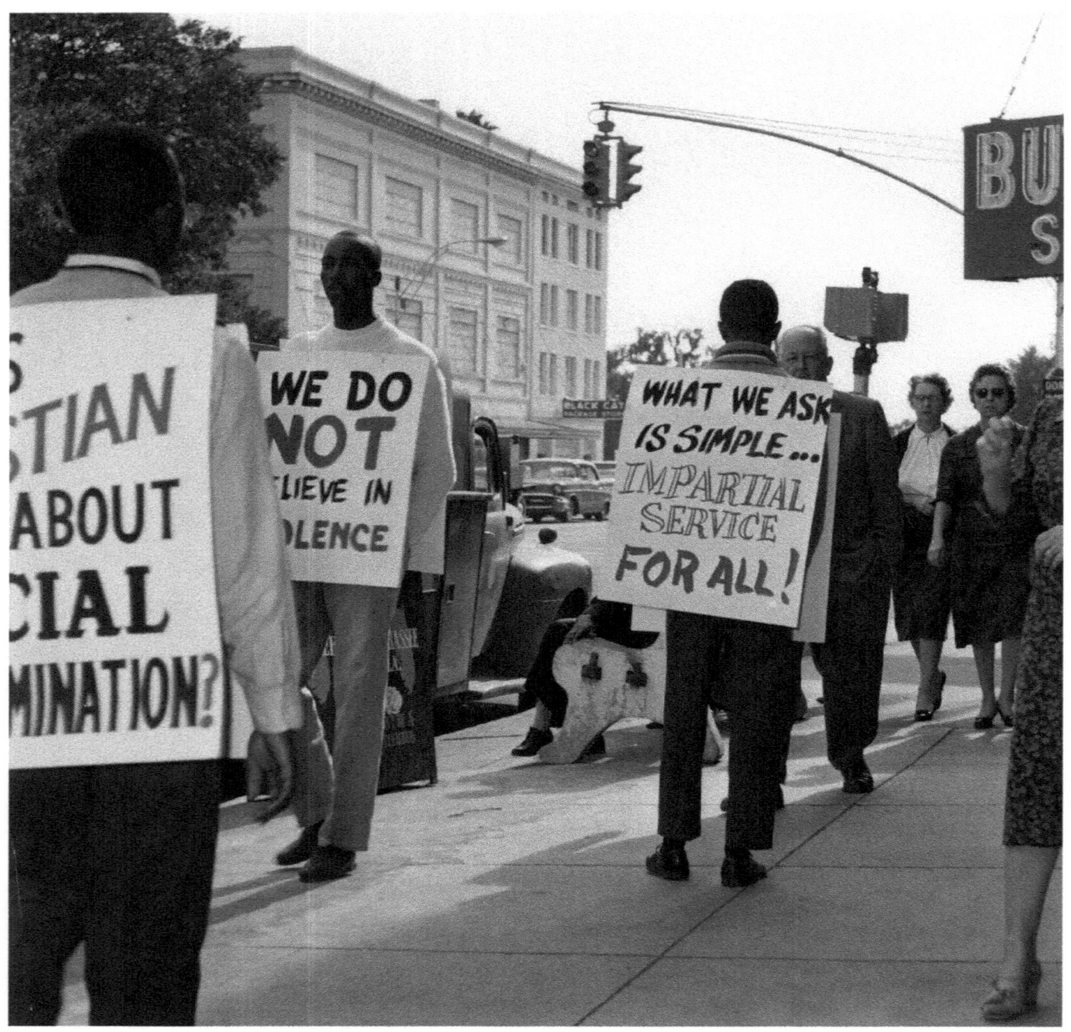

Civil rights protesters, many of them students from Florida A&M University, let their signs make their point during a December 1960 boycott and picketing of downtown Tallahassee stores. The protests were designed to point out the lack of progress in desegregating the lunch counters at downtown stores.

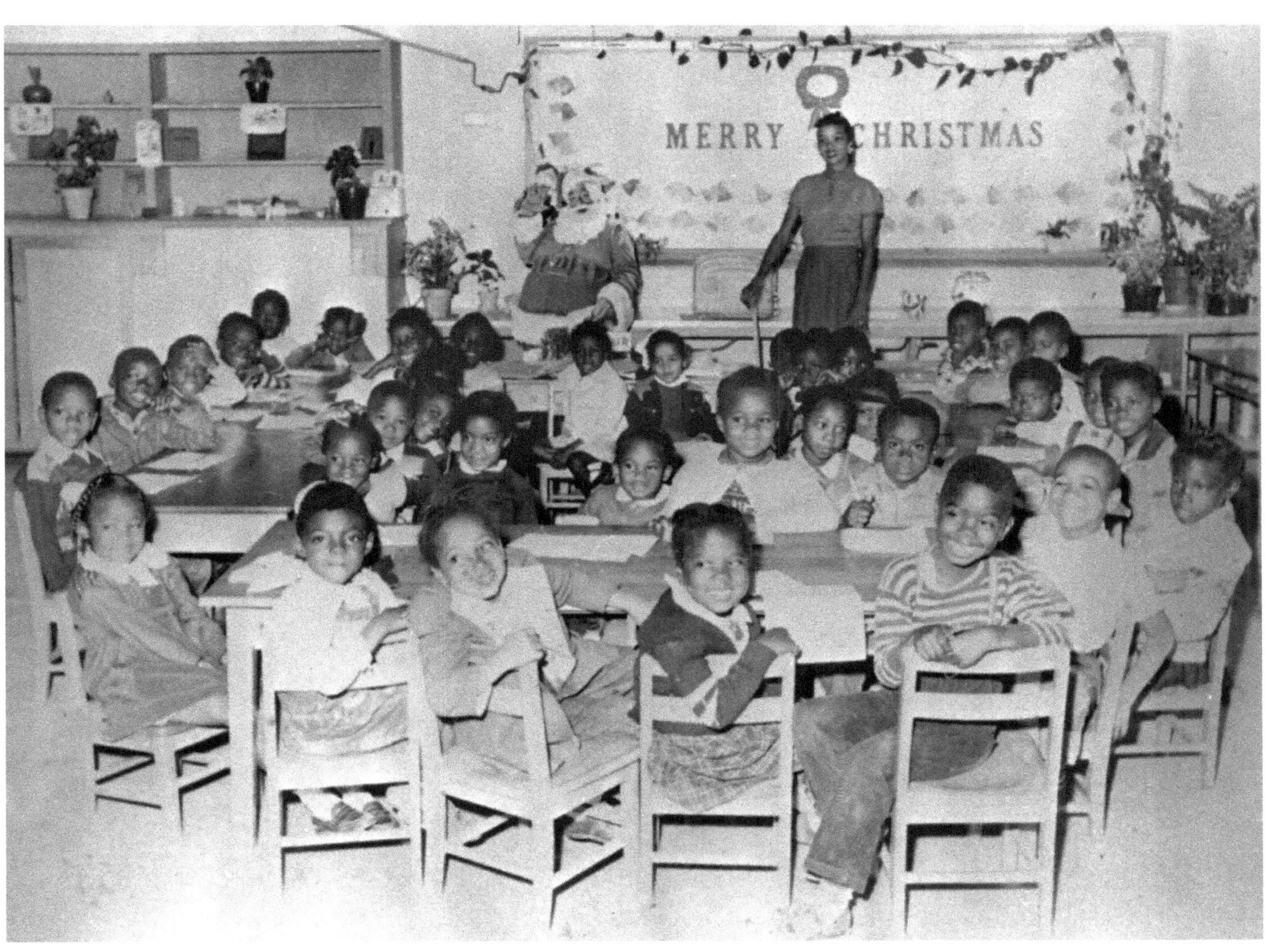

A class photograph of Kate Warren Condra with her Riley Elementary School students. In 1956 Leon County still had 10 all-black schools. As a result of the 1954 U.S. Supreme Court ruling declaring school segregation unconstitutional, the Civil Rights Act of 1964, and other efforts, Leon County had an integrated school system by 1970.

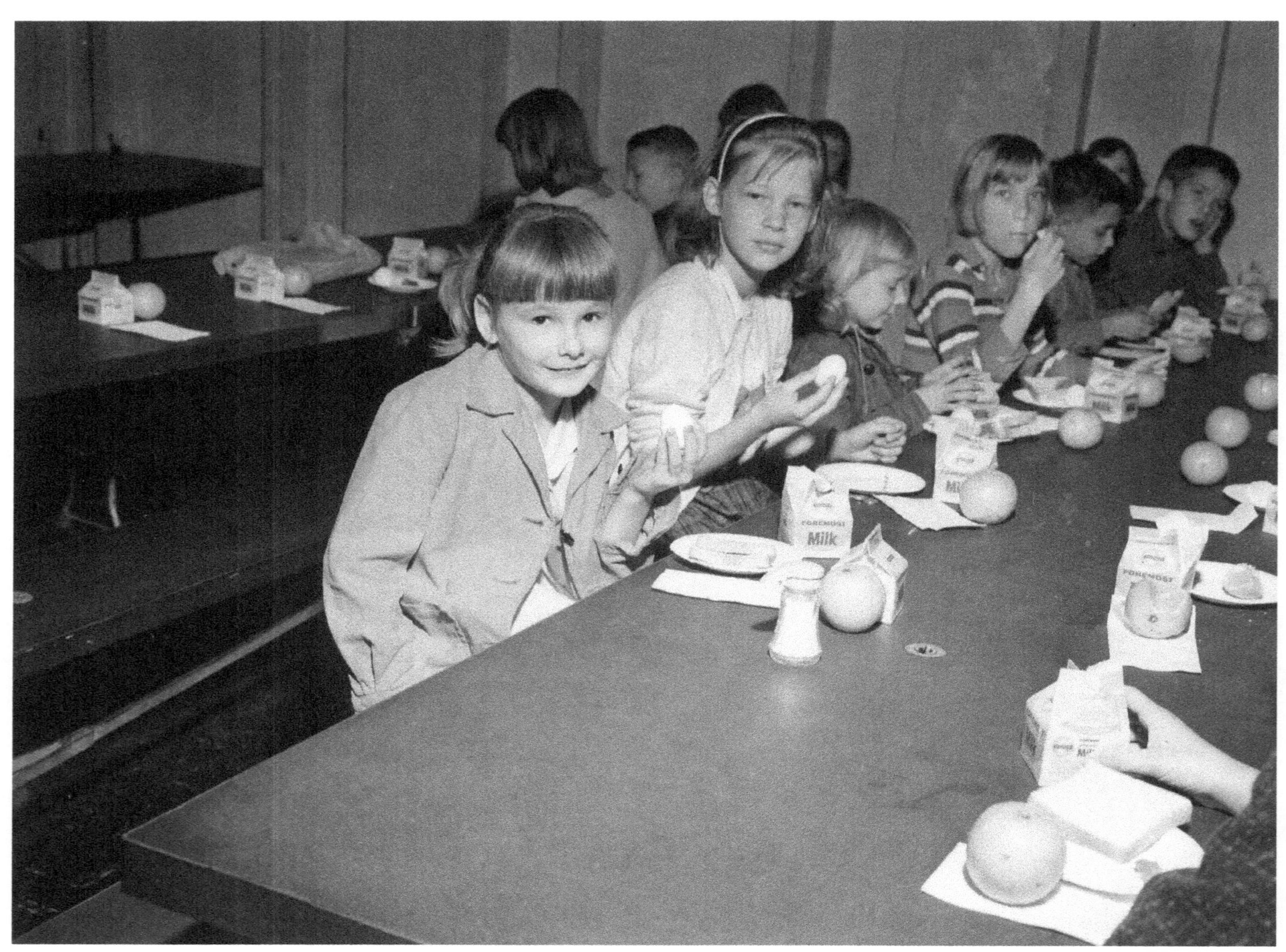

Students try a new diet at the cafeteria at Leonard A. Wesson Elementary School in 1961, located near a new subdivision. It opened as Prince Murat school at Dale Mabry Field in 1946, was moved and renamed South City School in 1949, and finally renamed after Leonard Wesson, a former School Board member, in 1956.

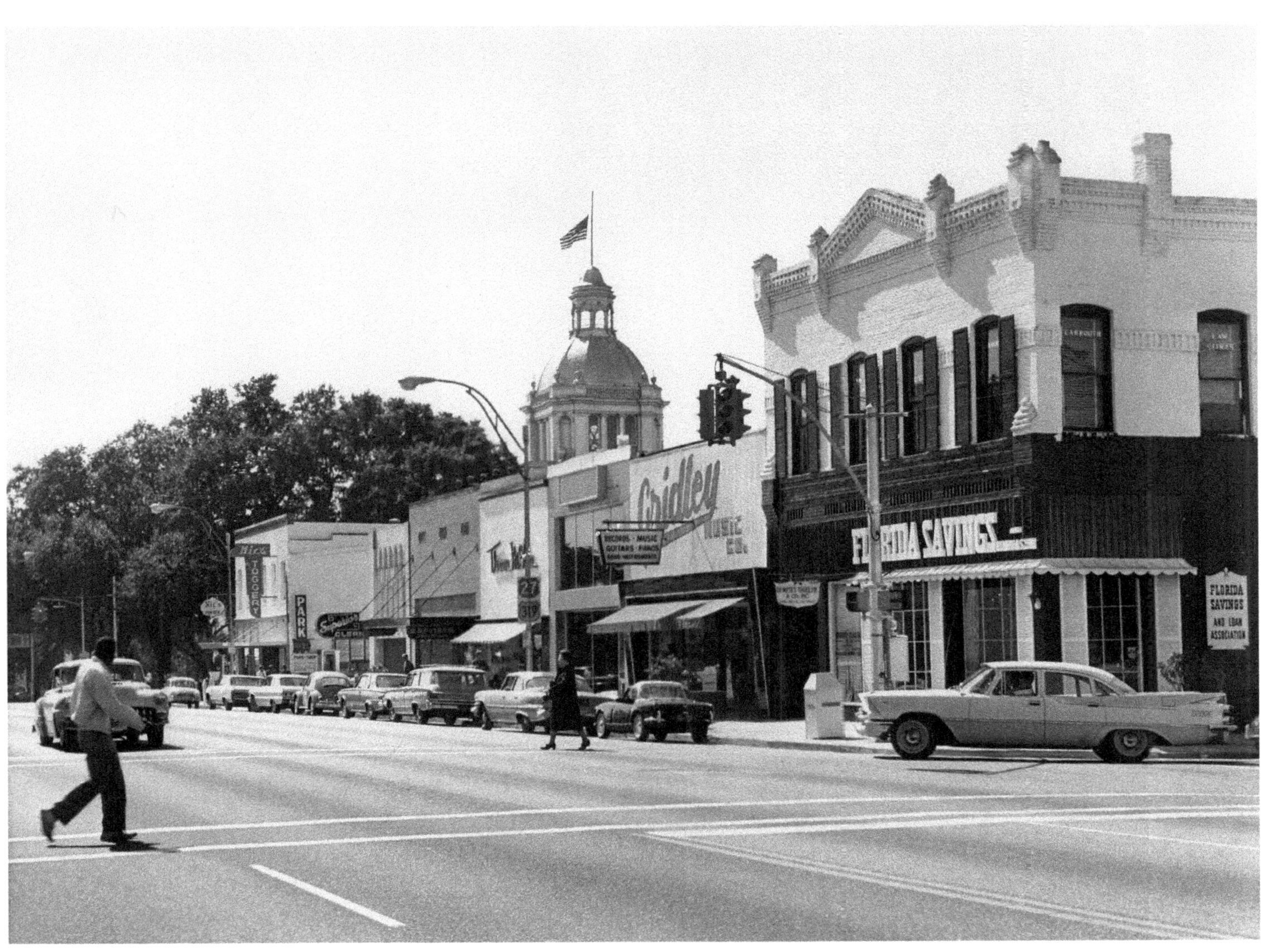

Since its founding in 1824, Tallahassee has survived many attempts to relocate the capital. Throughout the years, the city has responded by taking measures to retain the capital. This business district along Monroe Street was leveled to make way for the State House of Representatives office building in the 1970s.

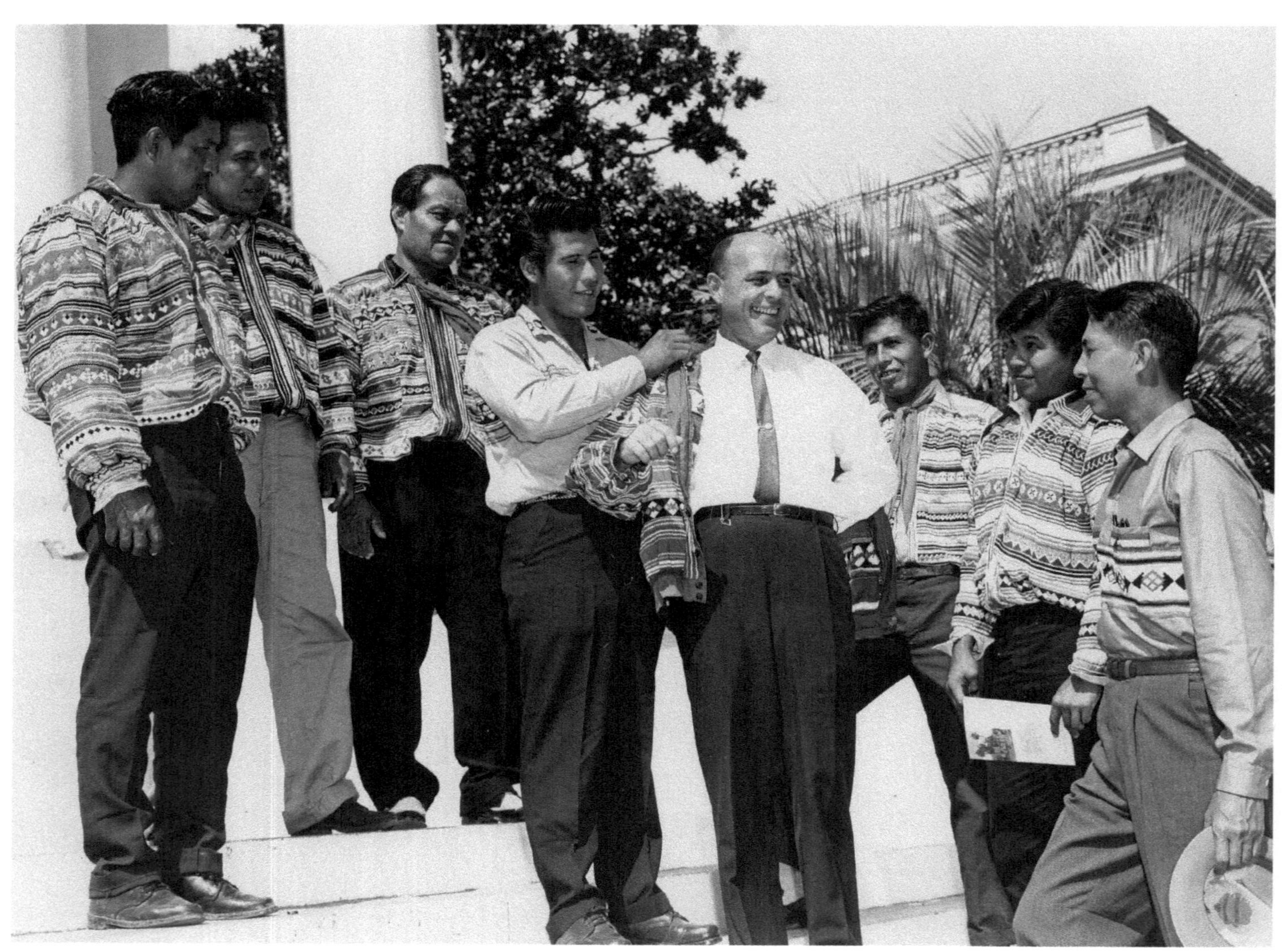

Miccosukee Seminole tribal leaders present William Kidd, an engineer for the state, with a colorful Indian jacket on the steps of the state capitol on October 16, 1961, as a memento for being given enough state land for a commercial development. Left to right are Stanley Frank, Jimmie Tiger, John Poole, John Willie, William Kidd, Tommy Tiger, Calvin Sanders, and Buffalo Tiger.

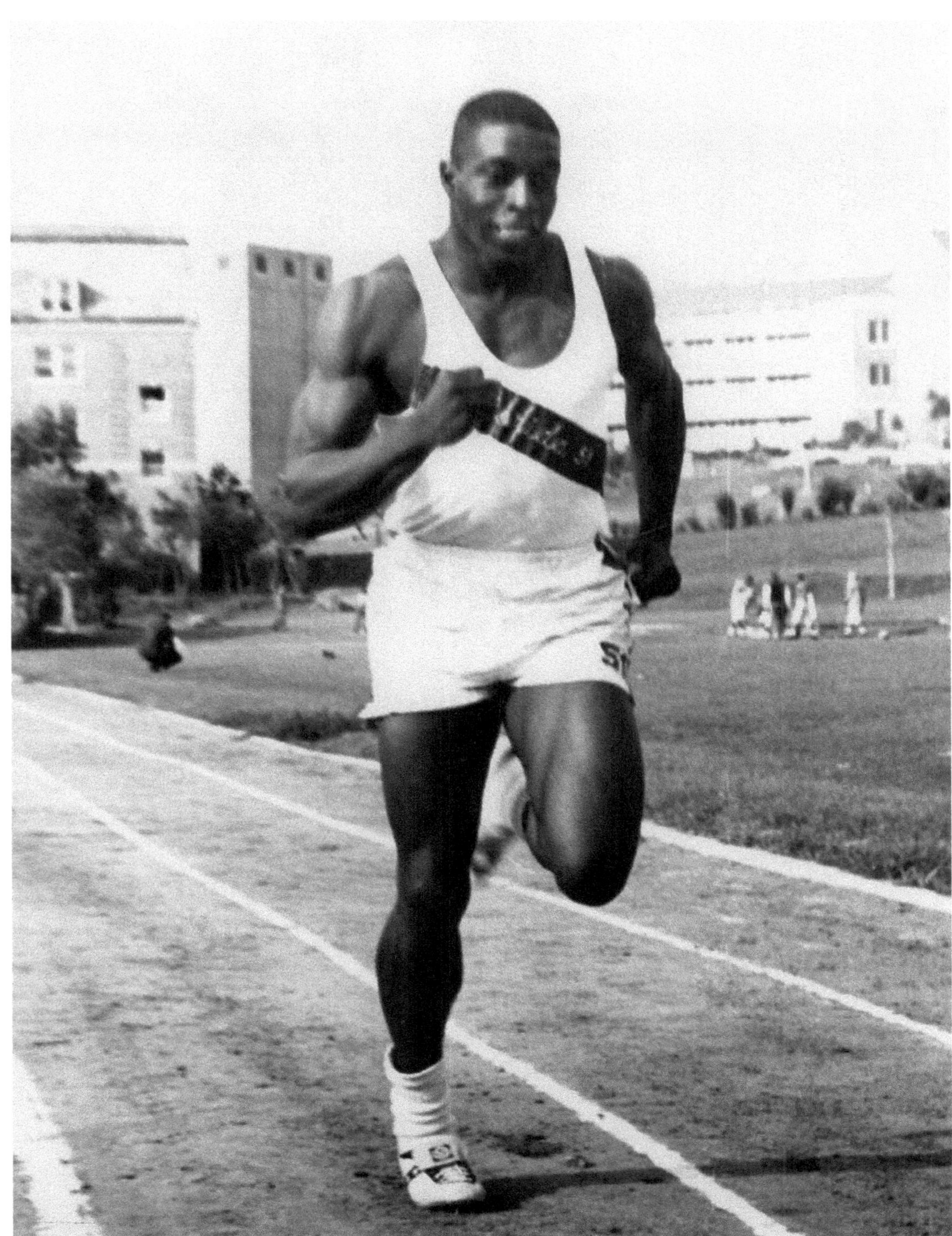

Florida A&M athlete Robert Hayes practices in 1962. He later set a world record in the 100-yard dash and won 2 gold medals at the 1964 Olympic Games in Tokyo. Unofficially titled the "World's Fastest Human," Hayes starred in the legendary Jake Gaither's FAMU Rattlers football teams, from 1960 to 1964. Their record was 36-4.

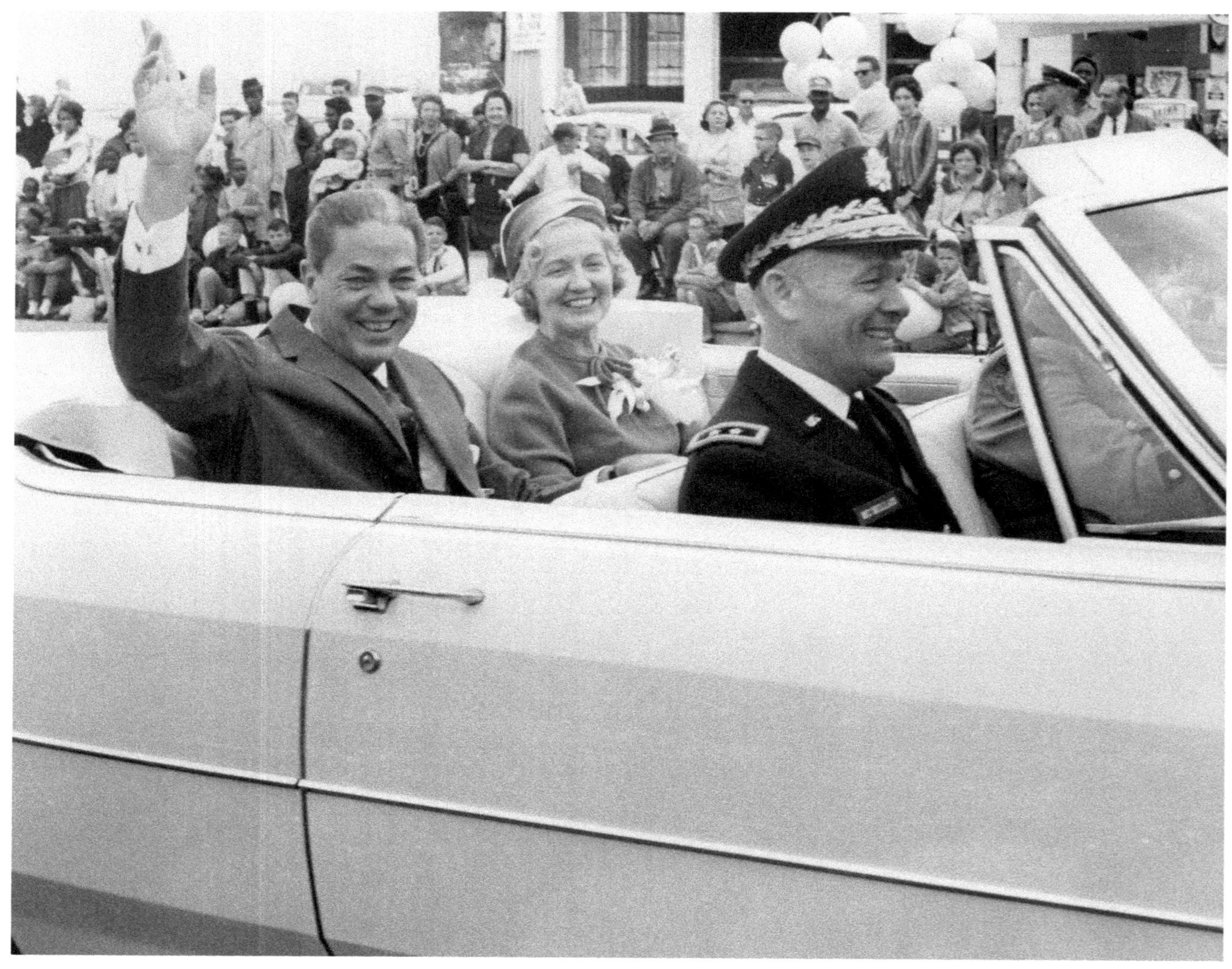

Governor and Mrs. Haydon Burns ride in the inaugural parade with Adjutant General Henry W. McMillan to the reviewing stand. Burns served as Florida's governor from January 5, 1965, to January 3, 1967. Governor Burns had a short term because the cycle of gubernatorial elections was changed so that it would not fall on presidential election years.

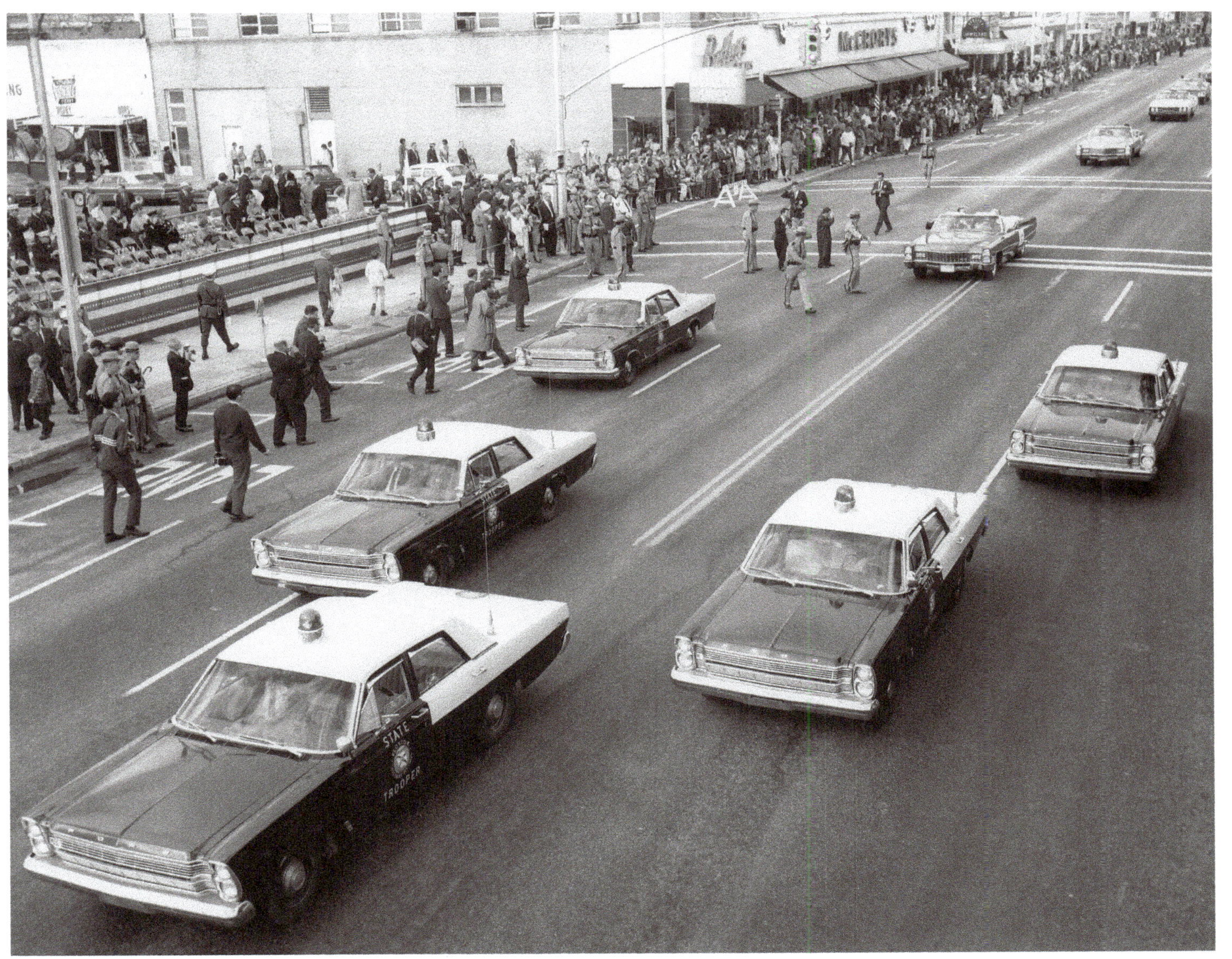

Police escort Governor Kirk to the inaugural parade viewing stand on Monroe Street, January 3, 1967. He was the state's first Republican governor in 90 years. During inauguration day activities, the unmarried governor introduced his companion as "Madame X." The governor later married "Madame X," Erika Mattfeld.

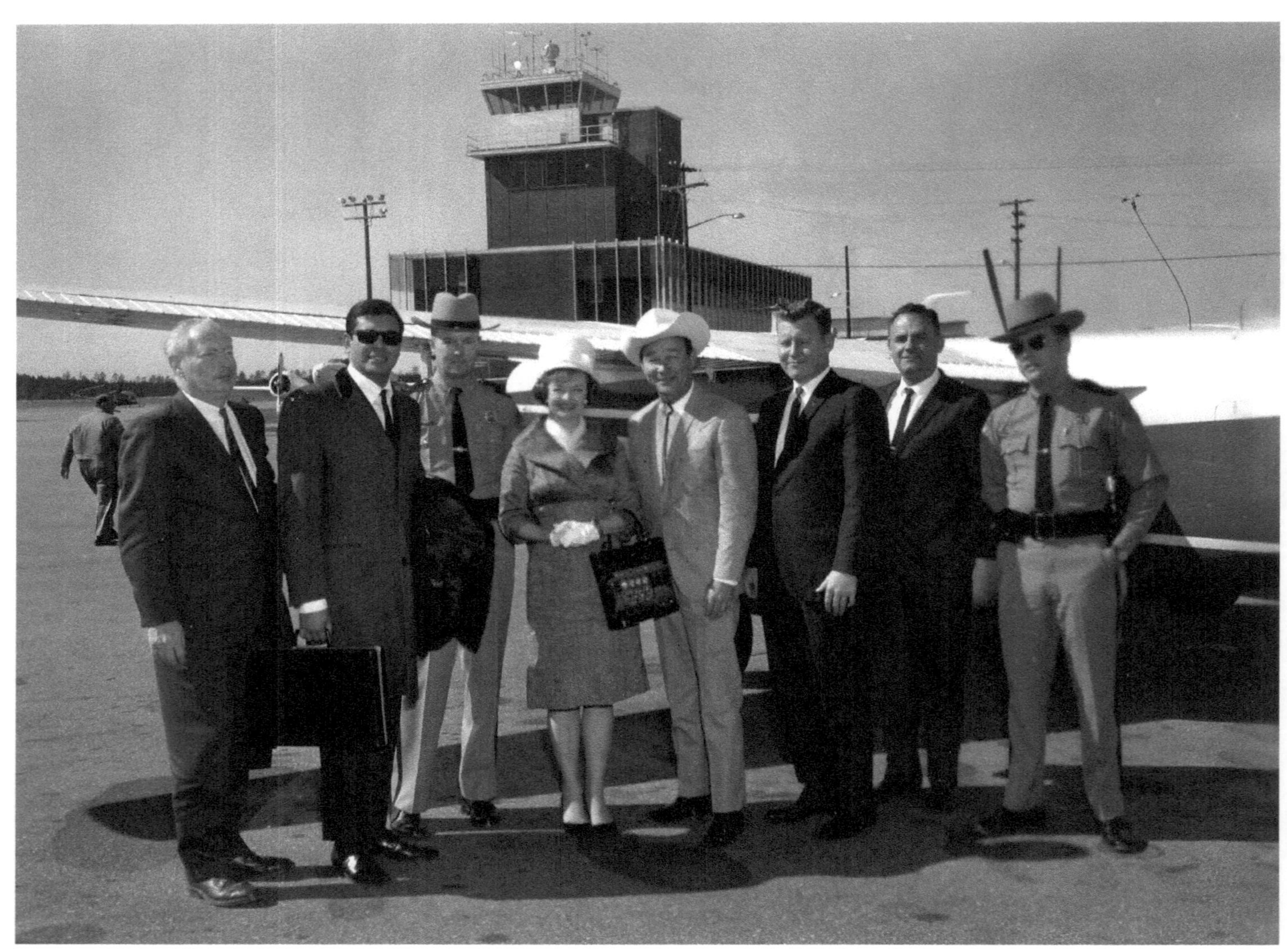

Dale Evans and Roy Rogers arrive at the Tallahassee Regional Airport on January 31, 1966. They visited Governor Burns at his office in the Capitol and then toured the Governor's Mansion with Mrs. Burns. As the capital city of a growing state, Tallahassee has hosted many dignitaries and celebrities throughout the years.

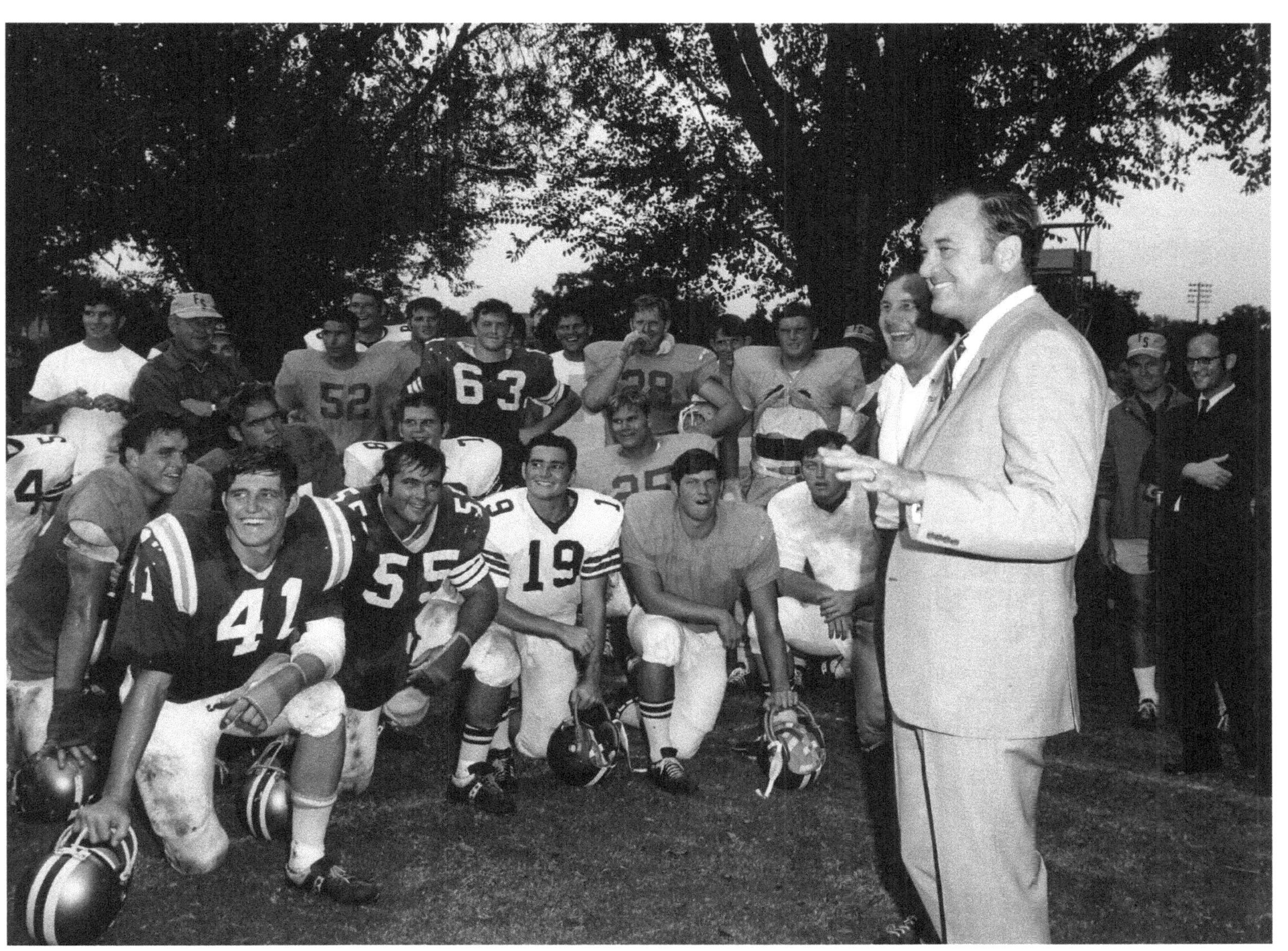

Governor Claude Kirk meets with Florida State University coach Bill "Pete" Peterson and the football team in September 1969. Coach Peterson, with a young Bobby Bowden on his staff, brought a young football program into national college football prominence, a tradition later continued by Bobby Bowden as head coach at FSU.

Notes on the Photographs

These notes, listed by page number, attempt to include all aspects known of the photographs. Each of the photographs is identified by the page number, photograph's title or description, photographer and collection, archive, and call or box number when applicable. Although every attempt was made to collect all available data, in some cases complete data was unavailable due to the age and condition of some of the photographs and records.

II **Corner of Adams and Jefferson Streets**
State Archives of Florida
rc02075

VI **View from the Capitol**
State Archives of Florida
rc02421

X **Mola on a Truck**
State Archives of Florida
GE1759

2 **Horse-drawn Wagon**
State Archives of Florida
Rc09760

3 **Ox Carts**
State Archives of Florida
Rc02491

4 **Harrison Reed Home**
State Archives of Florida
PR12227

5 **Wedding of Florence Holland**
State Archives of Florida
PR11861

6 **First Leon Church**
State Archives of Florida
Rc02493

7 **The Columns**
State Archives of Florida
PR12009

8 **Morgan Hotel**
State Archives of Florida
Rc03612

9 **African American with Mule Cart**
State Archives of Florida
Rc09758

10 **Old Capitol**
State Archives of Florida
Rc00569

11 **Portrait of Perez B. Brokaw**
State Archives of Florida
PR11625

12 **Trinity Methodist Church**
State Archives of Florida
Rc02006

13 **Union Bank Building**
State Archives of Florida
Rc08904

14 **Governor Stearns Greeting Harriet Beecher Stowe**
State Archives of Florida
Rc00551

16 **The Grove**
State Archives of Florida
PR12068

17 **Florida House of Representatives**
State Archives of Florida
Rc00834

18 **Selim W. Myers Home Built by William Cutler**
State Archives of Florida
N043119

19 **St. John's Episcopal Church**
State Archives of Florida
Rc02007

20 **African American People at Market**
State Archives of Florida
Rc04819

21 **Church of St. Mary**
State Archives of Florida
Rc05411

22 **Old City Cemetery**
State Archives of Florida
Rc12223

23 **Inspection Team with Engine #28**
State Archives of Florida
Ha00028

24 **Thomas Blake Byrd**
State Archives of Florida
PR11996

25 **Scene in Governor Bloxham's Parlor**
State Archives of Florida
Gv000424

26 **F. H. Flagg Home**
State Archives of Florida
PR12168

27 STEAMBOAT "WALKATOMICA"
State Archives of Florida
Rc13686

28 FLORIDA'S 14TH GOVERNOR E. A. PERRY
State Archives of Florida
Rc00629

29 WEST FLORIDA SEMINARY BUILDING
State Archives of Florida
Rc04562

30 VINEYARD
State Archives of Florida
HA00097

31 FLORIDA SENATE
State Archives of Florida
Rc12194

32 BOYS AND CREW WITH FLORIDA RAILWAY
State Archives of Florida
HA00076

34 NEW LEON HOTEL
State Archives of Florida
HA00058

35 LAKELAND PLANTATION
State Archives of Florida
Rc04034

36 FOX HUNTING GROUP
State Archives of Florida
Rc01983

37 FLORIDA LEGISLATURE
State Archives of Florida
Rc04337

38 GEORGE GWYNN, JR., AND "UNCLE" LIBERTY
State Archives of Florida
Rc08036

39 EIGHT MEN WITH PENNY-FARTHING BICYCLES
State Archives of Florida
Rc00877

40 JOHN WARD HENDERSON
State Archives of Florida
Rc03072

41 FOUR CHILDREN ON AN OX CART
State Archives of Florida
Rc03032

42 OFFICE OF THE WEEKLY FLORIDIAN
State Archives of Florida
HA00011

43 ALVAN S. HARPER AND HIS PONY
State Archives of Florida
HA00221

44 BROKAW-MCDOUGALL HOUSE
State Archives of Florida
Rc04342

45 TEACHER AND HER STUDENTS ON STEPS
State Archives of Florida
Ha00400

46 HORSE AND BUGGY
State Archives of Florida
Ha00106

47 LABORERS BOILING CANE SYRUP
State Archives of Florida
HA00073

48 SAWMILL
State Archives of Florida
Ha00018

49 STREET SCENE
State Archives of Florida
PR12401

50 WINTHROP CHILDREN ON HORSEBACK WITH THE MERRITS
State Archives of Florida
Ha00223

51 ON PARK AVENUE
State Archives of Florida
PR12413

52 LEWIS PARK
State Archives of Florida
PR11574

53 JOHN D. CAY
State Archives of Florida
Rc13243

54 COLLEGE AVENUE
State Archives of Florida
PR12412

55 GOVERNOR VISITING NATIONAL GUARD
State Archives of Florida
N046158

56 BROWN HOUSE
State Archives of Florida
PR11994

57 FREIGHT DEPOT
State Archives of Florida
N042983

58 CHILDREN IN YARD
State Archives of Florida
Rc04871

60 POST OFFICE CONSTRUCTION
State Archives of Florida
Rc00991

61 FOWLERS WITH GROUP
State Archives of Florida
Rc03248

62 SUPREME COURT JUSTICE GEORGE P. RANEY
State Archives of Florida
Rc02464

63 THE LEON
State Archives of Florida
Rc06725

64 MANAGER MR. OGLESBY AT LOBBY DESK
State Archives of Florida
Rc03005

65 BALL BROS. & DEMILLY GENERAL STORE
State Archives of Florida
Rc02518

66 HORSE AND BUGGY AT WINTHROP HOME
State Archives of Florida
N043160

67 TALLAHASSEE RAILROAD COMPANY'S MULE-DRAWN TROLLEY
State Archives of Florida
Rc08644

68 **Group Picture on a Porch**
State Archives of Florida
N042938

69 **Stores on West Side of Monroe**
State Archives of Florida
Rc06723

70 **St. James Hotel**
State Archives of Florida
Rc00014

71 **Men and State Treasurer James B. Whitfield**
State Archives of Florida
Rc03243

72 **Market/City Hall Building**
State Archives of Florida
Rc00005

73 **Cyclists**
State Archives of Florida
N029579

74 **Alvan S. Harper**
State Archives of Florida
Rc02417

75 **Governor Bloxham in Carriage**
State Archives of Florida
Gv003244

76 **College Hall at he Florida State College for Women**
State Archives of Florida
PR13013

77 **Dirty Smith**
State Archives of Florida
Rc00026

78 **Wanish Cigar Factory**
State Archives of Florida
Rc04813

79 **West Florida Seminary Football Team**
State Archives of Florida
N044028

80 **William Hodges' Office**
State Archives of Florida
Rc02917

81 **President**
State Archives of Florida
Rc00025

82 **Frozen Fountain on Capitol Grounds**
State Archives of Florida
Rc00730

84 **Georgia, Florida & Alabama Railway**
State Archives of Florida
N039185

85 **College Avenue**
State Archives of Florida
Rc00674

86 **School of the South**
State Archives of Florida
N042788

87 **Horse drawn buggy**
State Archives of Florida
Rc13806

88 **Bank Interior**
State Archives of Florida
N042108

89 **Surveying and Engineering**
State Archives of Florida
Rc01124

90 **Dealership of Ford Overland Automobiles**
State Archives of Florida
Rc12203

91 **Florida's 18th Governor, William S. Jennings**
State Archives of Florida
Rc08264

92 **Capital City Bank**
State Archives of Florida
Rc02558

93 **Confederate Veterans**
State Archives of Florida
Rc11577

94 **Seaboard Air Line Railway**
State Archives of Florida
Rc02248

95 **T. B. Byrd Grocery Store**
State Archives of Florida
Rc09795

96 **Firemen**
State Archives of Florida
Rc03440

97 **Leon County Courthouse**
State Archives of Florida
Rc00731

98 **Zach Fenn, Phelps Wilson, and John P. Brown in a 1903 Panhard**
State Archives of Florida
Rc10294

99 **Florida College Graduates**
State Archives of Florida
Rc01138

100 **Ox-drawn Cart**
State Archives of Florida
Rc03046

101 **Parker Brothers**
State Archives of Florida
Rc00556

102 **Governor Napoleon B. Broward**
State Archives of Florida
Gv000423b

103 **Dinner**
State Archives of Florida
Rc03074

104 **Mary Louise and Annie Collins Houstoun**
State Archives of Florida
Rc00899

105 **Turpentine Still**
State Archives of Florida
PR12641

106 **Tobacco**
State Archives of Florida
Rc04890

107 **F.S.C. Football**
State Archives of Florida
Rc01140

108 **Wakulla Springs**
State Archives of Florida
pr18602

109 **The Breeze Hotel**
State Archives of Florida
Rc10829

110 **Henry Beadel**
State Archives of Florida
N038139

111 **Boy Scout Troop**
State Archives of Florida
PR11445

112 **Former Governor William D. Bloxham**
State Archives of Florida
Gv002547

113 **Winthrop Home**
State Archives of Florida
N042929

114 **Leon Academy Girls Basketball Team**
State Archives of Florida
N043226

115 **Decorated Car on Monroe**
State Archives of Florida
N048403

116 **Monroe Street**
State Archives of Florida
Rc04132

117 **John P. Brown Driving Mr. Lewis**
State Archives of Florida
Rc10298

118 **Aviation**
State Archives of Florida
Rc02915

120 **Willis Jiles Crossing Street**
State Archives of Florida
Rc00110

121 **Golfers**
State Archives of Florida
Rc00978

122 **Shot Putting at Field Day**
State Archives of Florida
N046546

123 **James E. Bowdoin**
State Archives of Florida
Rc07200

124 **Goodwood Plantation**
State Archives of Florida
pr12121

125 **Float in Centennial Parade**
State Archives of Florida
N047417

126 **Firefighters and Child**
State Archives of Florida
Rc03447

127 **Middle Florida Ice Company**
State Archives of Florida
Rc12144

128 **Ryan Monoplane**
State Archives of Florida
Rc12120

129 **F.S.C.W. Students**
State Archives of Florida
Rc01237

130 **Knott House**
State Archives of Florida
PR12131

131 **The Carnegie Library**
State Archives of Florida
PR12683

132 **Celebration**
State Archives of Florida
n046315

133 **Floridan Hotel**
State Archives of Florida
Rc10836

134 **Florida National Guard 124th Infantry**
State Archives of Florida
N030676

135 **Florida's Governor John W. Martin**
State Archives of Florida
GV008238

136 **Supreme Court**
State Archives of Florida
Pc4194

137 **President and Mrs. Conradi**
State Archives of Florida
N044118

138 **Baptist Church**
State Archives of Florida
Pc4157

139 **Scene Inside Senate Chambers**
State Archives of Florida
RC00869

140 **Masonic Building**
State Archives of Florida
Fc4159

141 **Corinne Turner**
State Archives of Florida
N043416

142 **Dale Mabry Municipal Airport**
State Archives of Florida
Rc12119

143 **Venetia Restaurant and Hotel**
State Archives of Florida
PR12388

144 **Old Capitol**
State Archives of Florida
Rc03310

145 **Calhoun Street**
State Archives of Florida
Rc10330

146 **Busy Bee Cafe**
State Archives of Florida
Rc12163

147 **Florida's 25th Governor Doyle E. Carlton**
State Archives of Florida
Rc13392

148 **Log Deck and Sorting Shed**
State Archives of Florida
024310

149 **Gymnasium Building**
State Archives of Florida
PR12676

150 **Street Scene**
State Archives of Florida
N045877

151 **Automobiles**
State Archives of Florida
Rc20608

152 **J. L. Jordan Groceries**
State Archives of Florida
Rc12167

153 **Street Scene**
State Archives of Florida
N045874

154 **Christening of the Tallahassee Flyer Train**
State Archives of Florida
GV008253

155 **College Avenue**
State Archives of Florida
N043283

156 **Inauguration**
State Archives of Florida
GV013308

157 **Police Department**
State Archives of Florida
Rc03461

158 **First Eastern Airline Flight**
State Archives of Florida
Rc00691

159 **Dove Shoot**
State Archives of Florida
N047124

160 **May Party**
State Archives of Florida
PR11510

161 **Green Derby**
State Archives of Florida
PR11098

162 **FSCW's Astronomy Club**
State Archives of Florida
Rc01316

164 **Airplanes "on the line"**
State Archives of Florida
N044866

165 **Luella Knott**
State Archives of Florida
N043089

166 **Johnson-Butler-Caldwell House**
State Archives of Florida
PR12081

167 **Silver Slipper Restaurant**
State Archives of Florida
Rc09094

168 **Couples Say Goodnight**
State Archives of Florida
RC01339

169 **V-J Day Parade**
State Archives of Florida
N044828

170 **Ivan Munroe**
State Archives of Florida
N042097

171 **National Airlines Airplane**
State Archives of Florida
Gr0596

172 **Lee Hall at Florida A&M**
State Archives of Florida
c007751

173 **Monroe Street**
State Archives of Florida
RK0198

174 **Florida Governor Millard Caldwell**
State Archives of Florida
PT00233

175 **Southeastern Telephone Company Traffic Operating Room**
State Archives of Florida
Rc06641

176 **Seven Seas Restaurant**
State Archives of Florida
Rc09766

177 **Gulf Life Insurance Co.**
State Archives of Florida
Gr1282

178 **Brothers Swimming**
State Archives of Florida
N048813

179 **1953 Florida State University**
State Archives of Florida
Rck00095

180 **Police Destroying Confiscated Liquor**
State Archives of Florida
Rc12859

181 **Auction**
State Archives of Florida
Rc00560

182 **The Mecca**
State Archives of Florida
Rc01084

183 **Acting Governor Charley E. Johns**
State Archives of Florida
Rck00348

184 **Fire**
State Archives of Florida
N043180

185 **McClay Gardens**
State Archives of Florida
GR0852

186 **Governor Collins**
State Archives of Florida
c020348

187 **Governor's Mansion**
State Archives of Florida
c029066

188 **FSU Students**
State Archives of Florida
Rc06635

189 **Florida A&M Students**
State Archives of Florida
Rc12419

190 **Civil Rights**
State Archives of Florida
Rc12396-7E

191 **Class**
State Archives of Florida
N047216

192 **New Diet**
State Archives of Florida
C035240

193 **Business District**
State Archives of Florida
Rc06721

194 **Seminole Indians**
State Archives of Florida
Rc11826

195 **Robert Hayes**
State Archives of Florida
Rc02964

196 **Governor and Mrs. Haydon Burns**
State Archives of Florida
GV036091

197 **Police Escort**
State Archives of Florida
C800000-11

198 **Dale Evans and Roy Rogers**
State Archives of Florida
c651587-92

199 **Governor Claude Kirk at FSU**
State Archives of Florida
C65000-63

HISTORIC PHOTOS OF TALLAHASSEE

By the late nineteenth century, the city of Tallahassee was a vibrant cultural center of the South. Through changing fortunes, Tallahassee has continued to grow and prosper by overcoming adversity and maintaining the strong, independent culture of its citizens.

Historic Photos of Tallahassee captures this journey through still photography selected from the finest archives. From the Adams-Onis treaty to the 1905 Buckman Act, the accreditation of Florida A&M to the construction of Dale Mabry Air Field, *Historic Photos of Tallahassee* follows life, government, education, and events throughout the city's history.

This volume captures unique and rare scenes through the lens of hundreds of historic photographs. Published in striking black and white, these images communicate historic events and everyday life of two centuries of people building a unique and prosperous city.

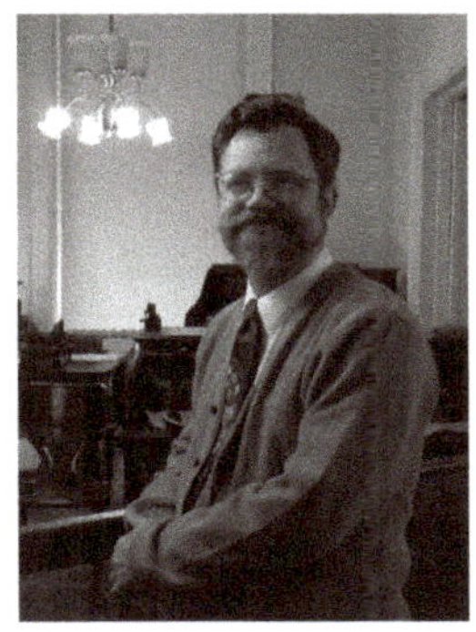

Andrew N. Edel, a retired twenty-year Air Force veteran from Jacksonville, Florida, spent his childhood in Tallahassee and north Florida. After retirement he enrolled in a Masters of Administration in Public History program at Florida State University. He has worked as independent research historian for museum exhibits: "San Marcos De Apalachee" for Florida State Parks; "The Florida Center of Political History & Governance" for the Florida Department of State; and "The Evolution of Justice in Florida" for the Supreme Court of Florida. Currently he holds three part-time positions: interpretive program specialist at the Historic Capitol Museum, the Archivist of the Supreme Court of Florida, and a ranger and lighthouse historian at St. Marks National Wildlife Refuge. He is also President of the Tallahassee Historical Society.

WWW.TURNERPUBLISHING.COM

www.ingramcontent.com/pod-product-compliance
Lightning Source LLC
LaVergne TN
LVHW060607110826
845154LV00003B/49

9781683369394